Beyond the Modern-Postmodern Struggle in Education

Toward Counter-Education and Eternal Improvisation

By

Ilan Gur-Ze'ev
University of Haifa, Israel

SENSE PUBLISHERS
ROTTERDAM / TAIPEI

A C.I.P. record for this book is available from the Library of Congress.

ISBN 978-90-8790-071-7 (paperback)
ISBN 978-90-8790-072-4 (hardback)

Published by: Sense Publishers,
P.O. Box 21858, 3001 AW Rotterdam, The Netherlands
http://www.sensepublishers.com

Cover photograph: Udi Edelman. Udi is a research student at Tel-Aviv University's Cohn Institute for the History and Philosophy of Science and Ideas. His work focuses on the grammar of practice of Direct Action and the possibility of alternative political space, bodies, and relations.

Printed on acid-free paper

To Alonik

CONTENTS

ACKNOWLEDGEMENTS

I would like to thank the following journals and publishing houses for permitting the publication of the following reworked articles:

EDUCATIONAL PHILOSOPHY AND THEORY:

1. Gur-Ze'ev, I. (2000). Critical education in the cyberspace? *Educational Philosophy and Theory*, 32: 2, 209-231.

EDUCATIONAL THEORY:

1. Gur-Ze'ev, I. (1998). Toward a nonrepressive critical pedagogy. *Educational Theory*, 48:4, 463-486.
2. Gur-Ze'ev, I. (1999). Cyberfeminism and education in the era of the exile of spirit. *Educational Theory*, 49: 4, 437-455.
3. Gur-Ze'ev, I. (Summer 2001). Philosophy of peace education in a post-modern era, *Educational Theory*, 51: 3, 315-336.
4. Gur-Ze'ev, I. (2005). Adorno and Horkheimer: negative theology, diasporic philosophy, and counter-education, *Educational Theory*, 55:3, pp. 343-365.

JOURNAL OF PHILOSOPHY OF EDUCATION:

1. Gur-Ze'ev, I. (Summer 2002). Bildung and Critical Theory facing Post-modern Education. *Journal of Philosophy of Education*, 36:3, 391-408.

JOURNAL OF THOUGHT:

1. Gur-Ze'ev, I. (1997). The vocation of higher education: modern and post-modern rhetoric in the Israeli academia on strike. *Journal of Thought*, 32:2, 57-74.
2. Gur-Ze'ev, I. (1997). Total Quality Management and power/knowledge dialectics in the Israeli army. *Journal of Thought*, 32:1, 9-36.
3. Gur-Ze'ev, I. (2000). The metaphysics of traffic accidents and education towards an alternative public sphere. *Journal of Thought*, 35: 3, 37-66.
4. Gur-Ze'ev, I., (2005). Feminist critical pedagogy and critical theory today. *Journal of Thought*, 40: 2, 55-72.

STUDIES IN PHILOSOPHY AND EDUCATION:

1.　Gur-Ze'ev, Masschelein, J. and Blake, N. (2001). Reflectivity, reflection, and counter-education. *Studies in Philosophy and Education*, 20: 2, 93-106.

EDUCATIONAL PHILOSOPHY AND THEORY:

1.　Gur-Ze'ev, I. (2000). Critical education in the cyberspace? *Educational Philosophy and Theory*, 32: 2, 209-231.

PETER LANG PUBLISHERS INC.:

1.　Gur-Ze'ev, I. (2003). Holocaust/Nakbah memories as Israeli/Palestinian homeland. Gur-Ze'ev, I., *Destroying the Other's Collective Memory*, New York: Peter Lang Publishers, pp. 25-50.
2.　Gur-Ze'ev, I. (2003). Adorno, Horkheimer, Critical Theory, and the Possibility of a Nonrepresive Critical Pedagogy. In Peters, M. and Lankshear, C. (ed.). *Critical Theory and the Human Condition - Founders and Praxis*. New York: Peter Lang, pp. 17-35.

ROWMAN & LITTLEFIELD:

1.　Gur-Ze'ev, I. (2002). Martin Heidegger, transcendence, and the possibility of counter-education. In Peters, M. (ed.), *Heidegger, Education and modernity*. Oxford: Rowman & Littlefield, pp. 65-80.

CHAPTER 1

DIASPORIC PHILOSOPHY, HOMELESSNESS, AND COUNTER-EDUCATION IN CONTEXT: THE ISRAELI-PALESTINIAN EXAMPLE

JUSTICE AS A THREAT TO THE VERY EXISTENCE OF ISRAEL

The Israeli condition has already begun to display this hard truth: after more than a hundred years of Israeli-Palestinian coexistence the Jews cannot avoid paying in the coin of *worthy life* to safeguard their mere *existence*. In other words, even if the structure of the State of Israel survives it will endure, most probably, only in the form of Sparta of the wicked.[1] It is so painful and hard for me to face this reality, as I am as much the grandson of Keyla Goldhamer, who barely survived the 1903 *Pogrom* of Kishiniev, and whose stories and lessons are so meaningful for me until this day, as the son of Robert Wiltchick, who lost almost all his family in the Holocaust and was spared the Nazi death industry only after being thrown into the mass grave from which he literally emerged all on his own, and the son of Hanna Wiltchick, who lost her marriage to her first husband as her share in the Holocaust; all these experiences are formative for my Diasporic horizons. Yet I think all of us, even the Zionists among us, should today rethink our old conceptions about Jewish life and the Jewish mission in Israel and in the Diaspora. Perhaps a good beginning would be to rethink central conceptions such as "Diaspora", "homeland", and "homecoming". Such an elaboration presents us with nothing less than the present day Jewish *telos* and our responsibility toward its fulfillment as well as toward the overcoming of its fulfillment and of what we presently are. It is of vital importance to conceive Diasporic human possibility as rooted in Judaism only as part of richer and deeper roots of human possibilities that transcend Judaism and overcome Monotheism, Western concepts of light-truth and triumphant patriachalism, even in the form of radical feminist alternatives in the McWorld. In the Israeli-Palestinian context, to my mind, the current historical moment already enables us critically to summarize the last hundred years' attempt to turn away from the Diasporic Jewish goal by the Zionist barbarization of the Jewish Spirit within the projects of "annihilating the Diaspora", "homecoming", and "normalization".

Under current historical conditions, as Israelis, Jews are structurally almost prevented from facing the possibility of living in light of the Messianic impetus, as the world's

---

1   Ilan Gur-Ze'ev, "Before we become Sparta in Kapotott", *Panim*, 4, (1998), pp. 73–80.

universal moral, intellectual, and creative vanguard. This special Jewish mission was
made possible by the Jews' unique *homelessness*—a Diasporic existence as a realized
ideal of a community that is not a collective. Diasporic life is ultimately a kind of life
in which the *yahid* (individual, not found in liberal terminology) is afforded, as an
ecstatic way of moral life, an existence that allows a universalistic moral *responsibility*
and intellectual commitment to overcome any dogma and content with the world
of "facts" and to reject the promises of mere power, glory, and pleasure. All this has
changed in face of the successes of Zionist education and its political realizations.

It is no wonder that there is no Israeli Ibn Gavirol, Baruch Spinoza, Karl Marx,
Sigmund Freud, Franz Kafka, Albert Einstein, Theodor Adorno, Emmanuel Levinas,
or Jacques Derrida. One can experience the immanent violence and the insipidness
of Israeli life just by driving on the roads. One can meet its devoted anti-humanist
values and passions by facing the unchallenged attacks on "the inefficiency and lack
of patriotism of the Israeli universities".[2] Another example might be the silence of
the current culture heroes and the popular satisfaction by which the cuts in funding
for high culture are accompanied. Still another example could be the unchallenged
crusade against the high court and the ideal of a rational, open, free, and equal public
sphere. And this is before facing the brutal realities of the treatment of foreign workers, or the structural repression of the Palestinians. I write this with great pain, not
because Israeli society is among the cruelest or the intellectually poorest of all societies
on earth. At this very moment there are so many worse examples that the politically
correct bible forbids us to address, in favor of concentrating moral, political, and
armed attacks on Israeli society.

The ongoing genocide in southern Sudan, the daily Russian assaults against the
Chechen people; the Beijing human-organs-industry based on taking the parts from
spiritual and political dissidents before systematically killing them on a mass scale; the
uprooting of the Tibetan people; the oppression of Christians and the conditions of
women, homosexuals and other minorities in Saudi Arabia; or the subjugation of the
Russian minority in Estonia are only a few examples of today's lack of courage and
widespread dishonesty in the treatment of Israel. At the same time it is true, and one
should face it, hard as it is to acknowledge, that Israel has become a space where there
is less and less room for genuine creative spirit and for social justice. Israel has become
the ultimate Diaspora of the Jewish Spirit. Here, more then anywhere else, there is
no room for "the Jewish heart", or for Jewish intellectual independence and avant-
garde creativity. It is a sad actuality, but I cannot avoid, must not avoid, facing it even
if it is so hard for me to acknowledge: there is no room for a just State of Israel. St.
Augustine knew this was so for all manifestations of "the earthly city".[3] In the case of
Israel it has become so clear that *unreserved siding against injustice inevitably endangers
the very existence of Israel*, not solely its current policies. The latest example of this is
the Second Lebanese War.

---

2   Ilan Gur-Ze'ev, "The Catch of Limor Livnat", *Ma'ariv*, 13.1.2002, p. 6.
3   St Augustine, *Concerning the City of God Against the Pagans*, translated by Henry Bettenson, London:
     Penguin Books, 1984, pp. 593–597.

Israel, as a normal state that is committed to its security and sovereignty, had to adopt terrible means to ensure not only social and economic stability on its northern border but its very existence, in light of the explicit Iranian-Hizbullah commitment to annihilate the Jewish state on religious grounds. So Israel had to respond in a harsh manner to the consistent unprovoked missile attacks on its northern cities while being condemned by world media and public opinion for a "disproportionate" reaction. The postcolonialists see Israeli policies in this respect (insisting on Lebanese sovereignty and its responsibility to ensure no private army will bombard Israeli cities at will) as another manifestation of its immanent brutal colonialist existence. On the one hand these are unjustified denunciations, based on misinformation, pragmatic interests in the Arab world, founded, reflecting and realizing the old and the New Antisemitism. On the other hand, Israel did commit terrible acts, so many terrible deeds, during that war, some by mistake, some intentionally. Given the military methods of the Hizbullah militia, which systematically uses villages in southern Lebanon not only to hide but actually to launch missiles against Israel, the IDF (Israel Defense Forces) was faced by dilemmas such as the following: identifying a present-moment launch of a Katyusha or a Zelzal II toward an Israeli city from the roof of a house in a southern Lebanese village, *should it bomb the house and save the Israeli victims while killing at an instant an entire Lebanese family (even if the mostly Shiite population of southern Lebanon normally enthusiastically welcomes the Hizbullah militia on its terrain) or should the Israeli army be morally committed to avoid any killing of Arab civilians, even at the cost of its own civilians' lives?* Is it morally right to discriminate against innocent Israeli civilians in favor of Lebanese civilians? In such instances should we morally go into the question of proportionality, namely what number of innocent Lebanese civilians killed justifies the prevention of the killing of innocent Israeli civilians? And so on. Should we, when faced with such dilemmas, go into questions such as the amount of unlimited cooperation and support by the civilian Shiite population in southern Lebanon for Hizbullah as a partial criterion for a decision on the immediate question of firing or not firing on a civilian house and its inhabitants to prevent the killing of Israeli civilian population targeted by a terrorist organization that uses civilian installations and ground for attacking the Israeli civilian population? Should moral considerations impel us to consider questions of the degree of separation and the measure of responsibility between Hizbullah and the southern Lebanese farmers, who in many respects are part of the Hizbullah organization, and sometimes also of its military organization and operations, taking part in the military attacks against the Israeli civilian population across the border? Even if the answer is affirmative, how do you actually reduce the degree of cooperation with a terrorist organization to degrees of responsibility, and how do you reduce the degree of responsibility to a specific order to the pilot in the warplane who needs to know if he should bomb the house or abort the attack? Such moral dilemmas were *not an exception* but the general rule in the practice of the military operations in the Second Lebanese War (August 2006). And the Second Lebanese War, how unfortunate, is only a microscopic example for the very existence of Israel in the region as a moral dilemma.

As anti-determinists, we should understand the present historical moment as *open*, since inevitably it also contains the possibility of a radical shift toward a more humane, rational, and moral existence in Israel, as well as in Palestine. Referring to the most recent example of the Second Lebanese War we might ask: why should we not be optimistic as to the possibility of an imminent peace treaty between Israel and Lebanon, if there are no fundamental border disputes between the two countries, joint economic interests can lead to cooperation and mutual prosperity, and a broad consensus in Israel (which includes even the extreme political right) favors cooperation and peace with Lebanon? Why should not the interests of post-Fordist economy, if not a humanistic vision of mutual respect and cooperation, lead us to a better future of creativity, prosperity and peaceful coexistence, stronger and more relevant than the fanatic religious and ethnocentric agendas? Addressing such a question beckons us into world politics, the interests of emerging regional powers such as Iran, and the specifics of Lebanese cultural and political realities. These might show us that in effect Lebanon is not a state in the modern sense of the word. But we will not go there. Instead, let us elaborate more on some central trends in Israeli reality.

When even for a moment, or to a certain degree, the direct threat to the very existence of Israel decreases (in the spaces where it is actualized) the plurality, openness, creativity and pragmatism of the McWorld have the upper hand. Yet in Israel the world of Jihad threatens not only beyond the border: it is a vital part of the constitution of the new Israeliness. In face of partial, deep post-idealist and anti-ethnocentristic-oriented tendencies most major politically organized powers in Israel manifest stronger ethnocentrism and weakening of democratic and liberal values, with very little interest in education for a mature humanistic, reflective, moral, coexistence. The rival groups and the separatist agendas are, as in Lebanon, and unlike the dominant tendencies in Palestinian society, which is speeding toward a fundamentalist consensus under the guidance of the Hamas educational-political leadership, unable to come up with a consensus about "the common good". They are certainly incapable of agreeing on a specific educational program aimed at a worthier reality. In face of this we may ask: *What has gone wrong with the State of Israel?* To answer this question we should return to the Zionist constitutive idea of "homecoming".

WHAT HAS GONE WRONG WITH ISRAEL?

The Zionist negation of Diaspora is a turn away from Jewish moral destiny. History corrects this deviation not without inflicting such enormous loss and suffering, which includes a threat to the soul and physical existence not only of the largest Jewish collective in the world but also—as September 11 manifested so clearly—of the entire world.

A century on, Zionist education has lost its naivety, and its optimism is doomed. In retrospect it has become clear to me that from its very beginning Zionist education failed in its major mission: to give birth to a durable grand truth and to its master-signifiers. Its genealogy shows that it was never equipped with the "right" violence, nor was it ready to be inhuman to the degree that would vouchsafe Jabotinsky's dream of "*geza gaon venadiv veachzar*", or a genuine realization of the myth of the *Sabra*, who, like the *Sabra* fruit, would be "coarse" on the outside yet "sweet, soft, and moral" in his innerness. Promising spiritual and moral Zionist alternatives, such as the project of Ahad Ha'am, were pushed aside, even if today some are still being followed in Israeli reality. The violence of Zionist normalizing education did not contain an enduring birth-giving vitality: it was not strong enough to actualize its constitutive idea, the idea of "the new Jew"; it was not effective enough to purify the Israeli, the *Sabra*, of the Ghetto mentality. It was not sufficiently potent to constitute a non-patronizing Jewish generosity that would extend its hand to the Arab world. Nor was it at peace with itself about conquering Palestinian space in a relentless storm that would erect Jabotinski's "Iron wall" against Arab fear, hatred, and violence.

Today it is actually impossible for disillusioned educators to look into the pupils' eyes and honestly say: "I promise you, dear children, soon it will be so much better". Secular mothers and fathers are unable to extract *meaning* from the fears and suffering of their children. Many of them are rethinking even the standard answer they have given themselves and their children in the last two years: "If only we harden our hearts and be more brutal and apply less moral restraints, we will win after all, and you, my child, will have a safe future in Israel". The Israeli formal and informal humanist educational apparatuses face rapid degradation. In today's Israel, in face of the spirit of global capitalism on the one hand, and of the Israeli-Palestinian violence on the other, the prospects are gloomy for an effective recruitment of the soul for protecting, cultivating, and enhancing at all costs the ideals and practices of secular humanistic-oriented Zionism.[4] Postmodern post-Zionists and humanistic-oriented anti-Zionists alike are united in their understanding that there are no prospects for a democratic reality in Israel.[5] Some are close to revealing the bitter truth that the prospects for a Palestinian democracy (in a future liberated greater Palestine or in any other format) are much worse. The two strongest, spiritual and politically growing rival forces are the projects of establishing a Jewish Spartanic-oriented theocracy on the one hand, and an Islamist militaristic theocracy on the other. Even if the Israeli middle class is still stronger than its enemies, and is not as racist as its victims and rivals claims it is, it is rapidly losing its fragile liberal tier, its vitality, its self-confidence, its life-impulse, and surely its Jewish heart. In face of this dynamic actuality I must say: *Can't you see that the time has come in Israel for a counter-education that will prepare for a self-initiated Jewish displacement and for a Diasporic way of life?*

TOWARD SELF-INITIATED ISRAELI DISPLACEMENT

In its narrower sense Diasporic education should prepare our children for worthy life in *eternal exile*. Counter-education should provide Israeli youth with tools that will enable them to avoid being pushed to the economic, social, and cultural margins of the techno-scientific and capitalist arenas to which their self-initiated displace-

---

4   Uri Ram, The *Globalization of Israel*, Tel Aviv: Resling pub. 2005.
5   Uri Ram, *The Time of the Post*, Tel Aviv: Resling Pub. 2006.

ment will impel them. It should facilitate the second Israeli exodus, to take them into
homelessness as their home, to the possibility of finding home everywhere, to life as
ecstatic, unsecured, open, creative, moral, life-loving citizens of the world. Linguistic
competence, intellectual and artistic creativity, improvising sensitivity and competence, and courageous border-crossing of existential, cultural, and philosophical differences become central to such counter-education. Unlearning hegemonic education becomes of vital importance here.

It is important, indeed very important, to stress this: the self-initiated displacement
of the Jews from Israel is a dialectical project. On the one hand, in order to secure "effectiveness" in terms of changing the fate of the Israelis as doomed victimizers, there
is a need for an institutionalized, collective, counter-educational effort. The Israeli
self-initiated evacuation of Israel is conditioned by many levels and dimensions of
successful violent distorting, manipulative politics, and normalizing education, which
will make possible productivity, consensus, concerted effort, and relative stability, or
peace. On the other hand, genuine Diasporic philosophy is never to be reduced to
any kind of collectivism, and as a counter-education it cannot avoid being nothing
more than an open possibility *for the individual*, solely for the individual and by the
individual. Diasporic nomadism is open always only for an individual as an erotic,
creative improviser, in the sense of the one who gives birth to and is enabled by *tefilat
hayahid* (the individual-improvised prayer, as against the institutional prayer of the
collective, the *minyan*). This openness is a possibility whose realization is to be struggled for every moment anew and is never a secured "home". It is an invitation to a
never guaranteed but always dangerous and costly possibility.

Diasporic philosophy is relevant for counter-education in current Israel as a dangerous attempt at creative improvisation with the Other and the given "facts". It is
of vital importance for the enhancement of new beginnings that are also unpredicted
and never controlled responses to the present possibilities and "calls of the moment".
At the same time, however, it is part of reclaiming, negatively, the lost intimacy with
the cosmos, with the law, and with tradition and togetherness. In other words, it is
not one of the conflicting alternatives. It is other, it is *essentially different* from the
various attempts to transcend all versions of normalizing education, cultural politics,
and other manifestations of imposed "consensus".

As a genuine dialectical realization of Diasporic philosophy, counter-education in
Israel cannot become instrumentalized, cannot become a collective self-imposed mass
immigration, as so many of my postcolonialist friends would like me to suggest. It is
not solely a moral-political concrete dilemma facing us nowadays; it is fundamentally
a philosophical and existential antinomy. Ultimately, it begins and ends in and by the
individual, who is willing to overcome his or her self and to open the gates to the nomadic existence of a brave lover of Life and creativity. But as a historical, political, and
collective project, the self-initiated new exodus, which gives a new meaning to the Exodus from Egypt to Israel and to the subsequent exiles of Jews to the Diaspora, is very
hard for another reason. There is no way to guarantee a deluxe exile: discrimination,
marginalization, and victimization await the exiled Israeli Jews. The postcolonialist
New Antisemitism most probably will not be content with the destruction of Israel

as a victory of its coalition with the world of Jihad. Already now the postcolonialist "anti-Israeliness" goes down to the roots of criticizing the essentials and the telos of Western culture and monotheism. Following here the young Marx, and today's post-colonialist heroes such as Chaves and Ahmadinejad, the Jewish return to its Diasporic existence and cosmopolitan nomadism will probably face fresh forms of exile as well as young, postcolonialist, forms of discrimination and exclusion, if postcolonialism is to maintain its consistency.

THE EXODUS FROM ISRAEL AND FROM JUDAISM TO DIASPORIC WANDERING

The new exodus is from Israel and the Zionist nation-building project as a present-day "Egypt" as a home. It is an exodus from a distorted concept of Diasporic life, from the concept of "Egypt" in the form of all versions of "homecoming" and a monotheistic way, to rebuild or go back to the Garden of Eden. It is an exodus to "Zion"; not in the sense of a national sovereignty imposed on a certain territory violently controlled, but to the infinity of the entire world of human existence and transcendence as the genuine "Zion". This too is only to be transcended into an ecstatic, totalistic, creative, existence within which Diaspora signifies the abyss of existence, meaninglessness, suf-fering, and the presence of the absence of God as a transcending impetus. The Jews at this historical moment are given this actual present as a tragic *universal mission*, which is fundamentally religious and cosmopolitan, in a Spiritless post-modern world. Indi-viduals of all nations must be invited to join this anti-religious, anti-collectivist telos of overcoming Judaism and monotheism in all its forms, in order to preserve and struggle for the realization of the essence of its creative truth.

The condemnation and oppression of the Jews might increase under the new his-torical conditions in two levels: **1.** As an assault against the Jews in the traditional sense. Here it is worth mentioning the present prosperity of the publication of *The Protocols of the Elders of Zion*, in places such as Japan, Venezuela, Pakistan and Egypt. The last-named recently opened its new national library with a central display of this ultimate modern antisemitic piece, while simultaneously prohibiting the screening in Egypt of films such as *Schindler's List*. **2.** As an assault against the new Diasporic human, the cosmopolitan nomad of our generation that will be both homeless and at home everywhere, even in the infinite dimensions and levels of existence in McWorld, cyberspace—in other words in the new historical era wherein he will exile. As a Di-asporic who is not at home in the current historical moment, yet takes responsibility, he or she will most probably be attacked by traditional humanists and patriots, by fundamentalists, by postcolonialists, and surely by the logic of the system. Diasporics not welcomed. They are the ultimate Other, they are "the Jews" of the postmodern era. They, the Diasporic humans who challenge both "colonialist" and "postcolonial-ist" dogmas and their respective violences, are the ones to be redeemed, emancipated or destroyed, even before the total purification of Palestine of all Jewish presence and forms of Israeliness.

The evacuation of all our "homes" and territory of Israel is in a certain sense a vic-tory of the Palestinian narrative and the postcolonialist agenda in more general terms.

As such it is only part of the future suffering which awaits the Israelis in their future fields of exile. Growing antisemitism impatiently awaits its new stage of development. But traditional and New Antisemitism is only part of the suffering that a self-initiated displacement might bring about. It might create new forms of suffering in light of individual evacuation of all kinds of "homes", by individuals of various nations, cultures, and faiths, who decide to struggle for their edification and *Love* as the impetus for rhizomatic creation and worthier intersubjectivity. Humans of all walks of life might meet, as Diasporic persons who have overcome monotheism, if they are genuinely to meet as creative nomads who take a different approach to responsibility, meaning, togetherness, creativity and self.[6] As Diasporic individuals they will have to overcome even the progressive idea of the Jewish *minyan*: in face of the absence of God, of the absence of a temple constituted by a self-evident dogma, and in the absence of a relevant, binding *Halacha* as a manifestation of laws interpreting-directing all walks and levels of life, they create a new kind of togetherness by repositioning themselves toward **the totally other** in face of the historical moment and relevant traditions.

Their prayer is *avodat kodesh*, whose essence is not its fulfillment but the possibility of the individual's being transcended by it: the essence of the prayer is the possibility of prayer. This kind of prayer, this *tefilat hayahid* (the individual's prayer—not determined by any text or conventional code of the community), invites a different concept of responding to a Diasporic existence and a different kind of *togetherness* with the world and with the Other. It is a precondition of philosophical life as presented by Plato and a precondition for a non-ethnocentrist community. As partners in such a community of individual de-territorialists, humans might meet each other in the presence of the absence of the otherness of **the totally other**.

The two kinds of prayer represent the two opposing conceptions of Diaspora and "homecoming". The conventional, institutionalized, collective prayer in the *minyan* in the form of *tefilat harabim* maintains a positive "homecoming" attitude. It is very much connected to the attitude to the law. Genuine Diasporic humans do not disregard the law and the importance of tradition. The other kind of prayer, *tefilat hayahid*, is fundamentally spontaneous and improvisational, of the kind that pre-assumes Life as an unbridgeable creative abyss. The law and the improvisation, *tefelat harabim* and *tefilat hayahid*, have their depths and heights and are very much connected. There is no meaningful improvisation and creativity without responsibility, tradition and laws. Traditional Judaism emphasized the importance of the Law yet maintained the tension between the *Halacha*, *tefilat hayahid*, and freedom of interpretation, as a manifestation of responsible improvisation and Diasporic Life. Diasporic life in a post-modern condition might be called to continue the Diasporic freedom of *the responsible improviser* as a Diasporic human. This, however, is far less than a satisfactory precondition for genuine Diasporic life since in Judaism this freedom of interpretation, nomadism

---

6   Ilan Gur-Ze'ev, "Critical theory and critical pedagogy today", in: Ilan Gur-Ze'ev (ed.), *Critical Theory and Critical Pedagogy Today—Toward a New Critical Language in Education*, Haifa: Faculty of Education, University of Haifa, 2005, pp. 7–34.

and improvisation was fertilized and enabled by the uncompromising *commitment* to religious law, the *Halacha* and the Jewish tradition even if as an object of alterity and edification. This fruitful tension constituted, enabled, and activated the Jewish concept of law as a relevant, religious director, to live in all its aspects, levels and dimensions. It was certainly a constitutive element for the fruitful tension between the Jewish law and the living art of interpretation for Diasporic moral avant-gardism. But how is this kind of Diaspora, nomadic life and eternal-improviser possible in a postmodern era? How is such a rich dialectics of commitment and improvisation possible in face of the absence not only of God and Godly truths, but in face of the absence of *Torah* and *Halacha*? How possible might become responsible improvisation and Diasporic life, or genuine responsibility as such, in face of the absence of monotheism and the exile of the concept of *Halacha*, in face of multi and hyper presence of rival infinities, conflicting gods, bibles, codes, laws, temples, quests, emancipatory projects, pleasures and Diasporic alternatives?

In Judaism both tendencies are free of any optimism about "homecoming" or "bridging narratives", and as such it manifests genuine religiosity much more than normally permitted by institutionalized Diasporic sensibility in institutionalized monotheistic religions. As such, Diasporic individuals become a community of creative, solidarian, humans, who create in the infinity of the present moment ever new, yet connected, responding, and dialogical, possibilities.

Diasporic life is made possible by Being as Diasporic *becoming*. Being is ontologically exiled of itself, and human beings are never genuinely "at home" with their telos, with their essence, with the truth of Being. Most philosophical, religious, and political projects are "homecoming" *calls* that enable humans to forget their exile, sometimes by becoming devotees of false, collective, dogmatic, domesticating versions of Diasporic philosophy, and sometime by forgetting their forgetfulness of Diasporic existence. In epistemology it is signified by the unbridgeable abyss between a question and "its" answer, by the unbridgeable abyss between concepts and things, language and world. In ethics it is represented by the infinite gap between the *ethical I* and the *moral I*. But Diasporic existence is to be reduced neither to an epistemological challenge nor to a question concerning the possibility of ethics in a postmodern world. Being as Diasporic becoming makes possible philosophical discourse—it is not one of its manifestations. It allows and conditions human existence and its moral essence. Diasporic individuals are made possible, not threatened, by unending displacements and boundless manifestations of creationism and clashes with the imperatives of the law and the "facts" of the historical moment. It is here that *redemption and Diasporic existence meet*. But "why should they do so?" one might ask. "Why should a bodily, psychologically, morally, aesthetically, and intellectually productive and prosperous, fully domesticated person respond to such *a call* for transformation that might entail loss of security and pleasurable self-forgetfulness?"

At another level one might articulate this question differently: "Why should the Israeli people go into a self-initiated displacement as long as militarily, economically, technologically and socially they are not yet defeated by the Palestinian violence and by the world's disgust, and morally they are not overcome; and the New Antisemitism of the postcolonialists and the disciples of the world of Jihad only awaits their self-imposed exile only to oppress them morally (as eternal, unredeemed victimizers[7]) and politically in ways currently prevented by the very existence of the State of Israel?"

Still, it seems to me that history insists already now on self-initiated displacement as a nomadic way of life for the better-off Israelis who can afford to flee, accompanied by big capital and relevant education for the McWorld. One of the most astonishing experiences in the last war was the sense of insistence on staying in Israel and willingness to fight for it even in light of the fragmentation and privatization processes. There is still room for illusion that somehow things will take a turn for the better and "we" will not have to evacuate "our home". Its justification is ultimately grounded not in practical individual or collective gains and losses. It is here that the Jewish Diasporic idea and its moral vanguard telos oppose Zionist education and clash with the reality of Israel as the Sparta of the wicked. Worthy life, or transcending mere life as the aim of life as a Jewish telos, is what is here at stake. This is the impetus of Diasporic life as an imperative.

COUNTER-EDUCATION IN LIGHT OF DIASPORIC PHILOSOPHY

Counter-education in light of Diasporic philosophy should not be limited to the preparation of self-initiated evacuation of Israelis from Israel. In its broader and deeper sense it is not an exclusive Jewish mission. It should become a universal alternative for individuals, always and only individuals, that is existential, philosophical, aesthetic, moral, and political in its realization. As such it should overcome the Christian claim to realize the Messianic essence of Judaism. It should disprove Christianity and all other forms of monotheism by realizing among the nations the idea of Diaspora, or the presence of the absence of the redeemer, as an infinite, negative, Utopia: an endless moral, creative, philosophical way of life beyond immanence and transcendence, in a Godless, unredeemable, "holy" cosmos.

Such a counter-education is part and parcel of an attempt to transcend monotheism, not Judaism exclusively. Monotheism in all its manifestations, even in the form of humanism: to transcend the quest for the appropriate, unquestionable, static, "meaning", collectivism, and an orderly, rationalized, consensual "home". It is a preparation for homelessness as a manifestation of ecstatic love of life, of creative meaning formations, of courageous intellectual life against the conventional manifestation of solidarity and truth, and of a dialogical relation with the otherness of the Other, even in face of his insistence on being part of the "we" against "them". As the realization of the Jewish ideal of Diasporic life it is an affirmation of the danger and happiness of endless new human possibilities in face of infinite responsibility regarding injustice, regarding ongoing fabrication by the system of truths, dreams, quests, and even of the self. It should prepare humans, all humans, for *tefilat hayahid*, in a Godless world as partners in a transformed *minyan*— to meet the world as creative, moral nomads, as truly religious human beings, who are liberated: exiled lovers of Life, displaced from

7   Ilan Gur-Ze'ev, *Edward Said as an Educator* (forthcoming).

any dogmatic passions, ideals, and practices of a certain "religion" as their "home-land". This means that this counter-education should also prepare Diasporic life for those people, like myself, who insist on living in Israel at all costs, even as it becomes before my eyes a Zionist Sparta of the wicked. This means that the interconnected-ness between *Gola* and *Geula* (Diaspora and redemption) should offer a very specific, concrete, and detailed counter-education in current Israel, for preparing not only the exodus from Zionism and the State of Israel but, what is even more important, *the possibility of Diasporic life in Israel itself.*

DIASPORIC LIFE IN ISRAEL

As the unification of an ongoing moral struggle for the realization of the essence of Judaism, and transcending it into a universal alternative human existence, and as a courageous, creative, Love, such a counter-education might open the gate to new possibilities to challenge concrete existential, moral, psychological, economic, and political manifestations of the present Israeli condition. It might edify, even in face of the exile of Spirit in a post-modern world, the old-new Jewish mission by overcom-ing it and realizing it as *a universal human telos.* It does not search for redemption as transcendence into the lost Garden of Eden or the establishment of an earthly positive utopia such as a strong, prosperous state. It is a telos which challenges the institutionalized and instrumentalized monotheistic religiousness, on the one hand, and the reified "secular" symbolic and non-symbolic commodities and passions of the post-modern culture industry on the other.

It should not be satisfied by introducing quests and tools for unveiling the manipu-lations of normalizing education, of the structural injustice of global capitalism on the one hand, and Israeli and Palestinian nationalism on the other. It should not limit itself to criticizing instrumental rationality and the reduction of the human subject from some-one to some-thing. In the present moment, under any conditions, it must open the gates of love and affirmation, of creativity and responsibility, in face of the omnipotence of the current production of meaninglessness (which appears as truth, as desired objects of consumption and representation, or as hopelessness). It must enhance the possibilities for improvising in the totality of the moment without aban-doning historical consciousness, without disregarding the Other's unfinished saying/need, without abandoning the utopian quest for creating new concepts, possibilities, and wanderings. As such, counter-education becomes a potential "redemptive" ele-ment even under almost impossible philosophical, cultural, and political conditions.

By transcending the truth of Judaism it becomes relevant for all homeless humans: for all truly religious humanists, who affirm Life, Love, creativity, the danger of un-ending self de-territorialization, and moral responsibility for the otherness of the Other and for the otherness within the self.

In current Israel, counter-education of this kind might culminate into a bridge for Jews and Palestinians. They might enter a non-violent dialogue only as partners in worthy suffering and love of Life, as homeless, as Diasporic persons, who are committed to overcome all versions of ethnocentrism and all projects of "homecoming", at all levels and dimensions of life. *A new way is opened for rebuilding "Yavne".*

Building the "New Yavne" is inescapably contradictory: to be true to itself it cannot be restricted to any specific place, mission or memory. It must be universal, and be realized in all dimensions and levels of human life. As such not only might it be realized even without the evacuation of Israel: it can never be reduced to mere geographic displacement. It must transform itself into a universal nomadic, creative, everlasting, way of life, without a *Torah* or a sacred truth but Love in the totality of every moment, which contains infinite possibilities in the infinite *terra* that is not merely the "innerness" of the individual, or the "exterior reality". It is the nowhere space, the *Utopia*, the space that is not "in between" the "I" and the Other, "innerness" and "external reality", "true meaning" and "meaninglessness". It is this special mode of creative self-constitution that makes possible a non-"linear" focused, instrumental, gaze, hearing, production, and representation. It offers a different existence, an erotic self-constitution that is also a totalistic, holistic, ecstatic, manifestation of the world. Only within the framework of a transcending Diasporic philosophy can one enter this ever-unfinished, creative, effort at dialogical self-constitution with the otherness of the Other and with the infinite richness of the cosmos as a worthy Diaspora. But such an Odyssey cannot take place outside a *form*, disregarding what Judaism calls *Halacha*. The tension between *Halacha* and *tefilat hayahid* or between the *Ethical I* and the *Moral I* is not solved by Diasporic philosophy and counter-education. In Israel all we can do today is nothing more then address it with no "solutions", "recommendations" or "relevant curriculum".

As a *negative utopia*[8] for and of Diasporic humans it fosters a genuine new partnership between "Israelis" and "Palestinians". Both are called upon. They are called upon to overcome the violence of the power-relations within which, and by whose productive manipulations, their collective identities have been violently reproduced by normalizing education in the last hundred years. They are called upon to overcome the negation of the Other, the commitment to destroy, exile, or re-educate "them". As Diasporic persons, as individuals who are responsible for the Other, Israelis and Palestinians are called upon to enter this dialogic, dangerous, totalistic way of life and transcend both Palestinian national identity and Israeliness, Islam and institutionalized Judaism, narcissism and self forgetfulness. But will they respond before it is too late?

---

8   Ilan Gur-Ze'ev, *The Frankfurt School and the History of Pessimism*, Jerusalem, Magnes Press, 1996, p. 147.

CHAPTER 2

CRITICAL THEORY, CRITICAL PEDAGOGY
AND DIASPORA TODAY

Critical Pedagogy faces today a very strange situation. While being positioned in a seemingly comfortable position and warmly received by so many liberals, post-coloni-alists, multi-culturalists, postmodernists, and feminists (to name only few of the long list of its adorers), it is being domesticated, appeased, or even castrated by the present order of things. It became too successful, under different titles, while under the flag of Critical Pedagogy it became domesticated, disoriented, or dogmatized. Today it has become difficult to speak of "Critical Pedagogy"; it is quite ambitious even to ar-ticulate the essential elements common to the various and conflicting pedagogies that propagate themselves under the banner of "Critical Pedagogy".

Critical Pedagogy was constituted on the central concepts of Critical theory and on the material, social, and cultural conditions that enabled the critical Utopia. It was part of a rich Western tradition, not just a sign of a dramatic crisis in modern thought and reality. If in classical times the whole was conceived as prior to the parts, and harmony preceded differences and otherness, the imperial Roman era already acknowledged the turn away from the wholeness of the cosmos. Stoa and Gnosis represented it in rich, different, ways. For Gnosis *Being is temporary*, not eternal. *Being is essentially split* and antagonistic to itself. The temporary of Being and its infinite not-identical-with-itself is acknowledged also by St. Augustine in the tenth book of his *Confessions* as well as in the first Letter to Thessalonians in the New Testament. Without abandoning truth, it faced the retreat of classical togetherness of humans and the wholeness of the cosmos, as well as the priority and supremacy of the whole over its individual parts. Cosmic intimacy and unproblematic self-evidence were replaced by alienation; alienation between the parts and the whole, and alienation within the individual himself. Medieval Christianity offered an alternative—via the "home-re-turning" project. With the assistance of dogma and well kept walls between classes in society, and between Christian Jewish sacred truth and existence, it maintained a fairly stable illusion of coherent, steady, relations between the intellect, moral faculty and the aesthetical dimensions of life, and the body. This relative stability was per-ceived as part of a redeemed, yet fragile and threatened whole: between the Christian, the world, the Other, and knowledge about worthy knowledge. This stable hierarchy, which divided Spirit and body, supra-human and worldly-life, was never genuinely harmonious, stable, coherent, or wholly penetrating. In actuality it did not safely protect the hegemonic social order and its realms of self-evidence: it was actually questioned time and again by rebellious poor farmers, well-educated heretics, witches, madmen, children, women, Jews, and other Others. And yet, it enjoyed relative success in hiding its *immanent violence*, which offered, aside from inequality (after death), suffering, ignorance, and effective silencing of the free spirit. At this price, however, it offered *meaning* to the given reality and *hope* for transcendence. The demolition of the medieval Western Christian world was brought about by the strengthening and universalization of two versions of its arch-rival: the alliance of classical Greek thought and Judaism. Herman Cohen emphasized the *universal realization of Judaism as the expression of the critical spirit and humanism*[1]—Karl Marx[2] emphasized the *universal realization of Judaism as manifested by the logic and practice of capitalism.*[3] The medieval Christian world could not very long resist such united, erotic, transcending powers.

The medieval order could not sustain durable resistance to the new philosophical and scientific revolutionary developments,[4] or to the economic, social, technological, and national challenges imposed by the spirit of capitalism. In modernity the critical project was aimed at a positive mission: reestablishing the world as a "home"; *offering a "home returning" project for humans, back to a (pre)meaningful wholeness* enhanced by rational, solidarian, dialogical, individuals. Within the framework of Enlightenment individuals committed themselves to re-constitute the Garden of Eden on earth via critical thinking and collective rational-political praxis. The Critical Theory thinkers of the Frankfurt School were faced with the problematic of the unattainable metaphysical assumptions for this mission. They also acknowledged the new, irrelevant, social conditions for the realization of the Enlightenment's educational project—and along with Heidegger and existentialism, they not only refused any metaphysic, they further developed a *Diasporic philosophy*—one that addressed humans' ontological *Diasporic existence*. They responded to the human condition as "being-thrown-into-the-world", meaninglessness, and omnipotent-cannibalistic-violence that enhances "culture" and "progress" only as new forms of nihilistic negation of love of Life in its wholeness.

For late Adorno and Horkheimer, this was the beginning of a new, vivid, thinking, not the end of their utopian undertaking. Even if they were not aware of it, we can still identify in their later work that the dissolution of the promise of modernity became, actually, a gate for a new beginning. Earthly, Diasporic, life disconnected from the Exile-Redemption narrative, became an entry for a renewed, negative, ecstatic, intimacy with the world. Out of awareness of the existential situatedness as *being-thrown-into-the-world* they articulated a concept of *living-toward-the-not-yet-in-*

---

1   Hermann Cohen, *Religion of Reason out of the Sources of Judaism*, translated by Simon Kaplan, New
     York: F. Unger Publications, 1972.
2   Karl Marx, *Zur Judenfrage*, Berlin: Rowohlt, 1919.
3   Ilan Gur-Ze'ev, "The university, the eternal-improviser, and the possibility of meaning in a post-
     modern era", in Ilan Gur-Ze'ev (ed.), *The End of Israeli Academia?* Haifa: The Faculty of Education,
     University of Haifa—*Iyyunim Bachinuch*, 2005, pp. 256–299.
4   Max Horkheimer, "Bedrohungen der Freiheit", *Gesammelte Schriften* VIII., Frankfurt a.Main 1985,
     p. 276.

a-Godless-world, in the totality of each moment. Living, here, is not so much in the sense of self protection and reproduction as in the sense of "becoming", of commitment for self-constitution and edification. Diasporic life enabled creative improvisations and births, which made meaninglessness an impetus to new possibilities for happiness, meaning, aim, and togetherness.

Within the framework of mature Critical Theory the concept of *Diaspora* was developed even beyond the Gnostic division between the exiled, hidden, God and the evil God of creation/reality; a division between evil nature and meaningless laws and fabrications—and the wholeness and supremacy of nothingness/chaos. The contribution of Critical Theory to the history of Diasporic Philosophy was made possible by the change of stance of the concepts, ideals, symbols, strivings, and other signifiers which were dissolved, ridiculed, or forgotten in the era of advanced capitalism and its fully administered world in which progress paralleled the broadening of the possibilities for emancipation on the one hand, and the empowerment of the oppression of the individual to the level of the instincts, on the other.[5] Not only the promise of Enlightenment became irrelevant: the traditional Gnostic rejection of the world of facts and its entire negative alternative became anecdotal at best, in face of the life conditions dictated by the omnipotence of Instrumental Rationality and advanced capitalism and its Culture Industry.[6]

Some Critical Pedagogy thinkers such as McLaren, Gruschka, Mason, Tubbs, De-Olivera, Zeichner, Roth and Weiler insist on the modernistic-oriented humanist project. Others, such as Michael Peters, Patti Lather, and Gert Biesta, emphasize the new possibilities within the framework of the postmodern discourses and the postmodern conditions. Still others, such as Colin Lankshear, Wendy Kohly, Nicholas Burbules, Raquel Moraes, Mark Olssen, Elisabeth Heilman, Eduardo Duarte and Henry Giroux, search for a creative synthesis between modern and postmodern sensitivities, conceptions, practices, technologies and paths for communication, existence and education. But this is far from being the only dichotomy. Other dichotomies crisscross Critical Pedagogy today on the level of gender, multiculturalism, post-colonialism, and queer conflicting theories. Sometime the line of division crisscrosses not solely critical thinkers and agendas—they oppose each other even in their own educational philosophy. Other critical philosophers, such as Jan Masschelein, refuse to identify themselves further with Critical Pedagogy, and search for a worthier alternative by long meditative walking in silence and in other paths. Regardless to the degree of identification with Critical Pedagogy, it seems to me that many critical pedagogues are today ready for, or actually searching for *a new critical language in education* that will go beyond the achievements and limitations of Critical Pedagogy.

In itself this is nothing to regret or to be sorry for. What is regrettable, however, is that so much of Critical Pedagogy has become dogmatic, and sometimes anti-intellectual, while on the other hand losing its relevance for the people it conceived as victims to be emancipated. Why is this regrettable? Because the erotic telos of Criti-

5   Max Horkheimer, *Eclipse of Reason,* New York: Oxford University Press, 1974, p. 141.
6   Max Horkheimer, *Gesammelte Schriften,* VII, Frankfurt a.Main: Fischer, 1985, p. 29–30, 159.

cal Pedagogy insists on poetic, religiously anti-dogmatic, worthy Life as a manifestation of Love, not of fear or of heated "critique". Because it symbolizes the quest for freedom and refusal of meaningless suffering in face of the *loss of naïve intimacy with the world* and with the truth of Being, and because, sometimes, it actually enhances equality and resists oppression; even if actually it normally promotes new forms of oppression and enhances new ways for *self-forgetfulness*. In detaching itself from the rich works of Adorno, Benjamin, Horkheimer, and the other thinkers of Critical Theory, Critical Pedagogy in its different versions has abandoned its attunement to *Life* itself in so many respects.

Currently next to no attempts are being made to confront Critical Pedagogy with reality in actual, enduring, pedagogical engagements. No wonder then that next to no attempts are being made to articulate an educational framework for critical teachers' training either, and certainly no ongoing practice of teachers' training at schools. Important exceptions here are the theoretical and practical contributions of Kenneth Zeichner,[7] Daniel Liston,[8] and Andreas Gruschka.[9] All this, in face of deceptive calls from the various symbols, strivings, and technologies of globalizing capitalism, and alongside the actuality of anti-reflective and ethnocentric-oriented construction of collective identities of many of the oppressed groups that are so enthusiastically idolized by many disciples of Critical Pedagogy. These are but fragmentary examples of the detachment of current Critical Pedagogies from the wholeness, depths, abysses, dangers, and richness of Life.

Critical Pedagogy contributed more than its fair share in an ongoing attempt to be relevant to political challenges, especially for marginalized and oppressed groups. This is an attempt of vital importance, especially when it is conducted in the wider context of the current crisis in the stance of humanistic-oriented knowledge and its dynamics (as in the work of Burbules, Peters, Heilman, Biesta, Tubbs, Rimon-Or, Marshall, Mason, Gruschka, and Masschelein), or within the context of historical cultural, and economic changes (as in the case of McLaren, Apple, Kellner, and Duarte). The present historical moment, however, needs so much more than that. And overcoming any historical moment and its imperatives, walls, and possibilities calls for even more than that. We cannot, however, offer, arbitrarily, new master signifiers, strivings, or openness, nor a new critical language, at the present historical moment.

A new critical vocabulary, and not-yet-born master-signifiers, along with other genuine manifestations of **the totally other**,[10] cannot appear out of the blue, on demand.

---

7   Kenneth M. Zeichner, "Traditions of practice in U.S. preservice teacher education programs", *Teaching and Teacher Education* (1993), 9, 1, pp. 1–13.
Kenneth Zeichner, "Changing Directions in the Practicum: looking ahead to the 1990's", *Journal of Education for Teaching*, (1990), 16: 2, pp. 105–131.
8   Dan Liston, "Love and despair in teaching", *Educational Theory* (2000) 50, pp. 81–102.
9   Andreas Gruschka, *Negative Paedagogik—Einfuerung in die Paedagogik mit Kritische Theorie*, Muenster, Pandora, 1986.
10   Martin Heidegger, "Letter on humanism", *Basic Writings*, London: Routledge, 1993, p. 258.
Max Horkheimer, "Die sehnsucht nach dem ganz Anderen", *Gesammelte Schriften*, VII., Frankfurt a.Main: Fischer, 1985, p. 385–404.

Master-signifiers, new horizons, and historical shifts are parts of the rich affluence of Being and are manifested differently in all parts and dimensions of the cosmos, preceding any abstraction, law, or control. They might be approached by humans as *manifestations of Love vs. Metaphysical Violence*, or as the infinite/restrained presence of *affluence as Metaphysical Violence*. In any case, these do not behave like domesticated pets, and are never at humans' mercy. They are true manifestations of the infinity and freedom of Being. The new master-signifiers are essentially unforeseeable, uncontrollable, and never totally deciphered, or truly to be mobilized for further productivization, preservation, or enrichment of the instrumental ways for being-in-the-world. They burst into reality—or do not appear at all, beyond determinism, contingency, and unpredictability. Their possible appearance enables freedom and necessity, yet it is not conditioned by laws of freedom, determinism, or representation.

When **the totally other** bursts into a specific historical moment the realm of self-evidence is cracked by this manifestation of "messianic time",[11] and "now-time"[12] is irreparably shattered by "redemption"; the epoch of the essentially newly born possibilities becomes not only possible but actually inevitable. It is the moment for untouched horizons, fresh master-signifiers, and fruitful, dynamic, new creations, reactions, and life-and-death wars. The truth of Being and the hidden violence of the historical moment might become unveiled by poetry, philosophy, art, dance, and singing. At such a rare moment dialogue with the world (that conditions any genuine human communication and "dialogue") and self-reflection face newly born possibilities. The very possibility of such a moment is a precondition for transcendence and for counter-education, which will uncover fresh forms of intimacy and creation with and amid distorted Being.

The possibility of a new critical language in education and of spanking new possibilities for approaching the nearness of truth and the richness of Life are always a matter for human concern. But even at the best of times it is in our hands only partially and always merely conditionally, fragmentarily, and frigidly. And this too, only for a fleeting moment. This is an important positive dimension of Negative Utopia: it means that there is so much that we can do, under the present conditions —actually, under any conditions! And yet, essentially, there is always a limit not only to our possibilities within the historical moment: the very existence of meaningful horizons and their specific material, symbolic, and existential characteristics are essentially *not ours* but a challenge to overcome, a potential to transcend.

Present-day Critical Pedagogy faces, as the authors of this collection manifest, challenges of different kinds, and it responds to these challenges in various, different, and at times conflicting, ways. Among these challenges the contributors to this collection note globalizing capitalism, the introduction of new technologies in communication, the change in the stance and function of knowledge, the dramatic shift in the struc-

---

11   Walter Benjamin, "Ueber den Begriff der Geschichte", *Gesammelte Schriften*, I.2, Frankfurt a.Main: Suhrkamp, 1980, pp. 695.
12   *Ibid.*, p. 701.

ture of society, and the transformation of relations between work, finance, and the state in the era of the MacWorld.[13]

Old conceptions of class-struggle and traditional emancipatory sensitivities, vocabularies, and practices are deconstructed, consumed, reified and neutralized in the present historical moment, while marginalization, suffering, injustice, and structural blocking from cultural and political capital become ever more sophisticated and harsh for ever more people around the globe. Under these circumstances normalizing education becomes a vital element of the oppression, not solely as part of the direct and indirect violence inflicted on the poor, the homeless, minority races, ethnicities, cultures, and other Others. It becomes at the same time an almost *omnipotent de-humanizing power* by the minorities, the oppressed, and the marginalized—against their own Others, against their oppressive powers and against free spirit, thinking, and Life.

Critical Pedagogy, in its different versions, has usually failed to meet this challenge of emancipatory pedagogy, becoming part and parcel of normalizing education.[14] Its identification with the marginalized and the oppressed, and its commitment to a positive Utopia, allowed it to sharpen its critique and become instrumental in many academic radical circles. Committed to its various positive Utopias in the fields of feminist, multi-cultural, race, class, post-colonial, and queer struggles, the different versions of Critical Pedagogy have more than once become dogmatic, ethnocentrist, and violent. Concurrently, they have become increasingly popular in ever widening academic circles, and decreasingly relevant to the victims it is committed to emancipate. What is to be done, for that which the different versions of Critical Pedagogy treat to be seriously re-approached? For a genuine rejection of injustice and the nearness *to truth as Love and as violence, as affluence and as scarcity/fright, as the presence of Eros and the presence of Tanathus*, not to be abandoned in favor of fashionable, domesticating "radical" rhetoric? I limit myself to six aspects of this manifold and rich challenge, from the perspectives of Diasporic Philosophy and counter-education.

1. Critical Pedagogy and Critical Theory. I believe I do not run the risk of exaggeration by asserting that in fact *all current versions of Critical Pedagogy have lost their intimate connections to the Critical Theory of the Frankfurt School*; not much is left of its original relation with the Frankfurt School that was an enrichment so fruitful for the very possibility of Critical Pedagogy; for Paulo Freire and early Henry Giroux, Peter McLaren, Michael Apple, Ira Shor, and other founders of the unexpected present popularity (and irrelevance) of the different versions of Critical Pedagogy. This historical and philosophical gap is not a regretful condition per se; if only a fruitful transformation and a rich, elevating, alternative had lifted Critical Pedagogy beyond Critical Theory! How regrettable that this promise is still not-actualized. It has not happened, even if the influences of postmodernism, post-structuralism, post-colonialism, new versions of feminism, multiculturalism, and queer theories have indeed

---

13   Benjamin Barber, *Jihad vs. MacWorld—How Globalism and Tribalism Are Shaping the World*, New York: New York Times Books 1995.

14   Ilan Gur-Ze'ev, "Toward a nonrepressive critical pedagogy", *Educational Theory* (Fall 1998), 48: 4, pp. 463–486.

enriched many aspects of current Critical Pedagogy. What is it that is lost, and should be courageously addressed?

Most versions of Critical Pedagogy opened themselves up to the influences of postmodern and post-colonialist academic rhetoric, which has become so popular in American and European universities. In their rush to become politically active and relevant in the field of education the Critical Pedagogy thinkers overlooked the essential instincts, ideals, and telos of Critical Theory that Critical Pedagogy, at its best moments, committed itself to "realize".

Critical Pedagogy thinkers forgot that mature Critical Theory was utopian, yet its Utopia was a *Negative Utopia*—not a Positive Utopia.[15] Later Horkheimer and Adorno dismissed any "revolutionary", "radical", or "emancipatory" project that promised reconciliation, "just peace", an "end to suffering", "salvation" for the victims, or even advancement on this road. Demolition of terror would inevitably result in cultural and social deconstruction, according to Adorno and Horkheimer,[16] and Benjamin asserted that there is no cultural document that was not a manifestation of barbarism.[17] Even the idea of approaching "truth" via ideology-critique was problematic for them, since, according to Adorno, cultural critique itself had become reified, and critical spirit, when content with itself, cannot challenge the total reification of the present historical moment.[18]

The mature work of Adorno and Horkheimer is not optimistic, yet it insists on the utopian axis of *Life* in all its manifestations—as a Negative Utopia. Philosophical pessimism makes the Messianic impulse possible, and redemption is what is being addressed here,[19] while insisting on what in Negative Theology was conceived as *the presence of the absence of God*. Horkheimer notes explicitly in his diary entry for 5 July1923 that this is his personal impetus for philosophizing.[20] There is such a rich, infinite, space for creative courage, Love of Life and transcending power in awareness of the presence of meaninglessness in face not of the absence of truth—but on the contrary, in face of the presence of the successful (contingent) production of truths, values, and yardsticks for evaluation of rival values, truths, and passions! All this in the service of a life-and-death struggle between rival arenas of truths-and–values-production, in support of nihilistic *self-forgetfulness* of humans' being-toward-life.

In light of the tradition of Diasporic Philosophy the mature Critical Theory of Adorno and Horkheimer conceived meaninglessness, suffering, and unbridgeable tension between equality and freedom and the abyss between human culture and the

---

15   Ilan Gur-Ze'ev, "Walter Benjamin and Max Horkheimer: from utopia to redemption", *Journal of Jewish Thought and Philosophy* (1998), 8, pp. 119–155.

16   Theodor Adorno and Max Horkheimer, *Dialektik der Aufklaerung*, Frankfurt a.Main 1988, p. 225.

17   Walter Benjamin, *Illuminations*, translated by Harry Zohn, New York: Schocken, 1969, p. 256.

18   Theodor Adorno, "Culture critique and society", in Theodor Adorno and Max Horkheimer, *The Frankfurt School*, Tel Aviv: Sifriat Poalim 1993, p. 157 (in Hebrew).

19   Max Horkheimer, "Pessimismus heute", *Gesammelte Schriften* VII, Frankfurt a.Main: Fischer 1985, p. 231.

20   Max Horkheimer, "Notizen", *Gesammelte Schriften* XI., Frankfurt a. Main, 1987, p. 235.

harmonic, beautiful-meaningless self-contentment of nature as a starting point for their (negative) Utopia; without being swallowed by false promises to overcome the dialectics of Life, the abysses and dangers facing true love and genuine creativity, and certainly *without promising social "emancipation" or "revolution"*[21] or a true, unproblematic, educational alternative of the kind Critical Pedagogy educators normally are so quick to promise us in so many voices and agendas.[22]

When Horkheimer declares his abandonment of Marx in favor of Schopenhauer[23] he actually comes very close to some of the central Gnostic conceptions within the framework of a Diasporic Philosophy. The foundations and the telos of the Enlightenment's modern emancipatory tradition and its Marxian versions are fundamentally challenged in the later works of Adorno and Horkheimer. Even the young Horkheimer already noted in his diary that he was most uncomfortable with the tranquilizing dimension of the Marxian Utopia.[24] This part of their work is too often ignored by today's radical and emancipatory educators. Here it might be worth bearing in mind that for the Gnosis authentic freedom is never to be related to the human mind or psyche—which are constructed and policed by historical power-relations and violent manipulations (much in the same manner as the body is enacted by the physical law). Solely the Spirit, the *pneuma*, the foreign, never-to-be-defined-nor-controlled element in Life manifests genuine freedom. Human psyche and mind are part of the evil creation of the *Demiurgus* that rules over all the world of individual existence and thingness.

Late Adorno and Horkheimer did not satisfy themselves in recycling a Gnostic concept of salvation within the framework of the reformulated late Critical Theory; they further developed (a beginning) of a *Diasporic Philosophy*, which refuses to offer any "solution", "method", or "salvation".[25] Their later work acknowledges the *Diaspora* as the gate to rich alternative thinking and becoming-toward-the-world.

This gate I understand as an important starting point for a present-day Diasporic counter-education. Of special importance here is their refusal of any version of Positive Utopia and of all calls for "salvation", "emancipation", "effectiveness", or "success". This is also a refusal of any kind of nihilism and abandonment of hope and Love of Life. For Diasporic humans, here the return to the (absent) wholeness and richness of nature is part of (re)establishing (negative) cosmic intimacy. Adorno and Horkhe-

---

21   Max Horkheimer, *Gesammelte Schriften*, VII. P. 341. See also: Max Horkheimer, "Kritische Theorie gestern und heute", *Gesammelte* Schriften, VIII, Frankfurt a.Main: Fischer, 1985, p. 346.

22   Ilan Gur-Ze'ev, "Toward a nonrepressive critical pedagogy", *Educational Theory* (Fall 1998), 48: 4, pp. 469.

23   Max Horkheimer, "Kritische Theorie gestern und heute", *Gesammelte* Schriften, VIII, Frankfurt a.Main: Fischer, 1985, p. 339.

24   Marx Horkheimer, "Notizen", *Gesammelte Schriften*, XI., Frankfurt a.Main 1987, p. 269.

25   Ilan Gur-Ze'ev, "Critical theory, critical pedagogy and the possibility of counter-education", in Peters, M., Lankshear, C., and Olssen, M. (eds.), *Critical Theory and the Human Condition: Founders and Praxis*, New York: Peter Lang, 2003, pp. 17–35.

imer are much closer here to Hans Jonas and Immanuel Levinas than to Heidegger, who, as Jonas rightly noted, had no respect for nature.[26]

Parallel to their intensive efforts to become "relevant", "involved", "effective", and "emancipating", the current different versions of Critical Pedagogy lost not only Negative Utopia. Today's Critical Pedagogy lost another essential element of Critical Theory—the attempt to transcend itself and to enable a worthier nearness to dialectical intimacy to the richness of Life in its wholeness. Critical Pedagogy abandoned the Negative Utopian kind of commitment to transcendence in favor of another: commitment to successful political activity and effective practical involvement that will ensure us being successfully swallowed by the continuum of the immanence; a successful return into thingness. This is a switch from a Diasporic project, which is committed to a never-concluding-effort of *transcendence*, to a different one, which while paying lip service to "resistance" and "emancipation" is totally committed to a nihilistic devotion to the closure of *immanence*. It runs away from eternal worthy suffering that is part and parcel of Diasporic nomadism and its struggle for a never-concluding-effort at transcendence—not for a reconciling "home-returning" project (which frequently praises exile too—only to end in nirvana, "redemption", "tragic heroism", "consistent nihilism" or other forms of Tanathus). This turn was paralleled in the last thirty years by overemphasis on either the intellectual aspects of education (ideology-critique, conscious awareness enhancement, and so forth), or on the subjective "experience" of the oppressed pupil and the self-evidence of diverse conflicting, marginalized collectives that strive for hegemony and "emancipation" that will ultimately effectively enslave their Others, without leaving traces or exacting too high a price.

Contrary to this trend, the Frankfurt School critical thinkers, while opposing the tradition of "life-philosophy", took all kinds of existential self-evidence and philosophical self-contentment as a challenge that might effectively destroy or exile the transcending potential of human existence.[27] They did not try to establish intimacy with the self-evidence of hegemonic or marginalized collectives. They conceived *self-evidence* as collective closure and as a great danger for the free human spirit. Intimacy, patriotism, and dogmatism for them were threats of being swallowed by thingness, nature, and myth.

As Diasporic thinkers, they centered their thought on the relation between the human subject and the world. Subject and object were not mere abstract theoretical categories for Adorno and Horkheimer. The human and nature, and especially the estrangement between the two, enforced by Western Instrumental Rationality, were a starting point for Enlightenment, and therefore also for Critical Theory, which acknowledges that all along history humans had to decide between two possibilities: enslaving nature or being enslaved by it.[28] For them the acknowledgement of humans' homelessness in a Godless world was the gate to the elaboration of possibilities for a

26 Hans Jonas, *The Gnostic Religion*, Boston: Beacon Press 1992, p. 339.
27 Max Horkheimer, "[Lebensphilosophie: Bergson, Simmel, Dilhey]", *Gesammelte Schriften*, X., Frankfurt a.Main 1990, pp. 276–299.
28 Adorno and Horkheimer, *Dialektik der Aufklaerung*, p. 71.

worthy response and for the possibility of cultivating what I call *Diasporic response-ability*.

Diasporic response-ability addresses the affluence of meaninglessness and violence since the destruction of the chaos/nothingness and the history of Godly creation/human "progress". Response-ability in this sense is not merely passive and not solely active; it is not a mere manifestation of affluence in Life, nor is it exclusively a manifestation of human scarcity. If, true to its Diasporic essence, it does not offer counter-violence against nature and against humans, nor does it offer what Nietzsche called slave morality as a gate for transcendence: it refuses all calls for escape in self-protection and pleasure/truth as the ultimate goal of Life. Here response-ability acknowledges meaninglessness and suffering, and does not try to escape them or the danger of self-destruction: it transcends them within the creativity of Love, Diasporic, non-sentimental Love of Life and its abysses.[29] It transcends them in the sense that it challenges the traditional lines of division between "transcendence" and "immanence", "home" and "homelessness". The various conflicting collective Positive Utopias, and individual escapist, nihilist, and relativist "home-returning" projects, were for them a manifestation of the forgetfulness of human forgetfulness; not a worthy response to this challenge, which in advanced capitalism became stronger and more sophisticated than ever. In their mature work, after the publication of the *Dialectic of Enlightenment*, they searched for a third, Diasporic, path between the Scylla of collectivism-dogmatism and the Charybdis of selfish, relativist-oriented Instrumental Rationality that sees nature and the Other as a mere standing reserve, an object of manipulation or a source of danger. The Diasporic counter-education that we can reconstruct from the tradition of Diasporic Philosophy (and here Adorno and Horkheimer are of special relevance to us) challenges modern nihilism, in all its forms. It maintains both dualism and dialectics, yet insists on Love and intimacy in a Godless world, where human rationality cannot establish any alternative Garden of Eden, meaning, aim, or an authentic "I".

Current Critical Pedagogy either continues the anti-Diasporic conception of the human as a mere "rational animal", or is swallowed by the sweet soporific power of the reformulated Sirens who call us with their irresistible beauty, as with Odysseus in his day, to come back *"home" to harmonious nature*: to the homogeneous-totalistic-infinity of the thingness; a safe "home-returning" to the infinity and the beauties of nature and harmonious thingness; back to nothingness, after finally defeating and abandoning the wonder, danger, and openness of otherness in Being and in the human being. In these two versions of Critical Pedagogy, its thinkers reveal a lack of attention and the importance of their avoidance; the significance of neglect of a theoretical, practical, physical, and existential synthesis.

This neglect offers a synthesis between human and world; a synthesis, yet never a symbiosis, between the moment and eternity, signifier and signified, becoming and

---

29 Horkheimer positions the centrality of this kind of love against the institutionalized religion that abandons sensitivity to real suffering in the world. Max Horkheimer, "[Diskussion ueber die Augabe des Protestanismus]", *Gesammelte Schriften*, XI., p. 366.

nothingness, Diaspora as an ontological, epistemological, existential attunement to the call to self-creation, as against self-forgetfulness; as an alternative to being swallowed by all "home-returning" appeals and all salvation/emancipation agendas and educational projects that offer to constitute the "I" via the "we" and the self-evident, true, or relevant values, truths, ideals, and strivings.

Critical pedagogy's abandonment of Critical Theory's Diasporic Philosophy is constructive indeed. This desertion enables its easygoing disregard for the educational connections between and among dance, poetry, play, singing, responsibility, intellectual edification, and non-oppressive political involvement. Critical Theory's Diasporic Philosophy's addressing the richness, meaninglessness, and potentialities of being-toward-the-Godless-world, with no absolute, with no undeceiving "home-returning" telos, is the only gate for hope.[30] Here we should remind ourselves that hope was so central to Critical Theory,[31] not part of a normalizing education that calls us to be swallowed by ethnocentrism and dogma as an alternative to an irrational intimacy with the cosmos, but on the contrary, as the only open gate to a mature, Diasporic, intimacy with loving, creatively improvising, Life in a Godless world. It is a Godless world not in the sense that there is no meaning to God but in the sense of the meaningful absence of God, and the *presence of creative metaphysical violence*,[32] suffering, and meaninglessness in a human life.

Critical Pedagogy, in all its versions, did not even try to develop a serious response to the theological and philosophical challenges presented by "environmental" education at its best.[33] This absence also signifies the lack of courage to search for a connection between (**A**) passions, intellect, the ethical-I, imagination, responsibility, and creative-improvisation; (**B**) human and nature, or Being and human beings; (**C**) the totality of eternity and (the totality of) "the moment"; (**D**) signifier and signified (which are dissociated only as an abstraction). This neglect is not a mistake, a shortcoming, or an abandonment, to be "fixed" by the new masters of Critical Pedagogy. It is essential to the very philosophical foundations of current Critical Pedagogy.

The various versions of current Critical Pedagogy do not continue the attempt of Critical Theory to offer a holistic (negative) Utopia, within which new, yet, essential, *connections are established between the aesthetic, the ethical, the intellectual, the existential, and the political.* Surely it does not follow Horkheimer's critique of Marx, according to which his work misses too much when it disregards Love.[34] Current

30 Ilan Gur-Ze'ev, "Max Horkheimer's political theology as a new Jewish diasporic philosophy", in: Christoph Schmidt (ed.), *Political Theology Today* (forthcoming).

31 Max Horkheimer, *Gesammelte Schriften*, VII., p. 386.

32 Jacques Derrida, "Violence and metaphysics", *Writing and Difference*, translated by Alan Bass, Chicago: University of Chicago Press, 1978, p. 86.

33 Bowers, C. A. *Education for Eco-Justice and Community*, Athens: University of Georgia Press 2001; Gerhard de Haan, Julia Mann and others (eds.), *Educating for Sustainability*, Frankfurt a.Main: Peter Lang, 2001; Joy A. Palmer, *Environmental Education in the 21ˢᵗ Century—Theory, Practice, Progress and Promise*, London: Routledge 1998.

34 Max Horkheimer, "[Disskussionen ueber die Theorie der Buduerfnisse]", *Gesammelte Schriften*, XII., p. 569.

Critical Pedagogy, so it seems, rejects any effort to become an actual attempt at a counter-educational eros, that refrains from becoming "a project", a "system/dogma", or a new form of collectivism.

And last but not least, current Critical Pedagogy has lost the connection to *Love of Life*. I have to say these hard words even when they refer to some of my best friends: their "critique" does not manifest love and distances itself from Life, packs itself into the mechanical, abstract, and violent level of the political and the historical; it is not only far from becoming creative—it is ultimately even irrelevant, dogmatic, and normalizing, and of the kind it is committed to emancipate us from.

Critical Theory in its mature form manifested *religiosity* as a relation to the cosmos. It was aware and proud of it. The present versions of Critical Pedagogy, while normally being committed anti-traditionalist and anti-religious, tend to assume an anti-religious position to the kind of religiosity that Adorno and Horkheimer praised in Judaism.[35] At the same time Critical Pedagogy itself has become more of a religion in the traditional, institutional, dogmatic, and oppressive sense.

Much more than a religious-creative-cathartic experience and an erotic dialogical edification, the "implementations" of the ideas of Adorno and Horkheimer by Critical Pedagogy masters tend to become rival, close ideologies, reproduced by closed sects of naïve, fanatic devotees. Their coldness, mechanism, and commitment to "effectiveness" distance them not only from the Critical Theory, but from *Life* and from possibilities of genuine creativity and worthy struggles to transcend educational violence.

Present-day versions of Critical Pedagogy tend to reproduce and defend collectivism and self-evidence (even if only that of the oppressed and not that of their victimizers). In their commitment to defend the victims and support their efforts to regain security, honor, wellbeing, and possibilities for rich development, Critical Pedagogy masters tend so often to justify and enhance the self-evidence and ethnocentrism of the marginalized and the oppressed. Here too in distancing themselves from the mature Critical Theory they have aligned themselves with greatest threats to the autonomy, happiness, responsibility, creativity, and solidarity of humans, as understood by Benjamin, Adorno, and Horkheimer. And they have surely missed the self-irony that was so much part of the religiosity of Adorno, Horkheimer, and Benjamin. That is why these versions of Critical Pedagogy, for all their importance—and they are so important in so many ways, are to be considered much more as part of normalizing education and less as part of current worthy counter-education.

What is there to be said about counter-education in relation to the current versions of Critical Pedagogy? Much is to be said about the relation between the possibilities of present-day counter-education in relation to Critical Pedagogy. This is because Critical Pedagogy, even when it collapses into dogmatic, non-creative, and ethnocentrist practices of "emancipation" and "critique", still symbolizes the quest for **the totally other**; a refusal to be swallowed by the temptations, imperatives, and fashions of the world of facts, the productivity of its power-relations and the limits set by its historical

35   Max Horkheimer, *Gesammelte Schriften*, VIII, Frankfurt a.Main 1985, pp. 170; 182–183.

horizons; transcending what Gnosis considered the manifestations of the (evil) presence of the God of creation. Even in face of an anti-utopian "reality" it still symbolizes the essence of the utopian commitment—even if against its own will. Its critical impulse[36] still symbolizes in its essence the possibilities for genuine, transcending, anti-collectivistic, and anti-instrumental-oriented reflection; its essence still insists on calling for *the birth of the nomadic eternal-improviser*. Critical Pedagogy, when true to itself, might still summon humans to overcome the reality it serves and represents; its call, however, if true to itself, is always negative, and it could only become a not-yet-deciphered *invitation*. As such, and only as such, it should send an invitation to transcend the numerous assorted temptations and practices that each moment join forces anew to push humans back into thingness; into the meaningless continuum of the immanence. This is where genuine counter-education might embark on its awakening; here is the potential starting point of Diasporic philosophy and its relevance to the field of education. This is where today's Critical Pedagogy, at best, is silent. This is where, at its best, it could learn so much from Critical Theory.

2. Critical Theory and Diasporic Philosophy. Critical Theory of the second stage in the development of the Frankfurt School[37] might be considered part of a philosophical tradition with roots much deeper than those of critical philosophy and modern revolutionary praxis; one might consider its roots in Gnosis, or even in the philosophy of Heraclites; maybe even in that of Anaximander and the problematization of Being and nothingness, thinking, and cosmos in light of the principle of individuation and Life and its inevitable suffering, punishments, and redemption.[38] Here I shall be content with only few words on Diasporic Philosophy and its implications for counter-education in light of the shortcomings and relevance of current Critical Pedagogy. To this topic I have devoted some effort on other occasions.[39]

I begin with the assertion that Diasporic Philosophy is more than a philosophical "stance" or "orientation"; it has a rich, deep, and wide-ranging past—if we dare to re-construct and re-interpret in this light works of thinkers such as Heraclites, Markion, Pascal, de Montagne, Kierkegaard, Nietzsche, Schopenhauer, Kafka, Heidegger, Adorno, Camus, Derrida, Levinas, Rushdie, and Deleuze, to name only a few. Some non-Western cultures have given rise to other important Diasporic thinkers. Not all cultures have done so, however, certainly not in the same forms and with equal richness. Nevertheless, their philosophical importance is vital for any further enhancement of a future genuine cosmopolitic Diasporic Philosophy that will offer a serious

---

36   Even when articulated in a manner that serves nothing more than an alternative, rival, violent realm of self-evidence that will enhance the violent productivity of the "we" against the "they" and their otherness.

37   Ilan Gur-Ze'ev, *The Frankfurt School and the History of Pessimism*, Jerusalem: Magnes Press 1996 (in Hebrew).

38   Anaximander, in: Jonathan Barnes, *The Presocratic Philosophers*, London and New York: Routledge 1986, p. 29.

39   Ilan Gur-Ze'ev, "Diasporic philosophy and counter-education" Website see: http://construct.haifa. ac.il/~ilangz/new/

counter-education. What we are facing here is the possibility of counter-education in a multicultural world governed by Instrumental Rationality, global capitalism, and the reactions of the world of Jihad to the MacWorld in face of the speedy, daily, McDonaldization of reality.[40]

Diasporic Philosophy—of which I consider Critical Theory in its second stage of development a part—has no starting point; nor does it have a telos or a territory; and it undoubtedly distances itself from all forms of "home-returning" projects.[41] Still, above all Diasporic Philosophy manifests *the erotic essence of Being*. Love of Life—not "critique" or a claim for justice to the oppressed, or revenge, is essential to it. Eagerness and dynamism, creation and renewal of creation in face of production toward nothingness; creation as a birth of Love, as a loving impetus—all these are essential. Its very existence, however, inevitably faces violence, meaninglessness, anti-creative horizons, and de-humanizing preconditions for any authentic creativity, for any quest for nearness to the truth of Being, for any responsibility that is more than an echo of the original, innovative, violence that enforced it, and for thinking itself.

Not being at "home" at all cost; refusing becoming swallowed by the self-evidence, self-content, and the negation of the Other at "home" and "there" is essential to Diasporic Philosophy. Refusing any identity thinking[42] or any positive Utopia is essential here ontologically, epistemologically, ethically, existentially, and politically. This runs counter to the historic tension between the concepts of Diaspora and Redemption, which was traditionally conceived within a framework of a promised synthesis, "salvation", or "solution"; even if in the form offered by Pyrrho the skeptic, who insisted on a concluding, total, silence; or Philipp Mainlander, who asserted that the act of suicide of entire humanity and the destruction of all the world will invite a a renewed pre-creationist harmonious nothingness.[43]

Diasporic Philosophy refuses all forms of positive Utopia in theory and practice. It overcomes any theoretical or political "home", self-evidence, truth, self-content, nirvana, and all other manifestations of Tanathus. In this sense it insists on consistent negativity as a form of Life.

Diasporic Philosophy emphasizes, but does not idolize, difference, *improvised continuation* as an alternative to *deterministic-mechanistic continuum*; it seriously faces *immediacy* in its intimate relation to *eternity, meaninglessness, violence, and historical productivity*. At the same time, it refuses relativism, nihilism, and pragmatism, and insists on religious existence, poetic creativity and courageous nomadism. It calls for a responsible self-constitution and reflection as one of the manifestations of human uniqueness in an infinite cosmos that is present in eternity as well as in the totality of

---

40   Scot Lash and Urry John, *The End of Organized Capitalism*, Madison Wisconsin: The University of Wisconsin Press 1991; Stuart Hall, "Brave new world: the debate about post-fordism", *Socialist Review* 2: 1, pp. 57–64.

41   Ilan Gur-Ze'ev, *Toward Diasporic Education—Multiculturalism, Post-colonialism and Counter-Education in the Post-Modern Era*, Tel Aviv: Resling 2004, p. 71.

42   Theodor Adorno, *Negative Dialectics*, translated by E. B. Ashton, New York: Continuum, 1999.

43   Philipp Mainlaender, *Philosophie der Erloesung*, Berlin 1876 (a new reprint: Hildesheim 1996).

each and every moment. It is focused on the presence of **the not-yet**, the potential, **the totally other**, and its wholly-presence in a Life which, ultimately, is not to be totally represented, controlled, or predicted.

The human being, as part of the infinite openness of Being, is essentially *free* because it is lost; it is lost in the cosmos, and as such it is in the state of becoming-toward-the-world and becoming-in-the-world alike. The human is potentially open to overcoming the successes of normalizing education, which is committed to turn him or her from **some-one** into **some-thing**.

3. Subject and cosmos. Critical Pedagogy keeps aloof from the birth-giving tension between humans and cosmos. This challenge was essential to Critical Theory throughout its evolution. Critical Pedagogy abandoned even the standard topics that are regularly dealt with in the framework of "environmental education": issues such as global responsibility for conservation of natural beautiful sites and important recourses; sustainability of the planet and resistance of humanity to dangerous practices of control and consumption of nature; education to critical reconstruction of economic and political interests that legitimate and drive the destruction of inner and outer nature and resistance to their treatment of ecology; and finally, education to responsibility for the future coexistence of humanity and nature.

Until today, Critical Pedagogy almost completely disregarded not just *the cosmopolitic aspects of ecological ethics* in terms of threats to present and future life conditions of all humanity. It disregarded the fundamental philosophical and existential challenges of subject-object relations, in which "nature" is not conceived as a standing reserve either for mere human consumption or as a potential source of dangers, threats, and risks. In many respects the ecological dimensions of Ulrich Becks' concept of "the risk society"[44] are much more advanced and promising than the ecological dimensions in the work of Henry Giroux.

Critical Pedagogy disregarded the *intimate* relations between humans and the cosmos, an intimacy that Diasporic Philosophy conceives as an abyss and mystery, and at the same time as an impetus for Life, Hope, Love, and creativity. Here "nature", "environment", and "ecology" are conceived in a much deeper and wider sense, and are identified in the Other, in one's self, and in the world of representations and their fruits. Counter-education that takes the tradition of Diasporic Philosophy seriously begins here, in the fundamentals of existence, as Heidegger articulated it, in the relations between Being and human beings, or the challenge that humans face according to the myth of Odysseus and the Sirens as interpreted by Adorno and Horkheimer. According to them, this dichotomy is the precondition for the dialectic of Enlightenment and the possibility of the enslavement of humanity to Instrumental Rationality that was supposed to enslave and consume nature in the service of humanity. Effective conquest of the cosmos as a form of "home-returning" after **the Fall** is revealed historically as an anti-diasporic stance that ultimately internalized violence and is in the end is directed not solely against brute "nature" as potential human "resources"

---

44 Ulrich Beck, *Risk Society—Toward a New Modernity*, translated by Mark Ritter, London: Sage Publications 2004.

but against other humans and against the individual himself or herself. Diasporic philosophy might offer here hope, imagination, alternative logics and alternative creative responses to the human situatedness between *cosmic exile and* scarcity (from human's point of view) and *inhuman cosmic affluence.*

Counter-education that takes the tradition of Diasporic Philosophy seriously makes an attempt to establish a Diasporic relation with the "successful", instrumental, enslavement of "nature". The governing borders, disciplines, dichotomies and life possibilities that are founded on instrumental subject-object relations are transcended. Homelessness in the various manifestations of the subject-object dichotomies enable a kind of diasporic life that reopens (negative) intimacy in the cosmos. This intimacy in and with the cosmos is enriched by alienation, sensitivity for suffering and enslavement of other people, creatures, and representations, and opens the gate to Diasporic hope. This hope makes possible Diasporic morality and Diasporic creativity, which manifest love of Life, and not dissatisfaction, greed, fear, and colonialism as a starting point for an alternative relation to the world.

4. Love. Love, as the opposite of violence, stands along with hope, imagination, and authentic, improvising creativity in contrast to fear, self-forgetfulness, greed, and conquest. Diasporic Philosophy represents a kind of homelessness that is opposed to the *self-forgetfulness* manifested in love of God, dedication to control-oppression-mere survival and to any other forms of enslavement to Tanathus.

Contradiction, negation, and tension are not in opposition to Love. On the contrary, according to Diasporic Philosophy *Love* is manifested in Life; and there is no Life but amid, within, and against contradictions, abysses, dangers, and self-constitution amid suffering, meaninglessness, and dialectical dynamics. Love of Life is love of creativity from, against, and towards difference, plurality, impasse and contradiction; yet it represents being-towards, becoming, and transcendence. This is why counter-education, as a manifestation of love, transcends meaninglessness and insists on revealing as creating meaning, aim, and alternative togetherness with the world and Others. Precisely because homelessness is its home it enables (negative) intimacy with the world and its realities and with the Others without a false promise of final reconciliation that actualizes nirvana, or "home-returning". This is the gate to counter-education that enhances genuine creativity that is fertilized by sensitivity to suffering, imagination, hope, and commitment to self-constitution and transcendence; a kind of creativity that is so much more than "art education" or "critical cinema studies" of the kind that are sometimes advanced within the framework of current Critical Pedagogy. Here creativity is an *ecstatic* experience that is essentially religious and manifests love of Life that might become poetically meaningful, good, and beautiful because there is no final point for the "home-returning" project nor any "solution" to meaninglessness, suffering, and loneliness. Love of Life, here, accepts Life as the rich presence of the absence, the absence of the absolute, the endlessly new manifestations of the "not-yet", the potential. This is why the Diasporic human, as a loving, creative, human, is actually an enduring improviser.

5. Creativity. Diasporic Counter-Education might offer new possibilities for human creativity that goes beyond the limits of "art education" which even in its limited form was foreign to most versions of Critical Pedagogy. Diasporic Philosophy faces the instrumentalization of eros and poiesis as a precondition for culture and successful social structures. Creativity is recruited in the service of teleological collective and dogmatic "projects", represented and served by all versions of normalizing education. The autonomy of the human subject and genuine creativity, in all spheres of life, not solely in the arena of what is determined as "art", are a threat to normalizing education, to "law and order", and to "peace". Critical Pedagogy is no exception here.

For Critical Pedagogy too, authentic creativity and its affluence in all spheres of life are a huge threat. Original creativeness is a great peril to the ideology of "emancipation" and to the truths, values, and collectives it is committed to. Genuine counter-education, however, will offer a Diasporic relation to the present achievements of cultures and ideologies, their truths, interests, symbols, agendas, and enemies. In face of meaninglessness, from the edge of the abyss of homelessness in the world of representations, abstractions, and violence it might enable the attendance or at least the quest for the eternal-improviser. The eternal-improviser does not simply abandon "critique". Neither are responsibilities as a citizen and a fellow human neglected: they are transcended.

The eternal-improviser tries to develop an alternative *gaze* and an alternative *eavesdrop*. Such a Diasporic existence makes possible much more than an alternative "art education"; it opens the gate to *Life as a form of art*, while offering a kind of homelessness than enables a new, nomadic, intimacy with the cosmos and all its forms of creativity/destruction. For the Diasporic human, as an eternal-improviser, this new embrace of Being is not in the sphere of abstraction. It is not an ideal to live by, or a mere "inner absolute imperative"; it is beyond "external" and "internal" power; it transcends the dividing line between two versions of metaphysical violence: scarcity as manifested by alienation and fear of the totality of the moment on the one hand, and being swallowed by/open to the *affluence* of intimacy with/against the infinity of eternity on the other. Creativity as a manifestation of Love of Life, for the eternal-improviser here is a manifestation of challenging metaphysical violence in the name of hope by the power of Love and creativity, without being overwhelmed by an optimistic, sentimentalist, or abstract conception of life, art, and education.

Counter-education here goes beyond the best achievements of Critical Pedagogy, yet it does not abandon them. Here ideology critique and empowering the skills and tools of deciphering the politics of cultural reproduction become an important part of art education; and art education becomes integrated with physical education, environmental education, critical cyberspace education, cooking, car repairing education, history lessons, literacy, economics, and so much of the canon. And yet, counter-education transcends all these not solely on the pedagogical level: it transcends all these in a religious sense by re-introducing poiesis in a postmodern world.

Re-approaching the original act of the human hands and reintroducing the body, poetry, play, and erotic togetherness are not abstract and mere fantasy. They are actual life possibilities for mature, religious humans, especially when they are young. As such, they are innovative and inviting. They invite creativity of the kind that opposes and overcomes the reification of art in face of globalizing capitalism and its culture industry. Counter-education here is Diasporic, refuses the calls for consensual reception and embrace by the fashion and hegemonic ideologies and institutions. Here too creativity, if true to itself, must be homeless and not strive for domesticating acknowledgement, consensus, admiration, and domesticating rewards. At the same time, however, it is part of a *nomadic life*, whose happiness and creativity amid suffering, meaninglessness, aimlessness, and misrecognition on the way to an alternative togetherness are enabled by the affluence of Love and the imaginative potential of hope. This path does not lead to nihilism, relativism, solipsism or cannibalistic joy, nor to irresponsibility. On the contrary, for the creative, nomadic, eternal-improviser, response-ability is a precondition for genuine creativity, for re-entering togetherness in a mature manner, and for caring and edifying all loving and transcending manifestations of courageous Life.

6. Response-ability. Diasporic Philosophy is in a sense immoral. Still, it negates all forms of nihilism. It is beyond the hegemonic moral politics because it relates seriously to the possibility of an "*ethical I*".[45] It relates in the most intimate way to the infinite richness of the world and its beauty, meaninglessness, and suffering in the totality of the moment on one level, and to the Other and the political arena on another, historical, level, as one, unifying (yet not systematic), Diasporic existence. On the one level it relates primarily to *response-ability*. On the other level it relates primarily to *respond-ability*.

Response-ability precedes respond-ability. It is related more to the ethical sphere and to the existential more than to the moral-historical-political arenas of human existence and human work. The two are not opposed to genuine responsibility, while they are opposed to the hegemonic social conditions, philosophical foundations, political practices, and fruits of normalized morality. An unsolvable tension, if not an abyss, exists between the two, even if both are authentic manifestation of the richness of Life.

Situated in Diaspora as a Utopian existence, Diasporic responsibility unites response-ability and respond-ability. It addresses the *infinity of the moment* in its endless creative possibilities, dangers, and abysses. It calls for a fundamental communication with the otherness of the Other, which precedes cultural borders, political interests, race, national, gender, and other differences. It precedes yet enables truly rational moral elaborations and critiques. As such it relates to the most intimate manifestations of *becoming-toward- the-world*, the Other, and one's self as a challenge and as an object of shared responsibility, love, creation, and happiness (which might include suffering).

At the same time, however, Diasporic responsibility must also be ready to address the historical moment. And when the moment comes, also to position itself against injustice and even join a wider political practice. It must be relevant to the cognitive, historical, and political dynamics. Yet *it cannot ensure a non-violent consensual histori-*

---

45   Emmanuel Levinas, "The ego and totality", *Collected Philosophical Papers of Emmanuel Levinas*, translated by Alphonso Lingis, Dordrecht: M. Nijhoff, 1987, p. 56.

cal action concerning the ongoing silenced genocide in Southern Sudan, and so much more.

For Diasporic Philosophy, all calls to respond are manifestations of Life as a *call*, as a challenge, as a potential to be addressed and creatively surmount. In face of *the abyss between the ethical and the political* it insists on nomadism and love, creativity and negativity. And as such, it cannot share the positive utopia of Levinas, who to a question in an interview replied: "Yes, an agreement between the ethics and the State is possible. The just State will be the work of just people and the saints, rather than of propaganda and preaching". It insists on what Adorno told us so many years ago, namely "a philosophy forswearing all of that must in the end be irreconcilably at odds with the dominant consciousness. Nothing else raises it above the suspicion of apologetics. Philosophy that satisfies its own intention, and does not childishly skip behind its own history and the real one, has its lifeblood in the resistance against the common practices of today and what they serve, against the justification of what happens to be the case".[46]

Diasporic Philosophy tries, negatively, yet as a form of Love of Life, to address the question of **The Good**. Benjamin, Adorno, and Horkheimer are of vital importance for us today, in responding in a worthy way to the calls of Life and their challenges. Responding here is active. While acknowledging the importance of contemplation, reflection, gaze, openness, and silence, it is directed *giving birth*. It concerns actual activity not philosophical challenges as a closed arena; it directs philosophy as an art of life to calls and challenges that are material, physical, emotional, and spiritual, "inner" and "exterior" ethical, aesthetic, existential, and political. It relates also to the conditions of "the call" as well as to the possibilities of a worthy response and their all-embracing practices.

Responding in a worthy manner is never given, easy, or without a price. Nor is it a skill to be developed by normalizing education. By itself it is a *possibility* as well as an *imperative* for worthy Life that resists becoming swallowed by any "home-returning" project; nor does it abandon responsibility to creation and Love. As such, it is "practice oriented". Its ultimate test is in actuality, in creation, deeds, actions, endeavors that are fundamentally authentic or inauthentic, relate to worthy eavesdropping or to its negation—to its replacement by instrumentalist-oriented focusing. Its actuality is in the attempt to approach new ways to gaze, overcoming the calls to satisfy itself in mere "rationalist" and instrumentalist-oriented use of the eyes. It even directs itself to abandon the collective and positive attempts to unveil the inner truth and the potentials of "the object" of manipulation. Active, responsible, involvement in the world presumes response-ability. In its absence humans' poiesis deteriorates into instrumental-oriented consumption and oppression that begins in self-oppression and concludes in the neglect or oppression of fellow citizens of the cosmos.

Response-ability is born each moment anew among the plants, among the animals, and in the birth of each new human baby. The human, however, treats this potential

---

46 Theodor Adorno, *Critical Models*, translated by Henry Pickford, New York: Columbia University Press, 1998, p. 6.

in a unique manner. So normally, this potential is robed, reworked, and productivized by the system at the instant of the new baby's birth. For humans within sophisticated cultural systems it is a neglected potential, not a given skill. In the framework of the political arena it is to be historically re-created, edified, cultivated, and protected only at the cost of its transformation into its opposite.

Response-ability is not only a potential: for the *ethical I* it is a gate to being true to oneself, a way for self-constitution as some-one and not as some-thing. Response-ability is a potential transcendence that does not disregard the whole and the call to retreat into the infinity of immanence. It aims at transcending thingness. At the same time, it is committed to *overcoming the division between immanence and transcendence.* It acknowledges this challenge as an ethical moment that is also an ontological sign. It does so even if in postmodern conditions humans are urged to self-forgetfulness and loss of genuine response-ability in the most efficient ways, in the name of promised pleasure, economic, emotional, and political rewards, and other agents of self-forgetfulness that work in the service of normalizing education. Diasporic Philosophy offers ontological signs and ethical calls that enable re-facing response-ability, at least as a (negative) Utopia. It enables a kind of counter-education that will call for, never ensure, overcoming self-forgetfulness and normalized morality, nihilism, ethnocentricity, and other "homes" that guard the hegemonic legitimacy of the discourse concerning moral and responsibility.

Diasporic nomadism invites the human; it cannot do more than that. It cannot guarantee or offer anything, not even a clear dividing line between its alternative and other, more attractive or "rewording" alternatives. If true to itself it can only invite the human to follow indirect paths to re-work his or her gaze while widening it and enriching it in new ways and towards more manifestations of Life, in the infinity of each moment. It invites the cultivation of a gaze that is beyond the industrialized focus, as it is developed within the framework of the system that is committed to the fabrication of the "rational human". It invites a different kind of focus; a focus that opens itself to attunement, to a happy attunement to each every degree out of the 360; an attunement that relates also to that which is absent but not from a standpoint of anger, revenge, or greed. It is a focus that enhances new kind of listening. Eavesdropping to each and every voice of the cosmic music, like the one we had as babies and lost with the success of normalizing education. Like the one poetry, music, and dance offer us again and again at rare moments of transcendence. Diasporic life here questions, deconstructs, subverts, yet preserves, accepts, and transcends. It does not offer an abstract negation, abandonment, or forgetfulness of politics, culture, habits, friendships, or experiences—it relates to them differently and overcomes their limiting, domesticating, enclosing effects. In this light it also relates to the category of responsibility.

By *overcoming responsibility in terms set by patriotism, devotion to the class, commitment to a race (or against a certain race), dedication to individual "achievements" or narcissistic-oriented enjoyment,* this counter-education does not put forward an ethical desert: it presents an alternative kind of ethics, a new, Diasporic, response-ability. Diasporic response-ability goes beyond the normalized responses to the post-modern reality on "authentic" paths that enable penetration into "the real"[47] or new age "spiritual" moral transcendence.[48] The gate to genuine response-ability is opened at the moment of accepting responsibility for overcoming the fruits of the violence of normalizing education in the form of aggression, fear, greed, narcissism, and "responsibility" in light of the self-evidence and the other manifestations of "home".

Homelessness without the promise of an emancipatory "home-returning" project in face of the presence of the absence of "God" opens the gate to *true responsibility*. This kind of responsibility is not only opposed to the one constructed by the various human "homes" and "home-returning" projects. It is opposed to the fundamental philosophy of "home", which also offers a kind of psychology that pretends to justify "home" and clarifies its inevitability from a psychological point of view. Diasporic Philosophy opposes the philosophical foundations of this psychology while offering a dialectical critique of the concept of "home" and the kind of responsibility it offers.

Responsibility, within the framework of Diasporic Philosophy, is part of and enables The Good, yet it is a Diasporic Good, not a domesticated good. The Good here accepts and responds to *Life* in an *eternal Diaspora* as a starting point for any reflection on historical and political arenas of human life and the possibility of an alternative philosophy of education. Responsibility here is grounded in Diasporic response-ability as a worthy response to Diaspora in history and Diaspora in politics, and only as such is it true responsibility that enables *The Good*. A true response to the infinite, uneducable otherness of the Other and a worthy response to the richness and meaninglessness of Life unite here in a new, Diasporic, kind of responsibility.

True responsibility is aware of the absence of God, it faces the withdrawal of the Absolute, the arbitrariness of master-signifiers, and the contingency of omnipotent effectiveness of meaninglessness. Today, it must challenge, beyond the dichotomies between modernism and postmodernism, immanence and transcendence, the very possibility of meaning and human activity as becoming-toward-the-world. It must search for new, Diasporic, ways to question that which produces (contextual) truths, (contextual) valid values, (contextual) yardsticks, and (contextual) safe havens and realms of self-evidence. This is the starting-point for a Diasporic *responsible response* to humans' being-in-the-world as becoming-toward-the-world. There is an abyss between *being-in-the-world* and *becoming-toward-the-world*. This tension, however, is a possible gate to caring for the self, for the edification of one's own difference in its relations to the world and to the otherness of the Other.[49]

But how relevant is it to the ongoing silenced genocide in the Southern Sudan, to the systematic starvation of entire populations by the interest rate of loans sent by "the

47 Slavoj Zizek, *Welcome to the Desert of the Real—Five Essays on September 11 and Related Dates*, Tel Aviv 2002, p. 20 (in Hebrew).

48 Hanan Alexander, *Reclaiming Goodness—Education and the Spiritual Quest*, Notre-Dame Ind. University of Notre Dame Press, 2001.

49 Emmanuel Levinas, "Is ontology fundamental?", in Adriaan T. Perezk, Simon Critchley and Robert Bernasconi (eds.), *Emmanuel Levinas—Basic Philosophical Writings*, Bloomington and Indianapolis: Indiana University Press, 1996, p. 9.

free play" of world exchange centers? Or for the future of women's, or children's rights in the Arab world? It is exactly in light of *the abyss between the ethical and the political* that a Diasporic responsibility might enable responsibility also in the historical moment; as an active citizen and as a politically engaged man or woman who is not a prisoner of the Platonic cave, who is not a mere echo/construct/product/agent of contingent power relations and violent educational manipulations. Such a citizen is a Utopia. It is, however, a concrete utopia. It is so far from what (even at their best) the hegemonic program of democratic education, peace education, and Critical Pedagogy offer us today.

The political aspect of Diasporic responsibility is not relevant solely to the politics of the construction of the human and the effective reproduction of her impotence for reflection, self-constitution, and worthy response-ability to its Diasporic situatedness in Life. It is at the same time of vital importance for the relation between this kind of becoming-toward-the world and worthy *response-ability* as against being-in-the-world and the possible *respond-ability* as a human situatedness in a specific historical moment, as a counter-educator.

Diasporic response-ability in the physical, psychic, spiritual, existential, ethical, and poetical aspects is a precondition for a worthy respond-ability in the social arena. In many respects it challenges the political dimensions of life and enables the nomadic eternal-improviser to free herself from the limits, imperatives, and manipulations of "the political". Diasporic counter-education must be very clear on this point: it is political in the sense that it challenges the political. It does not disregard the historical moment and the specific material, social, political, and cultural context. It relates to the historical sphere and the social arena in the most specific and concrete manner—in order to avoid being swallowed by their manipulations.

Does this mean that Diasporic counter-education is escapist and apolitical, and actually offers a tempting retreat into the "inner" world of the elect?

Politics. This is a fair question. It was not easy to answer even for late Horkheimer and Adorno. Late Horkheimer explicitly asserts that not "the revolution" is the aim of mature Critical Theory but the struggle of and for the autonomy of the "spiritual" individual.[50] My reply would be that such a counter-education would become politically involved and would not abandon politics. But it will become politically involved in the most responsible manner, namely engaging the contextual social realities in order to enable the individual to realize his or her respond-ability; respond-ability whose actualization will offer creative possibilities for doing **The Good** while *overcoming the logic of the politics altogether.* Here many of the fruits of Critical Theory would be very relevant and productive. Again, all this only to direct a critique and to respond to injustice not within the framework of an alternative collective or worthier dogma. Counter-education here offers an invitation to a kind of political involvement that manifests the situatedness of the ethical within the framework of the political only to overcome the political and to transcend the historical moment—not to enslave one's life to the imperatives, limits, and possibilities of the political. Again, it is not

---

50   Max Horkheimer, *Gesammelte Schriften*, VII., p. 341.

the bridge between the ethical and the political; it is the situatedness of the Diasporic eternal-improviser in the specific historical moment that enables his or her involvement in the social arena. And such an involvement is not only unavoidable, it is a worthy manifestation of the attempt to approach the truth of counter-education and the Diasporic existence.

In another sense, the "realization" of Diasporic counter-education in the social arena in each historical moment is never solely critical of and negative toward politics. It must become dialectically engaged in manners that will give birth to new possibilities for human togetherness. Of special importance it is for such a counter-education to open the way to *new kinds of togetherness* amid suffering, injustice and manipulations, for victims and victimizers alike, freeing them from their "homes" and normalized responsibilities. There should be a way for forgiveness and charity to all humans—yet not for all human deeds.

Central to a Diasporic counter-education are the sensitivity and self-directedness to human life as *becoming-toward-the world*. It manifests self-accepted transcendence as Love of life, and not as a mere echo, or a reaction of fear. As counter-education it does not educate to fear *loneliness in the Godless world*. As a Diasporic alternative it tries to offer concrete practices for edifying skills, sensitivities, knowledge, and practices that will enable the existence of the nomadic human that maybe we could call *the eternal-improviser*. The nomadism of the eternal-improviser enhances skills and knowledge of various kinds. Of vital importance among these are the response-ability to a changing and ever-veiling dynamics. Authentic responses are potentials of Life as a serious play, as a form of art;[51] they edify creativity as an ethical, physical, and intellectual becoming-toward-the-world. It is a nomadic becoming on all levels, and as such it challenges the fruits of normalizing education and the subjectification processes that precondition "home", "responsibility", stable "I", social order, and cultural progress. Like freedom, however, the connection between response-ability and respond-ability cannot be guaranteed, delivered or "correctly realized" in advanced—it must be freely decided, struggled for, each moment anew under odd conditions.

And yet, responding in a worthy manner to the call of **the totally other** and the new possibilities, it might (or might not) introduce/impose a potential that might be learned and cultivated. But it assumes a different kind of learning and a new kind of thinking.[52] It relates very much to what Adorno conceived as educated maturity.[53]

Here the responsibility of the counter-educator will be actualized in self-education and in inviting other individuals to self-education in manners, by skills, with and against methods, and practices that are already elaborated and partially realized in the history of counter-education. Here too, Critical Pedagogy, when it is true to Critical Theory, might become of much relevance. But ultimately response-ability

51   Herbert Marcuse, "Die Zukunft der Kunst", *Neues Forum*, (November-Dezember 1967), pp. 863–870.

52   Martin Heidegger, "The end of philosophy and the task of thinking", in: David F. Krell (ed.), *Martin Heidegger—Basic Writings*, London: Routledge, 1996, p. 449.

53   Theodor Adorno, *Erzihung zur Mundigkeit*, Frankfurt a.Main: Suhrkmp, 1971.

and respond-ability as manifestations of Diasporic responsibility are not to be ensured or authentically delivered. Openness, danger, and eros, here too, must have the last word. It is always put to the test in relation to the connection of human life to the moment, to history, and to eternity. Critical Pedagogy restricted itself to the historical sphere and the social arena. Diasporic counter-education that takes seriously the work of the Frankfurt School thinkers, however, might contribute so much if it related to the tensions, gaps, and connections of the moment, history, and eternity, for humans, animals, plants, and other manifestations of Life as a source of hope and transcendence, not solely as different manifestations of the Platonic cave. Politics, or the world of contingent power-relations and violent symbolic and direct dynamics, here becomes a very relevant factor, yet never has the upper hand. The Diasporic eternal-improviser, when true to himself or herself, is never a totally controlled citizen of **The Earthly City**; he or she resists becoming-swallowed-by-the-system, the historical facts, or the social horizons. He or she crosses from the infinity of each moment to eternity, or from eternity retreats to the historical sphere and to the infinity of a fleeting moment. Parallel to the asymmetry and the absence of hierarchy and determined order between the *moment, history,* and *eternity* is the absence of hierarchy and determinism between *reality, its hermeneutical depths. It parallels also* the *"cosmic music"* of that which is symbolized by " reality", its representations, its courageous-edifying critique and its creative-transformative interpretations. These two levels are parallel, but do not constantly relate to each other in the same order. So "the moment" relates to "the deeper meaning of reality"; "history" relates to "reality" and its power-relations; and "eternity" relates to "that to which the meaning and telos of history/reality refers too. This third element is not a mere abstract metaphysical category. Not only does it enable the moment and history—it also bursts into the continuum in all its richness, from time to time, in the form of Hope, **The Totally Other**, or the not-yet. For the Diasporic eternal-improviser, as a genuine nomad, this third, uneducable, uncontrollable, element of Life is of outmost importance. It enables the Diasporic existence to become-toward-the-world in infinite ways beyond being swallowed by the immanence and beyond being fragmented and disappearing in one of the "home-returning" projects that promise transcendence and an end to homelessness. Only within this framework is politics challenged from a Diasporic perspective in a way that enables **The Good** in its concrete material, historical and social context.

    Togetherness. Counter-education from the sources of Diasporic Philosophy counters collectivism, combats dogmatism, and opposes all other "homes". It refuses any plea or call for recycling, defending or enhancing the present order of things and its realms of self-evidence. Normalizing processes cannot but end up in collectives that surrender themselves to the destruction of the otherness of the Other as a concrete form of "salvation".[54] Diasporic existence is anti-collectivist-oriented and anti-dogmatic. It refuses the self-abandonment of the individual that is so vital for the historical production of a stable collectives and progressive cultures. This is true not solely in pre-modern and modern spaces, which are so quick to summon their armies,

---

54   Ilan Gur-Ze'ev, *Destroying the Other's Collective Memory,* New York: Peter Lang 2003, pp. 1–24.

habits, and temptations against the otherness of the Other. It is valid also in post-modern spaces such as the cyberspace. Maybe the Hacker, or that which the Hacker symbolizes, is one of the very few exceptions.[55]

Here, in light of a never-ending struggle for overcoming any "home" and collectiv-ism, new possibilities are opened. New prospects are given birth not solely for the self-constitution of the eternal-improviser as a genuine nomad: new leeway is opened for genuine solidarity and for new kinds of togetherness.

The new kinds of togetherness are not committed to the imperative of normalizing education to destroy the otherness of the *"ethical I"* and the otherness of the Other. *Becoming-toward-the-otherness-of-Being* and the infinite expressions of Love of Life might enable a kind of togetherness with the cosmos and all other Life manifestations on new paths that Diasporic self-constitution will pave. This new, Diasporic, togeth-erness with the otherness within the "I", the Other, and the world might crisscross "the moment", "history", and "eternity".[56] Such a self-positioning amid and against Being might enable a better eavesdropping to *the call*, when and if it comes. It might enable a worthy response in the right moment toward and with other Diasporic hu-mans in ways that will give birth to *a new, Diasporic, togetherness*.

A community, not a collective, is here enabled, for a moment, solely for a fragile moment, among Diasporic individuals. If true to themselves they will cherish mo-ments of togetherness as creative, improvising, responsible, Diasporic, individuals, yet will refuse any institutionalization or dogmatization of their—yes, their togetherness. The moment such counter-education is self-content and domesticated it will imme-diately transform itself into nothing but an old-new collective and an old-new form of normalizing education.

---

55   Ilan Gur-Ze'ev, "The Hacker as a counter-educator", in: Ilan Gur-Ze'ev, *Toward Diasporic Education*, Tel Aviv: Resling, pp. 77–92 (Hebrew).
56   See #8. "politics".

CHAPTER 3

ADORNO AND HORKHEIMER: DIASPORIC PHILOSOPHY, NEGATIVE THEOLOGY, AND COUNTER-EDUCATION

CRITICAL THEORY AS A MANIFESTATION OF DIASPORIC PHILOSOPHY

From today's perspective, the work of the Frankfurt School thinkers can be considered the last grand modern attempt to offer transcendence, meaning, and religiosity, rather than "emancipation" and "truth". In the very first stage of their work, up to World War II and the Holocaust, Theodor W. Adorno and Max Horkheimer interlaced the goals of Critical Theory with the Marxian revolutionary project. The development of their thought led them to criticize orthodox Marxism and it ended with a complete break with that tradition,[1] as they developed a quest for a religiosity of a unique kind, connected with the Gnostic tradition and emanating, to a certain extent, from Judaism. This religiosity offers a reformulated *negative theology* within the framework of what I call "*Diasporic philosophy*".[2]

As I have tried to explain elsewhere, Diasporic philosophy represents a *nomadic*, hence "Diasporic", relation to the world, to thinking and to existence.[3] Its starting point is the presence of the *absence* of truth, God, and worthy hedonism. Diasporic philosophy is positioned against any secular and theist philosophical, existential, and political projects that represent positive utopias and reflect "homecoming" quests. While thus calling for the creativity, love of Life and responsibility of *the enduring improviser* it is also committed to rejecting all dogmas and other forms of closure and sameness, it also refuses all versions of nihilism and relativism. In my view, later Critical Theory was in its essence such a Diasporic philosophy, as an existential self-positioning and counter-educational erotic endeavor that opens for us the possibility of non-repressive creation, happiness, responsibility, and worthy suffering that is most relevant to our life in face of global capitalism. This is especially so in face of contemporary postmodern rhetoric and fundamentalist calls for worthy homelessness and a reestablished Garden of Eden.

---

1   Ilan Gur-Ze'ev, *The Frankfurt School and the History of Pessimism,* Jerusalem: Magnes Press, 1996, p. 115 (in Hebrew).

2   Ilan Gur-Ze'ev, *Destroying the Other's Collective Memory,* Peter Lang: New York, 2003. See also: Ilan Gur-Ze'ev, *Toward Diasporic Education,* Tel Aviv: Reseling, 2004, p. 3 (in Hebrew).

3   *Ibid., p.* 9.

The present constitution of the "risk society" and the McWorld that is being cele-brated all over as part and parcel of the capitalist globalization, its culture industry, its technologies and logics, also open new possibilities for Diasporic existence and coun-ter-education. These material conditions and their ontological foundations present new possibilities for counter-education in the most concrete and specific terms and realizations. Improvisation, as one example, here becomes part and parcel of a no-madic existence of today's Diasporic human; and within the framework of counter-education, improvisation in its Diasporic-critical sense may be developed, thought, edified, and implemented as a new self-positioning and de-territorialization in the spirit of Adorno and Horkheimer's religiosity.

CRITICAL THEORY'S ANTI-REVOLUTIONARY END

In establishing Critical Theory as a Diasporic philosophy, Adorno and Horkheimer articulated a unique interpretation not only of the Enlightenment and Marxism, but also of religion and monotheism more generally. Judaism was of special importance for them, as a manifestation of a non-dogmatic and non-violent existential and philo-sophical possibility. In this respect, they continued the interpretation of Jewish pre-monotheistic nature as developed by thinkers such as Theodor Lessing[4] and Jakob Klatzkin,[5] who brought into Jewish thought some of the central conceptions of Ni-etzsche and Ludwig Klages.[6]

In their later work Adorno and Horkheimer came to regard Marx's project as a positive utopia, which by then both had rejected. Horkheimer explicitly declared this trend away from the Marxian thought to that of Schopenhauer and the tradition of philosophical pessimism.[7] By then his thought was plainly anti-revolutionary. It is the nature of the revolutionary, every revolutionary, to become an oppressor.[8] In his view, every revolution, especially a "successful" one, is a manifestation of power. And jus-tice, when it becomes powerful, is realized only at the cost of its transformation into oppression.[9] Adorno had very similar articulations: "civilization itself produces anti-civilization and increasingly reinforces it".[10] Adorno understood that "moral ideas [...] are directly derived from the existence of the suppressors".[11] Likewise, the early conditions for mature independence, by which every free society is predetermined—are already set by the powers and dynamics of the reality of the absence of freedom.[12]

---

4   Theodor Lessing, *Untergang der Erde am Geist (Europa und Asien)*, Hanover: G. Meiner, 1924.
5   Ya'akov Klatzkin, *Shekiat Hachaim*, Berlin: Eshkol, 1925 (in Hebrew).
6   Ludwig Klages, Um Seele und Geist, Muenchen: Ernst Reinhardt Verlag, 1951.
7   Max Horkheimer, *Gesammelte Schriften* VII., Frankfurt a. Main: Suhrkamp, 1985, pp. 339–340.
8   *Ibid.*, p. 418.
9   *Ibid.*, p. 341.
10   Theodor Adorno, *Critical Models,* New York: Columbia University Press, 1998, p. 191.
     Theodor Adorno, *Minima Moralia—Reflections from Damaged Life*, translated by E. F. N. Jephcott, London: Verso, 1999, p. 184.
12   Theodor Adorno, *Erziehung zur Muendigkeit* (Frankfurt a. Main: Suhrkamp) 1971, p. 135.

In contrast to the Marxian tradition, it is now conceived that as long as even some remnants of freedom survive violence will flourish.[13]

> In the end, whatever hopes Marx did hold on behalf of true society, apparently they seem to be the wrong ones, if—and this issue is important to Critical Theory—freedom and justice are interrelated in mutual opposition. The more justice there is, freedom will diminish accordingly.[14]

For both thinkers this truth is ontologically and not historically grounded, and sometimes Adorno articulates it in the language of the Gnostic tradition: "space is nothing but absolute alienation".[15] For him this is the framework for viewing the whole historical reality of advanced technological society, in which everything has become a commodity, and life, with all its layers and dimensions, is nothing but "a fetish of consumption".[16] In their *Dialectic of Enlightenment* Adorno and Horkheimer are not content to target the capitalistic logic and its realization in itself, or representations of totalitarianism such as National Socialism and Stalinism. Ultimately they target the essence of *culture* itself:

> Culture has developed with the protection of the executioner [...] All work and pleasure are protected by the hangman. To contradict this fact is to deny all science and logic. It is impossible to abolish [...] terror and retain civilization. Even the lessening of terror implies a beginning of the process of dissolution.[17]

The conception of revolution and Critical Theory within the framework of historically progressing human emancipation is conceived here within a double-layered philosophy of history, one layer linear, the other circular. From the viewpoint of the circular conception of time there is no room for progress in the Kantian, Hegelian, or Marxian sense, and there is certainly no room for a genuine revolution.

According to Benjamin, there is no document of culture that is not at the same time a document of a barbarity.[18] For Adorno and Horkheimer all substantive levels of "progress" manifest an oppressive regression. In this sense Adaptation to the power of progress involves the regression of power. Each time anew 'progress' brings about those degenerations. They manifest not the unsuccessful but successful progress to

---

13   Max Horkheimer, *Gesammelte Schriften*XIII. (Frankfurt a. Main: Suhrkamp) 1989, p. 247.

14   *Ibid.*, p. 340.

15   Theodor Adorno, *Gesammelte Schriften* X. (Frankfurt a. Main: Suhrkamp) 1970, p. 205.

16   Adorno, *Gesammelte Schriften* III., p. 243.

17   Theodor Adorno and Max Horkheimer, *Negative Dialectic,* Frankfurt a. Main: Fischer, 1988, p. 255.

18   Walter Benjamin, *Gesammelte Schriften* 1.2, Frankfurt a. Main: Suhrkamp, 1972, p. 696.

be its contrary.[19] On the other level of "progress", the explicitly historical one, unless an unpredictable interference occurs the good intentions and progressive talents of educators devoted to revolutionary education are of little use in halting the enhancement and sophistication of barbarism: actually they are its manifestation. In such a reality there is no room for non-repressive "progressive", positive, utopianism, or for an objective, justifiable, education and praxis for resisting and overcoming the present reality.[20] Adorno warns us *against the drive of emancipatory education* to culminate in an anti-mature human positioning[21] of the kind that present critical pedagogy only too often is driven into, in the name of "emancipation", "critique", and "the victims' justified counter-violence".[22]

Adorno and Horkheimer gave up the Marxist conception of progress, and in this sense their optimism as to a social revolutionary change, and even the goal, and to a certain degree also the means, of critique. But they did not abandon Utopia and the essential imperatives of Critical Theory as a counter-education and *political emancipatory praxis*. However, their definition of emancipation and the stance of realization of intellectual autonomy as praxis changed dramatically to become more in line with its early Jewish eschatological sources in the Qumran sect and other Jewish and Christian adherents of the Messianic tradition.

In Horkheimer's work the change from a Marxian Critical Theory to a Diasporic philosophy is paralleled by an articulation of Critical Theory as a new, Jewish, *Negative Theology*. Adorno's *Negative Dialectics* follows the same path, attempting to present what I call "counter-education" as a worthy addressing of the present absence of the quest for transcendence and meaning, and as a Diasporic form of awaiting as a self-education for the human stance of readiness to be called upon. It is a central dimension of "counter-education"[23] within the framework of present-day Diasporic philosophy. This is so in the sense that while refusing any dogma it reintroduces the exiled seriousness about that which is called "redemption" in Christian theology. "'It is even part of my good fortune not to be a house-owner', Nietzsche already wrote in the *Gay Science*. Today we should have to add: it is part of morality not to be at home in one's home".[24]

This is where the Diasporic dimension is so central to the mature thinking of Adorno and Horkheimer. The refusal to dwell in peace in the present order of things, the negation of the "facts" of the actuality, are but a manifestation of the rejection of metaphysical violence and of all kinds of "homes", dogmas, and self-satisfaction in a world of pain, injustice, ugliness, and betrayed love. Since they refused a positive Utopia, their mature thought could not promise a better world as a justification

---

19   Horkheimer and Adorno, *op. cit..*, p. 42.
20   Max Horkheimer, *Eclipse of Reason*, New York: Oxford University Press, p. 26.
21   Theodor Adorno, *Erzieung zuer Muendigkeit*, p. 147.
22   Ilan Gur-Ze'ev, "Toward a nonrepressive critical pedagogy", *Educational Theory*, 48, no. 4 (1998), p. 484.
23   *Ibid.*, p. 484.
24   Theodor Adorno, *Minima Moralia*, p. 39.

for resistance to normalizing education and the quest for pleasure, "success", and hegemony. Homelessness and the moral importance of suffering are here grounded ontologically and become a religious way of life. In this they followed Benjamin's lead: it is a kind of religiosity which is Messianic without a Messiah.[25] As a counter-education it holds out no promise of salvation or of redemption. But it might offer a *Messianic moment*, which will overcome the violence of the governing "now-time"[26] and open the gate to an alternative way of life, an alternative thinking in which challenging Spirit is reclaimed and the de-humanization of humans by the manipulations of the system is resisted as part of the regeneration of Life and its redemption from the all-celebrated triumph of "Spirit" and its cannibalistic-oriented offspring such as Instrumental Rationality.

In this counter-education, *Love* becomes possible, again, as different from the codes, passions, and ideals which are set by the omnipotence of the ruling culture industry. Within the framework of this counter-education the otherness in the self is reclaimed, the otherness of the Other becomes not only legitimate—it becomes an indispensable element in a new kind of Life, in which nomadism is realized on the intellectual and social levels, paralleled by infinite responsibility—with no God, dogma, or party central committee to guide the individual to "the good". **The totally other** bursts in—or does not—and refutes the consensus, unveils the accepted truths, values, passions, and the other manifestations of the self-evidence. It is a Diasporic, ecstatic, dangerous way of life, within which new possibilities are opened but no guarantees are available; no optimism, no room for assured overcoming of the suggestive power of the self-forgetfulness of the human. This does not mean that the human is doomed to passivity. Even if the actuality of **the totally other** is not to be guaranteed, and it is never an object of manipulation, there is still so much to do in order to prepare one's ears to listen to the unfamiliar music of the presence of **the totally other**. Here the Diasporic philosophy of Adorno and Horkheimer is of much relevance for this self-preparation, self edification, self-reflection, responsibility, and creativity within the framework of a present-day Diasporic counter-education.

AGAINST EDUCATIONAL OPTIMISM

To my mind, while the first stage (the revolutionary-optimistic) of Critical Theory became the foundation of today's Critical Pedagogy, the second stage is a brilliant manifestation of *counter-education*, committed not only to criticize, but also to overcome all versions of normalizing education. Adorno's and Horkheimer's later work offers a framework for counter-educational praxis whose religiosity is fertilized by the alarming recognition of the impossible realization of the imperative of human "homecoming" to God, or domesticating absolute Spirit or Reason; the establishment of a genuine "home" or "homecoming" to the advancing true knowledge of genuine human interests and realization of their potentials is here a constitutive element of

---

25 Benjamin, *op. cit.,* p. 203.
26 Walter Benjamin, *Zur Kritik der Gewalt und Andere Ausaetze,* Frankfurt a. Main, 1971, p. 701.

philosophy and politics. The current work of Slavoj Žižek, who writes that "the para-dox of self-consciousness is that it is possible only against the background of its own impossibility",[27] is very close to this later work of Horkheimer and Adorno. In this sense the later Critical Theory writings, which I consider essentially Diasporic in the sense that they try to overcome the quest for "homecoming" in all its manifestations, became prima facie counter-educational, even if the word "education" is rarely men-tioned and schooling is hardly tackled at all.

The big challenge for the critical mind and for humanistic education is not so much the fruit of alienation but the disappearance of (the consciousness of) aliena-tion within the totality, which is governed by Instrumental Rationality. This quest for alienation and the challenges of the exile of critical Spirit and Love of Life mark the difference between a critique of orthodox Marxist ideology and Horkheimer's and Adorno's conceptions. Governing Instrumental Rationality leaves no room for non-efficient and non-pragmatic considerations, and drives out the concepts, ideals, and traditions that allowed speculation and critique of the self-evident, and offered transcendence from the oppressive practices of all master signifiers. Instrumental Rationality is responsible for the current reality, in which the more progressive the processes of de-humanization become, the more efficient becomes the concealment of the oppression by present Culture Industry.[28] The exile of Spirit and Love of life, and the bridging of the abyss between substance and subject, existence and meaning, creation/work and aim, Diasporic self-positioning and quests for "homecoming", are trivialized, and Spirit is again presented; but only as a commodity that has lost its connection to its use value and functions primarily as a violent symbolic interchange, as part of what I call "the pleasure machine" that normalizing education is so quick to celebrate as "reality".[29] Reified consciousness[30] which is fabricated with less and less antagonistic dimensions by the present culture industry reaffirms "spirituality" and "spiritual education" as a power of anti-love-of-life, and occultists are celebrating their victory all over Western culture, especially when it presents itself as the redemptive Diasporic power at the present historical moment.[31]

According to Adorno and Horkheimer there is no stable ground or anchorage to moor optimism or even the very premises of Critical Theory, and a philosopher wor-thy of the name must become what I call "a Diasporic human being". The seeming political freedom, free opinion, and tolerance within present Western society conceal and actually serve the process of totalistic de-humanization.

27   Slavoj Žižek, *Tarring with the Negative—Kant, Hegel and the Critique of Ideology*, Durham: Duke University Press, 1993, p. 15.
28   Theodor Adorno, "Culture industry reconsidered", in Brian O'Connor (ed.), *The Adorno Reader*, Oxford: Blackwell, 2000, p. 233.
29   Gur-Ze'ev, *Destroying the Other's Collective Memory*, p. 2.
30   Adorno, *Critical Models*, p. 200.
31   *Ibid.*, p. 244.

Not only does the mind mould itself for the sake of its marketability, and thus reproduce the socially prevalent categories. Rather, it grows to resemble ever more closely the status quo as its "home" even where it subjectively refrains from making a commodity of itself. The network of the whole is drawn ever tighter [...] It leaves the individual consciousness less and less room for evasion, performs it more and more thoroughly, cuts it off as it were from the possibility of differentiating itself as all difference degenerates to a nuance in the monotony of supply.[32]

The critique of traditional Marxist ideology cannot be of much use since culture itself "has become ideological".[33] "Today", Adorno says, "ideology means society as appearance [...]".[34] However, since ideology is no longer conceived as a socially necessary appearance which veils the "facts", critique of ideology can no longer offer an emancipatory deciphering of "reality" and cannot claim to empower humanistic-oriented resistance to social oppression and to manipulative representations of histories, identities, and realities. Adorno offers a view that does not allow this kind of optimism, since

Ideology today is society itself in so far as its integral power and inevitability, its overwhelming existence-in-itself, surrogates the meaning which that existence has exterminated.[35]

Horkheimer is on the verge of acknowledging that there is no longer justification for a Critical Theory. In a personal letter to Adorno he says that nowadays "reflection [has become] senseless. Actually the world to which we saw ourselves as belonging is destroyed".[36] Elsewhere he writes that serious talk itself has become senseless and that those who refuse to listen—to the attempts to save meaning—are not totally wrong.[37] Truth in this context is not absent; it is rather revealed in, and swallowed by, the present reality. It can, however, offer only technological and scientific advance—not meaning, direction, or responsibility to resist injustice. The issue at stake here is not solely truth or justice but the very *quest* for truth and the commitment to justice, or, in other words, the possibility of transcendence[38] from meaninglessness and from

32 Adorno, "Cultural criticism and society", *The Adorno Reader*, p. 198.
33 *Ibid.*, p. 206.
34 *Ibid.*, p. 207.
35 *Ibid.*
36 Max Horkheimer Archive VI., 13, p. 511.
37 Max Horkheimer, *Dawn & Decline—Notes 1926–1931and 1950–1969* (New York: The Seabury Press, 1978, p. 129.
38 Adorno, "Meditations on metaphysics: after Auschwitz", *The Adorno Reader*, p. 85. See also: "Negative dialectics", *ibid.*, p. 65.

"sameness"[39]—or what Levinas calls the Same[40]—from the mere thingness of Being. Addressing the absence of the foundation for the quest for transcendence and facing its infinity as negative utopia is an ontological sign of Diaspora that Critical Theory offers as an impetus for a possible present-day counter-education.

In the work of later Adorno and Horkheimer, two very different conceptions of truth emerge. One is the hegemony that is established on the existing world of facts, which ultimately represents "power".[41] Here human existence in its essence is revealed at its full price: practical involvement, within which ideals transform into oppression.[42] The implicit negation of any optimistic positive emancipatory educational project of the kind that standard Critical Pedagogy is presently actualizing is mercilessly manifested here.

Within the framework of Critical Theory Adorno offers an alternative. He positions his philosophy against the fundamental assumption of all positive utopias and all "homecoming" philosophical projects: the assumption that the power of thought is sufficient to grasp the totality of the real.[43] In regard to an alternative concept of truth, homelessness and Diasporic existence are here connected to Adorno's central conceptions, among which a special role is reserved for dialectics, non-identity, negation, and reflection. For him

> The name of dialectics says no more, to begin with, than that objects do not go into their concepts without leaving a reminder, that they come to contradict the traditional norm of adequacy [...] It indicates the untruth of identity, the fact that the concept does not exhaust the thing conceived.[44]

In light of the centrality to Adorno's later thought of the concept of nonidentity, it is of vital importance to state that for him what I call "Diaspora" is not a merely epistemological dimension. It is even much more than a way of life, and surely it is not a temporary punishment of humans by God only to be overcome by redemptive "homecoming" to a cosmic harmony and non-alienated human existence. As in the Gnostic tradition, Adorno's rearticulated "exiled good God" is present as an *absence* in the reality of the evil God of historical existence and creative reality. This is why for him, while dialectics is the consistent sense of nonidentity it also assures the impossibility of *any* stable ground for a "standpoint"—not only the "wrong standpoint".[45] The aim of Adorno's Diasporic philosophy is *Diasporic self-reflection*, and self-over-

---

39   Adorno, "Culture industry reconsidered", *The Adorno Reader*, p. 236

40   Emmanuel Levinas, *Collected Philosophical Papers*, translated by Alphonso Lingis, Dordrecht: M. Nijhoff, 1987, p. 55.

41   Adorno and Horkheimer, *op. cit.*, p. 236.

42   *Ibid.*

43   Adorno, "The actuality of philosophy", *The Adorno Reader*, p. 24.

44   Adorno, "Negative dialectics and the possibility of philosophy", *ibid.*, p. 57.

45   *Ibid.*

coming, which will make possible transcendence, with no ground, ultimate end, or appeasing nihilistic pleasure, rational conclusion, totalizing synthesis, or any other kind of "home" or redemption.

In an imaginary conversation between the philosopher—an implicit reference to the masters of Critical Theory themselves—and the practical man, the philosopher is the one on the defensive, not his practical interlocutor. The genuine philosopher is introduced by Adorno and Horkheimer not as a promising educator but as a neurotic, who manifests his refusal to be cured when insisting on continuing his project of curing normal, realistic-oriented, sane, people.[46] Facing these conclusions one should ask, what, if any, is the justification for Critical Theory and for Critical Pedagogy as emancipatory education in action, under conditions in which "serious philosophy has come to its end"?[47] One may ask if there is a secure or insecure yet worthy non-religious "home" even for counter-education, if Adorno is right in saying:

> Whatever wants nothing to do with the trajectory of history belongs all the more truly to it. History promises no salvation and offers the possibility of hope only to the concept whose movements follows history's path to the very extreme.[48]

CRITICAL THEORY AS A JEWISH NEGATIVE THEOLOGY

The later Horkheimer presents mature Critical Theory as a Jewish Negative Theology. This change carries major educational implications. Following Benjamin, it was for him of vital importance that Judaism did not present God as a positive absolute. The negativity of this utopianism is constituted of two elements: the first is rejection in principle of the possibility of a positive realization of any Utopia. Horkheimer refuses to imagine a positive picture of future society prior to its realization.[49] The second is his commitment to confront Critical Theory with its own negativity and its own impossibility. This is a challenge worthy of a Diasporic philosophy that cannot satisfy itself in a concluding synthesis, not even in its essential homelessness or negativity. It is this challenge that opens the gate to counter-education, and in many respects it is the gate itself. In Adorno's words

> The plain contradiction of this challenge is that of philosophy itself, which is thereby qualified as dialectics before getting entangled in its individual contradictions. The work of philosophical self-reflection consists in unrevealing that paradox. Everything else is signification, secondhand […].[50]

46 Adorno and Horkheimer, *op. cit.*, p. 255.
47 Horkheimer, *Gesammelte Schriften* VII., p. 404.
48 Adorno, "Why still philosophy?" *Critical Models*, p. 17.
49 Horkheimer, *Gesammelte Schriften* VII., p. 382.
50 Adorno, "Negative dialectics", *The Adorno Reader*, p. 60.

As genuine Diasporic philosophers, both Adorno and Horkheimer refuse any philosophy that leads to consensus, synthesis, and the end of dialectics and worthy suffering. Yet at the same time they refuse to abandon the quest for the Messiah or human
emancipation. The *quest*, as a Messianic tension, is central here, not its "successful"
fulfillment. The messianic quest so often is interwoven in a positive Diasporic philosophy that it makes possible the institutionalization of religion and normalizing,
repressive, religious education, which challenges genuine religiosity and authentic
Diasporic existence. Adorno and Horkheimer are careful to position in the center of
their counter-education a different Diasporic attitude to Messianism, reflection, and
transcendence. In his *Minima Moralia* Adorno concludes that

> The only philosophy which can be responsibly practiced in face of de-
> spair is the attempt to contemplate all things as they would present
> themselves from the standpoint of redemption. Knowledge has no
> light but that shed on the world by redemption: all else is reconstruc-
> tion, mere technique. Perspectives must be fashioned that displace and
> estrange the world, reveal it to be, with its rifts and crevices, as indigent
> and distorted as it will appear one day in the messianic light.[51]

That is why Judaism was so important for Horkheimer. He saw in it "a non-positive
religion", "a hope for the coming of the Messiah".[52] Judaism, within this framework,
is not a reality but a symbol for—non-violent—solidarity of the powerless.[53] As a Jewish Negative Theology, Critical Theory expresses, in his view, "a refusal to recognize
power as an argument for truth".[54] Horkheimer's contribution to the Diasporic perspective is here crystal clear when he identifies "Judaism", as a "non-positive religion",
with Critical Theory. Adorno too understood the refusal of power, effectiveness, and
domestication in the "Same" of the world of facts as a precondition for genuine counter-education that would challenge the present reality.[55]

The conception of being in the continuum of *ontological Diaspora* was vital for presenting late Critical Theory as a Jewish Negative Theology. The uniqueness of Judaism
lies in its permanent demand for justice, emerging out of a hope with no real historical anchor: "Jewry was not a powerful state, but the hope for justice at the end of the
world".[56] The idea that *the demand for justice essentially cannot obtain power*, and that
justice can be realized only at the cost of its transformation into its opposite—injustice, is
central to the educational implications of this version of Critical Theory.

In my mind it implies that counter-education must not attempt to transcend negativism; it is committed to anti-dogmatism and it must resist any manifestation of the

---

51   Adorno, *Minima Moralia*, p. 247.
52   Horkheimer, *Gesammelte Schriften* XIV., p. 331.
53   *Ibid.*, p. 140.
54   Horkheimer, *Gesammelte Schriften* XIV., p. 139.
55   Adorno, *Erziehung zur Muendigkeit*, p. 147.
56   Horkheimer, *Dawn & Decline*, p. 206.

self-evident, even that of the oppressed and the persecuted. It must resist populariza-tion and political victories. At the same time its Messianism is directed to resisting actual injustices in the present reality as the only manifestation of the quest for truth and justice. This version of Negative Theology as a mature Critical Theory in Horkhe-imer's thought complies with Adorno's concept of Negative Dialectics.

It was not in opposition to the view of the philosopher as a neurotic who refuses to be cured, but in compliance with this vision that Adorno articulated the "categorical imperative of philosophy".[57] There he concludes: "it does not hold the key to salva-tion, but allows some hope only to the moment of concept followed by the intellect wherever the path may lead".[58] Yet Adorno's Diasporic philosophy is not consistent enough with itself, and actually Adorno presents Critical Theory as a path to salva-tion after all. This, however, is within a negative framework that leaves no room for any positive Utopia or actual salvation in the sense that traditional positive utopias or optimistic-oriented Critical Pedagogy can promise its disciples. In most of his educa-tional texts Horkheimer too is short of consistent Diasporic philosophy and he offers optimism on the possibility of a worthier education—at the expense of counter-edu-cation, which if genuine must be truly Diasporic and refuse any optimistic version of normalizing education. The explicit philosophical texts of these thinkers in their sec-ond stage of development represent a much more consistent Diasporic philosophy.

Regardless of its situation, according to Adorno philosophy has not concluded its mission. However, it does not have any foundation, self-evidence, social strata, or pain on which to establish its critical education: "Philosophy offers no place from which theory as such might be concretely convicted of the anachronisms it is suspected of, now, as before".[59] Adorno, in accordance with Benjamin and Horkheimer, presents another kind of dialectics that stands in contrast to the orthodox Marxist concept of dialectics and its version of Ideology Critique (as an emancipatory overcoming of al-ienation and false consciousness, and as a precondition for a revolutionary praxis). As a genuine counter-educator he refuses any concept of dialectics that promises victory, emancipation, or peace.

According to Adorno's ontology, human's homelessness is neither a temporary situ-ation nor a punishment, and ontologically it is rooted in the infinite rootlessness, in what Deleuze calls "becoming"[60] or "the rhizomatic", that opens the gate to nomadic existence. Adorno and Horkheimer are united here in refusing any manifestations of the absolute, the totality, the truth, or a positive justice on earth.

Adorno is very much aware of the contradictions at the heart of his project. His Diasporic project rests here, on these contradictions precisely, as a way of overcoming meaninglessness and self-evidence of various kinds, including the revolutionary kind. "The work of philosophical self-reflection consists in unraveling that paradox. Eve-

57 Adorno, "Why philosophy?" *The Adorno Reader*, p. 53.
58 *Ibid.*
59 Adorno, "Negative dialectics and the possibility of philosophy", *ibid.*, p. 55.
60 Gilles Deleuze and Felix Guattari, *A Thousand Plateaus—Capitalism and Schizophrenia*, translated by Brian Mussumi, Minneapolis: University of Minnesota press, p. 294.

rything else is signification, secondhand construction, pre-philosophical activity".[61]
What then remains for philosophy to do? Is there still a mission it can devote itself
to—without transforming itself into its negative and become a new, sophisticated,
version of normalizing education?

Adorno, like Horkheimer, constituted his utopian thought on his philosophical
pessimism, so Negative Dialectics became the last way to save the struggle to challenge
the self-evident and to transcend meaninglessness.

> To change this direction of conceptuality, to give it a turn toward no-
> nidentity, is the hinge of Negative Dialectics. Insight into the consti-
> tutive character of the nonconceptual in the concept would end the
> compulsive identification, which the concept brings unless halted by
> such reflection. Reflection upon its own meaning is the way out of the
> concept's seeming being-in-itself as a unit of meaning.[62]

In this sense, and solely in this sense, "philosophy can make it after all".[63] Adorno's
Diasporic philosophy in this respect becomes the only way to resist the process of
destruction of the autonomy of the human subject.[64] It becomes the only manner of
resistance to being overwhelmed by the one-dimensional functionality and thingness
of the system[65] and its deceiving message of freedom in accordance with the laws of
the market and the current world of facts.[66] As such, within its negativity, it incubates
an alternative to the hegemonic educational message propagated by the Culture Industry: it offers nomadic, creative, religious existence and love via the possibility of
refusal of the present process of subjectification; resistance to the reality of constructing the de-humanized agent. As such Diasporic philosophy offers a kind of thinking
which allows hope of overcoming the current educational reality[67] of which today's
Critical Pedagogy is an important part.

Diasporic philosophy enabled Adorno and Horkheimer to not only effect a radical
critical reconstruction of the present historical moment but to go further into offering
an existential-philosophical counter-educational refusal of all manifestations of power
in the present culture and society. The Diasporic philosophy they constructed was
actually a non-positivistic and anti-optimistic alternative; as in the Gnostic tradition,
it was a call to overcome the omnipotence of the presence of "the evil God". Such an
alternative opened up when they insisted on transcendence, and (against the deceiving call for relativism, nihilism, or pragmatism) on love, meaning, responsibility, and

61   Adorno, "Negative dialectics and the possibility of philosophy", *The Adorno Reader*, p. 60.
62   *Ibid.*, p. 63.
63   *Ibid.*, p. 60.
64   Adorno, *Critical Models*, p. 5.
65   Adorno, "Culture industry reconsidered", *The Adorno Reader*, p. 234.
66   Adorno, "Culture criticism and society", *ibid.*, p. 198.
67   Adorno, "Culture industry reconsidered", *ibid.*, p. 238.

creativity, which are not a mere echo of the hegemonic power-games of the totally administered world.

Critical Theory here becomes an introduction to a renewal of poiesis and ecstatic religiosity without becoming a new dogmatic religious, philosophical, or political "home". At the same time, however, dogmatic and institutionalized religion comes to have special relevance for the Frankfurt School thinkers: they struggled for the very possibility of Diasporic sensitivity to the pursuit for **the totally other**. Only within this Diasporic philosophy and its counter-educational alternatives are we to understand its refusal to abandon the imperative of responsibility to the yet unrealized human potentials. To this imperative, as to the presence of hope out of suffering, they offered only one possible way: that of religious negation.

The message here has its origins in the Jewish messianic impulse, the commitment to transcendence from any consensus, and from any manifestation of the self-evident and the Same; it is a call for a struggle to overcome meaninglessness in a Godless world. In this sense, here any possible educational "implication" should be negative, if it is to be true to itself. At the same time, as genuine counter-education it is a manifestation of love and a concrete realization of joy and creativity, *tikun olam*.[68] In this sense later Adorno and Horkheimer are so important in any attempt to keep alive the quest and the actual appearance of counter-education as a concrete Utopia of education for love in a postmodern condition.

For Adorno and Horkheimer, the transcendental dimension and the concept of the horizon as a limit that does not have the last word determine the frame of struggle which constitutes the "genuine" human—a position that comes close to mystic tradition. According to Adorno, and here he is very close to Heidegger, from whom he and Horkheimer were so concerned to distance themselves[69], what is incubated, that which awaits in the objects themselves needs such intervention to come to speak, while acknowledging and within the framework of the perspective that the exterior forces inflict, offer and mobilize "outside" [...].[70]

This dimension is made especially clear in Horkheimer's unpublished works. In every single thing, he wrote in a private note, a higher aim dwells, which is channeled to external infinity, which transcends it. The negative utopia of Diasporic philosophy is expressed here, on the one hand, by the deeds of the genuine philosopher, which manifest openness and readiness to be called on, geared to a total negation of the given reality as the actuality of "truth, beauty, and goodness".[71] Horkheimer's starting point, however, includes the acknowledgement that these dimensions reflect the absolute, which will forever remain concealed, unreachable, and misconceived. One must

---

68   Gur-Ze'ev, *op. cit.*, p. 9.

69   Theodor Adorno, "Negative dialectics and the possibility of philosophy", *The Adorno Reader*, p. 75.

70   Ilan Gur-Ze'ev, "Critical theory, critical pedagogy and the possibility of counter-education", in Michael Peters, Colin Lankshear, and Mark Olssen (eds.), *Critical Theory and the Human Condition*, New York: Peter Lang 2003, p. 29.

71   Horkheimer, *Gesammelte Schriften* XIV., Frankfurt a. Main: Suhrkamp, 1985, p. 162.

clarify the status of this yearning, a clarification that Horkheimer himself avoided and Adorno did only very little to address. Here we come up against the limits of their mature Critical Theory even when it becomes an implicit rich Diasporic philosophy.

With Horkheimer, as with Adorno and Benjamin, the struggle for the possibilities of transcendence from the boundaries of the horizons of the hegemonic reality transforms this praxis into prayer, a holy deed. Here too, holiness is not conditioned or determined by the level of its "success" but by openness and possibility. In Franz Rosenzweig's views on prayer too,

> The question is not asked here whether the prayer will be answered and fulfilled. The context of the prayer is its fulfillment. The soul prays [...] for the capacity for prayer [...] this ability to pray is the highest gift given to the soul in revelation. This gift is nothing but the capacity for prayer. But by being superior it already passes the boundaries of the realm of capacity. For, with the ability to pray given, the necessity to pray is also included.[72]

In prayer, the yearning for a dialogue between the human as an infinite challenge to her finitude, and "God" as a representation of infinity, is realized. The central force, here, in my opinion, is not in the establishment of an unproblematic meeting with "God" but in the Diasporic facing up to his absence and in the meeting of the existential moment where Sisyphean overcoming of mere (pleasurable/painless/"successful") human life is the aim of human life. A self-contained, domesticated, human subject cannot make possible a true human, since he or she is essentially Diasporic; the human is conditioned by transcendence and *challenging the totality of the immanence.* The traditional concept of prayer[73] represented this idea in a manner still valid, especially in face of the absence of God. As happens so often with love, happiness, and creativity, prayer too, when instrumentalized and institutionalized, negates its own essence and becomes a devoted slave of the reality it is committed to transcend.

Even in order to realize the idea of the autonomous subject, the human is overwhelmed by inhumanity: a desire for power—a desire for "home" in the swallowing presence of the absolute immanence. Unless Diasporic counter-education is offered, no emancipation or redemption awaits but nihilism and disintegration of human culture. Within counter-education the Diasporic community enriches itself by actualizing *improvisation* in all spheres of life in light of the presence of the absence of the absolute, which constitutes the longing for it. This negative presence, the presence of the absence, might reconnect us with the essence of religiosity that is so often misrepresented by the institutionalized religions that constitute the false quest for Diasporic existence as a prelude to "homecoming" to the lost Garden of Eden, nirvana, ultimate pleasure, or other positive utopian versions of human's self-forgetfulness. Counter-education as opposed to the hegemonic Critical Pedagogy and the other manifestations

---

72   Franz Rosenzweig, *The Star of Redemption*, Jerusalem: Bialik Institute, 1970, p. 215 (in Hebrew).
73   Samuel H. Dresner, *Prayer, Humility and Compassion*, Philadelphia, 1970, p. 24.

of normalizing education does not call for "effectiveness", success", or "homecoming". It identifies and challenges the Instrumental Rationality in Critical Pedagogy, radical feminist pedagogies and all other critical optimisms about the emancipatory dimensions of the cyberspace, radical democracy, and post-colonial alternatives as advocated by critical educationalists such as Henry Giroux, Peter McLaren, Douglas Kellner and Patti Latter. As an alternative it can only be edified into a *prayer*. This kind of prayer, however, is articulated as a concrete way of Diasporic life where the eternal-improviser actualizes her relation to the otherness of the Other in all dimensions and levels of Life. Here counter-education makes *nomadism* possible and facilitates the posing of new philosophical questions, a lust which gave power to martyrs at the stake, to monks confronting ancient parchments as absent truths, or to women confronting the systematic oppression that was inflicted on them by the ever-growing sophistication of Western phalocentrism.[74] The desire for **the totally other** as impetus of Love and authentic creativity made possible the reality in the system while challenging it. It allowed transformation, transgression, and border-crossing from one system of self-evidence but also the "homecoming" project and the commitment to "victory", nirvana, closed "truth" and borderless nihilism. It was not only co-opted for the reproduction of the order of things: it also was a power of *change* and altered systems on the existential level of every individual as well as on the level of the rises and falls of entire cultures.

CRITICAL THEORY AS A PRAYER IN A GODLESS WORLD

As an expression of Diasporic yearning for **the totally other**, prayer was traditionally also a gate to the infinite Other, a gate to overcoming its quest for a positive "home", to the absolute. As such it made possible the birth of young ears that were able to respond to the wordless invitation to Diasporic existence. Prayer, when true to itself, incubates the religious quest, the existential readiness, for such an openness to infinity. As such, prayer also includes a type of special knowledge, and it already represents, in this world, a genuine remnant of the moment of creation. As Rabbi Moshe Sofer (Hatam Sofer) said: "The lamentation over the destruction is itself the building". This knowledge with which we are dealing is close to Gnostic knowledge—or rather the struggle for knowledge in the Gnostic sense of the word.[75]

Gnosis was the struggle for the knowledge of "the good exiled God", the understanding of which was unattainable, hence its noble Diasporic position. Adorno and Horkheimer viewed the "understanding" of the given reality as stipulated in connection with the absolute; an affinity which is viewed as a certain type of knowledge, or conditioned in a specific type of knowledge, which is different from that which is reproduced in the hegemonic realm of self-evidence. In this manner even they, in their Diasporic philosophy, like gnosis, sought after metaphysical knowledge, which

---

74 Ilan Gur-Ze'ev, "Cyberfeminism and education in the era of the exile of spirit", *Educational Theory*, 49, no. 4 (Fall 1999), p. 452.

75 Hans Jonas, *The Gnostic Religion*, Boston: Beacon Press, 1963, p. 32.

can be defined as the "knowledge of the secrets of the universe". Only in this sense can a human hope to achieve salvation.[76] Within the framework of Critical Theory this is the quest for the secrets of the universe, inasmuch as it is a human universe.

Horkheimer's Negative Utopianism as prayer and as Diasporic existence has three aspects. The first is the advent of an ideal Diasporic, anti-ethnocentristic-oriented community in which one can attempt to see levels of religion, or an established cult with a special jargon, rituals and gestures, common enemies, similar societal background, etc., within this Diasporic philosophy. Negative Utopianism is also an invitation to the Diasporic community as a sort of "praying congregation", present in writings of Rosenzweig, as well as the method of establishing this community. To a certain degree, this type of community already exists.

The second aspect is the establishment of the religious ecstatic dimension of this Diasporic philosophy in relation to the absence of the absolute. According to Heschel, the purpose of prayer in Jewish mysticism is to recall God to the world and to establish in it his kingdom.[77] In this respect, prayer is the ladder up to the perfection over the horizon. With Horkheimer, the resting point of this ladder is Diasporic existence and the awareness of the absence of the absolute. "The longing for heaven, where he will never enter"[78] relies on the existence of the absolute and supersedes it—and at the same time constitutes it. Horkheimer's endeavor as prayer is very close to that of the *Kabbala* concerning the relationship between mystical prayer and divinity.

According to Moshe Idel, one of the *Kabbala* texts illustrating this belongs to Rabbi Elazar of Worms:

> Let there be the sound of prayer of Israel—for prayer travels upward towards the heavens above their heads and travels and rests on the head of the Almighty and becomes for him a crown [...] for prayer rests like a crown [...] Human prayers are transformed by their relation that they are transcended and become part of the divine escort: Divine Presence, a wreath on the head of God, and 'like the crown'.[79]

Idel sees the composition of a "wreath" by means of prayer as a "crowning of a king". From this aspect he continues, "one can see the *Kabbala* not only as caring for the garden but also caring for the gardener himself".[80]

Adorno and Horkheimer's Diasporic projects are not very far from the essence of kabbalistic yearning—the yearning of the homeless for **the totally other** than the totality of the immanence of the present reality as the manifestation of Being; the yearning for what Levinas calls "the infinite Other", which is a condition for prayer, and at the same time its fruits. With regard to the affinity to the absolute, the Diasporic

76 *Ibid.*, p. 284.
77 Joshua Abraham Heschel, *Man's Quest for God,* New York: Scribner, 1954, p. 61.
78 Horkheimer, *Dawn and Decline*, p. 212.
79 Moshe Idel, *Kabbalah—New Perspectives*, New Haven: Yale University Press, 1988, p. 372.
80 *Ibid.*, p. 197.

project itself appears as a prayer of an eternal nomad, who refuses any positive God, refuses any of the positive utopias and all alternative kinds of "homecoming" projects to the lost Garden of Eden or to its worldly realization. As such there is no place in it for prayer as a separate activity. This is based on the Gnostic view of true prayer: "prayer as a type of higher communication with supreme reality must be quietness".[81]

The third aspect of this Diasporic philosophy is the establishment of the "genuine individual" in the ideal Diasporic community. The ability of the true individual (the philosopher) to send the invitation to the critical conversation—where lies the possibility of the struggle for salvation of the soul—is also the moral duty which Horkheimer imposes on the Diasporic philosopher, and maybe on himself:

> Both prayer and romantic love have a common past. Today both are fading, and there is no better manifestation of it than the propaganda taking place in their name... the praise and the condemnation, the sanctions against the skeptic. If he remains purely negative, he contributes to the validity of regression. To be devoted one to another as man intended, in the past, to do with the assistance of prayer, even though the impotence of prayer and the insignificance of man became a well known thing; to transform into much love... to drive aside the skepticism whenever the social and psychological conditions were exposed and understood and from awareness to them: to drive aside the skepticism without forgetting what these skeptical matters brought about—this is the only resistance the individual can offer in face of the vain progress. It will not cease the decline; it will, however, bear witness on the right thing during the period of darkness.[82]

This responsibility of the Diasporic, religious, human, who has no dogma, collective, pleasure, "truth", "revolution", Garden of Eden, or God to enslave himself to, is born out of an the existential decision—similar to the Kierkegaardian "Either-Or"—which creates dislearning and manifests Love of Life. Adorno and Horkheimer's anthropology understands existence as dependent on that which is beyond it, hence the erotic commitment to transcendence above any given reality or above life as the ecstatic aim of life.

THE DIASPORIC PHILOSOPHY OF ADORNO AND HORKHEIMER

When we elaborate on the religious aspects of Adorno and Horkheimer's Diasporic philosophy it is appropriate to distinguish three terms: religion, religiousness, and theology. The relationship between Critical Theory and theology, especially in the later Adorno and Horkheimer, is very clear. First, many of their foremost peers were declared theologians. Second, they presented theology as a basis for a moral alterna-

81   Raul Mortley, *From Word to Silence*, II., Bonn: Hanstein, 1986, p. 37.
82   Horkheimer, *Dawn and Decline*, p. 206.

tive and for a critique of the present as a whole, and as dealing with historical research and philosophical judgment of the connection to a God in different religions. Third, they use much theological jargon: "martyr", "the resurrection of the dead", "original sin", and "the burning bush". Fourth, Horkheimer defines his Critical Theory and that of Adorno as "negative theology". Fifth, their work fits the theological category, at least by definition of the members of "radical theology". And sixth, their work became important for many theologians—those who did not consider themselves "radicals", and those who not only enriched their theological matters, but also saw the texts of Benjamin, Adorno, and Horkheimer, and even of Habermas, as theological work per se.[83]

Much more problematic is the definition of religion. It is difficult to state if one can see Adorno and Horkheimer's projects as religious. A clue can be found in the comments which Horkheimer wrote for himself one day in March 1969, and did not publish. In these writings he refers to his project as a bona fide religious undertaking, and he plans the last articles of the writings with the purpose of illuminating various aspects of new religiousness. Horkheimer wishes to express four ideas: solidarity; the love of the Other as equal to the integration of theology and science; the basis of fanaticism; and a non-violent solidarity.

These four ideas were supposed to be passed on through these essays: "Our home-land—the Planet"; "He—Like you" (a distortion of the Hebrew usually rendered "Love your neighbor as you would yourself"); "On Output"; and an additional essay which was planned, but never written, supposedly inspired by the condition of Jews in the Diaspora. He sums up the project: "These four ideas must be formulated in such a manner that they will lead to [the advent] of a new praxis which unifies science and religion".[84]

Since the concept of religion seems to us problematic and this connection is not meant to be decided through such an intricate problem—a problem to whose clarification neither Adorno nor Horkheimer devoted proper attention, we shall concentrate on a different kind of problematic: religiousness.

The Diasporic religiousness, which I credit to Adorno and Horkheimer, is similar to the existential religiousness that I find in Kierkegaard—something Adorno clearly states when speaking of Kierkegaard. Adorno and Horkheimer's religiousness is nothing but an interpretation of reality which becomes an ecstatic way of life that not only transcends the historical reality but even transforms the historical moment itself in the sense that it reveals its self-negation in face of the infinite Diasporic essence of Being itself.

As a way of life Diasporic philosophy is not religiousness based on the fear of life but on the affirmation of life, while facing meaninglessness, suffering, and the rejection of all other calls for "homecoming". This refusal makes *nomadism* possible as a

83   E. Arenas, *Kommunikative Handlungen—Die Paradigmatische Bedeutung der Geschichte Jesu fuer eine Handlungstheorie*, Düsseldorf, 1982, p. 379.
84   Horkheimer, "[Nachgelassene Notizen 1949–1969]", *Gesammelte Schriften* XIV, Frankfurt a. Main: Suhrkamp, 1985, 140.

religious way of life. It gives life justification, not through purposefulness of the kind from which the concept of oppression is constituted. This justification is a manifestation of love of life and is a Sisyphean one, in the sense of the religion of the Greeks according to the Nietzschian interpretation. The Diasporic human, then, like the Nietzschian super-human, may be truly happy (which is in opposition to satisfaction by the furnishing of phony needs) through this tragedy. The Greek hero, Nietzsche's super-human, and Horkheimer's philosopher all affirm Life despite their suffering and meaninglessness, but still more out of meaninglessness, suffering, and the absolute absence of the Other.

The Diasporic identification of the possibilities for transcendence from the tyranny of the facts of the present reality is also present in Nietzsche's Dionysianism. While opposed to conventional religion, this nevertheless is "the road towards life", which is essentially "religious", a tragic-"holy" struggle, an "aim" that overcomes "God" and redeems Life and "earth".[85] Horkheimer, for all his criticism, sees Nietzsche as a thinker who symbolizes a will and a way to salvation.[86] The Diasporic religiousness to which we refer to is not stopped by the awareness of "death of God"; on the contrary, this is its starting point. Of this may be said what Victor Nouvo said of radical theology: "a new liberty is formed from the recognition of the death of man and the death of God. It is radical theology which opens the way to this new liberty".[87]

Adorno and Horkheimer's Diasporic philosophy does not lack a belief in the deity: it turns the overcoming of the belief in all forms of "God", the absolute or the positive, into a starting point of a re-articulated Gnostic counter-education for love. As such it abides well with the dealings of modern critical theologians who express true religious tension, which is dependent on "waiving the concept of God as the basis for work", in the words of Dietrich Bonhoffer.[88] This disbelief is close to the religiousness of Karl Barth, who states that today "[true] religiousness is disbelief".[89] Even so, the denial of belief should not be seen as a forgoing of the absolute. It is *this* denial of dogmatic belief which makes possible a burst of vital, absolute belief which wills a life of wandering upon the skeptic. The holy deeds of the skeptic form the totality of his existence and the permanence of his Diasporic community. Historically, this is the difference between weak-spirited skepticism, which is pragmatic or carries the suffix "post", and skeptical religiousness, which enriches that same major religion—one which usually produces power and at the same time promises new eroticism. This Diasporic skepticism is the burning bush of the kind out of which God spoke to Moses (Exodus III, 4). This call out of the burning bush will never be easy to identify as other than the echo of the governing power-games and an effect of the immanence of the symbolic exchange. It will never be totally deciphered, classified, or evaluated; it

85   Friedrich Nietzsche, "Goetzen/Daemmerung", *Werke* II. Muenchen: Carl Hanser Verlag, p. 978.

86   Horkheimer, *Gesammelte Schriften* XIII., Frankfurt a. Main: Suhrkamp, 1985, p. 258.

87   Victor Nuovo, "Some critical remarks on radical theology", *Union Seminary Quarterly Review* XXII. No. 1, (November 1966), p. 25.

88   Dietrich Bonhoffer, *Widerstand und Ergebung*, Muenchen, 1965, p. 191.

89   Karl Barth, *Kirchliche Dogmatik* I., Zuerich, 1932, p. 327.

will always remain beyond, other, an abyss, as understood by the deep religiousness of Moses, Pascal, Schopenhauer, Nietzsche, Benjamin, Adorno, Horkheimer, and Levinas. The idea of "the bush that is never consumed" is to be understood in its connection to Utopian tradition as well.

Adorno and Horkheimer's Diasporic religiousness is closer to the Gnostic tradition than to atheism. In light of the loss of the relevance of the traditional religions as a manifestation of the overcoming of the bad God over Life, or over the primordial, exiled, God, they sought to give "theism a new meaning [...] from within atheism itself".[90] This is in order to save the "Judeo-Christian" Utopia of "unification of truth, love and justice, as expressed in the Messianic idea".[91]

Central to Adorno and Horkheimer's Diasporic philosophy is *Negative Utopianism*. This is Negative Utopianism geared to the human field of struggle over the realization of its potential for being different, and in a sense more, than merely directed by the system. However, it is not the attainment of power that is here stressed but the Diasporic acknowledgement of the impotence of justice and of the human who challenges injustice.

Adorno and Horkheimer's Diasporic religiousness calls for "unification of religion and philosophy in the realm of true solidarity".[92] This type of solidarity is supposed to include science as a central element and to perceive it as a threatening enemy. This is not the concept of utopian science which we find in Marcuse's "principle of the new reality", whose maximal utopian version is supposed to be realized in the future society.

Within the framework of Adorno and Horkheimer's Diasporic philosophy the given reality is not in the realm of "the absolute", nor is it the place that one can decide in connection with this reality itself. Both thinkers came out against "dogmatic atheism" on the one hand and against dogmatic theism on the other.[93]

Utopianism is vital for all versions of Diasporic philosophy, and Negative Utopianism is quintessential for Adorno and Horkheimer. They stress it with special clarity when treating the implicit predecessors of Diasporic philosophy. That is why Horkheimer went so sharply against "Schopenhauer's dogmatic atheism", in which, in his opinion, the idea of "the nil" is no less subjective than the idea of "God", which he refuses to present in a positive manner, in line with the hermetic tradition, Master Eckhart, and Nicolas of Cusa's *De Docta* Ignoratia and its Negative Theology.[94] He made a crucial decision, and because of this refused to give up the utopian desire. The only argument which can be found for this is a moralistic one: a refusal to acknowledge the reality of evil, which characterizes this world. In this context he explicitly speaks of "belief"—belief which is capable of unifying in a moralistic manner the

90   Horkheimer, *op. cit.*, p. 185.
91   *Ibid.*, p. 186.
92   Horkheimer, *Gesammelte Schriften* III., p. 223.
93   Horkheimer, *ibid.*, p. 238.
94   Nicholas of Cusa, *On Learned Ignorance*, translated by Jasper Hopkins, Minneapolis: The Arthur J. Banning Press, p. 84–85.

community that holds that the terrible reality in the world will not have the last word. In other words, in some respects this is a yearning for "true" reality—that intended by the utopian tradition and the tradition of religious salvation. Thus we conclude that ultimately, despite their important contribution to the history of Diasporic philosophy, Horkheimer and Adorno are not consistent in their Diasporic philosophy even in the second stage of their work.

As against this element in their thought it is important to stress that from a consistent Diasporic point of view the Diasporic essence of Being and human essential homelessness when true to itself is the possible arena for dancing with the immanence of the absolute. Only when overcoming the limits of their own work might Adorno and Horkheimer offer us such a transcending dance; a religious counter-education that will insist on transcendence from mere power-relations and meaninglessness. This will be within the framework of Negative Dialectics and nomadism as a way of life. It will be a mode of existence that develops special relations with the Jewish concept of an absent God and traditional Jewish anti-dogmatism and the rejection of any call to establish a national, intellectual or moral "home". This is only ultimately to overcome Jewish Messianism and all other forms of monotheism.[95] This refusal of any attempts at domestication and normalization is the terra to which the negation of the present reality is anchored. Eternal and infinite Diaspora as the manifestation of the absolute makes possible **the grand refusal** and empowers the overcoming of the call to reconcile with the reality and Being swallowed by the historical moment. But what is the non-contingent framework or foundation of "the last truth" or of the negation of its production? Horkheimer's answer is: "the religion".[96] Here the struggle for the salvation of religiousness appears to him synonymous with the struggle for realizing the essence or the aim of Western culture.

DIASPORIC EXISTENCE, JUDAISM, AND COUNTER-EDUCATION

Even if only implicitly, Adorno and Horkheimer accept the Diasporic essence of Being and human life as a starting point for their mature, religious-oriented Critical Theory.[97] This enables them to insist on their critique and on their reconstruction of the omnipotence of power and meaninglessness (namely the apparatuses that produce meanings, values, and drives) in current life, on the one hand, while insisting on transcendence from the present reality and insisting on creativity and moral responsibility on the other.

> We must all be unified by the yearning, which takes place in this world, injustice and horror will not be the final word, what was the other…

95   Gur-Ze'ev, *Toward Diasporic Education*, p. 200.
96   Horkheimer, *op. cit.*, pp. 238–289.
97   Adorno, *Gesammelte Schriften* X., Frankfurt a. Main: Suhrkamp, 1970, p. 137.

what is called religion […] the idea of infinity, which was developed by
religion—we must need it and not give up on it.[98]

The second idea comes to light in the commandment of Jewish religion not to present
a positive description of God,[99] an idea diametrically opposed to the Marcusian utopia as a whole and that realizes the Jewish commandment "Thou shall not make a
statue or mask".[100] These are at the foundation of the Diasporic **grand refusal**, which
contains the same special knowledge that is included in the criticism in the laws of
prayer; this is a privileged knowledge, an erotic response to the sudden possible- break
out-of **the totally other**.

Already, the first phase of Adorno's and Horkheimer's contemplation includes a
Diasporic recognition that one must not establish the truth value of values and goals
and it is impossible to prove objective truths; that already here is the decision to believe; that only from the act of *deciding* to believe can the counter-educational project
spring. The criticism that positions this decision as an experiment to save the moral
must still explain rationally how it is possible to see the preference of this move over
remaining in relativism or subjectivism or replacing a specific belief system with one
of its rivals. The absurd in the decision of Adorno and Horkheimer is that in the absence of the possibility to validate their decision rationally, the project takes place in
the realm of struggle for the salvation of enlightenment—which they criticize in an
extreme manner as an expression of power and oppression. Their decision exists within the realm of their own religiousness, and only it can be used as a systematic base,
just as it provides a utopian purpose as well. But *is it a decision, an act of free choice—or
the reaction to the persuasive power of the arbitrariness of the voice of* the totally other,
that forced itself on them and made possible their free choice to believe? And in what
sense is this arbitrariness and power essentially different from the deceiving power of
present-day Sirens that counter-education directs us to overcome?

The explicit purpose of Adorno's and Horkheimer's Diasporic religiousness in the
second phase of their thought is no longer a revolution, but a struggle for "the autonomy of the individual". [101]

In the struggle for salvation, Horkheimer's *animal symbolicum* overpowers mere
reality and continues on the paved way of the Cabbalists while he sees himself as continuing the position of Schopenhauer. According to this position reality is essentially
not absolute and Life is not governed or reduced to "facts", but the product of the
mind, symbols and allegories, objects for infinite creative interpretations.

> Each thing which turns into a symbol has the ability to bring us down
> into a gutter which cannot be described, to the aspect of nil. In all
> things and every phrase in the world a concealed brilliance of hidden

---

98   Horkheimer, *Gesammelte Schriften* VIII., p. 343.
99   *Ibid.*
100 Herbert Marcuse, "Marx, Freud und der Monotheismus", *Herbert Marcuse Archiv*, 241.00, p. 11.
101 *Ibid.*, p. 341.

life manifests itself for the Cabbalist, infinite life glows inward [...] It is possible to say that the whole world and all acts of genesis are nothing but style of speaking, as a symbolic expression of that layer of what the thought cannot afford, from it a post or a corner of each building which can be achieved by thought.[102]

The place of *Diasporic hope* in Horkheimer's thought also matches its understanding by the theologians of salvation within genuine religiosity: salvation is, first and foremost, a *promise* that "its realization might remain no more than a hope".[103] His "practical optimism" is not attuned to cosmic salvation. It is not even expressed in response to a utopian invitation to an ideal dialogue; within the Diasporic project, on the basis of the hope which it generates, the purpose and the end result of counter-education. Then, and only then, is there room for "practical" optimism in relation to the text and the Other as partners to a responsible, creative, loving, nomadic way of life. In other words, the "optimism" spoken of is found in the context and expresses a dimension of its action, and it is not a force or external condition which establishes this religiousness, which, in the long run, is devoted to an existential decision, which molds a way of life which, in the eyes of the believers, is moralistic. Adorno's and Horkheimer's Diasporic project expresses first and foremost yearning and belief which do not require approval and cannot be negated by the present reality and its logic.

What the new Diasporic philosophy that Adorno and Horkheimer offer us is of the kind traditionally Judaism offered to the world. Today, however, it is offered to us under the evil conditions set by the coalition between global capitalism, the world of Jihad and the postcolonialist agenda. This coalition currently develops along new destructions and distorted creative also new possibilities for counter-education and *active cosmopolitanism*. Of special importance is here the new psychological, philosophical, political and educational potentials of improvising.

This new cosmopolitanism transforms the Gnostic and Messianic traditions in face of postmodern and pre-modern fundamentalist-oriented postcolonialist alternatives. This Messianic moment, even as a potential, is normally distorted, misused, or forgotten. But in face of a cultural, economic, political, and, ultimately existential crisis, it awakes. When and if awoken, it might become an impetus for counter-education exactly against the exile of Spirit, the instrumentalization of reason, and the reification of the human relations. In opposition to the optimists, who establish great hopes for "the chosen ones" or even for all humanity in the cyberspace or on the foundations of globalizing capitalism,[104] I offer a dialectical reconstruction of our historical moment: it is the same globalizing capitalism which rationally sends entire populations into a "flexible job economy", rationalized starvation, structurally guaranteed poor health, and loss of self-respect in the margins of the affluence of "the risk society", which also

---

102 *Ibid.*, p. 227.
103 *Ibid.*, p. 244.
104 Ulrich Beck, *Risk Society—Towards a New Modernity*, translated by Mark Ritter, London: Sage, 2004, pp. 234–235.

opens the door for the instant, global, visibility of suffering, for universal needs and
values, and for new possibilities for creative, loving, responsible, improvising counter-
education and a Diasporic way of life that transcends ethnocentric solidarity, political
borders, and contextual pragmatism and cynicism.[105]

Their work is an important manifestation of counter-education in the Gnostic sense.
As such it manifests a Diasporic Philosophy that refuses all calls for "homecoming", to
God, to the Garden of Eden, to the Patria, to truth, or to mere-pleasure and practical
nihilism. Adorno's and Horkheimer's negative theology, while addressing the relevance
of Jewish traditional anti-dogmatism and anti-collectivism, offers us today, more then
ever, a goal, meaning, and love—without being swallowed by any "pleasure machine",
"truth" or "we". As Diasporic humans we are called upon by their counter-education
to insist on transcendence, to actualize love in creativity and in a kind of togetherness
that is dialogic and refuses any collectivism and all dogmas. In other words this is the
moment of birth of the eternal-improviser. Improvisation is to be thought, cultivated
and actualized in all spheres of public and individual life experiences. It is a precondition, as well as the manifestation, of genuine creativity that transcends the *Same*.
Transcendence here is an ethical act of the eternal-improviser, the Diasporic nomad.
The transcendence of the eternal-improviser, as in the case of the genuine hacker, is
a non-reified creativity; and even in a post-modern arena it is an open possibility. As
Levinas shows us in *Totality and Infinity* the transcendence of the otherness from the
continuum of the *Same* is an act of self-constitution that resists even the philosophical
logos. The Diasporic philosophy should become a source of dislearning and alterity as
well as a gate for authentic religious, creativity and Love that counter-education will
develop in the most concrete and specific ways. Improvisation has many aspects that
are to be thought, developed, edified and actualized: breathing, reclaiming forgotten
and repressed voices, responding to changing situations while holding on to a Gnostic
remembrance of (pre)history and the responsibility to the cosmos and eternity each
moment anew are vital for today's *ethical I*, who opens herself to the poiesis of Godless
religiosity within troubled Life. As such, the later work of Adorno and Horkheimer
makes a genuine contribution to counter-education, which is so much needed in face
of the recent success of the violence of capitalism, postmodernism, and postcolonialism. One of the first steps of current counter-education should be the synthesis of
Adorno's and Horkheimer's critique of Western society and the logic of capitalism
with present day analyses of capitalist globalization processes within the framework of
"risk society" that at the same time opens for the eternal-improviser new possibilities
for Diasporic existence and new realizations of nomadism of the kind that a re-articulated Gnosis might make relevant. Such a counter-education should not abandon
the critical tradition, yet it should insist on Love. It should develop new connections
between the aesthetic and the ethic, the intellectual and the physical, the political
and the religious dimensions of life of a non-dogmatic creator. How ironic it is that
global capitalism, while exiling human spirit and enhancing the omnipotence of the

---

105 Gur-Ze'ev, *Towards Diasporic Education*, pp. 179–202.

creative "evil God", also opens new possibilities for new forms of Gnosis and for new Diasporic individuals and communities.

CHAPTER 4

TOWARD A NON-REPRESSIVE CRITICAL PEDAGOGY

"Critical Pedagogy" has many versions today, as does "critical theory".[1] With important differences between critical theories and the variety of "critical pedagogies", identifying the problems of current Critical Pedagogies becomes difficult, and the development of a positive utopian alternative Critical Pedagogy becomes impossible. For all their differences, all current versions of Critical Pedagogy function as part and parcel of normalizing education and its violence. In this article I suggest an alternative critical education as *counter-education*. Within counter-education no room exists for a positive Utopia, and it does not promise collective emancipation under present circumstances, but counter-education suggests possibilities for identifying, criticizing, and resisting violent practices of normalization, control, and reproduction in a system which uses human beings as its agents and victims. Counter-education opens possibilities for refusing to abandon human potential to become other than directed by the system and the realm of self-evidence. It offers a chance—to be struggled for again and again—to challenge normalizing education in all its versions, including Critical Pedagogy. As I shall show, positive utopianism is the main weakness of current critical pedagogies that challenge the present philosophical, cultural, and social reality. Philosophical negativism, I argue, is a precondition for the development of a non-repressive Critical Pedagogy, which is essentially different from normalizing education. Current versions of Critical Pedagogy lack this negative dimension; all are united by a commitment to positive utopianism, even when explicitly denying it. For all their differences, today's versions of Critical Pedagogy are all based on weak, controlled, and marginalized collectives for their common optimistic view of the possibilities of changing reality and securing unauthoritative emancipation, love and happiness: they forget that the violence of self-evidence and power are the main obstacles to the human's transcendence and realization of her/his potential autonomy. The possibility and the nature of a non-repressive pedagogy is at the heart of my project. Here I suggest an initial step: to explore the exact relation between the philosophical framework and the social tasks of Critical Pedagogy. I begin by concentrating on the Critical Theory of the Frankfurt School as a historical and conceptual framework for developing a non-repressive Critical Pedagogy. I hope thereby to encourage a counter-education

---

1   Henry Giroux, "Radical Pedagogy as a cultural politics: Beyond the discourse of critique and anti-utopianism", in Peter McLaren (ed.), *Critical Pedagogy and Predatory Culture: Oppositional Politics in a Postmoden Era*, London and New York: Routledge 1995, pp. 29–57.

to hegemonic education and to oppose the dogmas and illusions of the hegemonic versions of Critical Pedagogy.

CRITICAL THEORY

The possibilities of the counter-education, which here will be only briefly suggested and generally characterized, are connected to central conceptions and philosophical orientations of critical philosophy, and more specifically to the project of the Frankfurt School thinkers. Their basic concept was the utopian; here I do not refer to a vision of a perfect future human order but to its dual philosophical foundation, namely the centrality of the transcendental dimension of their thought and their denotation of the category of potentiality as an essential element of the thing. According to this conception, the thing is not to be understood from itself. The given is to be evaluated in light of its potential, in light of the "not yet realized" that it incubates within itself. The realization and the blocking of these potentialities were understood in a dialectical historical and material context.

Another central dimension is the Frankfurt School's understanding of the connection between the utopian "hope principle" and the obligation to "the total otherness" from present reality.[2] In this tradition, negation is not a pose but a philosophical stand and a methodology elaborated in the Frankfurt School's concept of knowledge. This negation is inherent, in principle and in practice, philosophically and politically. This is the origin of the negation of the positivistic conception of knowledge that treats the "facts" of current reality as the supreme yardstick for desirable scientific work.

The Critical Theory thinkers saw themselves as committed to a struggle over the total transformation of present reality and not solely over its reconstruction.[3] They emphasized human emancipation as the vital dimension[4] of Critical Theory. This concern arose from the central ideals of Enlightenment, whose realization the Frankfurt School thinkers called for by means of technological possibilities whose absence had made them an abstract Utopia in the past.

Historically, "Critical Pedagogy" was perceived as a realization of the Critical Theory of the Frankfurt School in schools. This can be shown by a thematic and historical reconstruction of the classical manifestations of Critical Pedagogy in the thought of Paulo Freire, Wolfgang Klafki, Michael Apple, Peter McLaren, Ira Shor, Carmen Luke, Jennifer Gore, and Henry Giroux. The Frankfurt School thinkers did not have a narrow "Critical Pedagogy" but all their work concerned education in the subjects of

---

2   Max Horkheimer, *Gesammelte Schriften* 7 Frankfurt a.Main: Fischer Taschenbuch Verlag 1985, p. 385–404.

3   Herbert Marcuse, "Liberation from the Affluent Society", in David Cooper (ed.), *The Dialectic of Liberation*, London: Penguin Books 1971, p. 185.

4   Max Horkheimer, *Traditionelle und Kritische Theorie: Vier Aufsaetze*, Frankfurt a.Main: Fischer Taschenbuch Verlag 1977, p. 37.

knowledge, autonomy, reflectivity and agency, transformation/production/reproduction, and representation of reality, namely education in the broader sense.[5]

Some important questions arise in light of this understanding. First, can this philosophy be reduced to pedagogical theory and practice? Can it frame a didactic setting for use with the very young, the poorly educated, or non-Western cultures ignorant of the cultural tradition and social reality in which Critical Theory was formed? Even if the answers are affirmative, the principles of Critical Theory may not be implementable in present-day institutional schools, which are responsible for the cultural reproduction and normalization of the subject which Critical Theory negates. If the answers to the questions are negative, then standard Critical Pedagogy has to be challenged by today's Critical Theory, which rejects a Critical Pedagogy that is not a "negative pedagogy".[6] In any case, standard *Critical Pedagogy is inappropriate for a defensible Critical Theory of today*. Education in its narrower and broader sense has become a central philosophical issue. In an anti-philosophical era Philosophy is again appearing at the center of political and theoretical public and private spheres of life. Here I shall try to examine these issues by treating two main versions of Critical Pedagogy, one by Paulo Freire and one by Henry Giroux.

CRITICAL PEDAGOGY: PAULO FREIRE

The pedagogy of Paulo Freire is known as "Critical Pedagogy" and, like the pedagogy of Giroux, it also sees the Critical Theory of the Frankfurt School as one of its main sources; others are radical theology and the ideology critique of Antonio Gramsci. Education, according to Freire, is about cultural action for emancipation.[7] In Giroux's language, Freire combines "the language of critique" with "the language of possibilities".[8] Freire emphasizes the concept of education as political practice in the control of "language" and consciousness as a part of and as a condition for the subjection of individuals and groups by the rulers. Freire examines education as an aspect of the relations between critique and domination. He educates against the ruling group's claim that schools are centers for distributing relevant knowledge in an objective and neutral manner.

According to Freire, the model characterizing normal pedagogy's function is the bank. It is designed to reproduce power relations that dominate current society and realize the hegemonic ideology in school. He asserts that normal pedagogy accomplishes this project while blocking possibilities for dialogue. In dialogue he sees equal,

5   Gueter J. Freisenhahn, *Kritische Theorie und Pedagogik: Horkheimer, Adorno, From, Marcuse*, Berlin: Express Edition 1985, p. 1.

6   Hellmut Becker, "Durch paedagogische Aufklaerung den Menschen helfen—Hellmut Becker ueber Kritische Theorie und Pedagogik", *Pedagogische Korrespondenz* 8 (Winter 1990–91), p. 70.

7   Paulo Freire, *Cultural Action for Freedom*, Cambridge: Harvard Educational Review 1974, p. 1.

8   Henry Giroux, "Introduction: literacy and the pedagogy of political empoerment", in Paulo Freire, *The Politics of Education: Culture, Power, and Liberation*, Massachusetts: Bergin & Garvey Publishers 1985, p. xii.

open, and critical intersubjectivity between students and their world, and between teachers and students and the space in which they are situated, as an alternative to power relations in the school and the apparatuses and hierarchies that constitute it.[9] In Freire's opinion, it is of vital importance to transform these powers, hierarchies, and procedures into counter-educational praxis, one which his Critical Pedagogy is committed to constitute. On this level, Freire's understanding of Critical Theory and his Critical Pedagogy unite.

Freire's Critical Pedagogy did not grow out of mere principles but out of his direct involvement with Brazil's poor farmers. He saw that their social and economic misfortune and their lack of a "voice" and of competence to conceive reality critically and comprehensibly could not be separated from their inability to act correctly for a change in their existence. In his second stage of development, Giroux made much use of Freire's emphasis on communality, collective knowledge, and counter-education, which aims to challenge the silencing hegemonic education. Such an education guarantees the weakness and the silence of marginalized groups even when they comprise the majority of the population. Note that unlike Giroux, Freire still formulates his Critical Pedagogy in modernistic categories of class struggle.

The postmodern and the multicultural discourses that influenced Giroux took a one-dimensional attitude to the counter-violence of postcolonialism and to *power* as such. They denoted the importance of deconstructing cultural reproduction and the centrality of relations of dominance for the "voices" of groups whose collective memory, knowledge, and identity were threatened or manipulated by power relations and knowledge conceptions that reflected and served the hegemonic groups. Freire was not aware that this manipulation had two sides, a negative and a positive. The negative side *permitted the realization of violence by guaranteeing possibilities for the successful functioning of a normalized human being and creating possibilities for men and women to become more productive in "their" realm of self-evidence.* Their normality reflected and served this self-evidence by partly *constituting* the human subject as well as the thinking self. Giroux easily extracted from Freire's Critical Pedagogy the elements denoting the importance of acknowledging and respecting the knowledge and identity of marginalized groups and individuals. In fact, this orientation and its telos are in contrast to the central concepts of postmodern educators on the one hand, and to Critical Theories of Adorno, Horkheimer, and even Habermas on the other. But many similar conceptions and attitudes are present as well.

The aim of Freire's Critical Pedagogy is to restore to marginalized groups their stolen "voice", to enable them to recognize, identify, and give their name to the things in the world. The similarity to postmodern critiques is already evident in his acknowledgment that to coin a word correctly is nothing less than to change the world.[10] However, to identify this conception with the postmodern stand is over-hasty because the

9   Paulo Freire and Donaldo Macedo, *Literacy: Reading the Word Reading the World*, London: Routledge and Kegan Paul 1987, p. 49.
10 Paulo Freire, *Pedagogy of the Oppressed*, translated by Ramos Bergmann, New York: Herder and Herder 1968, p. 75.

centrality of language in Freire's thought relates to his concept of "truth" and a class struggle that will allow the marginalized and repressed an authentic "voice",[11] as if their self-evident knowledge is less false than that which their oppressors hold as valid. Implicitly, Freire contends that the interests of all oppressed people are the same, and that one general theory exists for deciphering repressive reality and for developing the potentials absorbed in their collective memory. An alternative critique of language which does not claim to empower the marginalized and the controlled to conceive and articulate their knowledge and needs on the one hand, and is not devoted to their emancipation on the other, is mere "verbalism", according to Freire.[12]

The purpose or common cause of the educator and the educated, the leader and the followers, in a dialogue between equal partners is called here "praxis". In education praxis aims to bridge the gap between theory and transformational action that effectively transforms human existence. This concept of transformation contrasts with the educational concept of Critical Theory and with the tradition of Diasporic philosophy. Here learning and education are basically the individual's responsibility and possibility, and are always an ontological issue while epistemologically concretized in the given historical social context. They are conditioned by an individual's competence to transcend the "father image", prejudices, habits, and external power relations that constitute the collective in order to attain full personal and human growth.[13] According to Freire, this personal development is conditioned by critical acknowledgment and should occur as part of the entire community's revolutionary practice. Only there can successful educational praxis realize its dialogical essence. The dialogue is an authentic encounter between one person and another, an educator and her/his fellow who wants to be dialogically educated, and the encounter should be erotic or not realized at all. "Love" is presented as the center and the essence of dialogue.[14]

Freire's Critical Pedagogy is foundationalist and positivist, in contrast to his explicit negation of this orientation. It is a synthesis between dogmatic idealism and vulgar collectivism meant to sound the authentic voice of the collective, within which the dialogue is supposed to become aware of itself and of the world. The educational links of this synthesis contain a tension between its mystic-terroristic and its reflective-emancipatory dimensions. In Freire's attitude to Fidel Castro and Che Guevara, the terroristic potential contained in the mystic conception of the emancipated "group", "people", or "class" knowledge is revealed within the concept of a dialogue. Freire introduces Che Guevara as an ideal model for anti-violent dialogue between partners to the desirable praxis. Che Guevara used a structurally similar rhetoric to that of Ernst Juenger and National Socialist ideologues on the creative power of war, blood, and sweat in the constitution of a new man, the real "proletar" in South America. Freire

---

11   *Ibid.*
12   *Ibid.*
13   Theodor Adorno, *Erziung zum Muendligkeit: Vortraege und Geschpreche mit Hellmut Becker 1956–1969*, Frankfurt a.Main: Suhrkamp Taschenbuch Verlag 1971, p. 144.
14   Paulo Freire *Pedagogy of the Oppressed*, p. 77–78.

gives this as an example of the liberation of the oppressed within the framework of new "love" relations which allow the silenced "voice" to speak.[15]

His uncritical understanding of power/knowledge relations led him to observe the de-colonization process in Africa and elsewhere (undoubtedly a progressive development in itself) as suitable contexts for national realization of Critical Pedagogy.[16] This is not mere naivety but a readjustment of the terroristic element of his Critical Pedagogy revealed earlier in his understanding of "Che" as an educator in his alliance with the national systematic oppression of "liberated" Third World countries. I do not claim that there is no need to support local struggles for democracy, equality, and development in such countries or that it is impossible for them to be regarded as inferior or undemocratic in principle. My claim does not refer even to a specific country, since it is possible that in some cases a Third World country will develop a flourishing democracy. However, for historical reasons, such as Western imperialism, local power structures, cultural traditions, and conceptual apparatuses, Western-style democracy is not likely to be realized in most of them. My argument refers to Freire's failure in the crucial theoretical and political element of the concept of dialogue and the relation between knowledge and power, consciousness and violence, as presented by Hegel, Marx, Adorno, and Foucault. That is why his emancipatory Eros sides implicitly with the anti-critical tradition of dogmatic revolutionary Christianity and voluntaristic revolutionary models of the anarchists, National Socialism, and South America's guerrillas. These are contrasted with the explicit devotion of his Critical Pedagogy to dialogue, non-functionalist Critical Thinking, as well as spiritual maturity.

Like the Frankfurt School's Critical Theory, Freire's project is also indebted to the negation of present reality. However, from the totality of reality and its power games it attempts to expropriate knowledge of repressive groups as possessing special validity; from the totality governed by Globalizing capitalism, colonialism and instrumental reason it attempts to save a certain "authentic will" and consciousness which are devoted to an erotic praxis. Within Critical Pedagogy they are supposed to be freed from the dynamics and internal logic of reality implicitly, in the name of the superiority of the essence of being. In contrast to Critical Theory's concept of love,[17] this kind of love is immanently violent, even in the sense of political terror and the control of collective and individual consciousness. Its interest in dialogue is not erotic and transcendent but is what Plato called "popular Eros",[18] as manifested by Alcibiades, the great disciple and lover of Socrates. Not surprisingly, Alcibiades became a traitor to his fatherland and even to those with whom he sided. Alcibiades' political acts of betrayal are but a manifestation of his treachery against "the heavenly Eros",[19] flaunting

---

15   *Ibid.*, p. 163–164.

16   Paulo Freire and Donaldo Macedo, *Literacy*, p. 154–157.

17   Max Horkheimer, *Dawn and Decline: Notes 1926–1931 and 1950–1969*, translated by Michael Shaw, New York: The Seabury Press 1978, p. 127.

18   Plato, "Symposium", in: Irwing Edman (ed.), *The Works of Plato*, New York: The Modern Library 1927, p. 344.

19   *Ibid.*

the earthly superiority of "the popular Eros"[20] and rejecting the struggle for spiritual maturity and transcendence. Freire acts as if he were Alcibiades, finding himself a Socrates who agrees to teach him "the truth". As in the case of Alcibiades, this "popular Eros" functions as an *impetus* to a political power game, seeking its expansion through philosophical education and entry into a dialogue that promises warm and easy love, after being frustrated in transforming "heavenly Eros" into a positive political power/ knowledge alternative.

My argument about Freire's project is that non-critical and automatic preference for the self-evident knowledge of the oppressed to that of the oppressors is dangerous. The self-evidence of "the people" or a social or cultural group, even when developed to reflectivity by a grand leader-educator, is not without a terroristic potential. On the one hand, the idea is that the educational leader is responsible for the success of the project, while by the same token he (not she) has to be a total lover and be totally loved. This is within the framework of a praxis whose starting point is the self-evidence of the group and earthly politics. This opens the gate to totalitarianism as earthly heaven. These poles, with violence as their secret connection, are manifested in other poles in the system, as personified in the identification of Freire with Che Guevara or Fidel Castro and his own acceptance by his followers as a guru who encourages the groups and creates the horizon of their dialogues.

It seems to me that the thinkers of both the first generation of the Frankfurt School, such as Adorno and Horkheimer, and of its second generation, such as Juergen Habermas and Karl Otto Apel, acknowledged the danger of this kind of education. They understood the difference between negation of social conditions alien to ideals of solidarity, understanding, and transcendence and the positive utopia of "love". The latter was a false promise that in effect yielded a kind of "dialogue" reproducing the inner logic of existing power relations; it prevented transcendence and struggle for autonomy of the individual. Such an education blocks the possibility of counter-education, which is conditioned by an alternative critique. Counter-education as a starting point for a non-repressive critique does not rush into easy optimism, positive utopianism, and "love" of the kind that Freire promised. Within the framework of such a positive utopia, education constitutes itself on either the self-evidence of the group or that of the leader-educator. That is why this kind of Critical Pedagogy is immanently endangered by overflowing into verbalism, dogmatism, or violence. Since Freire is careful to exclude the third option, his Critical Pedagogy is practically realized within the horizons of verbalism and dogmatism, which constantly threaten the project with unreflective acceptance of the false consciousness and knowledge of the repressed groups, who are unprepared for reflection on the dialogical process in which they are involved. Freire challenges this threat not within radical philosophical education but within political half-conservatism.[21]

There are also important emancipatory elements in the anti-elitism of Freire's and his followers' Critical Pedagogy. The fall into the peril of violence is not inevitable in

20 *Ibid.*
21 Paulo Freire, *The Politics of Education*, p. 178.

this project, even if it is immanent to the system. This version of Critical Pedagogy is of much value for groups and classes in the Third World and for marginalized and controlled groups in the Western world. To a certain degree, this pedagogy even incubates potential refusal of and resistance to the inner logic of capitalism and current technological progress, but because of its central problems it will never develop into anything more than a futile revolt set on precarious foundations for counter-totalitarianism.

The importance and the futility of this project are exemplified, for example, by one of Freire's best known American disciples, Ira Shor. Shor describes his experience in trying to criticize the self-evident knowledge of students at a communal college where one of America's greatest myths—the hamburger—was questioned.[22] However, lacking Critical Theory's "elitist" general theory, even the greatest achievement of this version of Critical Pedagogy is drawn into the order which it intended to rebel against. Lacking the need and the possibility of conceptualizing and articulating the critical "experience", this critique is compelled to become another commodity needed in American colleges so as to be successful in the present order of things.

CRITICAL PEDAGOGY: HENRY GIROUX

Henry Giroux's project might serve as another example of a Critical Pedagogy based on the Frankfurt School's Critical Theory. Giroux is quite explicit, justifying this connection by the revolutionary potential of Critical Theory.[23] The Critical Pedagogy that he formulated highlighted the optimistic dimension of the Frankfurt School's revolutionary stand, and he developed it to meet the needs of his version of Critical Pedagogy. In the Frankfurt School the optimistic revolutionary dimension was developed mainly by Herbert Marcuse. Even in the 1930s, when Critical Theory had ambitions of stimulating a change in political reality in addition to a theoretical shift in social and cultural critique, this dimension was dialectically set in a framework that had a competing, pessimistic, dimension.[24] Giroux's characterizations of Critical Theory are better suited to characterize his own theory than to reconstruct Critical Theory—even in its first stage of development.[25]

In the 1970s and 1980s Henry Giroux formulated a Critical Pedagogy that synthesized the more progressive elements of John Dewey's philosophy and the Critical Theory of the Frankfurt School. The emancipatory ambition of this Critical Pedagogy exceeded that of Dewey's philosophy of education. In *Theory and Resistance in Education* (1983), Giroux describes his project as a pedagogical realization of Herbert Marcuse's philosophical project. This Critical Pedagogy is indebted to the politicization

---

22   Ira Shor, *Critical Teaching and Everyday Life*, Chicago: University of Chicago Press 1980, p. 163.
23   Henry Giroux, *Theory and Resistance in Education: A Pedagogy for the Opposition*, Massachusetts: Bergin & Garvey 1983, p. 19.
24   Max Horkheimer, *Traditionelle und Kritische Theorie: Vier Aufsaetze*, Grankfurt a.Main: Fischer Taschenbuch Verlag 1977, p. 33.
25   Giroux, *ibid.*

of teachers and students and their empowerment as radical intellectuals who change their school as part of a general struggle over essential social change.[26] The important point here is that Giroux referred to and developed Marcuse's Critical Theory solely in its positive utopian dimension. This positive-utopian dimension was drawn into his system in isolation from the other, pessimistic, dimension in Marcusian philosophy. To my mind, understanding the dialectics between them is vital for a fruitful interpretation and development of Marcuse's work and its implementation in different fields of knowledge and life.

Marcuse's positive utopianism manifests itself on two levels. On the first level, his positive utopianism is realized by his characterizations of future society and the possible realization of human potentialities and their development.[27] This dimension is vital for the realization and justification of the "total refusal" and its concretization in specific historical situations. Political radicalism and anti-positivistic obligation, in the art of conceiving socio-cultural reality as a precondition for critique and transformative action, were incubated in Giroux's pedagogy, but not unproblematically. However, even in the new stage of his pedagogy's development, while influenced by the feminist and postmodernist discourses he adhered to this Marcusian positive utopianism.

Marcusian utopianism, which was the impetus to "grand refusal" of the present reality, was committed to constructing a **totally different** reality,[28] and he therefore rejected a "mere revolution".[29] The Marcusian *telos* pointed to a new human being and a new world where life is "art" and work is "play".[30] Here the "reality principle" loses its superiority to the "pleasure principle", and the dichotomy between the realm of must and the realm of freedom is overcome, as is the separation between subject and object, between sense and world.[31]

These aspects of Marcuse's positive utopianism are missing in Giroux's positive utopianism, and this makes his philosophical consistency highly problematic, if indeed possible at all. He did not offer an alternative to or further development of Marcuse's political radicalism or his philosophical coherence, which rendered the task of implementing Marcuse's Critical Theory in the field of schooling practically impossible. Noteworthy is his neglect of the element of transcendence in Marcuse's philosophy. In contrast to his repeated declarations, in his work he developed Dewey's concep-

26 Henry Giroux, "Radical pedagogy as cultural politics: Beyond the discourse of critique and anti-utopianism", in Peter McLaren (ed.), *Critical Pedagogy and Pedatory Culture: Oppositional Politics in a Postmodern Era*, London and New York: Routledge 1995, p. 30.

27 Herbert Marcuse, *One-Dimensional Man: Studies in the Ideology of Advanced Industrial Society*, Boston: Beacon Press 1964.

28 Herbert Marcuse, *Counterrevolution and Revolt*, London: Allen Lane 1972, p. 58.

29 Herbert Marcuse, "Liberation from the Affluent Society", p. 179.

30 Herbert Marcuse, *Eros and Civilization: A Philosophical Inquiry into Freud*, London: Routledge & Kegan Paul 1956, p. 176.

31 Herbert Marcuse, "Culture and Revolution", *Herbert Marcuse Archive* 406.00.

tion of "democracy as a way of life"[32] more than Marcuse's idea of "life as a work of art". Marcuse followed the messianic/revolutionary tradition, while Giroux, in his first stage of development, was more radical, pursuing the progressive middle-class tradition in America that applies the jargon of German Critical Theory to a different, namely liberal, orientation. This was so even prior to Giroux's second stage of development, when he explicitly distanced himself from Critical Theory[33] and declared his special interest in postmodern and feminist discourses. Hence, even the positive utopianism separated Marcuse and the most developed stage of the Critical Theory of Adorno and Horkheimer is distinctive from what Marcuse and Giroux had in common. There is another distinction, which is no less important: Critical Theory's philosophical pessimism was totally neglected by Giroux's Critical Pedagogy, even in its Marcusian version.

The positive Utopian dimension in Marcuse's thought had another level which was likewise disregarded by Giroux. Marcuse saw in the present and future uprisings of oppositional forces of his time an ontological sign. Neither hope nor confidence that it was possible to overthrow or even crack the present realm of self-evidence led him to praise the revolts of young students, feminists, and guerrillas in the Third World. His support can be explained by his understanding of these as heroic manifestations of the possibility to resist the constitution of a one-dimensional totality that controls world societies and false collective consciousness and psyche. Marcuse abandoned Marxian historicism, and theoretically was satisfied with the educational potential of preserving the revolutionary Eros for a future order of things when historical possibilities were again open. Then the myths of refusal and revolt as elements in the struggle for a true humanistic transformation of society would assume great importance.

From here a non-fashioned education theory is constituted that anchors its utopianism in the transcendent (as well as in the acknowledgment of the impossibility of essential social transformation in the present reality) on the one hand, and in the imperative of a dialogical struggle for the realization of (potential) reasoned human autonomy on the other. This is a teleological project committed to universal emancipation. Its limits are the historical horizons, and it treats the local event at the end through its meaning in and contribution to the total transformation of present reality. This position leaves no room for rapid anti-hierarchical relations between the educator and those whom he/she is committed to liberate. Marcusian "education" is committed to counter-manipulations and rejection of a quick and hasty revelation or creation of truth or consensus within the dialogical framework of ecstatic revolutionaries. This is in contrast to Nicholas Burbules, Paulo Freire, Giroux, and other disciples of Critical Pedagogy's concept of dialogue. The latent Marcusian philosophy of education is committed to Ephraim Lessing's concept of *Educating the Human Race* in a historical process in which truth does not reveal itself fully and directly; educators with good intentions are manipulated in the service of humanistic education as a trans-historical

---

32   Henry Giroux, *Border Crossings: Cultural Workers and the Politics of Education*, New York: Routledge and Kegan Paul 1992, p. 12–13.

33   *Ibid.*, p. 47.

process[34] that is understood merely in its fullest unfolding, as a Hegelian or Marxian metanarrative. Adorno and Horkheimer represented a different philosophy of educa-tion from the view point of their philosophy's commitment to a negative utopianism. Their transcendentalism was theoretically realized as an educational project denoting the absence of truth and negating the illusions and the over-optimistic and shallow encouragement of present and future revolutionaries, which uses standard theoreti-cal manipulations and terror, manifesting the power of the purpose principle against which they intended to revolt.

In the second stage in the development of Giroux's Critical Pedagogy, when he started to emphasize the jargon and the thematics of his theory as they relate to the conventions of current postmodernist and feminist discourses, he criticized Adorno and Horkheimer for taking conservative stands, and implicitly for even holding a repressive philosophy; he felt that their conception of emancipation was grounded on a modernist ideology, which demanded universal emancipation and the realization of the autonomous ideal subject in the name of a theory based on higher culture's superiority to popular culture.[35]

From the 1980s Giroux constructed an original version of Critical Pedagogy that is even less of a "negative pedagogy". It is a critique that challenges the ideals and funda-mental concepts of Critical Theory because it is also committed to the negation of the current order of things. The elements of the new Critical Pedagogy that Giroux cur-rently presents are committed to negating the ideal autonomous and reflective subject, as well as any "elitist" negative pedagogy. The Frankfurt School thinkers strove for a kind of education that would promote what Adorno called "*Muendigkeit*", coming of age,[36] a maturity that in present society would realize itself in critique, resistance, soli-darity, and transformation. He saw this project as conditioned by the development of the knowledge of Western cultures, canonical works, and the possibility of acquiring intellectual power by men and women struggling for spiritual autonomy, the capacity for conceptualizing interests, potentialities, and his negation and political resistance of which the normalized person is deprived.[37]

Giroux realizes and develops Critical Theory through schooling as a political arena with a major role in producing of discourses, meanings, and subjects, as well as in their control and their distribution. In the second stage of development, Giroux is strongly influenced by postmodernists such as Michel Foucault. In his projects he synthesizes elements from educational thinkers such as Nicholas Burbules, Paulo Freire, and Michael Apple, in suggesting the school for socio-cultural reproduction

34   Gotthold Ephraim Lessing, *The Education of the Human Race*, translated by M. Robinson, London Anthropological Cub. C. 1927
      Max Horkheimer, *Gesammelte Schriften* 7 p. 253.
35   Henry Giroux, *Border Crossings*, p. 183–184.
36   Theodor Adorno, *Erziung zum Muendligkeit: Vortraege und Geschpraeche mit Hellmut Becker 1956–1969*, Frankfurt a.Main: Suhrkamp Taschenbuch Verlag 1971.
37   Max Horkheimer, *Gesammelte Schriften* 8 Frankfurt a.Main: Fischer Taschenbuch Verlag 1985, s. 450.

and distortion of dialogical possibilities in current Western societies. Giroux does not present a one-dimensional postmodern position, whereby dynamic symbolic interchange and cultural reproduction use individuals and groups solely in the interest of the system. He addresses progressive modern critical themes such as ideology critique, which he presents as important practice for resistance to the hegemony of the school system and its normalization practices.[38] He also retains Critical Theory's ambition of enhancing students' reflective power and ability to reconstruct the socio-cultural context that blocks their abilities to create and realize their own meanings.[39] But he explicitly rejects the Enlightenment's and Critical Theory's concept of emancipation, and the essence of his pedagogy is to recognize the "other" in his/her culture and the full implications of difference.[40] Whereas Critical Theory recognized the "other" in its otherness, in its unfulfilled needs and untruthfulness, Giroux, in accordance with postmodern popular formulations, sees that "other" as the starting point of the non-repressive work of Critical Pedagogy,[41] and negates modernistic "metanarratives" and general theories that could have served as a framework for reasoned critique and dialogue, to which he remains committed. This draws him into the difficulties that Burbules identifies as challenging all "postmodern" critical thinkers.[42] Giroux's educational theory becomes non-dialectical and optimistic in a manner that enables him to declare his crossing from the language of critique to the "language of possibilities". Contrary to his assertions, he distances himself from the essentials of the Enlightenment's emancipatory project, while staying faithful to some of its harmful characteristics: its positive utopianism, its hasty optimism, and its arrogance as to the possibility of liberating the repressed and constituting a better world within current reality. While criticizing functionalist-positivistic attitudes, he abandons philosophy for political success in his Critical Pedagogy. In his own words, "schooling for self and social empowerment is ethically prior to questions of epistemology…".[43]

Giroux constructs an original synthesis of the Enlightenment's universalistic commitment to liberate the repressed and a rejection of the concepts as the universality of reason, the validity of a general theory, and resistance of constructions and dynamics that are to be reconstructed and negated, even if not defeated or domesticated. Today Giroux accepts the postmodern understanding of the plurality and inconsistency of time fields, the different epistemological structure of different communities, and the legitimacy of political and epistemic difference; yet he still insists on the possibilities of emancipation here and now. Implicitly, in his thought these possibilities for

38   Henry Giroux, *Theory and Resistance in Education: A Pedagogy for the Opposition*, Massachusetts: Bergin & Garvey 1983, p. 157.
39   Henry Giroux, *Ideology, Culture and the Process of Schooling*, Philadelphia: Temple University Press 1981, p. 81.
40   Henry Giroux, *Border Crossings*, p. 128.
41   Henry Giroux, "Radical pedagogy as cultural politics", p. 50.
42   Nicholas Burbules and Susanne Rice, "Dialogue across differences: Continuing the conversation", *Harvard Educational Theory* 61: 4 (1991), pp. 397.
43   Henry Giroux, "Radical pedagogy as cultural politics", p. 30.

emancipation are actual and universal, and his positive utopianism and his new epistemic assumptions are inconsistent. Here arise violent potentialities of his concept of dialogue between teachers and students. He has not found a theoretical solution to the conflict between the authority of the self-evident knowledge, criteria, goals, and interests of individual students of repressed collectives and the principles of his own Critical Pedagogy. While paying tribute to the self-evident knowledge of popular culture and criticizing elitist culture and Critical Theory, his own theory is elitist, sophisticated, and far from the reflective reach of those normalized and manipulated by popular culture and other manifestations of the culture industry.[44] It is a typical representative of both feminist and "patriarchal" Critical Pedagogy.[45]

Acknowledgment of difference as the foundation of the "language of possibilities" may justify the optimism and positive utopianism of such a Critical Pedagogy. Yet it guarantees that this critique will not contemplate deeply or problematize the roots of existence and co-existence, nor question the possibilities of reality, but will realize its potential for philosophical violence and political terror. Giroux combines two salient elements that guarantee the political success of his Critical Postmodern Pedagogy. He ignores Critical Theory's exposition of the systematic destruction of the individual's potential for autonomy and reflectivity[46] and neglects their exposition of the disappearance of Spirit[47] and the exile of reason which was replaced by instrumental rationality. In his work Giroux combines these two omissions with neglect of a central postmodern position: the relation of knowledge and power. This last omission allows him to disregard postmodern critique of "truth" claims of the intellectual as well as the emancipatory movement that "succeeds" in "liberating" individuals and collectives. The very concept of the "we", the "community", as a manifestation of the violence of education that constitutes the self-evidence and the identity of both the oppressors and the oppressed, remains non-problematic and is presented uncritically in this Critical Pedagogy. Precisely where he could use postmodernist understandings to reformulate some problematic modernist elements in his pedagogical ambitions, Giroux uses some of the most dangerous concepts. His concept of dialogue and alternative relations between teachers as intellectuals and students is based on modernistic attitudes to voluntarism and vitalism, but there is no defined concept of reason; this is philosophically and politically very dangerous.

The Common Ground of the Different Versions of Critical Pedagogy

---

44　Jennifer Gore, *Feminism and Critical Pedagogy*, New York: Routledge 1992, p. 62.

45　Peter McLaren 1988, "Schooling the postmodern body: Critical Pedagogy and the politics of Enfleshment", *Journal of Education*, 1970: (1988), p. 71.
Ira Shor, *Empowering Education: Critical Teaching for Social Change*, Chicago: The University of Chicago Press 1992, p. 57.
Kathleen Weiler, "Freire and a feminist pedagogy of difference", *Harvard Educational Review*, 61: 4 (1991), p. 450.

46　Max Horkheimer, *Dawn and Decline*, p. 161.

47　*Ibid.*, p. 134.

In his current version of Critical Pedagogy, Giroux emphasizes the importance of differences among groups, persons, knowledge, and needs.[48] Like thinkers of Feminist Critical Pedagogy and Post-Critical Feminist Pedagogy, Giroux denotes the centrality of repressive elements in modernistic emancipatory claims.[49] These different educational projects have in common the eschewal of challenging their own philosophical and political difficulties, which affect their educational alternatives.[50] They are committed to reconstruct or decipher the power relations that produce the subject, consciousness, identity, knowledge, and possibilities to act in and change reality. They demonstrate and challenge the production of marginality, impotence, and violence of individuals and groups, their control and activation for the sake of the present order of things. They all negate "neutral" positivistic and functionalist trends that prosper in Western societies and, with the help of formal and informal education, reproduce the present order. However, they all refuse philosophy and anything that hints of a "theory" or "elitism". This is the background to their political and educational impotence, which leads to nothing but empty negativism and fruitless pessimism.[51]

One of the philosophical and political weaknesses of the different versions of Critical Pedagogy is their positive utopianism and their commitment to optimism as a condition for a meaningful educational praxis. Optimism or "possibilities of emancipation" is presented as an argument for refusing a philosophical work as too "pessimistic". For Giroux, for example, this is an argument strong enough to negate Adorno and Horkheimer's late Critical Theory, while for Feminist Pedagogy, "political interests" and "the efficiency of the concrete struggle" are enough to sidestep theoretical challenges. Some feminists understand this anti-philosophical orientation as problematic, since they understand that today it is wrong to separate the struggle for liberating the consciousness and changing the social order of women and other oppressed groups from serious philosophical work.[52]

I do not claim that all the theoretical and practical work of Critical Pedagogy is useless or wrong, let alone that we should prefer hegemonic educational ideologies. However, philosophy cannot supply an alternative. The philosophy I suggest is a political issue, and its educational implication demands *vita activa* rather than *vita contemplativa*. Such public activism, theoretical work, and educational praxis are not "postmodern", "post-critical", "feminist", or "multicultural". The educational philosophy presented here is a negative utopianism. The "grand refusal" and utopia that demand transcendence from the current realm of self-evidence are here combined into a politico-philosophical deed. This is educational praxis as counter-education. I will try

48   Henry Giroux *Border Crossings*, p. 60
49   *Ibid.*, p. 56.
50   Robert Young, *A Critical Theory of Education: Habermas and our Children's Future*, New York: Harvester Wheatsheaf 1989, p. 57.
51   *Ibid.*
52   Nancy Fraser and Linda Nicholson, "Social criticism without philosophy: An encounter between feminism and postmodernism", in A. Ross (ed.), *Universal Abandon? The Politics of Postmodernism*, Minneapolis: University of Minnesota Press 1989, p. 86.

to demonstrate some of its historical and conceptual characteristics and elaborate on the potentials of some of these educational alternatives.

Critical Theory's Critique of Critical Pedagogy

In "The Future of Critical Theory" Horkheimer demarcated the dividing line between the first and the second stage of his intellectual evolution. In the first stage Critical Theory was characterized by positive utopianism: belief in the possibility of the revolutionary constitution of "the good society", whose establishment, Marx believed, would perfect human thinking, not to say human relations.[53] In the second stage Critical Theory presents a position matching central conceptions of postmodernism. On the basis of this position Critical Theory is mistakenly accused, and because of this the possibility of a non-naive and non-repressive Critical Pedagogy is denounced.[54] In the second stage of its development, Critical Theory presents an explicitly anti-revolutionary stand, according to which the revolutionary has succeeded in becoming an oppressor by the nature of "revolution".[55] The implications of such a theory are clear for Freire's Critical Pedagogy and his praise of Castro's guerrillas who finally "got the upper hand". Within the framework of their Diasporic philosophy Adorno and Horkheimer did not distinguish the Fascist project, the Marxist project, and the so-called capitalist-democratic projects. They saw in all of them different versions of modern rationality and conflicting versions of collectivism and self-forgetfulness, whose critique was their work.

The concept of reason in Critical Theory is very different from that on which Critical Pedagogy is founded, so the concepts of freedom and liberation differ too. In some respects late Critical Theory is much closer to the concepts of reason held by Martin Heidegger, Michel Foucault, and Lyotard than to those held by Juergen Habermas, Paulo Freire, Henry Giroux, and Ira Shor. This issue is studied in *The Dialectics of Enlightenment*. The Critical Theory that was overlooked, by Critical Pedagogy's supporters and their opponents, reconstructs historical evolution and the concrete social and cultural instrumentalization of reason as non-reversible developments. Within our Critical Theory, unless an unpredictable interference occurs, no good intentions or progressive talent of educators devoted to counter-education will be of much use in halting them. On the historical level, the instrumentalization of rationality is reconstructed as representing and serving the growing needs of technological progress and economic development. Instrumental reason becomes "a magic essence", and is correctly described as the return of *mythos*. In such a reality, there is no room for positive utopianism or for a positive critical stand on the present order or its apparatuses and powers.[56] The constitution of an order representing extreme and unchallenged rationality in such a context is irrational from traditional Objective Reason's point of view.[57] This rationality is realized by almost complete control of the psyche and consciousness

53 Max Horkheimer, *Eclipse of Reason*, New York: The Seabury Press 1974, p. 21.
54 Max Horkheimer, *Gesammelte Schriften* 7 1985, s. 415–418.
55 *Ibid.*, s. 418.
56 Max Horkheimer, *Eclipse of Reason*, p. 26.
57 *Ibid.*, p. 159.

of individuals and collectives. However, this does not mean that under such conditions there is no place for "pluralism" or false critical consciousness. From a Critical Theory point of view, this consciousness can be manifested in the naive emancipatory project of a "paternalist" Critical Pedagogy and in alternatives such as Feminist and Multiculturalist Pedagogies. The historical reconstruction of Instrumental Rationality's victory has an ontological dimension of vital importance for the possibilities of the hermeneutics of the self and the possibilities of a new educational dialogue based on sensitivity and understanding of "difference".

Already in its first stage the ontological dimension was central to Critical Theory in terms of the possibilities of emancipation and the success of counter-education in a reality where Instrumental Rationality celebrates its victory. It is manifested, for example, in Walter Benjamin's *On the Critique of Violence*,[58] in which political violence is elaborated in the historical context where there is no place for redemption but where, at the same time, the ultimate reality in history is absent. The real is conceived within a framework in which history is just one of its moments. Therefore, political struggle, as one of history's manifestations, is not the place where central issues and possibilities are determined. These, and others, are tested ultimately in the framework of the collision between God's power and the power of the *mythos*. Only in the Godly context is the ahistorical and "redemptive" dimension conceived not as a historical dimension but as part of overcoming history. Only here is it possible to seek "justice", since it is basically a theological category.[59] To my mind this is the starting point for a Critical Pedagogy that is not dogmatic or hastily optimistic.

For fully developed Critical Theory, the return of the myth within the framework of Instrumental Rationality is even worse today than it was in its ancient version in its penetrating possibilities.[60] The erosion of possibilities for the very existence of an autonomous subject, which Critical Theory thinkers understood as central to any alternative to present reality, is totally neglected by Critical Pedagogy's thinkers. Perhaps they avoid this major element of Critical Theory in order not to challenge the kind of optimism in which their projects are implicitly grounded. This does not mean that Critical Theory's thinkers have abandoned Utopia, or that one should ignore the educational meanings, some of which are quite close to some central conceptions and sensitivities of current postmodernism. However, one should realize that such a Critical Theory repudiates the central characteristics of Critical Pedagogy and its different alternatives. All three versions of Critical Pedagogy, albeit with different rhetoric, suffer the same weakness and for the same reason: Freire's admiration of "Che" as an educator is to be understood similarly to his admiration for African dictatorships as proper sites for possible national institutionalization of Critical Pedagogy. A latent terrorist potential is revealed here within his concept of "love" and "dialogue", in which

---

58   Walter Benjamin, *Zur Kritik der Gewalt und Andere Aufsaetze*, Frankfurt a.Main: Suhrkamp Taschenbuch Verlag 1971.

59   *Ibid.*, p. 57.

60   Theodor Adorno und Max Horkheimer, *Dialektol der Aufklaerung*, Frankfurt a.Main: Fischer 1985, p. 9.

all hierarchies disappear. In the Critical Pedagogy developed by Giroux, McLaren, and Shor, the dangers of positive utopianism are manifested in a more sophisticated way. On the one hand, the modernistic commitment to reason, empowerment, and revolution is kept, and it cannot be sustained without a general theoretical and political framework. On the other hand, there is acceptance of postmodern commitment to negate meta-narratives, general theories and transcendence as such. There is even an approval of an anti-Enlightenment critique of the Western concepts of subject, reason, and consensus, which is tantamount to negation of the free thinking itself. But more than that there is here a celebration of anti-Diasporic intellectualism, or, self-forgetfulness in the form of being swallowed by conventionalism and new forms of anti-"Western" or "postcolonialist"-oriented dogmatism.

Politically and philosophically, this antinomy is in constant danger of being resolved by violence because of its collectivist and positive utopianist attitude. The same antinomy is seen within the framework of Feminist Critical Pedagogy and other current versions of Feminist Pedagogy. Since the claim for liberation is grounded in a dialectical acceptance of the equality of different identities and cultures, the very possibility of defending and developing the category of "feminism" or "woman" becomes an impossibility. As a result, the commitment to solidarity, as the possibility of developing and defending feminine identity and knowledge, is to be decided by symbolic and other manifestations of violence. None of the three models of Critical Pedagogy has succeeded in synthesizing the problematics of essentialism, foundationalism, and transcendence, nor the recognition of the Other's suffering, rights, and potentialities, with the preconditions and claims of a philosophy demanding human reflectivity and emancipation. All three versions ignore Critical Theory, while neglecting the price of this disregard.

This can be exemplified by the issue of dialogue as a manifestation of Critical Education. The Critical Pedagogies of Freire, Giroux, Shor, and Burbules are constituted on education for a critical dialogue between educators and educated that is committed to demolishing hierarchies and power relations,[61] within which students are empowered (ideally) to the degree of being able to decipher the hidden codes, power relations, and manipulations that build and represent reality, knowledge, and identities. Basically, this concept of dialogue is part of the modernistic emancipatory project. The subject taking part in such an anti-violent dialogue is supposed to be rational and solidarian to the degree of being able to reconstruct reality and understand it within the process of the dialogue, even if the "understanding" here is not conceived as "objective truth" or a representation of "the thing in itself and for itself". This conception consensus is deconstructed by postmodern critique and is negated by Critical Theory's understanding of our historical situation. According to this argument, in our historical situation, even as an ideal, there is no place for such a subject whose assumed existence preconditions Critical Pedagogy's concept of dialogue. That is one reason why Critical Theory has no room for such an optimistic emancipatory concept. In these versions

61 Nicholas Burbules, *Dialogue in Teaching: Theory and Practice*, New York: Teachers College Press 1993, p. 8.

of Critical Pedagogy even the hermeneutic dimension, to which praxis education is implicitly committed, is not represented as it is: a project whose foundations and practice are both within the framework of high culture, as in the philosophy of Hans Gadamer, but as an open possibility of the given reality.

Fully developed Critical Theory understood the realization of the Enlightenment in our era as a mass deception within the framework of the culture industry, in which the subject too is transformed into a commodity, including critical knowledge. The rationalization of all levels and dimensions of life, and the progress of instruments and possibilities of controlling the subjects by the system,[62] brought to its peak the use of the subject as a totally committed agent of reproduction of the realm of self-evidence. Under such conditions, it is impossible to escape the omnipotence of the system.[63] The dynamics suitable for demolishing the ideal of the rational subject and its concrete possibilities are historically reconstructed here. On the theoretical level, according to Adorno and Horkheimer, from the very beginning "the individual" is nothing but an illusion that normally serves to enhance the control of people's consciousness, and to construct life possibilities maximizing their productivity in the service of the system in which they are activated.[64] This productivity is conditioned by the degree of their normalization, which is the real aim of education. This two-level concept of Adorno and Horkheimer is in agreement with Benjamin's two-level concept of time, revolution, and redemption.

From this perspective, the consensus reached by the reflective subject taking part in the dialogue offered by Critical Pedagogy is naive, especially in light of its declared anti-intellectualism on the one hand and its pronounced glorification of "feelings", "experience", and self-evident knowledge of the group on the other. Critical Pedagogy, in its different versions, claims to inhere and overcome the foundationalism and transcendentalism of the Enlightenment's emancipatory and ethnocentric arrogance, as exemplified by ideology critique, psychoanalysis, or traditional metaphysics. Marginalized feminist knowledge, like the marginalized, neglected, and ridiculed knowledge of the Brazilian farmers, as presented by Freire or Weiler, is represented as legitimate and relevant knowledge, in contrast to its representation as the hegemonic instrument of representation and education. This knowledge is portrayed as a relevant, legitimate and superior alternative to hegemonic education and the knowledge this represents in the center. It is said to represent an identity that is desirable and promises to function "successfully". However, neither the truth value of the marginalized collective memory nor knowledge is cardinal here. "Truth" is replaced by knowledge whose supreme criterion is its self-evidence, namely the potential productivity of its creative violence, while the dialogue in which adorers of "difference" take part is implicitly represented as one of the desired productions of this violence. My argument is that the marginalized and repressed self-evident knowledge has no superiority over the

---

62   Mark Poster, *Critical Theory and Poststructuralism: In Research of a Context*, Ithaca and London: Cornell University Press, p. 67.
63   Max Horkheimer, *ibid.*, p. 95–96.
64   *Ibid.*, p. 141.

self-evident knowledge of the oppressors. Relying on the knowledge of the weak, controlled, and marginalized groups, their memory and their conscious interests, is no less naive and dangerous than relying on hegemonic knowledge. This is because the critique of Western transcendentalism, foundationalism, and ethnocentrism declines into uncritical acceptance of marginalized knowledge, which becomes foundationalistic and ethnocentric in presenting "the truth", "the facts", or "the real interests of the group"—even if conceived as valid only for the group concerned. This position cannot avoid vulgar realism and naive positivism based on "facts" of self-evident knowledge ultimately realized against the self-evidence of other groups.

These conceptions are all historical, and do not take seriously the present Western system's capacity for shaping all collective consciousness, not only the ruling group's. The inner logic of the system is not relevant solely for the center. The system is to be understood as a complex of specific power relations and symbolic dynamics that contains and allows the potentials and limitations of groups and individuals, identities and interests, conceptual possibilities, and economic-technological realities. Within these limits, every element of the system is set, regulated, and activated, thereby receiving its "meaning" and aims. This is the case from the level of the different elements of the psyche to the level of the global sub-systems of production, mobilization, distribution, and conquest. It is made possible by the formation of social, economic, and technological circumstances, as well as by conscious and psychic ones, which are all contained within the limits of the present order of things. On the one hand, the premises and practices of current standard Critical Pedagogy, by emphasizing the knowledge of marginalized people (not necessarily marginalized knowledge), might look like the realization of Foucault's understanding of truth/power and the recognition that "each society has its regimes of truth....that is, the types of discourse which it accepts and makes function as true".[65] On the other hand, even from a Foucaultian perspective, the optimism of standard Critical Pedagogy neither recognizes nor challenges Foucault's common ground with Critical Theory's conceptions when he writes that "knowledge is also the field of coordination and subordination of statements in which concepts appear and are defined, applied and transformed...".[66] Deciphering these ways of constructing reality, identity, knowledge, and conceptual possibilities on a historical local and general level might release one from easy optimistic reliance on the vitalism that is implicitly understood to be contained in the alternative knowledge of the marginalized. A pedagogy that overemphasizes the importance of the effectiveness of revolutionary praxis and whose yardstick is power is not to be counted as part of Critical Education or Critical Pedagogy. A Critical Pedagogy that does not suffer from these weaknesses must present itself as an elaboration of the possibility of an alternative spirituality, and as part of an effort to transcend reality and the present realm of self-evidence.

---

65   Mischel Foucault, *Power/Knowledge: Selected Interviews and Other Writings 1972–1977*, translated by Colin Gordon, New Kork: Pantheon 1980, p. 131.
66   Michel Foucault, *The Archeology of Knowledge*, translated by Sheridan Smith, New York: Pantheon 1972, p. 183.

THE EDUCATIONAL IMPLICATIONS OF CRITICAL THEORY

The educational implications of Critical Theory draw on its metaphysical level that connects it to the philosophical tradition of Anaximandrus, Heraclitus, Plato, Schopenhauer, Nietzsche, Heidegger, and Foucault, as well as to the tradition from Democritus and Aristotle to Kant, Hegel, Marx, and Freud. Hence one can understand the strong link between Critical Theory and some central elements of postmodernism, as well as the basic contradiction between these two projects. Heidegger presented the human being struggling to realize his/her authenticity as a captive of the game of being, which, in the advanced technological era, is hidden more than ever. But Heidegger did not deny the possibility of an essential turn, though not the one frequently called "revolution". Technological progress is understood by Heidegger as the "spiritual fall of the earth", and his critique pinpoints one of humanity's manifestations of retreat from human "destination" through the drift of *tekhne* into modern technology and the context that makes this possible. The nihilism of Western science and technology, according to Heidegger, demands that one overlook the "meaning of being" and its concealment in the technological and scientific "progress" that mocks the human being. For Adorno and Horkheimer, Instrumental Rationality's characteristics are very close to Heidegger's characterization of reason and technology.[67] Yet Adorno and Horkheimer presented a general and systematic historical and contextual reconstruction of power apparatuses, symbolic dynamics, and manipulation instruments that constitute the conditions and the orientation of Westerners in the 20th century. Their reconstruction is historical and utopian, but not of the kind presented by orthodox Marxism or Critical Pedagogy's thinkers. An important affinity may exist between Critical Theory and the postmodern discourse in understanding apparatuses of truth production as well as understanding the subject as an agent of the system and a manifestation of the system's symbolic dynamics and power games; but they differ in their treatment of the socio-cultural network.

Foucault's disclosure of power/knowledge relations, which are manifested institutionally and produce subjects to be researched, punished, taught, and administered, and the practice of reproduction of the system does not totally contradict Critical Theory. The critical reconstruction of the culture industry, for example, does not exclude Foucault's research on clinics, prisons, schools, and hospitals, and the conclusions on the normalized subject and his/her possibilities for intellectual autonomy, "authenticity", or "freedom" have much in common. Understanding instrumental rationality as a dimension that is not an emancipator, and does not promise equality and justice but greater control over human beings, is another central element common to Foucault, Adorno, and Horkheimer. Even the surrender of traditional categories such as "class", estrangement, and "ideology critique" within a revolutionary theory and praxis that promises liberation is common to these projects. The two concepts of

---

67   Ilan Gur-Ze'ev, *The Frankfurt School and the History of Pessimism*, Jerusalem: The Magness Press 1996, p. 183.

power and signalization do not essentially differ. However, important differences do exist and they carry significant educational implications.

The most notable difference between Critical Theory and postmodern discourse is Critical Theory's commitment to the negation of the present order of things, to transcendence and human redemption essentially not conditioned by historical reality. This is so since its impetus is erotic and its "foundation" is religious and anti-metaphysical. In the final analysis, it implies a negative utopianism, in which the only possible appearance of justice is in the presence of its absence, in the acknowledgment of the violence of its negation. Not to mislead, Critical Theory cannot promise "liberation" but endless struggle over understanding, refusal, and resistance to the negation of dialogic existence. By contrast, Foucault's project, like many other postmodern projects, is anti-utopian and anti-erotic, and abandons "spirit", "justice", and "truth" even as regulative ideas or negative theology. As I will try to show, emphasizing the importance of kaleidoscopic points of view and the contest among the different parameters to criticize reality, its evaluation, the action within it, and its transformation does not negate Critical Education and Critical Pedagogy as I understand them.

Critical Theory is committed to universal emancipation, in the sense I have presented, and need not necessarily become dogmatic or negate the plurality of narratives and the acknowledgment of the life-or-death struggle of different narratives constituting the conceptual apparatuses and the consciousness of those enclosed within the horizons. Critical Theory has to acknowledge this plurality. However, this recognition must denote that it is not a mere plurality in which "everything goes"; such a plurality is possible and even necessary within the framework of a certain order that is to be reconstructed, criticized, and resisted.

The universality of capitalist production and the omnipotent power of technological progress and its needs are the foundation for the concrete appearance of "difference" today. They are the substratum of the obligatory and "objective" meaning of the power of fashion and the efficiency of the symbolic violence of narratives, identities, and different educational apparatuses. Critical Education should acknowledge this violence in the following manner: on the level where differences are denoted, the epistemological possibilities are determined by the violence of fashion and by the aggressiveness of educational practices. On the universal level, technological progress and capitalist development, as well as the local system's constructions, enjoy universal validity on the one hand and an omnipotent compulsory dimension on the other, as manifested in the motorized traffic roads, the roads on the Internet, or realized principles of the market economy. The dialectic between these two levels determines the possibilities and limitations of human beings, as well as the constitution of their concrete and most specific life possibilities. However, this is only a partial manifestation of the camouflaged game of being that hides itself from human beings, as Heidegger shows, or as a dimension of the storm that plays with "the angel of history", as described by Walter Benjamin in his "Theses on the philosophy of history". This is but a manifestation of the realm of self-evidence; within it there is room for systems such as the one that genuine Critical Pedagogy has to struggle against today.

THE POSSIBILITY OF A NON-REPRESSIVE CRITICAL PEDAGOGY

The educational implications of this understanding can be presented on two levels. On the first, educational implications deviate from confronting the bottom depths of self-evidence and the systems that reflect every realm of self-evidence, the hiding games of the camouflaged being. Such an acknowledgment is not "pessimistic" or "optimistic", even if historically it was elaborated within the framework of the history of philosophical pessimism.[68] The possibilities of understanding the limits of dialogue and the real horizons in which obligatory power rules are of vital educational potential, even for the ideal of dialogue and the struggle over its conditions and possible realization. The struggle to understand the ways in which the subject is produced, as well as knowledge, power, and the system's context of their realization, transformation, and determination, is weakened if one refuses to acknowledge this obligation as an imperative and to strike the lowest depths. Non-repressive education might then be tested only on its surface. Normal Critical Pedagogy is part of this bottom depth.

On the second level, human beings are called as individuals, and only as individuals, to decipher the current realm of self-evidence and to demystify the codes and the manipulations of the powers constituting their conceptual possibilities, their life conditions, and their concrete limitations, as well as their dialogical possibilities for struggle and change. On this level, the projects of Critical Theory and some post-modern and feminist thinkers might be partly united, at least in their sensitivities, as exemplified in the work of philosophers such as Seyla Benhabib and Charles Taylor, and educational thinkers such as Carmen Luke and Henry Giroux. The development of Critical Theory should be the development of critical philosophy, namely the development of philosophy. It should be theoretically interdisciplinary and politically committed to be involved in society. However, it is wrong to reduce it to mere political work and wrong to judge it according to its educational effectiveness in political terms, as is common in Feminist Pedagogy and in the "paternalistic" versions of Critical Pedagogy. As counter-education it is essentially committed to negate prevailing power games and any kind of strategically-oriented theory and praxis, even when enacted in the name of emancipation. It refuses all versions of educational violence, and as such it deserves the name counter-education. While refusing positive utopianism and violence, it does not abandon the quest for transcendence and for **the totally other**. It has a Utopian axis, yet its Utopia is negative.

The kind of Critical Theory presented here is liberated from the pretension of conventional Critical Theory to be "humanistic" or disconnected from the power games of capitalist symbolic dynamics and objective truths or facts of Instrumental Rationality. I say, clear as crystal: freed radical or critical schools will not be transformed into "a liberated zone". In this sense, my disagreement is not limited to the naivety of Freire and the pretensions of Giroux, McLaren, Shor, and their followers. Here my stand is closer to Foucault and Heidegger, who enlighten the all-penetrating presence of powers and conditions that constitute the human being, the conditions of

68   Michel Foucault, *Power/Knowledge*, p. 114–115.

his/her production, his/her possibilities and limitations. As a non-repressive version of Critical Pedagogy, counter-education should evolve out of this understanding into its struggle over the possibilities of non-repressive critical dialogue, not abstract refusal of the self-evidence, fashions, identities, and pedagogies that produce, distribute, and marginalize or execute these fashions, dynamics, and pedagogies, only in order to exchange them for others.

Here presents itself the Utopia on which Western reason was traditionally dependent, and on which the humanistic dimensions that are to be protected still depend. Within this framework counter-education dwells, with the "hope principle" and the understanding that in principle it cannot be realized in this world as refined, justified, and promising counter-violence. The anti-foundationalist concept of the counter-education presented here cannot suggest any counter-poison. It has no positive and evident alternative to false consciousness, such as "the memory" or "the knowledge" of women, minorities, or the marginalized and oppressed, as suggested in conventional Critical Pedagogy. The counter-education suggested here has no room for any one-dimensional positive alternative, or for any evident foundation for the critique as suggested in the Critical Pedagogy of Freire and Giroux. Even Foucault's or Derrida's abandonment of "meaning", "understanding", and "dialogue"[69] is negated for the sake of the struggle over the possibilities of a kind of praxis and dialogue that are concerned with the development of the partners and the change made by them in the conditions that prevent or deviate from critical dialogue. On this level, counter-education can offer no more than incomplete, local and painful successes of practical reason, even within the limits of current reality.

The counter-education suggested here differs from the normalization practices of hegemonic education in its responsibility to increase the awareness of the strategies and tactics of producing, controlling, representing, and activating reality, knowledge, and subjects as part of a revolt against the current realm of self-evidence, the deception of being, and the forgetfulness of challenging its deception as part of deception, namely as part of being human. Counter-education challenges self-evidence since, with Benjamin, it does not accept reality as having the last word. Understanding that there is no place for redemption within the framework of history—merely of revolutions—should not prevent counter-education from working out general historiosophic and historiographic theories and concrete social practices. The same is true as for the reconstruction of the system's efficiency: This does not necessarily imply the acknowledgment of the superiority of power apparatuses over the potential autonomy of the individual, or the superiority of the representation practices and symbolic dynamics over specific philosophical and political possibilities for emancipation. The system contains both (although the latter normally is seen just as a potential), and is activated by the dialectics between them. In this sense, as a non-repressive Critical Pedagogy counter-education should educate to decipher reality, to reconstruct it, and to articulate its practices, possibilities, and limitations, and to act within and on behalf of the ideal dialogue. Here I do agree with Charles Taylor who defends, quite

69   *Ibid.*

successfully, the possibility of practical reason within the framework of struggle for developing the reflective potential of human beings and their ability to articulate their world as a realization of their reason.[70]

Praxis education of this sort is conditioned by the possibility of developing people's competence to demystify reality, decipher its codes, and critically reconstruct the demolished potential for human solidarity, cooperation, and the realization of their dialogical essence while acknowledging that in the current historical stage these two missions contradict each other. This acknowledgment might become a power for moral elevation, as in the *Bildung* tradition to which it critically refers. This transcendence can receive its meaning only within the framework in which a dialogue is immanent, and might change it and make possible the self-realization of individuals as part of a solidarian partnership with other reflective politically-oriented human beings.[71] Until the establishment of conditions that will give birth to such a dialogue—conditions that are beyond the present historical horizon—such a non-repressive critical pedagogy might be realized only for isolated individuals and cannot become a matter of collectives. This conception of praxis is very far from the one common in today's standard versions of Critical Pedagogy; and it is committed and conditioned by spirituality, conceptual possibilities, and socio-cultural conditions that are described by standard Critical Pedagogy as "elitism". However, just as no human being has any shortcuts, counter-education should feel its way by acknowledging that such a spirit, such conceptual possibilities, and such socio-cultural conditions are still a Utopia.

The "elitism" of counter-education is indeed directed to demystify and negate any self-evident "knowledge", but it should criticize any version of elitism, reconstruct its function and aims and, at the same time, strive for conditions under which everyone will be able to become part of the human dialogue. The negation of the ethnocentrism of the oppressed improves the efficiency of intellectual and psychic impotence of people, such as the education that constitutes false dialogues. Such a dialogue must begin from a defined starting point, from the concrete possibilities and limitations of individuals within the framework of the system in which they are imprisoned. In this sense, such dialogue needs some of the achievements of standard Critical Pedagogies, which have to be transformed and de-contextualized. Then, and only then, will the human subject be able, though not "liberated" and "authentic", to confront the forgetfulness of being and the central questions and great and small difficulties of the given reality, which as a manifestation of the realm of self-evidence are not to be changed, yet might be identified and negated. Critique is in this sense a prayer that cannot change the world, but allows transcendence from it. This is the only non-repressive form of hope possible in such an educational project.

---

70   Charles Taylor, *Philosophy and the Human Sciences: Philosophical Papers II*, New York: Cambridge University Press 1995, p. 151.
71   Max Horkheimer, *Gesammelte Schriften* 8 Frankfurt a.Main: Fischer Taschenbuch Verlag 1988, p. 126.

CHAPTER 5

ADORNO, HORKHEIMER, CRITICAL THEORY AND THE POSSIBILITY OF A NON-REPRESSIVE CRITICAL PEDAGOGY

The direct and indirect influences of the Critical Theory on current philosophy of education are immense. The manifestations of these influences go far beyond the horizons of Critical Pedagogy as the concrete realization of Critical Theory in the schooling process. Even within the limited concept of education as schooling, feminist pedagogies, multicultural and post-colonial theories of education, cultural studies, as well as critical literacy or aesthetic education are all seen to be influenced by the ideas of Theodor Adorno, Max Horkheimer, Herbert Marcuse, Walter Benjamin, Erich Fromm, and the other members of the Frankfurt School. Some of the influences of Critical Theory are more obvious and explicitly acknowledged by central educational thinkers such as Paulo Freire, Peter McLaren, Henry Giroux, and Kathleen Weiler, and some are less explicit and are subterranean or are realized indirectly.

It is not uncommon that some of these influences are dressed in postmodern garb and are offered—how ironic—as an alternative to the modernity of Critical Theory and the Enlightenment's arrogance and self-defeating educational project.

The main argument below is that the foremost philosophers of education who were explicitly and even enthusiastically influenced by Critical Theory were influenced by the work of Herbert Marcuse and by the first stage in the development of Adorno and Horkheimer's thought. According to this argument, the second stage in the development of Adorno and Horkheimer's thought was disregarded by most philosophers of education and did not illumine the paths chosen by the various versions of Critical Pedagogy.

When the main version of Critical Pedagogy became defensive and apologetic in face of the critique of the academic left it turned to the postmodern alternatives for help.[1] This unfortunate situation was instrumental in allowing the development of original, influential, and progressive educational theories such as those of Giroux, McLaren, Weiler, Aronowitz, and Ellsworth. It was most unhelpful, however, for the task of establishing a reflective counter-education. For all its importance, it also contributed to the establishment of repressive properties and uncritical trends within Critical Pedagogy itself. The thoughts of Adorno and Horkheimer in the second stage

---

1   In this article I do not prove this claim. I try to show its validity only by referring to Henry Giroux, who is undoubtedly one of the central figures in this field.

of the development of their Critical Theory, I argue, could have been and still are potentially open to the creation of a genuine *counter-educational struggle*—of the kind that went beyond the prospects of hegemonic Critical Pedagogy.

The part in Critical Theory that was not ignored and was even praised by most educational theoreticians was fundamentally optimistic, revolutionary, and positive, at least at first sight. Its Marxist birthmarks where still very present at this stage. In the tradition of Critical Pedagogy this part of the work of Horkheimer and Adorno was conceived in a manner that deprived Critical Theory of its self-reflection and its dialectical dimension. The thinkers of Critical Pedagogy normally underestimate Adorno and Horkheimer's anti-utopianism and self-reflection. On the one hand, they over-emphasize their optimism about the possibility of the constitution of a theoretical and educational framework that will enhance a praxis which, on the other hand, will overcome the logic of capitalism and other forms of oppression.

The third issue of the sixth volume of *Zeitschrift fuer Sozialen Forschung*, the official journal of the Frankfurt School, which was published in 1937, can serve as a vivid manifestation of the complexity of the smilingly explicit anti-utopian commitment of Horkheimer of that time. In "a contribution" to Marcuse's main article in that issue he goes out of his way to criticize "those who call themselves critical theoreticians" -- namely Marcuse, whose utopianism "contradicts genuine Critical Theory".[2] He criticizes Marcuse's "philosophical utopianism", likening it to other dangerous versions of utopianism. He especially targets the liberal version—for manifesting "saintly egoism", which ultimately opens the way to nihilism and National Socialism, and the orthodox Marxist version, which is "mechanistic and non-dialectical".[3] Already in 1931, when the theologian Paul Tillich described capitalism as "the devil", both Adorno and Horkheimer were quick to criticize him for the kind of utopianism that constituted this unworthy critique.[4] The two colleagues attacked those intellectuals who attempted to find a philosophical ground for the revolution. They criticized those who saw capitalism as "the ultimate kingdom of evil, the bad form of human togetherness" and who "expect the ultimate truth on earth"[5] to be realized in actual history. Their evaluation and critique of the ideological dimensions of hegemonic knowledge, in that period, was still guided by the Marxist claim of anti-idealism and anti-transcendentalism, founded on materialist reality, class interests, and economic developments. At the same time Adorno and Horkheimer of that period favored the possibilities of a proletarian revolution and more than once even found themselves siding with the kind of utopianism they so strongly opposed. It was Horkheimer himself who wrote then, "Maybe they are right. Maybe socialism does bring with it the kingdom of the millennium and the prophecies of the Old Testament prophets will be realized after all".[6]

---

2   Max Horkheimer, *Gesammelte Schriften* V., Frankfurt a. Main 1985, p. 224.
3   *Ibid.*, p. 223.
4   Max Horkheimer, *Gesammelte Schriften* XI., Frankfurt a. Min 1985, p. 410.
5   *Ibid.*, p. 264.
6   *Ibid.*, p. 226.

The standard position of the Critical Theory thinkers of this period is, however, that theory is never neutral—and this is valid in respect of Critical Theory itself. The very foundation of Critical Theory is not justified merely on theoretical grounds: "a vision of a worthier human reality guides it".[7] And yet, with all its explicit anti-utopian commitment, already in his 1935 "Notes for philosophical anthropology" one encounters other trends, whereby Critical Theory commits itself to the mission of "a happier humanity".[8] In 1936 Horkheimer explicitly speaks of the possibility of "future circumstances [in which] efficiency and consciousness will constitute a common interest for human beings; 'the destruction drive' will no longer disturb them…".[9] This trend is visible even in "Traditional Theory and Critical Theory", probably the most important publication of Critical Theory in its first stage of development (1937). Critical Theory is here explicitly presented as "a moment" of revolutionary praxis towards "new social forms". While still founding his perspectives for future society on materialist grounds and not on philosophical speculations Horkheimer explicitly speaks here of the importance of the idea of a future free human community ("as much as it is allowed by the technical conditions"). At the same time, however, he develops a vision of the realization of reason and overcoming of alienation between thinking and reality, rationality and sensuality; in an almost Marcusian spirit he speaks even of "future freedom and spontaneity". This positive utopian trend is manifested also in "Montaigne and the function of skepticism" (1938). Here Critical Theory is presented as directed to nothing less than "the establishment of a brand new world".[10] At this period both Horkheimer and Adorno offer a promising, progressive, revolutionary theory of knowledge and of overcoming oppressive social realities and ideological manipulations. While doing very little in the field of explicit educational theory, their Critical Theory is of much relevance for criticizing established leftist and rightist pedagogical theories and they draw the framework for a possible revolutionary pedagogy. In this respect Paulo Freire, Peter McLaren, Henry Giroux, Patti Lather, Ira Shor, Kathleen Weiler and other teachers of Critical Pedagogy are not totally mistaken in their implementation of Critical Theory as Critical Pedagogy. Still, as I will show by referring to Giroux as a representative of this attempt, this project is far from unproblematic.

The pedagogical project of the early Giroux serves as an educational model that almost disregards Adorno and Horkheimer's later work. At the same time it makes productive use of the other, less optimistic and less foundationalist dimensions, even in the first stage of the development of Critical Theory.[11] Giroux explicitly notes that his educational project is founded on Critical Theory. The revolutionary potential of the latter is explicitly of special importance in the early stage of the development of

---

7   Max Horkheimer, *Gesammelte Schriften* III., Frankfurt a. Main 1985, p. 105.
8   *Ibid.*, p. 266.
9   *Ibid.*, p. 86.
10   Max Horkheimer, *Gesammelte Schriften* IV., Frankfurt a. Main 1985, p. 289.
11   Ilan Gur-Ze'ev, "Toward a Nonrepressive critical theory", *Educational Theory* 48: 4, (Fall 1998) pp. 463–486..

his thought.[12] In another place he says that a precondition for a worthy pedagogical work is a worthy reading of the work of the Critical Theory thinkers.[13] Here Giroux draws on the positive utopianism of early Critical Theory, and following Freire he develops his project in accordance with the requirements of an optimistic revolutionary pedagogy.

According to Giroux, in the Critical Theory of the Frankfurt School every thought and theory is bound to a specific interest in the development of an unjust society.[14] Of special importance for Giroux, as for other thinkers in Critical Pedagogy, is to present Ideology Critique -- which challenges hegemonic knowledge and its claims—as a fundamentally unproblematic tool, a tool for emancipatory education. As a prima facie Critical-Theory-in-action, Critical Pedagogy, in this sense, becomes a transformative process, controlled in a more humane future.[15] Giroux speaks here explicitly of Critical Theory as a transcendental power within which critical thinking becomes a precondition for human freedom.[16]

The central trend in Critical Pedagogy as here represented by Giroux contradicts the central massage of late Critical Theory as manifested by later Adorno and Horkheimer, but also even the central commitments of its first stage, as laid down in the works of Benjamin, early Adorno, and early Horkheimer. Actually Giroux follows Herbert Marcuse and ignores the reservations of Adorno and Horkheimer concerning Marcuse's easy-going revolutionary project.[17]

In the following I will show that in the second stage of the development of Critical Theory Adorno and Horkheimer not only abandoned their *positive utopianism*, they forcefully cast aside its philosophical foundations and historical justifications. They rejected the entire tradition, which supported and manifested optimism about the possibility of a non-repressive revolution and about an unproblematic emancipatory critique.

This is the theoretical arena out of which they developed their later negative Utopia and what I call their "Diasporic philosophy". It was based on the tradition of philosophical pessimism, which they elaborated into a transcendental dimension within their *negative utopianism*. Since they refused to give up the utopian axis they founded it in a most original way on philosophical pessimism.[18] This later work, as will be argued, is of vital importance in any attempt to develop current possibilities for counter-education in a postmodern era; Critical Pedagogy was deprived of such

12   Henry Giroux, *Theory and Resistance in Education: A Oppressed*, South Hadley, Mass. Bergin & Garvey 1983. p. 19.

13   Henry Giroux, Ideology, Culture & the Process of Schooling, Philadelphia 1981, p. 81.

14   Henry Giroux, Theory and Resistance in Education: A Pedagogy for the Oppressed, South Hadley, Mass. Bergin & Garvey 1983, p. 19.

15   Henry Giroux & Stanley Aronowitz, *Education under Siege—The Conservative*, Liberal, and Radical Debate Over Schooling, South Hadley, Mass. Bergin & Garvey 1981, p. 103.

16   Henry Giroux, *Theory and Resistance in Education*, p. 19.

17   Ilan Gur-Ze'ev, *The Frankfurt School and the History of Pessimism*, Jerusalem The Magnes Press 1996, p. 160 (in Hebrew).

18   *Ibid.*, p. 211.

possibilities since it ignored the mature part of Critical Theory. Nevertheless, when developing his Critical Pedagogy on Critical Theory's foundations, following Marcuse and avoiding the work of later Adorno and Horkheimer, Giroux offered an important contribution to the development of a progressive Critical Pedagogy that emphasized "possibilities" without neglecting "critique".

According to Giroux's Critical Pedagogy, when evaluating the schooling process it is wrong to disconnect the school curriculum and its other texts from its cultural and social contexts. In this sense school is a prima facie political arena, which plays an indispensable part in the production of discourses, meanings, identities, and subjects, and allows efficient control of their manipulated representation, distribution, and consumption. Following Critical Theory, Critical Pedagogy reveals the powers, interests, and ideologies beyond the *Maya* curtain of the school's declared commitment to the distribution of true/relevant knowledge/information. It critically reconstructs the abundant ways by which schools reflect and serve central social interests. This structural role of the school determines its function as a space dedicated to the organization of canonic knowledge, control of time, body, consciousness and conscious, and even constituting "valid" evaluation apparatuses, validating "the relevant" interpretive strategies. In this sense school functions as one of the cultural, social, and economic reproduction apparatuses in service of the dominant group and/or the hegemonic master signifiers and their realm of self-evidence.

In contrast to the hegemonic pedagogical rhetoric, which is committed to depoliticizing the predicates and the sources of the representations of schooling, Giroux -- following Adorno, Horkheimer, and Marcuse—acknowledges that at the present stage of capitalistic development there is no level or terra in society that is free of the presence of the hegemonic ideology.

Giroux presents ideology in two very different contexts: of distortion and perversion on the one hand, and as elaboration and enlightening power on the other. On the one level, ideology becomes hegemonic as the distortion of true deciphering of reality and as a prevention of true dialogue. On the second level, ideology contains a reflective moment and becomes a precondition for a dialogical process that leaves room for conscious and social emancipation. Giroux notes that given its enslavement to a conservative socio-cultural context, which does not search for contradictions and invisible powers and interests, the reflective potential of ideology is very limited and it prevents it from being a foundation for emancipation.[19] In light of this reconstruction, following Critical Theory in its first stage of development, Ideology Critique becomes for Giroux a central emancipatory educational apparatus.[20]

This is because he conceives the human subject as autonomous and open to critical overcoming of the social and ideological manipulations that limit his or her horizons. This is where his educational language of "possibilities" and "transformation" is situated.

---

19   Henry Giroux, *Theory and Resistance in Education*, p. 67.
20   *Ibid.*, p. 159.

Giroux expressly identifies his Critical Pedagogy with the work of Marcuse, and commits himself to realizing this work in the field of education in order to develop a radical new pedagogical theory.[21] Within this project, the Marcusian work is interpreted as a call for intellectual activism for teachers and students in the school arena. Teachers are called upon to become "transformative intellectuals" in schools and in society in general. As deeply committed intellectuals, they are obliged to develop every aspect of the formal educational process into an active and "popular" clash with the hegemonic order of society.[22]

In the mid-1980s Giroux made a turn, and postmodern influences became central to his Critical Pedagogy. This has conceptual manifestations, but it becomes clear even in other respects. Not surprisingly, therefore, in his 1981 *Ideology, Culture and the Educational Process* Marcuse is named on 22 pages, Adorno is mentioned on ten and Horkheimer on four. In his *Border Crossings* (1992), however, Adorno is mentioned only four times, and so is Horkheimer. From then on, Marcuse is not mentioned at all. Michel Foucault, who was mentioned only once in the 1981 text, has now become the hero of the reformulated Critical Pedagogy and is cited more than any other philosopher. Giroux, like McLaren, Weiler, Lather, Shor, and other prominent American thinkers in the tradition of Critical Pedagogy, and to a certain degree also Paulo Freire, did not just disregard the mature work of Adorno and Horkheimer. Even within the part of Critical Theory that they did relate to they selected the more optimistic and foundationalist parts, especially in the work of Marcuse. They disregarded the complementary skeptic-pessimistic-anti-foundationalist aspects of Critical Theory, which are of vital importance even for the understanding of the immanent dialectic of Critical Theory in its first stage of development. The inner dialectics between these two dimensions is the gateway to understanding Critical Theory and its educational implications.

This dialectic is present not only in the work of Adorno, Horkheimer and Benjamin.[23] It is there even in Benjamin's utopianism, which was challenged along with that of Marcuse, even if for contrasting reasons.[24]

The dialectical dimension between optimism and pessimism and between positive and negative utopianism is essential also for the work of Marcuse, whose supposed optimistic revolutionary project has been celebrated for more than thirty years now among leftist intellectuals and many of the 1968 generation. This misunderstanding of Marcuse, and certainly of the work of the other members of the Frankfurt School and their Critical Theory, is of special importance. It becomes a constitutive element in establishing Critical Pedagogy's educational optimism in respect of developing its

21   *Ibid.*, p. 2.
22   Henry Giroux, "Border pedagogy and the politics of modernism/postmodernism", in Henry Giroux, *Teachers as Intellectuals*, New York Bergin & Garvey 1988, p. 37.
23   Ilan Gur-Ze'ev, "Walter Benjamin and Max Horkheimer: from utopia to redemption", *The Journal of Jewish Thought and Philosophy*, 8 (1988), pp. 119–155.
24   *Ibid.*

central concepts such as "empowerment", "dialogue", "Ideology Critique", "transformative education", "agency", "possibilities", and "praxis education".

The limits of Critical Pedagogy were challenged within the tradition of Critical Pedagogy as well as "outside", by critics such as Elizabeth Ellsworth.[25] It is also in the center of a currently published book which addresses critical pedagogy and the possibility of a new critical language in education. Until now, however, these difficulties were hardly met by an attempt to rearticulate Critical Pedagogy in light of a new reading of Critical Theory as a first step in countering new critical theories and trends within postmodern, post-colonialist, feminist, multiculturalist and queer theories and discourses. The effort to rearticulate Critical Pedagogy was made explicitly to be in line with the latest fashions in current critical rhetoric. Among the very few prominent Critical Pedagogy thinkers who were not swallowed up by this trend McLaren deserves mention. But he too did not respond to the limits of Critical Pedagogy by rethinking his conceptions of Critical Theory. He preferred to rearticulate *orthodox Marxism* in light of the current capitalistic globalization processes and in face of the dehumanization and the suffering it brings along with the "prosperity" it offers its elected ones.[26]

To show how avoiding the essentials of Critical Theory, even in the first phase of its development, became a constitutive element for Critical Pedagogy is not difficult. It is easily demonstrated by reference to the silence of the critical thinkers in the field of education in face of the challenges of philosophical pessimism and of the implications of skepticism in the works of Benjamin, Adorno, and Horkheimer. Far harder, however, is to show these elements in Marcuse, who was the most influential thinker of the Frankfurt School among the 1968 generation of revolutionary students. This is the best reason for responding first to the Marcusian challenge, before proceeding to the later philosophy of Adorno and Horkheimer.[27]

For the Marcusian project the utopian dimension was of vital importance. In his thought there is no potential for the critique of culture and society that is disconnected from the utopian axis as a source of hope and as a total moral responsibility to resist injustice. This claim is valid in respect of immanent critique and as well as critique as the heart of transcendence. Art and art criticism were essential for Marcuse's utopian project. This is because only in art did bourgeois society tolerate its own ideals and present them as a general demand. What is conceived as utopian, fantasy, or an unforgivable revolt against the world of facts, in art is conceived as legitimate.[28]

---

25 Elizabeth Ellsworth, "Why doesn't this feel empowering? Working through the repressive myths of Critical Pedagogy", *Harvard Educational Review* 59: 3 (1989), pp. 297–324.

26 Peter McLaren, "Reconsidering Marx in post-Marxist times: a requiem for postmodernism?" *Educational Researcher* 29: 3 (April 2000), pp. 25–33.

27 This is still a much missing element in the critique of Marcuse's work. Here I offer only the main argument with brief references to its textual justifications. The dialectic between his philosophical pessimism and positive utopianism is extensively analyzed in: Ilan Gur-Ze'ev, *The Frankfurt School and the History of Pessimism*, Jerusalem 1996 (in Hebrew).

28 Herbert Marcuse, *Negations—Essays in Critical Theory*, London Penguin Press 1968, p. 114.

Concept such as "otherness" or "the totally other", which challenge the current world of "facts" and the "not-yet"—concepts that are so vital for the project of the Frankfurt School's Critical Theory—are realized in the work of Marcuse in respect of the category of beauty. "Beauty", says Marcuse, "is nothing less than the sudden appearance of another truth to the heart of the established reality".[29] Marcuse is very clear about his understanding of "otherness". In a still unpublished fragment in the Marcuse Archive he refers to nothing other than the urge toward or the manifestations of the trinity of "the beautiful, the good and the just".[30] Here Marcuse and Adorno are very close. Adorno too understood that it is art that is to approach "the very target of rationality" by its very structure or aim. Marcuse and Adorno are closer on this point to Heidegger[31] than to Horkheimer.

In his *One Dimensional Man* and in many other texts Marcuse manifests historical pessimism, which is very different from Benjamin's, Adorno's and Horkheimer's philosophical pessimism. It is, however, of vital importance for the educational implications of his work. Central to the Marcusian constitution of an emancipatory epistemology and to the critique of culture and society are a practice and theory of art within which "the aesthetic form of beauty" is manifested in sublimation.[32]

Marcuse, however, came to the conclusion that as part of the historical success of the repressive de-sublimation of the capitalist Culture Industry, this potentially transcending dimension of Western culture was being demolished by the omnipotence of the realization of the logic of capitalism. The traditional gap between art (and that which it points to) and the "factual" order of things that artistic alienation traditionally contained was vital for the emancipatory potential of art and for Critical Theory. However, Marcuse came to the conclusion that alienation itself was being impaired in the current technological society as an element of the total irrational rationalization of human space.

As part of this process, according to Marcuse, there was diminishing room for "the grand refusal" or indeed for any moral resistance and for meaningful critique. Not less devastating for the critical mind, according to Marcuse, was that the otherness, or "the other dimension", was being swallowed, and— after being castrated of its antagonistic potential—reproduced, as part and parcel of the present order.[33] The cultural reality of late capitalism, according to Marcuse, presents an ever more efficient attack on the very possibility of *transcendence* and of the very possibility of an *immanent critique*. After neutralizing the antagonistic dimensions in the culture and after deconstructing the possibilities for transcendence, this society targets human inwardness as a potential source for immanent autonomy and courageous critique. It transforms the human

---

29   Herbert Marcuse, "Culture and revolution", *Herbert Marcuse Archive* 406.00.

30   Herbert Marcuse, "[Epikur]", *Herbert Marcuse Archive* 100.25 (1936).

31   Martin Heidegger, "The question concerning technology", in: *Basic Writings*, London: Routledge and K. Paul 1996, pp. 311–341.

32   Herbert Marcuse, "Nachwort", in Walter Benjamin, *Zur Kritik der Gewalt und andere Aufsaetze*, Frankfurt a.Main Fischer 1971, p. 78.

33   *Ibid.*, p. 68.

psyche and its strivings. It domesticates it until it becomes an unproblematic dweller of current hegemonic one-dimensionality.[34]

While suggesting the possibility of the continuation of art as the only possible source of hope[35] he himself is very clear about the implications of his work: the words and the concepts which until recently allowed the presentation of a possible free society have lost their meaning today. They can no longer serve for introducing the human condition into a worthier society.[36]

A critical reconstruction of Marcuses' *One Dimensional Man* reveals two conceptions of progress in his work: one is conceived as "genuine" or "good", while the other is nothing less than the sophistication and progress of evil. And it is the latter, according to Marcuse, which is being realized unhampered in present post-industrial society.[37] In an unpublished text Marcuse presents this kind of progress, within which the productive powers are to be understood as representing "productive destruction" within a process which is "irreversible".[38] Summarizing this point in another unpublished text Marcuse concludes: "Western industrial society has no future".[39] And in yet another unpublished text he says in this light, "being today a realist is to become a pessimist".[40]

This neglected side in Marcuse's thought conceives pessimistically the presence of the idea of reason in its present historical setting. Today the idea of reason, which was central to the concepts of progress in humanistic projects of Kant, Hegel, and Marx, says Marcuse, "has itself become an illusion, like the prejudices that it was aimed to replace".[41] "Rationality itself", he concludes, "has become a repressive apparatus",[42] cultural progress is becoming less and less rational,[43] or in other words, irrational reality is becoming rational and resistance to it is becoming irrational. This is the triumph of what he calls "irrational rationality".[44] Resistance to this historical progress, as well as the critique of it, have accordingly become "unrealistic", and identification with the alternatives to the present order has become merely a matter of "personal preferences".

How then are we to understand Marcuse's identification with the students' revolt, with guerrilla warfare, and with the radical re-education of people within the frame-

---

34 *Ibid.*, p. 80.
35 Herbert Marcuse, "Art and literature in the one-dimensional society", translated by Oded Peled, *Proza* 10 (October 1976), pp. 18–19.
36 *Ibid.*
37 Herbert Marcuse, "Nachwort", in: Walter Benjamin, *Zur Kritik der Gewalt und andere Aufsaetze*, Frankfurt a..Main Fischer1971, pp. 20, 32.
38 Herbert Marcuse, "Fortschrit—Kategorien", *Herbert Marcuse Archive* 564.02 (1979).
39 Herbert Marcuse, "On pluralism, future, and philosophy", *Herbert Marcuse Archive* 569.00.
40 Herbert Marcuse, "Culture and revolution", *Herbert Marcuse Archive* 406.00, p. 36.
41 Herbert Marcuse, "Marx, Freud und der Monotheismus", *Herbert Marcuse Archive* 241.00 (8.6.1964), p. 12.
42 *Ibid.*, p. 11.
43 *Ibid.*, p. 13.
44 *Ibid.*, p. 14.

work of Critical Theory and its Ideology Critique? And how are we to understand in this light the founding of optimistic Critical Pedagogy on his thought while ignoring these essential parts of his philosophy?

Any reply to this challenge should, to my mind, address the dialectical tension between the positive-utopian and the pessimist dimensions in Marcuse's work. Such an attempt was not made by his disciples, such as the early Giroux, or by his numerous opponents. Entering this gate will afford us the possibility of seeing Marcuse as a sophisticated educator, of the kind of Marx and Lenin.

Neither Marx and Lenin was content with reliance on a genuine understanding of the explicit educational role of their texts by the oppressed. They allowed themselves to be manipulative and consciously to deceive their disciples. This was within the Jesuit pedagogical framework of the goals justifying the means. So they "only" tried to use the didactics that would make the oppressed think what they ought to think and want what they ought to want, if only for them to become free to recognize their own interests or meet their authentic/true self, identity, or consciousness.

In acting as arch-educators, whose "lessons" endure not hours or days but generations, Marx and Lenin functioned like servants or media in the human historical process, as presented by Lessing[45] and the other heroes of the Enlightenment. In this they followed the deepest eschatological trends in the Jewish and Christian traditions which the Enlightenment secularized under the flag of the emancipatory project.[46] So in the name of the eschatological logic of historical progress as the genuine educator and as the realization of the humanist Messianic commitment to future lasting human happiness, Marx, Lenin, and Marcuse trusted that they were allowed, even obliged, to conceal from the yet-unredeemed their real conclusions, ideas, and erotic imperatives. They did so with no qualms of conscience, like so many caring parents do with their beloved young children.

As *a self-appointed arch-educator*, Marcuse understood, like Marx at the time of the Paris Commune, that in the concrete historical conditions the students' revolt could not gain the upper hand. Yet he did not challenge the students' optimism and openly supported and encouraged them. How may we understand this in terms of realizing his responsibility as an arch-educator?

Within the framework of a one-dimensional society, what remained to Marcuse as an educator was to do everything to keep alive the very idea of *resistance* as a master signifier for a totally different reality and for a totally different relation between

---

45   Ephraim Gothold Lessing, *On the Education of the Human Kind*. Lessing's small book is only an example. Schiller's *On the Education of Man in a Series of Letters* belongs to the same tradition. My argument that even works that did not present themselves explicitly as representatives of this tradition, such as those of Karl Marx, should be considered, at least partially, members of this tradition, to which Marcuse also belongs. The parallels between the historical process as the educator of humanity and the personal approach to maturity within the tradition of the Bildungroman are of a real significance here.

46   Amos Funkenstein, "Knowledge as a key for salvation", in: *Zemanim* 73 (Winter 2000–2001), pp. 4–9 (in Hebrew).

humans, symbolic intersubjectivity, and history. He reflects how the mystic can become an effective magician and change reality—if not immediately then in future generations. As such, his historical role, as a devotee of the concealed and defeated master signifier of emancipation, was of outmost importance. It was especially so at a time when "the grand refusal" or the very idea of transcending the affluent society had become irrelevant, naive, or even ridiculous. As a master of magic in the field of normalizing education within the framework of radical social philosophy, and as a person responsible to the future stages of the struggle for human emancipation, he understood that *the students' failure, if grandiose and tragic enough, would become an important educational lesson* for future generations of revolutionaries. For an essentialist such as Marcuse this historically educational lesson was actually an ontological sign, a sign of the presence of a positive Utopia that one day might be realized. Keeping alive the very possibility of negation and the dream of a more humane reality became part of the awakening process of the defeated idea of the redemptive process itself. What could be more important than fulfilling this educational responsibility to the historical teleological imperative itself?

Marcuse's positive utopianism was articulated within a linear, progressive, concept of history. His non-optimistic conclusions were not founded, as were those of Adorno and Horkheimer, on philosophical pessimism. This is very relevant to his understanding of historical impasses and their educational implications. He understood the historical barriers to human progress as fundamentally historical, temporary in nature. They were therefore also historically to be overcome—when conditions changed and if humanistic-oriented intellectuals like himself responded to the call of history and realized their educational duty.

As will be shown in the following, Critical Pedagogy, as formulated by Giroux—which was explicitly founded on Critical Theory—*disregarded* the most important educational aspects of Adorno and Horkheimer. It even misunderstood the central elements of Marcuse's educational implications. In this respect it could not justify its claim to being the pedagogical realization of Critical Theory. Maybe these, and not the reasons presented by Ellsworth,[47] are the main reasons for the shortcomings of Critical Pedagogy.

In the following I try to show that the most important implications of Critical Theory are beyond the scope of the inner dialectics in the work of Marcuse. They are to be found in the work of Benjamin or in the second phase of the work of Adorno and Horkheimer.

In the first stage of Critical Theory both Adorno and Horkheimer interlaced the goal of Critical Theory with the Marxian revolutionary project. In the second stage the turn away from Marx's main theses is evident. Marx's project was regarded as an element in the positive utopian position, which by then they both rejected. Horkhe-

---

47   Elizabeth Ellsworth, "Why doesn't this feel empowering? Working through the repressive myths of Critical Pedagogy", *Harvard Educational Review,* 59: 3 (1989), pp. 297–324.

imer expressly declares that it is a trend from the Marxian thought to that of Schopen-hauer and the tradition of philosophical pessimism.[48]

In the second stage of the development of his thought Horkheimer is explicitly anti-revolutionary. It is the nature of the revolutionary, every revolutionary, accord-ing to later Horkheimer, to become an oppressor.[49] Every revolution, especially a "successful" one, is a manifestation of power. And justice, when it becomes powerful, is realized only at the cost of its transformation into oppression.[50] In contrast to the Marxian tradition, it is now conceived that as long as even some remnants of freedom survive violence will flourish.[51] "In the end, whatever hopes Marx did hold on behalf of true society, apparently they seem to be the wrong ones, if—and this issue is impor-tant to Critical Theory—freedom and justice are interrelated in mutual opposition. The more justice there is, freedom will diminish accordingly".[52]

The historical reconstruction of the Culture Industry with its limitations, about which Giroux was aware and from which he articulated important implications in his Critical Pedagogy, is conceived here within the framework of *philosophical pessimism*. For Adorno, "space is nothing but absolute alienation".[53] For him this is the frame-work for viewing the whole historical reality of advanced technological society, in which everything has become "consumption", and life, with all its layers and dimen-sions, is nothing but "a fetish of consumption".[54]

In their *Dialectics of Enlightenment* Adorno and Horkheimer do not target the capi-talistic logic and its realization in itself, or the other representations of totalitarianism such as the National-Socialist or the Stalinist. Ultimately they target culture itself: "Culture has developed with the protection of the executioner... All work and pleas-ure are protected by the hangman. To contradict this fact is to deny all science and logic. It is impossible to abolish...terror and retain civilization. Even the lessening of terror implies a beginning of the process of dissolution".[55] The conception of revolu-tion and Critical Theory within the framework of historically progressing human emancipation is conceived within a double-layered philosophy of history, one linear, the other circular.

From the viewpoint of circular conception of time there is no room for progress in the Kantian, Hegelian, or Marxian sense, which made possible the optimism of Critical Pedagogy.

According to Benjamin, there is no document of culture which is not at the same time a document of a barbarity.[56] For Adorno and Horkheimer all substantive levels

48   Max Horkheimer, *Gesammelte Schriften* VII., Frankfurt a. Main: Fischer, 1985, pp. 339–340.
49   *Ibid.*, p. 418.
50   *Ibid.*, p. 341.
51   Max Horkheimer, *Gesammelte Schriften* XIII., Frankfurt a. Main: Fischer 1989, p. 247.
52   *Ibid.*, p. 340.
53   Theodor Adorno, *Gesammelte Schriften*, X., Frankfurt a.Main Suhrkamp 1970, p. 205.
54   Theodor Adorno, *Gesammelte Schriften*, III., Frankfurt a. Main: Suhrkamp, 1970, p. 243.
55   Theodor Adorno & Max Horkheimer, *Dialektik der Aufklaerung*, Frankfurt a.Main: Fischer, 1988, p. 255.
56   Walter Benjamin, *Gesammelte Schriften*, 1.2, Frankfurt a.Main: Suhrkamp1972, p. 696.

of "progress" manifest an oppressive regression. In this sense, "adaptation to the power of progress involves the regression of power. Each time anew 'progress' brings about those degenerations. They manifest not unsuccessful but successful progress to be its contrary".[57]

On the other level of "progress", the explicitly historical one, unless an unpredictable interference occurs the good intentions and progressive talents of educators devoted to revolutionary education are of little use in halting the enhancement and sophistication of barbarism. The instrumentalization of rationality is reconstructed as representing and serving the growing needs of technological progress and economic development. Instrumental Rationality becomes "a magic essence". Instrumental Rationality is conceived here as a metaphoric revolt of instrumentalized nature, as a return of *mythos*, whose overthrow was the essential mission of Enlightenment. Mythical thought gave birth to Enlightenment as overcoming *Bildung* and human emancipation. This is the reason that Enlightenment today, in its most "progressive" form, returns to a more dangerous type of mythical thought[58] within what Horkheimer calls "the full-administered world".[59]

In such a reality there is no room for non-repressive "progressive", positive, utopianism, or for an objective, justifiable, education and praxis for resistance and overcoming the present reality.[60] Does this mean that Adorno and Horkheimer abandoned Utopia altogether, that they gave up the essential commitment of Critical Theory, or ended their transformative-educational imperative? Not at all. On the contrary, they became devoted more than ever to the Utopian call.

Adorno and Horkheimer gave up the Marxist conception of *progress*, and in this sense their optimism as to a social revolutionary change, and even the goal, and to a certain degree also the means of critique. But they did not abandon the utopian project and the essential imperatives of Critical Theory as an emancipatory dimension and political praxis. However, their definition of emancipation and the stance of realization of intellectual autonomy as praxis changed dramatically to become more in line with its early Jewish eschatological sources in the Qumran sect and other Jewish and Christian members of the Messianic tradition.

In Horkheimer's work, the change from a Marxian Critical Theory to a pessimistic philosophy is paralleled by an articulation of *Critical Theory as a new, Jewish, Negative Theology*. Adorno's Negative Dialectics follows the same path, attempting to present counter-education, attempting to face the present absence of the quest for and the awaiting for the human stance of readiness to be called-upon, a seriousness about that which is called "redemption" in Christian theology.

This is where the Diasporic dimension is so central to the mature thinking of Adorno and Horkheimer, following the lead of Walter Benjamin on this path. The refusal to dwell in peace in the present order of things, the negation of the "facts" of the ac-

---

57   Horkheimer and Adorno, *Dialektik der Aufklaerung*, p. 42.
58   Max Horkheimer, *Eclipse of Reason*, New York: Oxford University Press, 1974, p. 22.
59   Max Horkheimer, *Gesammelte Schriften*, XIII., Frankfurt a.Main: Fischer, 1989, p. 328.
60   Max Horkheimer, *Eclipse of Reason*, New York: Oxford University Press, 1974, p. 26.

tuality, are but a manifestation of dismissal of metaphysical violence and of all kinds of "homes", dogmas, and self-satisfaction in a world of pain, injustice, ugliness, and betrayal of love. Since they refused a positive Utopia, in their mature thinking they could not promise a better world as a justification for resistance to normalizing education and the quest for pleasure, "success", and hegemony. Homelessness and worthy suffering are ontologically grounded here and become a religious way of life. It is a kind of religiosity which is Messianic without a Messiah.[61]

It has no promise of salvation or of redemption. But it might offer a Messianic moment, which will overcome the violence of the governing "now-time"[62] and open the gate to an alternative way of life, an alternative thinking in which Spirit is reclaimed and the de-humanization of the human by the manipulations of the system is resisted. Here, and only here, Love becomes possible again as different from the codes, passions, and ideals that are set by the omnipotence of the ruling culture industry. Here, where the otherness in the self is reclaimed, the otherness of the Other becomes not only legitimate: it becomes an indispensable element in a new kind of Life, in a new kind of dwelling in which nomadism is realized on intellectual and social levels, paralleled by infinite responsibility—with no God, dogma, or central committee of the party to guide the individual towards "the good". "The totally other" bursts in and disconceals the consensus, unveils the accepted truths, values, passions, and the other manifestations of the self-evidence. It is a dangerous way of life, in which new possibilities are open but there are no guarantees, no optimism, and no room for self-forgetfulness of the human.

In the second stage of the development of their work, both thinkers offer a counter-educational praxis whose religiosity is fertilized by the alarming recognition of the impossible realization of the imperative of human advance toward God, absolute Spirit, or Reason; toward the progressing true knowledge of genuine human interests and realization of their potentials. The current work of Slavoj Zizek, who writes that "the paradox of self-consciousness is that it is possible only against the background of its own impossibility",[63] is very close to this later work of Horkheimer and Adorno. In this sense the later work of Critical Theory becomes prima facie counter-educational, even if the word "education" is rarely mentioned and schooling is hardly tackled at all.

At the same time, both Adorno[64] and Horkheimer[65] referred explicitly to education and to schooling and academic education quite specifically and explicitly, in more popular texts and radio interviews. On these occasions another aspect of their work is expressed, which is less sophisticated, less negativistic, and less utopian-pessimist.

61   Walter Benjamin, *Gesammelte Schriften*, 1.2, Frankfurt a.Main: Suhrkamp1972, p. 203.
62   Walter Benjamin, *Zur Kritik der Gewalt und andere Aufsaetze*, Frankfurt a. Main. 1971, p. 701.
63   Slavoj Zizek, *Tarrying with the Negative; Kant, Hegel, and the Critique of Ideology*, Durham: Duke University Press ,1993, p. 15.
64   Theodor Adorno, *Erziehung zur Muendigkeit—Vortraege und Gespraeche mit Hellmut Becker 1959–1969*, Frankfurt a. Main: Suhrkamp 1971.
65   Max Horkheimer, *Gesammelte Schriften*, VIII., pp. 361–456.

There is a permanent gap, sometimes an unbridgeable abyss, between these popular references to education in its narrower sense and the deeper aspects of their formulated Negative Dialectics and Negative Theology as a path to counter-education. Here I concentrate on their more refined and deeper elaborations and on their educational implications.

Adorno and Horkheimer's treatment of the challenge of modern historical progress, especially in the 20th century, assigns a special place to technological progress and its implication for human life. They contend in a profound and courageous manner the challenge of current dwindling possibilities for human autonomy, solidarity, and elevation. On this level they are surprisingly close to Heidegger—much closer than to Marcuse.[66] The elaboration of the present state of technology and its implications is realized here within a critical reconstruction of Western metaphysics since technology is understood by them as the zenith and the essence of Western metaphysics.

According to later Horkheimer, in the modern world everything is enslaved for the ennoblement and advancement of technological progress under the control of Instrumental Rationality. Within this process nature has lost its own meaning and humans have lost their transcendental mission. Only one aim is still valid, namely self-preservation: egoism, which ultimately is revealed as serving omnipotent mythical powers within and as part and parcel of the totally administered world.[67] Within this process of post-industrial society and its Culture Industry there is no room for the autonomy of the individual. This conception is vital for the understanding of Horkheimer's perspective on education in its narrower and its wider manifestations.

The big challenge for the critical mind and for humanistic education is not the fruit of alienation but the disappearance of (the consciousness of) alienation within the totality, which is governed by Instrumental Rationality. This quest for alienation and the challenges of the exile of Spirit make the difference between orthodox Marxist Ideology Critique and Horkheimer and Adorno's conceptions. Governing Instrumental Rationality leaves no room for non-efficient and non-pragmatic considerations, and drives out the concepts, ideals, and traditions that allowed speculation and critique of the self-evident, and offered transcendence from the oppressive practices of all master signifiers. Instrumental Rationality is responsible for the current reality in which the more progressive the processes of de-humanization become, the more efficient becomes the concealment of the oppression of the present Culture Industry.[68] *The exile of Spirit* and the overcoming of the abyss between substance and subject are trivialized, and Spirit is again celebrated after being equalized with the governing representations as "reality", "normality", and the (given or promised) pleasure-machine to which normalizing education is quick to surrender to.

The seeming political freedom, free opinion, and tolerance within this society conceals and actually serves the process of totalistic de-humanization.

66 Ilan Gur-Ze'ev, *The Frankfurt School and the History of Pessimism*, Jerusalem: The Magnes Press 1996, p. 83 (in Hebrew).
67 Horkheimer, *Eclipse of Reason*, pp. 101–102.
68 Theodor Adorno, *The Adorno Reader*, edited by Brian O'Connor, London: Blackwell 2000, p. 233.

Not only does the mind mould itself for the sake of its marketability, and thus reproduce the socially prevalent categories. Rather, it grows to resemble ever more closely the *status quo* even where it subjectively refrains from making a commodity of itself. The network of the whole is drawn ever tighter. It leaves the individual consciousness less and less room for evasion, performs it more and more thoroughly, cuts it off as it were from the possibility of differentiating itself as all difference degenerates to a nuance in the monotony of supply.[69]

Within this process traditional Marxist Ideology Critique cannot be of much use since culture itself "has become ideological".[70] "Today", Adorno says, "ideology means society as appearance...ideology is not simply reducible to partial interest".[71] However, since ideology is no longer conceived as a socially necessary appearance which veil the "facts", Ideology Critique can no longer offer an emancipatory deciphering of "reality" and cannot claim to empower humanistic-oriented resistance to social oppression and to manipulative representations of histories, identities and realities, as Critical Pedagogy claims to offer in the name of Critical Theory. Adorno offers a view that does not allow this kind of optimism, since

Ideology today is society itself in so far as its integral power and inevitability, its overwhelming existence-in-itself, surrogates the meaning which that existence has exterminated.[72]

Horkheimer is on the verge of acknowledging that there is no more justification for a Critical Theory. In a personal letter to Adorno he says that nowadays "reflection [has become] senseless. Actually the world which we saw ourselves as belonging to is destroyed".[73] Elsewhere he writes that serious talk itself has become senseless and that those who refuse to listen—to the attempts to save meaning—are not totally wrong.[74] Truth in this context is not absent; it is rather revealed in and swallowed by the present reality. It can, however, offer only technological and scientific advance—not meaning, direction, or responsibility to resist injustice. The issue at stake here is not solely truth or justice but the very quest for truth and the commitment to justice, in other words *the possibility of transcending from meaninglessness and the Same—from the mere thingness of being.*

In the work of later Adorno and Horkheimer, two very different conceptions of truth emerge. One is of the kind of the existing world of facts, which ultimately

69 *Ibid.*, p. 198.
70 *Ibid.*, p. 206.
71 *Ibid.*, p. 207.
72 *Ibid.*
73 Max Horkheimer, letter to Adorno 26 May 1960, *Max Horkheimer Archive* VI., 3, 511.
74 Max Horkheimer, *Dawn & Decline—Notes 1926–1931 and 1950–1969*, New York: The Seabury Press 1978, p. 129.

represents "power".[75] Here human existence in its essence is revealed at its full cost: practical involvement, within which ideals transform into oppression.[76] The implicit *negation of any optimistic positive emancipatory educational project* is mercilessly manifested.

In an imaginary conversation between the philosopher—an implicit reference to the masters of Critical Theory themselves—and the practical man, the philosopher is the one on the defensive, and not his practical interlocutor. The genuine philosopher is introduced by Adorno and Horkheimer not as a promising educator, but as a *neurotic*, who manifests his refusal to be cured when insisting on continuing his project of curing normal, realistic-oriented, sane, people. Facing these conclusions one should ask: what, if any, is the justification for Critical Theory and for Critical Pedagogy as emancipatory education in action, under conditions in which "serious philosophy has come to its end"?[77]

The texts of later Adorno and Horkheimer reconstruct a cultural moment, which resembles an Arab story about a vicious magician who poisoned the well whence all the tribe drew its water. Everyone drank from the well—and went mad. Only the king did not drink. It took no time before the rumor spread all over: "How sad, our beloved king went crazy...." The king, according to this story, who was a wise man, asked his servants to hurry as fast as they could and bring him water from the poisoned well, and when left alone he drank from it. In no time a new rumor spread all over: "How wonderful, our beloved king has come back to his senses...." And so, according to the story, the tribe was saved.

Adorno and Horkheimer present us with a diametrically opposite vision. It is a vision of a philosopher who refuses at all costs to integrate, to be normalized, and as a neurotic, within impossible conditions, keeps his commitment to his counter-educational mission which nothing in reality can justify.

The later Horkheimer presents mature Critical Theory as a Jewish Negative Theology. This change carries major educational implications. Following Benjamin, it was for him of vital importance that Judaism did not present God as a positive absolute. Following Benjamin, and in contrast to Marcuse, the negativity of this utopianism is constituted from two elements. The first is rejection in principle of the possibility of a positive realization of any Utopia. He refuses to imagine a positive picture of future society prior to its realization.[78] The second is his commitment to confront Critical Theory with its own negativity. He refuses any philosophy that leads to consensus, synthesis, and the end of dialectics and worthy suffering. And at the same time he refuses to abandon *the quest for the Messiah* or human emancipation. The quest as a Messianic tension is central here, not its "successful" fulfillment. That is why Judaism was so important for him. He saw in Judaism "a non-positive religion", it was "a hope

---

75   Horkheimer and Adorno, *Dialektik der Aufklaerung*, p. 236.

76   *Ibid.*, p. 255.

77   Horkheimer,*Gesammelte Schriften* VII., p. 404.

78   *Ibid.*, p. 382.

for the coming of the Messiah".[79] Judaism, within this framework, is a symbol, not a reality, a symbol for solidarity, a non-violent solidarity of the powerless.[80] As a Jewish Negative Theology, Critical Theory expresses, in his view, "a refusal to recognize power as an argument for truth".[81]

The conception of being in the continuum of *ontological Diaspora* was vital for presenting late Critical Theory as a Jewish Negative Theology. The uniqueness of Judaism lies in its permanent demand for justice, emerging out of a hope with no real historical anchor: "Jewry was not a powerful state, but the hope for justice at the end of the world".[82] The idea that the demand for justice essentially cannot obtain power, and that justice can be realized only at the cost of its transformation into its opposite—injustice, is central to the educational implications of this version of Critical Theory.

It implies that genuine education must not attempt to transcend negativism; it is committed to anti-dogmatism and it must resist any manifestation of the self-evident, even that of the oppressed and the persecuted. It must resist popularization and political victories, while at the same time its Messianism is directed to resisting actual injustices in the present reality as the only manifestation of the quest for truth and justice. This version of Negative Theology as a mature Critical Theory in Horkheimer's thought complies with Adorno's concept of Negative Dialectics.

It was not in opposition to the view of the philosopher as a neurotic who refuses to be cured, but in compliance with it, that Adorno articulated the "categorical imperative of philosophy".[83] There he concludes: "it does not hold the key to salvation, but allows some hope only to the moment of concept followed by the intellect wherever the path may lead".[84] Actually, he presents Critical Theory as a path to salvation after all. This, however, is within a negative framework that leaves no room for any positive Utopia or actual salvation in the sense that traditional positive utopias or optimistic-oriented Critical Pedagogy can promise its disciples.

Regardless of its situation, philosophy according to Adorno has not concluded its mission. However, it does not have any foundation, self-evidence, social strata, or pain on which to establish its critical education: "Philosophy offers no place from which theory as such might be concretely convicted of the anachronisms it is suspected of, now, as before".[85] Adorno, in accordance with Benjamin and Horkheimer, and contrary to Marcuse, presents another kind of dialectics, a Negative Dialectics. Note, however, that his position stands in contrast to the orthodox Marxist concept of dialectics and its version of Ideology Critique[86] (as an emancipatory overcoming of

---

79   Max Horkheimer, *Gesammelte Schriften*, XIV., Frankfurt a. Main: Fischer, 1988, p. 331.
80   *Ibid.*, p. 140.
81   Horkheimer, *Gesammelte Schriften* VIII, p. 158.
82   Horkheimer, *Dawn & Decline—Notes 1926–1931 and 1950–1969*, New York: The Seabury Press 1978.
83   Adorno, *The Adorno Reader*, p. 53.
84   *Ibid.*
85   *Ibid.*, p. 57.
86   This is the kind of Ideology Critique which is fundamental to hegemonic Critical Pedagogy.

alienation and false consciousness, and as a precondition for a revolutionary praxis). As a genuine counter-educator he refuses any concept of dialectics, which promises victory, emancipation, or peace.

According to Adorno, "contradiction is not what Hegel's absolute idealism was bound to transfigure it into". "It indicates the untruth of identity, the fact that the concept does not exhaust the thing conceived".[87] Adorno and Horkheimer are united here in refusing any manifestations of the absolute, the totality, the truth, or a positive justice on earth. Adorno grounds his concept of negativity in what in another philosophical tradition is called "the essence of being".

That is why even dialectics itself is not at peace with itself, nor brings appeasement or truth. "The name of dialectics", he says in his *Negative Dialectics*, "says no more, to begin with, than that objects do not go into their concepts without leaving a reminder, that they come to contradict the traditional norm of adequacy".[88] The gap will never be bridged, no theory will fully and adequately represent its object.

The very presence of the object separated from its representation apparatuses is problematized here in a manner that leaves no room for easygoing promises of "understanding", "empowerment", or "emancipation". Certainly not of collectives, as Critical Pedagogy never tires of promising the oppressed and the marginalized in the name of Critical Theory.

Adorno is very much aware of the contradictions at the heart of his project. The important philosophical and educational view of his rests here, on these contradictions precisely, as a way of overcoming meaninglessness and self-evidence of various kinds, including the revolutionary kind. "The work of philosophical self-reflection consists in unraveling that paradox. Everything else is signification, secondhand construction, pre-philosophical activity".[89] What then remains for philosophy to do, if there is still a mission it can devote itself to?

Adorno, like Horkheimer, constituted his utopian thought on his philosophical pessimism, so *Negative Dialectics* becomes the last way to save the struggle to challenge the self-evident and to transcend meaninglessness.

> To change this direction of conceptuality, to give it a turn toward nonidentity, is the hinge of Negative Dialectics. Insight into the constitutive character of the nonconceptual in the concept would end the compulsive identification, which the concept brings unless halted by such reflection. Reflection upon its own meaning is the way out of the concept's seeming being-in-itself as a unit of meaning.[90]

---

87 Adorno, *The Adorno Reader* 2000, p. 57.
88 *Ibid.*, p. 57.
89 *Ibid.*, p. 60.
90 *Ibid.*, p. 63.

In this sense, and solely in this sense, "philosophy can make it after all".[91]   Philosophizing, in this respect, becomes the only way to resist the process of destruction of the autonomy of the human subject.[92] It becomes the only manner of resistance to being overwhelmed by the one-dimensional functionality and thingness of the system[93] and its deceiving massage of freedom in accordance with the laws of the market and the current world of facts.[94] As such, within its negativity, it incubates an alternative to the hegemonic educational message propagated by the Culture Industry. In so doing, it offers the possibility of refusal of the present process of subjectification or resistance to the reality of constructing the de-humanized agent. As such philosophy offers a kind of thinking which allows hope of overcoming the current educational reality[95] of which Critical Pedagogy is an important part.

The later work of Adorno and Horkheimer is indispensable in the present historical moment of Western culture. In face of the exile of Spirit it represents an uncompromising quest for Utopia. Western Eros is not being destroyed but consumed and reproduced as part of the one-dimensional reified diversity of the preset cultural moment, which in some respects is already beyond the horizons of the Culture Industry that was challenged by Critical Theory.

In face of the current post-modern conditions, which are accompanied by modernist and even pre-modernist ones, the later work of Adorno and Horkheimer are of special value, and not solely as a theoretical and educational challenge to postmodern ideologies and educational alternatives. It is also important as an alternative to normalizing education and for the creation of a new kind of a Diasporic philosophy of the kind Judaism traditionally offered the world—under the evil conditions set by postmodern global capitalism that develops along new destructions and distorted creative Eros, which is governed by the logic of Thanatus—also new possibilities for cosmopolitanism. This *new cosmopolitanism* transforms and further develops the Messianic tradition. This Messianic moment, even as a potential, is normally distorted, misused, or forgotten. But in face of cultural, economic, political, and, ultimately, existential crises it awakens. It might become an impetus for counter-education precisely against the exile of Spirit, the instrumentalization of reason, and the reification of the human relations. In opposition to the optimists, who establish great hopes for all humanity on the foundations of globalizing capitalism, we offer a dialectical reconstruction of our historical moment: it is the same globalizing capitalism which rationally sends entire populations to starvation, poor health, and lost of self-respect on the margins of world affluent economy; which also opens the door to the visibility of suffering, to universal needs and values, and to new possibilities for counter-educa-

---

91   *Ibid.*, p. 60.
92   Theodor Adorno, *Minima Moralia—Reflections from Damaged Life*, translated by E. F. N. Jephcott, New York: Verso 1999, p. 5.
93   Adorno, *The Adorno Reader*, p. 234.
94   *Ibid.*, p. 198.
95   *Ibid.*, p. 238.

tion and Diasporic way of life that transcends ethnocentric solidarity, political borders, and contextual pragmatism and cynicism.

Later Critical Theory struggled for the very possibility of sensitivity to alienation, for worthy suffering, and for containing the pursuit for **the totally other**. Within this attempt, and only within it, are we to understand its refusal to abandon the imperative of responsibility to the yet unrealized human potentials. To this imperative, as to the presence of *hope* out of worthy suffering, Adorno, and Horkheimer offered only one possible way: that of religious negation.

The message here is the messianic impulse, or the commitment for transcendence from any consensus, or the self-evident, into a struggle to overcome meaninglessness in a Godless world. In this sense any possible educational "implication" should be negative, if true to itself. And in this sense later Adorno and Horkheimer are so important in the attempt to keep alive the quest and the actual appearance of counter-education as a concrete Utopia in a postmodern condition.

Counter-education, if true to itself, cannot be, as Critical Pedagogy would have us believe, an attempt to implement any "theory", as sophisticated or good-intentioned as it may be. If true to itself, counter-education must challenge any theoretical, ideological, or political "home", any master signifier, dogma, or ethnocentrism as manifestations of the Same, of the thingness in Being, which human beings are called on to guard and transcend.[96] Counter-education, in this sense, must be at once Messianic and negative at any cost. This means that it cannot satisfy itself even with identification with the negation of the self-evident, with the resistance to the ethnocentrism of the oppressed, and it cannot identify itself with the "worthier" violences they actualize against their own "internal" and "external" Others.

If faithful to itself, counter-education must concentrate on overcoming itself, negating its own theoretical assumptions, procedures, and conclusions. A special role is reserved here for a critical reintegration of ethics, aesthetics, and interdisciplinary critical scientific work in its cultural and social context. Its negativity must avoid being abstract and one-dimensional, and love is essential to its realization.

It must turn to realize solidarity in actual dialogical situations and make room for love and generosity in actual life situations. As a concrete Utopia, counter-education must acknowledge this world and the presence of politics and power-relations. And in this sense there is some affinity between it and Critical Pedagogy. However, it should not see itself as of this world, and it should refuse reduction to power-relations, group interests and implications of politically-correct vocabularies. It acknowledges itself as holy work (*avodat kodesh*), and only as such also as involvement in the political space.

Counter-education speaks only from the perspective of the Exile, as a homeless one who challenges the meaninglessness of the celebrated truths, values, and pleasures. It is facilitated by the possible appearance of grace in a Godless world. For such a project the later work of Adorno and Horkheimer is certainly not the sole source but

---

96 Martin Heidegger, "The question concerning technology", in: *Basic Writings*, London Routledge and Kegan Paul 1996, pp. 196, 234.

it is a worthy point of reference, and a relevant erotic experience. As an alternative to normalizing education, of which Critical Pedagogy is part and parcel, mature Critical Theory has "educational relevance": as a manifestation of counter-education and as a link in a worthy tradition that has not yet said its last word.

Only after developing these aspects is it worth reconstructing the later texts of Adorno on education after Auschwitz,[97] and Horkheimer's conceptions of higher education as the last barrier against the new barbarism enhanced by the culture industry.[98] Such work has not yet been done. That is why its initiation must pay special attention to the overcoming of the worthier parts of Adorno's Negative Dialectics and Horkheimer's Negative Theology.

---

97   Theodor Adorno, *Erziehung zur Muendigkeit—Vortraege und Gespraeche mit Hellmut Becker 1959– 1969*, Frankfurt a.Main Suhrkamp 1971, pp. 88–104.
98   Horkheimer, *Gesammelte Schriften* VIII., pp. 409–419.

CHAPTER 6

CRITICAL EDUCATION IN CYBERSPACE?

Critical educational thinkers who support recent advances in communicative technologies are of various ideological backgrounds: "hard" and "soft" postmodernists, neo-Marxists working within the framework of critical pedagogy, and those engaged in critical literacy, cultural studies, and feminist, post-colonialist, and multicultural discourses. Some conceive cyberspace as a

> space of a total textual environment based upon text-based computing, giving rise to the notion of the virtual text, new forms of interactivity, and emergent discourses which collapse in formal communication and traditional forms of scholarship.[1]

In this chapter I treat the response of critical educational theorists to the challenges posed by cyberspace. Part of this discourse does not go forward under the banner of "critical pedagogy" but under titles such as "critical literacy" or "critical media education". Here I refer to these attitudes as "critical".

I reconstruct the hopes of critical thinkers for cyberspace and try to show what specific elements are conceived as potentially critical and emancipatory, and I elaborate on its meaning. I conclude by challenging the concept of education and the concept of critique of the critical cyberoptimists; I articulate a different perspective on the educational potential of cyberspace within the framework of counter-education.

GREAT HOPES

Michael Peters, Michele Knobel, and Colin Lankshear have great hopes regarding cyberspace:

> the transition from print-based texts to electronic text forms and practices, which is continuing apace, opens up space for expanded and enhanced practices of critical literacy. We regard this as a matter, simultaneously, of educational urgency and possibility. Our prevailing

---

1   Michael Peters and Colin Lankshear, "Critical Literacy and Critical Texts", *Educational Theory* (1996), 46, 1, p. 61.

"enclosured" forms of consciousness may impede a fuller realization of
critical literacy within this changing textual environment.[2]

It is worth noting here that they explicitly relate their project to the tradition of critical pedagogy.[3] They argue that traditional critical pedagogy has to change some of
its central Freirean elements in the direction shown by Henry Giroux and George
Landow, and as such they are very optimistic about the future implementation of
critical pedagogy in cyberspace.[4] Knobel argues that these hopes are founded in actual
research, and that the chief goals of critical pedagogy and its methodology are to be
implemented within the framework of critical literacy as a radical praxis in cyberspace.[5]
Muffoleto holds a similar position.[6] On the other hand, some of the cyberoptimists
refer to "contemporary" critical theory as realized in cyberspace, with reference to Derrida and the network concept of knowledge as an (explicit) alternative to the classical
critical theory of Adorno and Horkheimer, and its alleged elitist concept of knowledge and transcendence.[7] Other cyberoptimists are already influenced by the ("soft")
postmodern discourse, yet they preserve stronger philosophical ties with the classical
critical theory tradition, its assumptions, goals and concepts via the new possibilities
opened up by the communication technologies. Douglas Kellner is a representative
of the first trend. Kellner, one of the best known students of the critical theory of the
Frankfurt School, is deeply involved in the attempt to realize classical critical theory
(in the form of Freirean critical pedagogy) within the framework of critical literacy in
cyberspace. In opposition to representatives of the second trend such as Knobel, Peters, and Lankshear, he does not think that central elements of critical pedagogy have
to be changed for successful realization of critical literacy in cyberspace.[8] Stanley Aronowitz shares this optimism regarding the possibility of implementing critical theory
in the postmodern condition.[9] Other critical thinkers such as Nicholas Burbules and

---

2   *Ibid.*, p. 53.
3   Colin Lankshear, Michael Peters and Michele Knobel, "Critical Pedagogy and Cyberspace", in: Hen-
     ry Giroux, Colin Lankshear, Peter McLaren, and Michael Peters (Eds.), *Counternarratives: Cultural
     Studies and Critical Pedagogies in Postmodern Spaces*, New York: Routledge, 1996, p. 149. Michael
     Peters and Colin Lankshear, "Critical literacy and critical texts", *Educational Theory* (1996), 46, 1, pp.
     52–53.
4   Ibid., 160.
5   Michele Knobel, "Critical literacy and the new technologies", http://www.schools.ash.org.au/litweb/
     michele/html 8.6.1998
6   Robert Muffoletto, "Towards a critical pedagogy of media education", http://muffoletto/coe.uni.edu/
     summer96/critical-pedagogy.html 1.17.1999
7   George Landow, *Hypertext: The Contemporary critical Theory and Technology*, Baltimore and London:
     John Hopkins Press:1992, p. 23.
8   Douglas Kellner, "Media illiteracies and critical pedagogy in a multicultural society", http://www.
     gseis.ucla.edu/courses/ed253a/newDK/medlit.htm 12.1997
9   Michael Menser and Stanley Aronowitz, "On cultural studies, science, and technology, in: Stanley
     Aronowitz, Maris Martinsons, Michael Menser and Jennifer Rich (eds.), *Technoscience and Cyberspace*,
     New York and London: 1996, p. 14.

Suzanne Rice participate in the optimism of other critical thinkers about cyberspace (not without some reservations), yet without seeing it as part of the realization of critical pedagogy; sometimes they even expressly depart from this tradition as influenced by educational thinkers such as McLaren and Giroux.[10]

CYBERSPACE AND EMANCIPATION

Under the influence of the postmodern discourse Landow is committed to accomplishing a realization of critical theory within cyberspace while emancipating it from its "repressive" modernist characteristic: "We must abandon conceptual systems founded upon ideas of center, margin, hierarchy, and linearity and replace them with ones of multilinearity, nodes, links, and networks".[11] Landow argues against the *hierarchical* concept of knowledge and a canon enforced on students by a set of books and hierarchical relations between the teacher as the one who knows. He asserts that cyberspace is an alternative to the traditional legitimating medium of the "correct" interpretation, which reflects asymmetrical social relations and oppression.[12]

According to many critical thinkers "post-structuralism and the common digital code seem part of the same event".[13] I agree with perceiving cyberspace as one of the manifestations of the postmodern condition. Critical pedagogy and its telos, however, I see as a manifestation of the Enlightenment's emancipatory project, and as such as an essentially modernist that there are problematic relations between its concepts of critique and emancipation and those offered by the various postmodernist trends. If I refer to the critical pedagogy of Freire and the early Giroux and to a certain degree to the current critical pedagogy of Peter McLaren, the modernist characteristics of the project are very much in the center.

For Paulo Freire the subject-object dichotomy and the possibility of knowing "the reality" of the oppression is a precondition for emancipatory pedagogy.[14] He believes in "objectivity"[15] and calls for education where "the genuine humanist educator and revolutionary"[16] will challenge hegemonic education and its context. Within critical pedagogy, a successful transcendence from hegemonic ideology is possible, and this is the aim of the dialogue, which will identify unfulfilled potentials that will be fulfilled or struggled for within critical pedagogy.[17] The early Giroux uses Marxist economic

10 Nicholas Burbules and Susan Rice, "Dialogue across differences: continuing the conversation", *Harvard Educational Review* (November 1991), 61, 4, p. 397.

11 George Landow, *Hypertext: The Convergence of Contemporary critical Theory and Technology*, Baltimore: John Hopkins Press, 1992, p. 2.

12 Lankshear, Peters, Knobel, "Critical pedagogy and cyberspace", p. 155.

13 *Ibid.*, 160.

14 Paulo Freire, *Pedagogy of the Oppressed*, Jerusalem: Sifrei Mifras 1981, p. 37 (in Hebrew).

15 *Ibid.*, p. 40

16 *Ibid.*, p. 84.

17 *Ibid.*, pp. 97–103.

categories to explain school as a cultural and political reproduction apparatus,[18] sees
critical theory as a foundation for successful social activism,[19] and sees in critical pedagogy the bridge between theory and practice. The teacher and the authority of critical
knowledge are irreplaceable here for the emancipatory project, which is conceived as
a collective effort.[20]

These characteristics of critical pedagogy collide with "soft" postmodern concepts
such as subjectivity, identity, difference, contingency, and fluidity, and certainly with
"hard" postmodern concepts such as incommensurability or the absence of a "subject"
or "reality". Giroux himself was aware of the tension between the two,[21] and suggested
a new critical pedagogy that would synthesize them. The amazing thing, however, is
that when thinkers who see themselves as part of the tradition of critical pedagogy
explicitly try to realize critical pedagogy in cyberspace they do not address the theoretical *gap* between critical pedagogy and its modernist context and cyberspace as a
manifestation of a postmodern condition. In their important "critical pedagogy and
Cyberspace", Colin Lankshear, Michael Peters, and Michele Knobel are aware of the
need to rearticulate critical pedagogy, but there is no systematic theoretical elaboration
of the gap and the tensions between a postmodern and an Enlightened educational
project. Addressing this tension, in other words elaborating the very possibility of a
critical theory and emancipatory education within a postmodern arena, especially in
the context of the cyberspace, is, in our view, of vital importance. The absence of this
activity is part of other problematics: the concept of critical pedagogy held by critical
cyberoptimists. *The kind of critical pedagogy they hold enables them to identify the central
anti-humanist and anti-critical characteristics of cyberspace and to develop unjustified
hopes and expectations regarding the critical possibilities of the cyberspace.* This paper tries
to contribute something in this direction. I attempt it by reconstructing the critique
of the critical cyberoptimists on the conception of high culture and the text as held by
the critical theory thinkers as well as by traditional critical pedagogy.

Within the postmodern discourse not only the hegemonic repressive ideology, but
critical pedagogy too, as a bona fide modernist project, is foundationalist-oriented
and was largely theorized around modes of consciousness based on the book as the
text paradigm. The institutionalization of the book as a representation of hierarchical knowledge and human relations within the modernist schooling process is sometimes conceived as a mystification of the Word-World relations and institutionalization of an enclosuristic orientation. According to this thinking, this mystification is
deconstructed in cyberspace.[22] There the book as the paradigmatic text is replaced by
hypertext: it is composed of blocks of text and the electronic links that join them.

---

18   Henry Giroux, *Ideology, Culture and the Process of Schooling*, Philadelphia: Temple University Press,
      1981, p. 70.
19   *Ibid.*, p. 82
20   *Ibid.*, p. 83.
21   Henry Giroux, "Border pedagogy and the politics of modernism/postmodernism", *JAE* (February
      1991), 44, 2, p. 72.
22   *Ibid.*, p. 161.

Landow does not distinguish hypermedia from hypertext: hypermedia simply extends the notion of the text in hypertext by including visual information, sound, animation, and other forms of data. Hypertext links a passage of verbal discourse to images, maps, diagrams, and sound as easily as to another verbal passage, expands the notion of text beyond the solely verbal,[23] and allows the realization of critical pedagogy in cyberspace within a postmodern concept of knowledge where multiplicity and not hierarchy is the most important characteristic. It opens possibilities that have been impossible in the modern world, in the sense of access to any information, unending possibilities of engaging the text, editing it, and appropriating it on-line. The authority of the author or the hegemonic ideology is deconstructed by the open possibility for limitless re-authoring of any text on-line. Hypertexts, in contrast to printed texts, says Burbules, are inclusive.[24]

According to Burbules the "link" has a special role in realizing critical literacy in cyberspace and contains an emancipating potential. Burbules, however, shows problematic dimensions of the "link" also: while enabling readers to design/author their own hypertexts, the initial contact that users have with hypertext is with materials created by unknown persons whose reasons, values, biases, motivations, and credibility are almost entirely beyond their awareness.[25]

Other thinkers, for whom the postmodern era is accepted less critically, see cyberspace as a textual totality where transcendence is already realized as a living absolute[26] and the Hegelian world is realized in the Web as *Geist*.[27] I think that Burbules is right when he warns us that the link is both a line that I follow and a line that draws us in "like a fish: the Web or Net is a set of paths that I explore, but also a web or net that catches us up".[28]

In their criticism of traditional (Freirean) critical pedagogy, Lankshear, Peters, and Knobel challenge its modernistic concepts of empowerment and its commitment for "problem posing", dialogue, and its critique of the hegemonic curriculum.[29] From a postmodern perspective, they claim that in contrast to its pretension critical pedagogy remains teacher-controlled and *paternalistic*, and at best create an illusion of dialogue. General theories, transcendental concepts of linear knowledge, and other modernistic characteristics made its ideals of "emancipation", "justice", "equality", and "radical democracy" abstract and decontextualized.[30] By contrast, they see as promising the realization of the critical pedagogy of McLaren and Giroux in cyberspace.

According to this view,

---

23 Landow, *ibid.*, p. 5.
24 Nicholas Burbules, "Rhetoric of the web: hyperreading and critical literacy", http://www.ed.uiuc. edu/facstaff/burbules/ncb/papers/rhetorics.html, p. 2. 8.11.1998
25 *Ibid.*
26 Mark Taylor and Esa Saarinen, *Imagologies: Media Philosophy*, New York: Taylor & Francis Books, 1994, p. 2.
27 *Ibid.*, Simcult 3.
28 Nicholas Burbules, "Aporias, webs, and passages" (to appear in *Curriculum Inquiry*).
29 Lankshear, Peters and Knobel, *ibid.*, pp. 151–153.
30 *Ibid.*, p. 154.

New forms of textuality and intertextuality—hypertext and multimedia—indicate promising directions for reconstructing consciousness,
and the subject. In the new reader-controlled environment the reader
manipulates the limits, scale, and topography of the text unit.[31]

Uncritical literature envisions cyberspace as an arena where identity is disengaged
from gender and ethnicity, where "users can float free of biological and socio-cultural
determinants"[32] and form solidarian virtual communities and virtual democracy. Under this influence, many educational critical thinkers abandon the critical orientation
in favor of a rhetoric which promises on-line, immediate, realization of their positive
utopianism that until recently was clothed by them in the jargon of the critical tradition. Within this optimistic view solidarity does not negate spontaneity and self-
constitution, and the dialogical ideal is realized in virtual communities researching
jointly, and reconstituting themselves and the identities of the participants as individuals: *realizing educational elevation within the hybridity, contingency, and fluidity of
cyberspace.* Not only are the modernist institutionalized spaces of enclosure opened up
to critique, its alternative is actually realized by the overthrow of the book, its culture,
and its social context. A new culture emerges where there are new possibilities for
interactivity and intersubjectivity between the readers-writers who participate in these
ever re-created and reformulated virtual communities.

> Regular users of bulletin boards, on-line discussion groups, and the
> like express enthusiasm for the possibilities of opening inside reels and
> relations that are more egalitarian, purpose-driven, and self-imposed
> and self-monitored than those which have come to characterize domi-
> nant educational practices.[33]

Many critical thinkers understand cyberspace as a "radical democracy".[34] While acknowledging the dangers of the technologies of this *electropolis*, Kellner envisions
"a positive postmodernity [that] would thus involve creation of a more egalitarian
and democratic society in which more individuals and groups were empowered to
participate".[35]

critical cyberoptimists are united by a vision of cyberspace as a realm where virtual
communities are formed "spontaneously", or arise by self-determination, and constitute free individuals participating in uncensored, chaotic, dialogical communication
that crosses borders of disciplines, identities, cultures, and concepts of knowledge. It

---

31   *Ibid.*, p. 161.
32   Mark Dery, "Flame wars", in Flame Wars: The Discourse of Cyberculture, Duke: Duke University
     Press 1994, p. 7.
33   *Ibid.*, p. 167.
34   Kellner, *ibid.*, p. 7.
35   *Ibid.*, p. 11.

creates new worlds through and within differences, and not, as in the modern concept of knowledge and intersubjectivity, through a drive to overcome or destroy differences. Spontaneity and egalitarianism are conceived as overcoming socially constructed asymmetrical relations and distorted communication based on race, sex, ethnicity, nationality, and class. [36]

Michele Knobel, for example, follows Manuel Castells and rightly emphasizes that the increasing integration of text, images, and sounds in the same system, interacting from multiple points, in chosen time along a global network, in conditions that she conceives as "open and affordable access", does fundamentally change the character of human communication.[37] Knobel believes, however, that a good moral education that will unite with the development of operational and critical skills in the critical tradition will realize the Freirean vision of critical pedagogy within cyberspace.[38] In the positive utopianism of the tradition of the critical theory of the Frankfurt School[39] the realization of the ideal of emancipation is conceived here as "art as a form of life".[40] Here "democracy" is conceived within the framework of a future possible erotization of existence, where "the pleasure principle" and the "reality principle" will stop being alienated but will merge into a new "reality principle".[41]

From another version of critical theory, a "purely" postmodern one, George Landow shares positive utopianism with Knobel, Kellner, Peters, Lankshear, Muffoletto, and other scholars of classical critical pedagogy. His version of *positive utopianism* transforms Richard Rorty's idea of the poetical hero into a model for life in cyberspace. It becomes a manifestation of "edifying philosophy", or "philosophy as a way of life".

> This hypertextual dissolution of centrality, which makes the medium such a potentially democratic one, also makes it a model of a society of conversation in which no one conversation, no one discipline or ideology, dominates or founds the others. It is thus the realization of what Richard Rorty terms "edifying philosophy", the point of which "is to keep the conversation going rather than to find objective truth. It is a form of philosophy... Hypertext, which has a built-in bias against "hypostatization" and probably against privileged descriptions as well, therefore embodies the approach to philosophy that Rorty urges. The basic experience of text, information, and control, which moves the boundary of power away from the author in the direction of the reader,

---

36   Peters and Lankshear, p. 65.
37   Knobel, "Critical literacy and new technologies", p. 6.
38   *Ibid.*, p. 9.
39   Ilan Gur-Ze'ev, "Walter Benjamin and Max Horkheimer: from utopia to redemption", *Journal of Jewish Philosophy and Thought* (1998) 8, pp. 119–155.
40   Herbert Marcuse, Die Zukunft der Kunst", *Neues Forum* (November-Dezember 1967), pp. 863–870.
41   Herbert Marcuse, "Liberation from the affluent society, in: David Cooper (ed.), *The Dialectics of Liberation*, London: Penguin, 1971, p.185.

models such a postmodern, antihierarchical medium of information, text, philosophy, and society.[42]

CRITICAL PEDAGOGY, CRITICAL LITERACY, AND CYBEROPTIMISM

Landow's enthusiasm for cyberspace is a manifestation of the relevance of postmodern thought to what I regard as a totalistic postmodern condition. This merger re-articulates the concept and the praxis of education. It is important, I think, to see the broader picture in historical, social, cultural, and conceptual terms. Historically, such a reconstruction should refer to the change in the stance of knowledge and to the general tendencies within modern culture and the postmodern conditions; in these, "hard" postmodern, "soft" postmodern, neo-Marxist critical theory and functionalist-oriented educational theorists articulate their cyberoptimism within feminist, post-colonialist, multiculturalist, and other discursive domains. Such a historical reconstruction is important for the analysis of the different kinds of optimism regarding cyberspace. Such a reconstruction will help us to contextualize the special kind of the cyberoptimism I see in the vision of non-critical concepts of education like that stated by US President Bill Clinton:

> Our effort to connect every classroom is just the beginning… But we cannot stop there. As the Internet becomes our new town square, a computer in every home—a teacher of all subjects, a connection to all cultures—this will no longer be a dream, but a necessity. And over the next decade, that must be our goal.[43]

This concept goes along with general right-wing concepts of capitalist globalization, free market, and new virtual prospects for a "Jeffersonian vision" of democracy in cyberspace. This will eliminate "the gap between the knowledge-rich and knowledge-poor", as evinced in the Magna Carta of the cyberoptimists.[44] As Langdon Winner Shows, the optimism of the Magna Carta writers about democracy in cyberspace and the new organization of society that will reflect the current technological and economical changes is deceptive as their claim that "Government does not own the cyberspace, the people do".[45]

---

42   Landow, *ibid.*
43   Bill Clinton, State of the Union Address, White House, http://www.whitehouse.gov.WH/SOU97/ (1997)
44   Esther Dyson, George Gilder, George Keyworth, and Alvin Toffler, "Cyberspace and the American Dream: A Magna Carta for the Knowledge Age", *Release* 1.2, Progress and Freedom Foundation, Washington, D.C., August 22, 1994, at
http://www.townhall.com/pff/position.html 2.8.1999
45   Langdon Winner, "Cyberlibertarian Myths and the Prospects for Community", http://www.rpi.edu/~winner/cyberlib2.html 8.17.1998

Ironically, this vision is not very different from the vision of critical educational thinkers like Mark Poster who reconstruct the history of Western democracy as leading from the Greek agora to the MOOs and the Internet as a genuine democracy. With some reservations, yet still in line with the current idea of other critical educational thinkers, Poster speaks very much like Clinton about cyberspace as a radical democracy based on the postmodern condition:

> Now, Internet news groups, MOOs, and other virtual communities are being promoted as nascent public spheres that will renew democracy in the 21st century.[46]

Poster concludes that the democratic vision of the critical theory of the Habermasian kind has become irrelevant today; there is no room for the public sphere where rational, autonomous citizens formulate and reformulate the common good. Not only must the question of democracy take into account new electronic modes of discourse; it has to reformulate the "subject".[47]

Techniques such as virtual reality and modes of communication and computer-mediated intersubjectivity such as the MUDs and MOOs allow and encourage functionalist-oriented and postmodernist-oriented cyberutopianism, which unites the optimism of Bill Clinton, Donna Haraway, and Douglas Kellner. I do not claim that the authors of the right-wing Magna Carta and Poster or Kellner share the same stance, yet their common cyberoptimism and the inability of the critical thinkers to mark a dividing line between them and the right-wing cyberoptimists is very important in our mind. It shows to what degree it is vital to understand the stance of technology per se, and especially current communication technologies,[48] the social changes and current cultural possibilities and limitations. It is not only a matter of theoretical possibilities: by the same token it is a matter of real urgency, action that should be taken, realizing our present responsibility and potential.

The issue of cyberspace and the problematic position of critical pedagogy, critical literacy, and critical educational thinkers in general enlighten the current demolition of traditional ideological divisions, philosophical and political traditions, and educational possibilities and limitations. They reflect the current degeneration of the concept.[49] In cyberspace the *concept is domesticated* by the realm of self-evidence and its practices and reintroduced as part of "reality" from which the critical eros is exiled. As a totalistic symbolic arena, cyberspace has a special role here and raises questions,

---

46   Mark Poster, The Net as a Public Sphere? http://www.wired.com/wired/3.11/departments/poster/if/html

47   Mark Poster, "CyberDemocracy: Internet and the Public Sphere", http://www.hnet.uci.edu/mposter/writings/democ.html p. 11 11.12.1998

48   Paul Standish, "Only Connect: computer literacy from Heidegger to cyberfeminism, *Conference Papers of the Philosophy of Education Society of Great Britain*, Oxford: GBPES, 1998, pp.100–116.

49   Adam Tenenbaum, "Prolegomena for a 'post-critical' education", in Gur-Ze'ev, I. (ed.), *Critical Theory and Education—Studies in Education* (1997), 2, 2, p. 93.

which should be addressed. These refer to the present and future of the concept and of the human subject, the will to meaning and the possibilities of challenging the self-evident while abandoning the call for **the totally-other**. Within this framework I should question the stance of knowledge and the possibilities still open for dialogical intersubjectivity within a system governed by the new technology, globalizing capitalism, and new social organization. It is wrong to separate critical pedagogy, critical literacy, or critical education and cyberspace from the issues of capitalist globalization. It is equally wrong, in our mind, to refrain from reformulating the questions of what is education today and what are the current possibilities for a critical philosophy of education within this context.

AN ALTERNATIVE VIEW OF CYBERSPACE AND CRITICAL EDUCATION

It is no wonder that critical thinkers such as Landow, who see their concept of hypertext and communication as a realization of the thinking of Roland Barthes, Michel Foucault, Jacques Derrida,[50] and other "hard" postmodernists, do not face their cyberoptimism with a critical reconstruction of globalizing capitalism, its technologies, and the culture industry, which reflects and enhances its further advancement. It is more difficult, however, to explain the optimism of "soft" postmodernists on this issue. "Soft" postmodern critical thinkers usually indicate the prospects for overcoming the marginalization of cultural, sexual, and ethnic groups and classes, empowering their potential self-positioning and "voice", opening new possibilities for dialogue among differences, cultural re-articulation, and radical democracy.

The difficulty I see in the position of the "soft" postmodernists who hail the new educational possibilities in cyberspace goes even further. It treats the issues of democracy and critical and emancipatory possibilities. It treats also the very possibilities of meaningful decisions and of responsibility in cyberspace. In these matters I should separate the stances of the "hard" and the "soft" postmodern cyberoptimists. Once we limit our elaboration to the "soft" postmodern cyberoptimists we can ask the question.

I claim that in various degrees and ways the influence of postmodernism and the suggestive power of the capitalist order has dissolved the revolutionary or the transcendental eros of these critical thinkers and domesticated the modes and the aims of their critical education. Within their cyberoptimism, dialectical thinking is overtaken by the faith in *paralogism* within the system. Here there is no room for the ideal of the subject or the transformative dialogue. In contrast with traditional critical pedagogy, the postmodern concept of paralogism and contingency cannot move beyond the possibility of change towards the Enlightenment's Utopia of emancipation. If I am right, then here these critical thinkers follow postmodernists such as Lyotard, who places his hopes in the *uncontrolled paralogism* of the capitalist system, and are on the verge of departing from the central aim of critical pedagogy. According to Lyotard,

---

50   Landow, *ibid.*, pp. 3, 25.

The computerization of society... could become the "dream" instrument for controlling and regulating the market system, expanded to include knowledge itself and governed exclusively by the performativity principle... But it could also aid groups discussing metaprescriptives by supplying them with the information they usually lack for making knowledgeable decisions.[51]

I think that the adoption of postmodern paralogism and language games[52] cannot be included within the critical project of critical theory and critical pedagogy without serious philosophical work. This work has yet to be undertaken by critical thinkers who have adopted postmodern attitudes to their critical pedagogy. Even if they took up this issue, the question might arise of in what sense it was still to be considered critical pedagogy or even critical education at all.

The historical explanation is to be actualized within a reconstruction which shows the shift from emphasizing and developing the educational implications of late Adorno's and Horkheimer's critical theory to the Freirean kind of critical pedagogy, and hence to Giroux's Postmodern critical pedagogy on the one hand, and McLaren's Contraband critical pedagogy on the other. Against the background of this development it is important to mention post-critical pedagogy thinkers, or non-critical pedagogy critical thinkers, such as Burbules and Ellsworth on the one hand, and Masschelein and Biesta on the other, each representing an original critical educational path. The formers address the possibilities of critique as central to current emancipatory education via "soft" postmodern, feminist and pragmatist discourses, while the later addresses this issue via revisiting continental philosophy even when relating to the postmodern discourses, where it is more at home with the problematic posed by "hard" postmodernism. Against this background I introduce counter-education, which I will elaborate here regarding its implications for the positive utopianism of the critical adorers of electropolis.

Peter McLaren occupies a special position in the sense that he has not abandoned the claim of the critical tradition for revolution, while he acknowledges the realities of postmodern society and the capitalistic globalization. On the grounds of Bloch's hope principle, he reintroduces "Che" as a model example for the critical ethical educator.[53] McLaren's optimism is unquestioned even by his own conclusions concerning the advancement of global capitalism:

> as symbolic economies continue to proliferate outside of a monolithic casual relationship with capital, creating a greater variety of subject-

---

51   Jean F. Lyotard, *The Postmodern Condition: A Report on Knowledge*, translated by G. Bennington and
      B. Massumi, Manchester: Manchester University Press, 1991, p. 67.
52   Landow, *ibid.*, p. 66.
53   Peter McLaren, Critical Pedagogy and Predatory Culture, London: Routledge, 1995, P. 226.

positions to assume, the possibilities have also increased for…global forms of cultural cross-dressing".[54]

Building on Frederick Jameson's reconstruction of the "global decentralization and small group institution",[55] like so many other critical educational thinkers, McLaren too has difficulty justifying optimism about the Internet. He has trouble safely grounding his hope for a new future international proletariat and revolution in a post-modern reality.

We have been exiled into a post-human hyperreality—into a condition the dimensions of which we fail to recognize and are too fearful to fully understand…To my mind, the post-modern era is an era where democracy becomes historically subverted by capitalism to a greater extent than ever before, where values become a trick of fiction and radically incommensurable. [56]

While he reconstructs the way global capitalism is conquering the local culture, he considers the otherness of other cultures within this globalization process an "authentic" part of cyberspace.

I really do believe that we live in a society now that is based on the management and articulation of moods. But we need to remember that our affective investment in material objects or consumer fetishes is related to relations of production and a politics of consumption that must be geo-politically and contextually specific. We no longer live in a society of goals, one that is goal-oriented. I think that was a society that was predominantly a print-oriented society linked to industrial capitalism in specific ways.[57]

Yet, McLaren does not abandon the emancipatory project of critical pedagogy, without the rearticulation that Lankshear, Peters and Knobel insist on.[58] Critical pedagogy, in his mind, can after all be implemented in the cyberspace and challenge the existing order.[59] But within his own reconstruction I see no contextual justification for it. I can understand his optimism only as a manifestation of the **principle of hope**, which he explicitly takes from Ernst Bloch's theological utopianism.[60] This kind of hope is transcendental, modernist, and religious. It is conceived as "metaphysical" and irrelevant by the postmodern writers he likes to read, it is abandoned by most critical cyberoptimists and it posits a tension between his project and that of Henry Giroux that to often is received as one and the same project.

---

54   *Ibid.*, 179.
55   *Ibid.*
56   Peter McLaren, *Revolutionary Multiculturalism*, Boulder, Colorado: Westview Press, 1997, p. 231.
57   *Ibid.*, p. 230.
58   Peter McLaren, "Che—the pedagogy of Che Guevara: critical pedagogy and globalization thirty years after Che", *Cultural Circles*, (Summer 1998), 3, p. 80.
59   Peter McLaren, (in press) "Traumatizing capital: oppositional pedagogies in the age of consent", in: Manuuel Castells, Ramin Flecha,, Paulo Freire, Henry Giroux, Donaldo Machedo., Paul Willis, *Critical Education in the New Information Age*, London: Roman & Litterfield, p. 30.
60   Peter McLaren, *Critical Pedagogy and Predatory Culture*, p. 52.

If cyberspace is fundamentally a mere part of the postmodern system which contains *no transcendence*, and as a manifestation of fast capitalism incubates no revolution or essential change of the system, how then, I may ask, should I understand the critical cyberoptimists and the affinity of their hope for freedom, equality, and democracy with the hope of the right-wing cyberoptimists?

Central to global capitalism are its flexibility in contrast to "Fordism"[61] and the disappearance of the physical market, facing the furthering of the identification of the commodity with its representation, of economics with culture. As Frederick Jameson shows us, it is a process within which the reception of the process of consumption is vital to *the Hollywoodization of reality*, which manifests the cultural logic of current capitalism.[62] This post-Fordist flexibility is required at all levels and arenas of life—from the global flow of finances to the production and consumption of commodities, identities, and knowledge (which is transformed into information) even at schools.[63] Electronic information technologies are vital in this process in terms not only of speed but also of diversity and flexibility of the kind in which everyone can take part, regardless of class, sex, ethnicity, race, disability, and age—as an effective consumer-producer in the capitalist market: only as such, and certainly not as a subject realizing her potential autonomy or her otherness. The special kind of diversity (of commodities and reified knowledge, identities, and passions) which is vital for global capitalism is not negated but is fertilized by the one-dimensionality represented by the logic of the current technology. This is a phenomenon that makes both distance and surface irrelevant, in favor of the time-span. And on the other hand we have global time, belonging to the multimedia, to cyberspace, increasingly dominating the local timeframe of our cities and our neighborhoods. One can speak with Paul Virilio of the "glocal" as part of a process in which "the local has by definition became global and the global, local".[64] Instrumental rationality faces no challenge here from the tradition of objective reason, as historically it faced the challenge in the history of western culture.[65] The triumph of instrumental rationality brings about the Commodification of knowledge, discourses, and human relations within a global culture industry which encourages "diversity", folklore (at the expense of traditional cultures, which are dissolved by it), locality, and popular culture. It does so through a "democratic" leveling process, which grinds everything into particles of sameness. This process covers the creation, storage, sorting, distribution, and consumption of information, passions, and reactions, acknowledging no national border, collective

61 Dona Harvey, The Condition of Postmodernity 1990, p. 47 (cited in Norman Fairclough, Global Capitalism and Critical Awareness of Language, http://www.schools.ash.org.au/litweb/norman1. html p. 2. 24.6.1999

62 Frederick Jameson, *Postmodernism, or the Cultural Logic of Late Capitalism*, Durham: Duke University Press, 1991.

63 Arnold, M. "The high-tech, post-Fordist school", *Interchange*, (1996) 27, 3–4, p. 229.

64 Paulo Virilio, Speed and Information: Cyberspace Alarm, *Le Monde Diplomatique*, translated by P. Riemens, (August 1995) in http://www.ctheory.com/a30–cyberspace_alarm.html p. 2. 8.17.1998

65 Theodor Adorno, und Max Horkheimer, *Dialektik der Aufklaerung*, Frankfurt a. Main: Suhrkamp 1988, pp. 1–2.

interests, censorship, transcendence, or privilege, which are problematic for economic or mathematical formalization[66] or digitalization and which resist entering cyberspace under its own conditions.

It is wrong, I think, to detach the "democratic" tendencies of "voice" and de-centralized symbols and passions floating in cyberspace from current development in global capitalism and the kind of "radical democracy" that Mark Poster and Kellner envision in the cyberspace. I think that *cyberspace and the globalization process of capitalism are inseparable*. Not only as an economic trend but also as a logic, as a world of passions, hopes, and human narcissistic coexistence where there is nowhere for the "totally other" than the present order,[67] and surely not for the otherness of the Other.[68] At the same time, and as part of the current culture industry, there is more need for hailing "free will", subjectivity, relativism, diversity, democracy, fluidity, pleasure, and critical thinking—as long as they are part and parcel of the same de-humanizing order. This attitude is supported by Gilles Deleuze and Felix Guattari, among the most influential postmodern thinkers who have made their mark on the work of today's critical educational thinkers. Following these thinkers, even from a postmodern point of view, there is no room for today's kind of optimism that most (postmodern) critical thinkers have regarding the Internet. Deleuze and Guattari argue that in the postmodern age philosophy as conceptual critical thinking is in its most problematic position in the history of Western culture:

> Finally, the most shameful moment came when computer science, marketing, design, and advertising, all the disciplines of communication, seized hold of the word *concept* itself and said: "This is our concern, we are the creative ones, we are the *ideas men!* We are friends of the concept, we put it in our computers". Information and creativity, concept and enterprise: there is already an abundant bibliography. Marketing has preserved the idea of a certain relationship between the concept and the event. But here the concept has become the set of product displays…and the event has become the exhibition that sets up various displays and the "exchange of ideas" it is supposed to promote. The only events are exhibitions, and the only concepts are products that can be sold.[69]

Globalizing capitalism is possible only in a postmodern world, yet the condition for the reproduction of postmodern conditions and their culture industry involves the reproduction of modern and pre-modern conditions in its margins: more efficient

---

66   Juergen Habermas, *Der Politische Diskurs der Moderne*, Frankfurt a. Main: Suhrkamp 1989, p. 136.
67   Max Horkheimer, "Die Sehnsucht nach dem ganz Anderen", *Gesammelte Schriften*, VII., Frankfurt a. Main: Fischer, pp. 385–404.
68   Emmanuel Levinas, "From existence to ethics", *The Levinas Reader*, Oxford: Blackwell, 1989, p. 47.
69   Gilles Deleuze and Felix Guattari, *What is Philosophy?* translated by H. Tamlinson, G. Burchell, New York: Columbia University Press, 1994, p. 10.

production of software cannot prevent the modernist and pre-modernist modes of production for those who have been pushed to the margins. All take part in global capitalism, but surely not all take part in a postmodern mode of production and distribution. The differentiation in modes of production parallels and re-creates different production relations and oppressive social organization on a global scale. It is not that class becomes an outdated category, or alienation irrelevant. They become more sophisticated, internalized, and veiled at the center of capitalist affluence or sharper at its margins in the west or in the third world. Concurrently they enhance the logic of oppression and consumption, and distribute it through its myths, drives, technologies, and commodities as a global process not only at the conscious level but also at the emotional level of its victims/agents.

In our view, cyberspace cannot but reproduce the logic of the one-dimensional system that has become totally rational, where all dialectics, alienation, and dissent are overtaken, digested, or destroyed. At its center, power-relations become disguised, as everything becomes visible, externalized, open, and "free" to all competent partners. The signifiers become identical with themselves and it becomes impossible to negate them in a totally rational arena, with no history, no eros, no traces of the otherness that is absent, no mystery and no transcendence—and therefore no meaning. According to Paul Virilio,

> what lies ahead is a disturbance in the perception of what reality is: it is a shock, a mental concussion… never has any progress in a technique been achieved without addressing its specific negative aspects. The specific negative aspect of these information superhighways is precisely this loss of orientation regarding alterity (the other), this disturbance in the relationship with the other and with the world. It is obvious that this loss of orientation, this non-situation, is going to usher a deep crisis which will affect society and hence, democracy.[70]

Within cyberspace, with technologies as virtual reality, the Internet, the MOOs, and the like reproduce a certain kind of representation, where there is room only for a "horizontal" diversity, contingency, temporality, fluidity, hybridity, and spectacle, which prospers as long as it efficiently supports the further productivization of the system. As such, cyberspace contends successfully with all traditional attempts to eternalize, mystify, and de-mystify reality, and allows a new kind of normalizing education. To our mind, it is the most advanced nihilistic normalizing education ever to challenge humanity.

Within cyberspace the production of myths and the control of information, identity, and consciousness are being shifted from the hegemony of ideological institutions, the state, a party, and so on, to other, more sophisticated powers, which are less visible, less open to criticism and resistance.[71] The logic of control, efficiency,

---

70 Paulo Virilio, *ibid.*
71 Zygmunt Bauman, "Is there a postmodern sociology?", *Culture and Society*, 5, 2–3, p. 222.

and productivity is present in cyberspace even when it distances itself explicitly from the discursive, linear, authoritative text and favors a metaphoric, "pre-textual" digital arena of free play of icons, intuitions, rhetoric links and spectacle.[72] Normalizing education does not disappear; it only becomes more sophisticated, productive, and effective, and less transparent as the need grows for the international system's ever greater sophistication, for ever more controlled and advanced reflectivity and flexibility, functional for capitalist reproduction and technological advance. Oppression, here, does not need the oppressor. It is internalized and enacted by its victims as the most enthusiastic agents of the system. High modernism needed a culture industry where passive consumers were effectively manipulated. The postmodern condition needs the initiative, creativity, flexibility, and critical potential of the consumers, who become efficient and creative producers within the system.

Critical educational thinkers who are aware of "the dangers" within cyberspace and call for education for critical thinking, critical literacy, and the like, should, in our opinion, contextualize these *hopes* in the present culture industry, and in its normalizing education apparatuses. But at the same time they should also ask the basic questions: what is the stance of the human subject? What are the present conditions for her struggle to realize her dialogical potential or her potential autonomy or self-creation—or the foundation for the meaninglessness of the concept of human potential autonomy? What is the stance of knowledge under these conditions, and is there today any room for the quest for dialogue? Under these conditions, is it possible that the subject will enter a dialogue and actualize reflection? Are there moments of negativity, which will decipher ontological signs and challenge the governing sameness? Is there room for transcendence in cyberspace and for an effort by the subject to be more than a mere object or de-humanized "subject"? And if the answer to some of these questions or all of them is negative, what does this imply for us as human beings?

NORMALIZING EDUCATION, THE SUBJECT, AND CYBERSPACE

I claim that the aim of education is the normalization of human beings and the leveling of all into mere *things*. It is a violent process, by which the otherness of the subject is banished, allowing her to function as an agent of the system, as some thing and not as some one. As such, the subject is supposed to be productive in reproducing the current order of things and the hegemonic realm of self-evidence. The more efficient hegemonic normalizing education is, the more passionately do people cling to the chains that prevent them from being what they could have become, and the more effective is the veiling of the apparatuses which constitute what they have become as agents of the system.[73] The aim of normalizing education is to make the subject forget **the totally other** than the present order and their unfulfilled human potential.

---

72   Richard Lanham, *The Electronic World: Democracy, Technology, and the Arts*, Chicago and London: University of Chicago Press, 1993, pp. 34–37.

73   Ilan Gur-Ze'ev, "The Exile of Spirit and Counter-Education, in Philosophy", *Politics, and Education in Israel, Haifa*: Haifa University Press 1999.

The target is not the people themselves as "others", but the "other" system, whose agents, servants, and worshipers they are. Traditionally, normalizing education was committed to "internal" and "external" colonization, so that the Other was of vital importance for it: the "subject" is used by the system within ethnocentrist frameworks for struggles against other "subjects" and systems and against the otherness of the "subject". The knowledge, identity, passions, social function, and productivity of the subject have to guarantee the successful reproduction of the system and its victories over internal and external oppositions. However, it also has to guarantee rivals who are equipped with their own normalizing agenda for the sake of efficient "education", "salvation", or "destruction" of their Others. *The symbolic violence* conquers or creates the centers of power-relations and dynamics and allows direct violence in its ecological, economic, military, and other forms. When victory is secured it allows the orchestration of the emotional structure, passions, conceptual apparatus, consciousness, and social functioning of the normalized subject who as such is never some one.[74] Moral knowledge and its relation to concepts of knowledge are a vital element within this kind of violence, which is the essence of education[75] as *subjectification*. Normalized human beings actually realize the death of the subject, in the sense that deprived of their otherness they are always replaceable.

These brief remarks about the essence of normalizing education are articulated from a perspective of counter-education, which suggests a philosophical, existential, and political negation of normalizing education. Counter-education, contrary to critical pedagogy and other versions of critical education, has no positive Utopia.[76] It insists, however, on the possibility of a struggle for dialogical self-constitution and moral responsibility to the otherness of the Other and of the subject's struggle to overcome herself as constituted by normalizing education.[77]

In our view, cyberspace is a prima facie postmodern environment. This determines the subject's possibilities and limitations, even if at the same time she can be involved in modern contexts, and even in pre-modern contexts crisscrossing cyberspace. It is typical to the critical cyberoptimists that Landow introduces a lengthy citation from Foucault at the beginning of his book and Lankshear, Peters, and Knobel begin their article by quoting Haraway saying that "we are living through a movement from an organic, industrial to a polymorphous, information system—from all work to all play, a deadly game".[78]

Haraway, a representative of critical thinkers who were overwhelmed by the "hard" postmodern discourse, is very clear on the issue of the postmodern subject, the cyborg:

74   Jan Masschelein, "Wandel der Oeffentlichkeit und das Problem der Indentitaet", *Zeitschrift fuer Paedagogik* (1992), 28, p. 62.

75   Ilan Gur-Ze'ev, "The morality of acknowledging/not-acknowledging the Other's Holocaust/Genocide", *Journal of Moral Education* (1998), 27, 2, p. 161.

76   Ilan Gur-Ze'ev, "Toward a nonrepressive critical pedagogy, *Educational Theory* (1998), 48, 4, p. 463.

77   Ilan Gur-Ze'ev, "Modernity, postmodernity and education (Introduction)", in Ilan Gur-Ze'ev (ed.), *Modernity, Postmodernity and Education*, Tel-Aviv: Ramot, 1999, p. 9.

78   Peters, and Knobel, *ibid.*, p. 149.

"a cyborg is a cybernetic organism, a hybrid of machine and organism, a creature of social reality as well as a creature of fiction".[79] The anti-metaphysics, anti-foundationalism, essentialism, universalism, and transcendentalism of "hard postmodernism" of this kind is manifested also in the thought of critical thinkers who still see themselves as part of critical pedagogy. They try to impart it to cyberspace as the arena for the emancipation that the critical theory of the Frankfurt School and critical pedagogy of Freire sought in vain in the modern social-cultural-economic -technological arena. According to Lankshear, Peters, and Knobel, "cyberspace calls into question the stability and coherence of the book and the forms of narration enacted upon it. Equally, it calls precisely these same features into question in relation to the subject".[80] With Haraway, Saarinen, and others,[81] they celebrate the postmodern "bottomlessness"[82] which makes possible the convergence of the machine and the subject into "shifting subjects", and the "fluidity of identity in the cyberspace"[83] that along with the other conditions of cyberspace will eventually allow the successful realization of the emancipatory project of critical pedagogy.

"Soft" postmodern influences such as those articulated in the critical thinking of Burbules and Rice (and certainly of Kellner, who still works within a modernist theoretical framework) reject the totality of mere contingency, hybridity, and fluidity of information, passions, identities, and relations, and indicate its threat to critical education.[84] At the same time, Burbules identifies room for great possibilities for the flourishing of the critical subject within cyberspace.[85] I think that on the issue of the subject, the reconstruction of the "hard" postmodernists among the critical educational thinkers describes the situation of the subject much better than that offered by "soft" postmodernists like Burbules and Rice. I cannot, however, share their celebration.

The normalization within cyberspace, I claim, is different from the reproduction of the traditional Western metaphysics and its grand narratives by great men of letters. The postmodern realm of self-evidence does not need legitimate writers and interpreters of the textual truth. Traditionally they prospered in religion, philosophy, art, science, and technology at the family, church, school, army, jail, and other disciplining

---

79   Dona Haraway, *Simians, Cyborgs and Women: The Reinvention of Nature*, New York: Routledge, 1991, p. 149.

80   Lankshear, Peters and Knobel, *ibid.*, p. 161.

81   Sherry Turkle, *The Second Self: Computers and the Human Spirit*, New York: Simon and Schuster, 1985, p. 276.

82   Jim Garrison, "Foucault, Dewey, and self-creation", *Educational Philosophy and Theory* (1998) 30, 2, p. 111.

83   Lankshear, Peters and Knobel, *ibid.*

84   Suzanne Rice and Nicholas Burbules, "Communicative virtues and educational relations", http:// www.ed.uiuc.edu/pes92_docs/rice_burbules.HTM 1.120.1999; Nicholas Burbules and Suzanne Rice, "Dialogue Across Differences: Continuing the Conversation", *Harvard Educational Review* (1991), 61, 4, p. 394.

85   Nicholas Burbules, "Rhetorics of the Web: Hyperreading and Critical Literacy", http://www.ed.uiuc. edu/facstaff/burbules/ncb/papers/rhetorics.html, p. 2. 8. 11.1998

and normalizing sites where "the truth" or the right values or yardsticks were revealed, transferred, and internalized.

The Enlightenment's universal conception of Reason and the human potential for autonomy, dialogue, and emancipation made possible the commitment to equality and dignity among differences.[86] Within this framework, where *Spirit* and the tradition of objective reason were the dominant factor along with instrumental rationality, there was room not only for modern, efficient, educational violence as the realization of the arrogance of truth, justice, beauty, and happiness. By the same token there was also a potential for counter-education, as a critical practice of *the ethical I* who, in the face of the unanswerable, confronted by openness, meaninglessness, and infinity, strives for dialogue, reflection, and transcendence. There was also room for the existentialist-oriented alternative and even for nihilism and pessimism as serious philosophical positions which realized the responsibility of the human subject and activated her potential for meaningful decisions and for self-creation even when this meant suicide as the greatest manifestation of sovereignty.[87] Here *the ethical I* has a responsibility to the otherness of the Other, and being human is actualized as other than being. Only as such, says Levinas, is the "I" irreplaceable.[88]

In postmodernity, where instrumental rationality has the upper hand, the possibility of struggling for autonomy, self-creation, and dialogue, and even for making a genuine choice among differences, becomes most problematic. In *The Ethics of Authenticity* Taylor asks, "Can a mode of life that is centered on the self, in the sense that involves treating our associates as merely instrumental, be justified in light of the ideal of authenticity?" He replies that on the social level—to which I will posit that cyberspace belongs in the postmodern condition—"the answer is a clear yes".[89] But can we see human relations as instrumental to our fulfillment, and thus as fundamentally tentative? "Here the answer is easier. Surely not, if they are also going to form our identity", says Taylor.[90] As long as the subject is deprived of her otherness and abandons erotic overcoming of the given diversity of sameness, the "subject" is a carrier of fluid identities and is replaceable by some of the other "subjects". As such she has no option of a judgment or a decision that will be more than a "creative" caprice or a reflection of efficient suggestive power of the system; she cannot be responsible even for the realization of her neglected humanity.

86 Charles Taylor, *Multiculturalism and "the Politics of Recognition"*, Princeton: Princeton University Press, 1992, p. 41.

87 Ilan Gur-Ze'ev, *The Frankfurt School and the History of Pessimism*, Jerusalem: Magnes Press, 1996, p. 21.

88 Emmanuel Levinas, *Ethics and the Infinite; Conversations with Philippe Nemo*, translated by Meir, E. Jerusalem: Magnes Press, 1982, p. 76 (in Hebrew).

89 Charles Taylor, *The Ethics of Authenticity*, Cambridge, Mass.: Harvard University Press 1991 pp. 50–51.

90 *Ibid.*, 52.

From this point of view the possibilities of the postmodern "subject" in cyberspace for creating uncensored, centerless, virtual communities and dialogues with others,[91] and for freely choosing information, critical and innovative strategies, aims, and identities, look very dubious. This is because both "hard" and "soft" postmodernism hold that in cyberspace "subjects" are *constituted* within an arena that is purged of modern and pre-modern remedies such as mystery, eros, meaning, responsibility, and aim. Non-instrumental, pragmatic, or "aesthetic" play is not to be disconnected from the metaphysical self-evidence, the hierarchy of values, narratives, and knowledge that have been demolished in the postmodern condition. Metaphysics as violence is a must in order to destroy/replace (visible) violence and normalizing education. It is a constitutive element in alienation that is challenged by *the ethical I* or by the Utopian quest which transcends sameness and the self-evident. As we have seen, even for the postmodern critical thinkers the celebration is about an alleged emancipation from the tyranny of the metaphysical pretensions about "human essence", "authenticity", "worthy aims", "moral commitments", and "human needs". Only thus, jailed within "their" narrative, are these critical thinkers "free to choose of everything that suits them" in cyberspace—as long as they abandon the metaphysic of the presence. By the same token they are required to abandon their otherness and their responsibility to the Other and the not-yet, and to forget the openness of being.

This kind of emancipation from metaphysics promises their being pleasurably drawn into a quantitative, deceiving openness and a false, meaningless, infinity. As part of productive, endless, sameness the subject becomes totally identified with the signifiers of an anti-essentialist system; not a creator of concepts, signifiers, and signified but a mere agent and a shadow of the movement of signifiers in an infinite simulacrum, one of endless manifestations of nothingness. She becomes an element in the sameness to which Socrates, Kierkegaard, Nietzsche, and Levinas offered admirable resistance.

I think that under such conditions a "free decision" to purchase a certain identity, a certain way of life, or knowledge manifests the success of the subject's de-humanization. Within such a dynamic the "subject" cannot struggle to realize her potentials of autonomy. There is not even room for such a concept as a regulative idea. Actually, there is no room for struggling for human life as more than mere power regulating itself.

In other words, in such an arena the subject cannot be other than she is constructed to be, even as an undefined, unstable, fluid "subject". She cannot relate to **the totally other** in herself and in the Other, and she cannot struggle to overcome her self, transcend the self-evidence, and change the present order of things. Within cyberspace, abandoning the negation of the current facts and the quest for realization of the not-yet or the Utopian axis are an imperative of the inner logic of the system. The post-metaphysical world does not give up the concept: it reintroduces it as passions, as drives. As part and parcel of the postmodern system these are anti-erotic: they demand the abandonment of the critical Spirit and of dialogue as a way of life. They

---

91   Sherry Turkle, *Life on the Screen: Identity in the Age of the Internet*, New York, London, and Toronto: Simon and Schuster, 1995, p. 20.

ensure the irrelevancy of dialogue as a struggle over the human subject as some one, as an *ethical I* who relates to eternity by her total responsibility for the otherness[92] than the given order of things.

Burbules tries to show that even on the Internet there is room for critical literacy in the sense that the subject is faced with a text and pre-constructed links whose hidden ideology, commercial manipulations, and so forth, she can critically try to reconstruct. While acknowledging the problems and the dangers of the Internet, we can, he argues, pragmatically educate for critical sensitivities and communicative virtues, not only critical skills, for critical literacy on the Internet.[93] But even this most reflective version of cyberoptimism does not question the very existence of a subject in cyberspace. Nor does it justify the possibility of non-manipulative or non-capricious yardsticks, ideas, or passions, which will regulate or make possible this critical evaluation or this process of critique of ideology.

In the absence of a perspective or *critical distance*, even as an ideal, what, we may ask, can allow one to hope within this framework that the critical praxis will not be a mere reflection of the suggestive power or inner logic of the system which is supposed to be criticized? From a counter-educational point of view, as long as there is no room for *transcendence*, reflection is impossible and therefore the subject becomes a "subject". For the *ethical I*, reflection is a life-and-death struggle for the humanist dimension that allows both negative and positive elements in the dialogical struggle, yes, struggle, of her subjectivity. The critical cyberoptimists represent the general characteristics of education as normalization and do not open the door for counter-education and for reflection in cyberspace.

For her as a normalized participant within cyberspace, the inescapability of normalization in the Internet ensures that dialogical relations within it will be impossible. The absence of the otherness of the Other secures the futility of the effort to empower marginalized groups and to give them a space to raise their silenced "voice". When it is heard it will be on a level with capitalistic one-dimensionality and under the logic of the system which will eliminate or at least jeopardize its uniqueness.

Dialogue, I argue, is impossible without a Utopian axis, without a common ethical and political effort to transcend the given reality. The dialogue is a special kind of human relations where the otherness of the Other is acknowledged by the *ethical I* not only as relevant and legitimate but rather as a condition for the struggle for self-positioning. Cyberspace as an anti-transcendental and as a contingent, anti-essentialist space makes impossible the will for the good and the negation of the production of the self-evident or the unveiling of the untruth as a moral commitment. In virtual reality, Internet, or the MOOs, hegemonic or self-understood apparatuses and its hidden logic create "truth", or the contingent "relevant information" and the governing passions which are unchallenged since there is no transcendental, uncontingent, or meaningful "position" or ideal to question them or their inner logic. To make efforts

---

92   Emmanuel Levinas, "God and Philosophy", *Collected Philosophical Papers*, Dordrecht: M. Nijhoff 1987, p. 166.

93   Rice and Burbules, "Communicative virtues and educational relations", pp. 4–6.

at de-mystification of the world and to resist the de-dehumanization of individuals and virtual communities become impossible. Even the negation of the false claims to relevancy, validity, or normality is impossible where there is mere contingent, fluid, information, identities, and relations as a "free game" that serves the "free market" and the aimless technological advance.

The constitutive element in cyberspace is sameness, which is camouflaged as infinite diversity, "difference", and contingency. There is no room for dialogue where the system pretends to manifest total openness, hence the end of alienation and oppression; from this perspective the struggle against oppression or the quest for transcendence, **the totally other**, or for the "not-yet", seems naive, obsolete, or even oppressive. However, the "openness" and the "free choice" or self-constitution, which cyberspace pretends to realize, actualizes an infinity that is totally different from the one which Kierkegaard, Rosenzweig, Adorno, or Levinas referred to: it is an openness which contains a quantitative infinity, not a qualitative infinity. In it, sameness is clothed as openness to "difference"—only as long as it is part and parcel of the system and its inner logic. Antagonistic logics cannot enter the system unless they are interpreted and transformed according to the requirements and roles of this totalistic system. There is no room for the otherness of the Other and for the infinity affluent from this otherness that Levinas reveals in the "face" of the Other.[94] Cyberspace as a pleasure machine is quite successful in digesting into its sameness the otherness, the transcendent, the alienation, the unanswered question, and Utopia. The success of this pleasure machine guarantees the impossibility of the erotic quest for dialogue, since Utopia was already achieved and realized. Now we are invited only to consume its pleasures and advance its realization into the infinite borders of its sameness.

Dialogue is the space where the struggle over reflection as an open possibility can take place. Within it, the otherness of the "external" and "internal" Other as a reflection of the infinity and the openness of being allows the realization of transcendence in the immediate moment. Negative Utopia as a positive quest is struggled for in concrete circumstances, and opens the possibility of a special moment of non-violent intersubjectivity. This non-violent intersubjectivity involves acknowledging difference, total difference, and therefore it is a *struggle*, not a celebration of white, rational, upper-class males, as usually conceived in the tradition of the Enlightenment. This is why counter-education can be struggled for only within the horizons of a dialogue.

One of the central manifestations of counter-education is reflection. Reflection is a special characteristic of *the ethical I* in her relation to another subject as some one, not as an object of manipulation, not as one whose otherness has to be destroyed. Within the dialogue moral commitments of the subject priors reason and her cognitive potentials. She struggles to re-articulate herself as part of the elevation of the Other as the manifestation of **the totally other**. In so doing the partner in the dialogue contributes to the effort to change the context of the dialogue in a way that will elevate the potentials of the dialogue which we are.

---

94   Levinas, "Philosophy and the idea of infinity", in: *Collected Philosophical Papers*, p. 55.

As part of human intersubjectivity and as a social process, reflection has not only a role but also a place. Language is the home of reflection yet it cannot offer transparency, "truth", "facts", or "authenticity"—nor a pleasurable "emancipation" for their arrogance. In a dialogue meanings are never "givens"[95] or bits of affects as in the symbolic space or at the symbolic speed which is the cyberspace communication.

The move from modern normalizing education to the postmodern normalizing education within cyberspace has not brought an end to normalizing education or to the relevance of oppression and emancipation, as the "hard" postmodernists claim. Neither has it opened new possibilities to negotiate or overcome class, race, gender, ethnicity, and other manifestations of oppression, mystification, and de-humanization of the Other and of the self, as claimed by "soft" postmodernists. As I have shown, it has made the struggle against normalizing education and the current order of things more problematic than ever.

COUNTER-EDUCATION AND CYBERSPACE AS A PLEASURE MACHINE

At its best, I claimed, cyberspace is a giant pleasure machine. Here, I asserted, the subject is dissolved of her otherness and there is no room for dialogue and transcendence from the given. How, then, I should ask, is it possible to challenge this pleasure machine, if at all? Is it possible to challenge the self-evidence or the given self within a pleasure machine which offers total pleasure and which contains advancement into new experiences and new pleasures initiated by the subject? One possible answer is no; it is impossible for the subject herself to plug out from the ultimate pleasure machine since where there is total, one-dimensional pleasure or quest for pleasure there is no autonomy whence responsibility to *the not-yet* or the evil is struggled for. Here, where otherness is abandoned, where the subject is abstracted from her possible autonomy and responsibility, there is no room for dialogue with the otherness of the Other. Counter-education, it seems, is impossible here since there is no room for eros and for the special kind of transcendence as an ethical act of negation of the sameness and the given.

I think, however, that even within cyberspace as a pleasure machine the subject becomes only a "subject", not a mere object—no matter how devoted she is to nothingness as her long-sought home. Even as a devoted citizen of cyberspace who becomes a mere "subject" she is exposed every moment to the openness of being: the "totally other" can burst in from "outside" the system and "plug her out". The unpredictable and uncontrollable which are incubated in being as infinite openness might reformulate the world, and resurrect that which is forgotten or be deconstructed in the Net: eros, reflection, transcendence, and *the ethical I* and her unsolved tiger jump into a historically situated dialogue.

This very possibility can force the agent of the pleasure machine to stand face to face with her (absent) humanity and the meaninglessness of life not only in cyberspace but

---

95   Ilan Gur-Ze'ev, Jan Masschelein, Nigel Blake, *Reflection, Conference Papers of the Philosophy of Education Society of Great Britain*, Oxford: GBPES, 1988, p. 224.

also in the Utopia of the dialogue. Negative Utopia might introduce it as an impetus for struggling from positive naive Utopia into human maturity and self-constitution without the naive essentialist predications and without the promised escapism of the postmodern pleasure machine. *The unpredictability of being* might open the possibility of facing the fundamental challenges of humanity. In one instant she might become a subject, and counter-education might be revealed as a concrete (negative) Utopia worth struggling for. This possibility is enough for maintaining counter-education as relevant even within cyberspace.

Another source of relevance is the social and cultural construction on which cyberspace is made possible. Citizenship in cyberspace as a pleasure machine is conditioned by global capitalism, which reproduces social inequalities between those that have cultural capital and dwell in the pleasure machine and those who are determined by the system to be left out. This inequality, this alienation and injustice, this refusal of dialogue, makes counter-education relevant not only for those who are left outside the pleasure machine, and knock on its doors to enter and "plug in". It makes it relevant also for those who are already within the new home that the postmodern condition has constructed. But the price is the oppressed striving to become part of the sameness and join their oppressors' meaninglessness, which is challenged only by their sufferings—not by their passions, hopes, and language. Counter-education, however, can only negate, overcome, and struggle for reflection and transcendence where the sameness is not complete, where there is still alienation and (potential) otherness which will allow the realization of *the ethical I* and the struggle for establishing a dialogue.

The realization of counter-education is conditioned by many components that the success of the postmodern condition has made impotent. When critical thinkers speak about overcoming the "dangers" and the constrains in-built in cyberspace they take for granted the humanistic subjectivity of the subject who can choose among different options, emancipate herself and others, and realize in the new arena the critical Spirit. In our view, critique in itself, as well as "choice" among "differences", can hide the sameness imposed by the system as part of its reproduction. In our view, the realization of the critical Spirit is not guaranteed, and certainly not self-understood. *The exile of Spirit* and the subjectification which produces the "subject" makes counter-education a Utopia, since the subject as well as the dialogue are today no more than a Utopia. This is exactly why counter-education is relevant, in face of the claim for the realization of Utopia in the pleasure machine and in face of the misery, pain, and unfulfilled passions which make possible the productivity of the capitalist system with cyberspace as its crown.

CHAPTER 7

MARTIN HEIDEGGER, TRANSCENDENCE, AND THE POSSIBILITY OF COUNTER-EDUCATION

Normalizing education has many faces. At its best it is power realizing its responsibility for the efficient subjectification of the subject and its pleasures. Within the process of *subjectification* it produces the "I". In the course of its production the "I" is constituted as a focus of selfhood in a manner that ensures the identification of the subject with the present order of things, reinforces its justifications, and makes possible the invisibility of the violence which constructs and represents it as "reality". *Normalizing education* guarantees efficient orientation in the given order of things, perfects competence in its classification and representation, and allows communication and functional behavior, success, security, pleasure, and social progress.[1] It distributes these competences, knowledge, and powers in a socially uneven manner, creating or reproducing social and cultural asymmetries and violences within the system. It not only permits human social life and its normalities, it even constitutes its telos. This success, however, has its price: it opens the gate to reflection, resistance, alternative orders, and unexpected new versions of normalization and standardization. Even in such situations, not solely in situations of stability, it must ensure the constitution of the normalized subject as a false not-yet-"I"; as an unproblematic product of the subjectification processes. As long as normalizing education is unchallenged the human comes upon her relation to the Other, to the world, and to herself while imprisoned in the framework of never-fully-deciphered representation apparatuses. Even if unconsciously, she faces the full toll of the efficiency of the representation apparatuses in the form of "the given" limitations and possibilities. As existential, political, and theoretical "realities", these horizons actually manifest her very existence as a constant downfall. This is so since "reality" and her own self are constructed by the manipulations, traditions, structures, and powers that she can reflect on or challenge only through the ways, tools, and manner imposed on her by the very system whose logic and "vocabulary" are to be questioned, resisted, and overcome. Normalizing education does not "influence" or "limit" the self: it actually produces the "I" and the self-evidence of the self. In this respect normalizing education produces the human subject as some-thing and prevents her from becoming *some-one*, a true subject. Normalizing education achieves this by internalizing in the subject from "outside" the conceptual

---

1   Ilan Gur-Ze'ev, "Introduction", in: Ilan Gur-Ze'ev (ed.), *Conflicting Philosophies of Education*, Dordrecht: Kluwer Academic Publishers 2000, p. 1.

apparatus, the moral yardsticks and ideals, the consciousness, and the main actual possibilities for reflectivity and social behavior. It governs even the human possibilities for encountering the otherness of the Other and knowledge about knowledge. Even knowledge and evidence about the otherness of the "I" are fabricated by normalizing education. *The annihilation of the subject's otherness* is a bona fide manifestation that the human subject is more than the product of the powers that fabricate and control her, that reduce her to an object of care, education, salvation, and oppression. She is much more than what she was directed to become.

But what if not only knowledge and knowledge about knowledge, but even yardsticks to categorize, evaluate, and receive/reject knowledge, values, fears, and quests are nothing but manifestations of the productivity of normalizing education, which is effective enough to hide its violence from its victims, who are created by, and to make them its most devoted agents? What if, in the end, our sense of evidence, certainty, and desirability manifest the efficiency of the creative violence of normalizing education? In this light we should ask: Is there room for "genuine", "authentic" reflection, dialogue, and transcendence from omnipotent meaninglessness? Is there room at least for a tragic sense of life, real nihilism, or even real overcoming of the quest for life, for meaning, or for happiness in such a closed system? There are several answers to this challenge, but here I offer only one, which is a conditional "yes". Yes—but only if this closure is not quite entire or unchallenged. That is, the world and the human are infinite in a way that also includes antagonistic elements of a kind that might fertilize an essential alternative to normalizing education, one that is not just another version of normalizing education. "But", one should ask, "is there any serious justification for talking about the possibility of counter-education as a different stance in life, which *transcends* the conflicting versions of normalizing education, many of which pride themselves on being emancipatory, different, ever more radical, or anti/counter-educations"?

Below I suggest that the philosophy of Martin Heidegger is of much relevance for the elaboration of an attempt to unlock the gate to counter-education as an open possibility. An attempt of this kind already challenges the triumph of normalizing education. From its part, counter-education is far from an unproblematic alternative. It is a very dangerous path, and the reconstruction of Heidegger's philosophy of education suggested here will manifest this danger.

The centrality of the concept of transcendence results from the severity of the struggle over meaning, from the despair invested in the search for a meaningful manner to relate to the human as a subject. Such a search is conditioned by the possibility of a very special moment. It is a moment of *transcendence from thingness*. This "moment" in itself is the beginning of elevation. It is immanent to life as an effort for overcoming the closure of contextualism, of the situateness of each perusal, quest, and act. Every such moment, indeed, every "moment", incubates a promise for transcendence. It is embedded within this special kind of relation to human existence as transcendence, as elevation in, but also from, the context which constructs the human as an object of manipulation, as one among countless beings, materials, or merchandize. Is it justified to speak about the human if she or he does not ask the question of Being and cannot but become but a mere manifestation of the violence of the context—be this as an effect of the manipulations, traditions, or present horizons that are arbitrarily imposed by social-cultural-technological structures?

If the context, the situation, or the human enframing merely reflect the omnipotent contingent arbitrariness of the context, then what it actually ensures is this: *a perfect de-humanization of the human subject*. If the situateness is totalistic, closed, and contingent, and has no invitation or room for the presence of the totally other, talk of de-humanization processes is unjustified. This is because from the very beginning, in her essence, the human subject has no room to exist as a subject or to engage in a meaningful relation to her stolen subjectivity as a manifestation of her humanity.

Nor is there any air for the human to breath within conditions of total "freedom"; where nothing within the "I", the context, or the transcendental can reveal/enforce alienation and sparse in terms of an aim, meaning, yardstick, or impetus—as in the Utopia of the cyberoptimists. The category of transcendence as an open possibility manifests or preconditions the humanity of the subject. It manifests itself as a social and individual process of overcoming the given horizons, the present conditions, or the fabricated/revealed truths, internalized strivings, fears, and hopes, as well as the power of the hegemonic representation apparatuses. The moderate minimalist claim is that the subject can be human as a subject of discourse, as a manifestation of a position he or she holds within a system, whereby she can offer resistance and re-positioning—although not transcendence. Yet even this claim is still grounded on a concept of transcendence.[2] But, one can ask, what if this quest or this reasoning too is nothing but one of the manifestations of the hegemonic representation apparatuses? What, then, would be the first step in challenging normalizing education, which often manifests itself in the form of extreme skepticism, relativism, escapism, and anti-philosophical orgies? For centuries Western and Eastern philosophies committed themselves to respond to this challenge, and Heidegger's contribution here is of special importance. It is particularly so in face of post-modern conditions in which traditional dichotomies such as subject-object, real-imaginative, center-margin, same-different, and even human-machine or culture-nature, have been transformed.

Heidegger too is occupied with the question that concerns us here in various articulations, relating to the possibility of overcoming meaninglessness or the possibility of transcending from unauthentic to authentic life.

At first glance Heidegger "solves" the traditional problem of the gap between the known/unknown object and the knowing/failed-attempts/vain attempts of the knowing subject. This is apparent in his refusal to develop the subject-object problematic within the framework of traditional Western realism, relativism, skepticism, and solipsism. Accordingly, in his philosophy the possibilities and limitations of transcendence from ignorance to knowledge or from evil to worthy life, or the question of redemption come to a turning point in Western thought.

---

2   Michel Foucault, *Power/Knowledge: Selected Interviews and Other Writings 1972–1977*, translated by Colin Gordon, Leo Marshal, John Mepham, Kate Soper, New York: Harvester Press 1980, p. 117.

According to Heidegger the human being as Dasein is not like a stone, one of the beings who is positioned as an object among other objects. The presence in the world of Dasein differs from that of a stone or a table in the sense that these are parts of Dasein's world who is the center of this world within which the Dasein works, concerns, uncovers, forgets, or transcends himself from or in face of nothingness. The world of appearances, or reality, is not to be understood as "objective", in the sense that its existence is unconditioned by the will or recognition of the human being. For Heidegger, the *being-there* of the Dasein is not to be understood as if it merely exists within a physical space or within another essential content. The human "being-there" is exclusively human. While rejecting the traditional attempts to overcome skepticism or produce proofs to the existence of reality,[3] Heidegger's being-in-the-world of the Dasein projects human creativity on all other beings. It is not "within" but part of being-in-the-world in which the human becomes a meaningful reality and reveals the world within a mode of existence as a human existential. "If Dasein is understood correctly, it defies such proofs, because, in its Being, it already *is* what subsequent proofs deem necessary to demonstrate for it" says Heidegger.[4]

Transcendence is the fundamental structure of the subjectivity of the subject. This is why in the traditional sense for Heidegger there is no transcendence: for him it is immanent in human existence. If the subject were not constantly on the move, did not transcend beyond the given, she would not be a subject.

> To be a subject means to transcend. This means that Dasein does not
> exist as something that transcends from itself from time to time—the
> fundamental meaning of his existence is the transcendence beyond the
> given.[5]

While being-in-the-world as a creator of the world and as concern (*Besorgen*) Dasein manifests itself simultaneously in authentic and in unauthentic life. Freedom manifests itself in both. This is how existence manifests itself not as a fact, reality, but as a possibility.

A dialectical tension exists between the concept of the constant partiality of the Dasein, as being-there which is committed to *self-overcoming*, and Heidegger's concept of the human subject who conceives herself as a constant *possibility* to become wholeness. This tension manifests the uniqueness of the human as a special being among beings, who as in the traditional concept of God creates/subordinates all beings, all non-human beings as a manifestation of her freedom.

Heidegger's concept of freedom avoids moral or other hierarchical models of concern. In his philosophy, authentic life possibilities do not stand in hierarchical relation

---

3   Martin Heidegger, *Being and Time*, translated by John Stambaugh, New York: State University of New York Press 1996, p. 248.
4   *Ibid.*, p. 249.
5   Martin Heidegger, *Gesamtausgabe, 26: Metaphisische Anfangsgruende der Logik im Ausgang von Leibniz,* Frankfurt a.Main: Klostermann, 1978, p. 33.

with unauthentic life. Both are but manifestations of the exile of Being. In this respect, at first glance "genuine" transcendence seems is impossible in Heidegger's philosophy, given the human condition. Later on we will see two versions of transcendence in his philosophy. These are two levels of problematizing the possibility of transcendence in the sense of confronting the possibility of overcoming meaninglessness. The two versions of transcendence are of special importance for the evaluation of Heidegger's contribution to philosophy of education, offering a theoretical framework for the elaboration of the possibility of counter-education.

The existential possibilities of normalizing education as well those of counter-education are always manifested in concrete relations and in specific historical arenas, even if they are never reducible to power relations and to efficiency of political struggles. This stance makes a special contribution to the attempt to avoid self-contained, easy going, "emancipatory" educational projects. Often these projects introduce pedagogies for the oppressed, for overcoming contextualism in the form of hegemonic consciousness and unjust structural power relations. They avoid being swallowed by instrumentalist-oriented educational projects. These are normally functionalistic in their nature and are committed to improving the adaptation of the human being to the governing facts, improving humans' productivity, "success", and pleasures while serving as an agent of the governing violences. Both "conservative" and "emancipatory" trends represent normalizing education, which counter-education should resist. A possible resistance should refer to Heidegger's concept of transcendence.

As we have seen for Heidegger transcendence is immanent to the Dasein, yet at the same time it has an ontological framework which positions as a normal human situation unauthentic concern and oblivion of the call of Being. Before examining Heidegger's conception of the ontological conditions for transcendence, which makes transcendence to authentic life or a worthy struggle such a rare situation on the one hand and ultimately imaginary and futile on the other, we should revisit his dividing lines between the categories of authenticity and unauthenticity.

For Heidegger, the human subject can exist only by self overcoming, which as an authentic existence reveals itself in the moment of conceiving herself—and her surroundings— as some-thing, and will open herself to the call, to her or his mission of revealing the openness of Being in beings—and in herself. She manifests herself as a *creator* in realizing the call of Being and manifests her uniqueness in disclosing the thingness of the world. Dasein is "the location of the truth of Being".[6] For Heidegger

> The essence of man consists in his being more than merely human, if this is represented as being a rational creature.[7]

This is revealed when he responds to the call of Being:

6   Martin Heidegger, "The way back into the ground of metaphysics", in: *Existentialism from Dostoevsky to Sartre*, ed. Walter Kaufman, Clevelend and New York: Meridian Books, 1969, p. 213.
7   Martin Heidegger, "Letter on humanism", in *Basic Writings*, London 1996, p. 245.

> Man is the shepherd of Being. Man loses nothing in this 'less'; rather, he gains in that he attains the truth of Being. He gains the essential poverty of the shepherd, whose dignity consists in being called by Being itself into the preservation of Being's truth.[8]

Man in his authentic existence, as the shepherd of Being, is in an *ecstatic "homelessness".*[9] This is the Heideggerian understanding of realizing human responsibility as "ecstatic dwelling in the nearness of Being"[10] which enables the Dasein to face meaninglessness, to confront the question of Being, and to exit authentically in face of the *Daseinfrage* (question of Being).

The possibility of authentic life is inseparable from the question of truth. But here the question of truth is not revealed as an epistemological question within a correspondence theory but as an erotic posing of the question of the truth of Being. As the shepherd of Being the human subject is not a mere thing, one of the beings which do not concern for the question of Being and the truth of his mission. He has a responsibility, an aim to fulfill—to face the *absence* of the call by which he is to be awakened. The response to the absent call fertilizes a creative self-positioning which is anti-instrumental or anti-goal oriented.

The Heideggerian concept of truth as *a-letheia* as *Ent-bergung* (dis-covery, un-covering, un-veiling) confronts *Verbergung* (concealment), closure and thingness. Transcendence in the authentic ex-istence realizes concern as un-covering, as opposed to the possibility of oblivion of human responsibility and being swallowed in an opposite, unauthentic concern in the given appearances as an alternative mode of existence.

Angst (anxiety) normally drives the human subject away from himself. It prevents him from facing his situateness as being-thrown (*geworfen*) into meaninglessness (as manifested in accepted truths, values, and ways of life), of the Man, of a way of being-in-the-world which is contrasted to itself, and as such realizes itself in an unauthentic existence (*Uneigentliches Dasein*).[11] Authenticity is here revealed as a human existential in which the presence of the absence of wholeness manifests itself as a human question. It is exactly the absence of the presence of wholeness which enables the authentic human subject to face the partiality and creative-meaninglessness which surrounds him—as a precondition to turning himself to the wholeness, to the infinity of nothingness beyond the given reality. This is manifested in being-towards-death.[12] Anxiety is not only the way for human to experience her or his authentic experience of death as being-towards-not-being. This is where, for Heidegger, freedom manifests itself: when deciding for authenticity and against unauthenticity not as a realization

---

8   *Ibid.*
9   *Ibid.*, p. 242.
10   *Ibid.*, p. 246..
11   Martin Heidegger, *Being and Time*, p. 233.
12   *Ibid.*, p. 234.

of a positive Utopia but as a manifestation of realizing responsibility for overcoming all false promises of optimistic-purpose-oriented projects. Freedom reveals itself in *letting-things-be*.[13]

To be authentic the human subject must overcome the governing world of facts, the realm of self-evidence or "proved" truths and resist the threats and temptations of security, pleasure, and success offered by the Other, by society. Then, and only then, in face of the anxiety,[14] of confronting the infinity of nothingness and of homelessness, will the overcoming of the given be possible and truth as uncovering realize itself in human transcendence.

> Da-sein means: being held out into the nothing. Holding itself out into he nothing, Dasein is in each case already beyond beings as a whole. This being beyond beings we call "transcendence". If in the ground of its essence Dasein were not transcending, which now means, if it were not in advance holding itself out into the nothing, then it could never be related to beings nor even to itself.[15]

This kind of unveiling as letting-things-be is essentially different from normal violence directed at imposing realities and meanings. It represents a concept of transcendence as enlightening—and not as a violent penetration. It is this alternative concept of transcendence, which allows this *Lichtung* (enlightening) in which Being, which is normally veiled and exiled, reveals itself.

Threatened and utterly disquieted as man is by the infinity of nothingness the authentic subject approaches the things in the world in a unique, never-determined or instrumentalized manner. In this sense she transcends from unauthentic existence, faces things in their veiled situatedness and sees in light of Being the original, not-yet-revealed meaning of the things, as they actually are. In this anti-utopian concept of transcendent freedom, in authentic existence, must at the same time be a binding-to what-is. Precisely the authentic human in an act of free creation manifests her infinite openness, letting-a-being-be what it actually is.

> But when the gods are named originally and the essence of things receives a name, so that things for the first time shine out, human existence is brought into a firm relation and is given a basis.[16]

This authentic self-positioning, while transforming the human condition and realizing transcendence from unauthentic into authentic existence, ultimately manifests human freedom as openness. This openness makes possible infinite possibilities and

---

13   Martin Heidegger, "On the essence of truth", *Basic Writings*, p. 125.
14   Martin Heidegger, "What is metaphysics?", *Basic Writings*, p. 106.
15   *Ibid.*, p. 103.
16   Martin Heidegger, "Hoelderlin and the essence of poetry", in *Existence and Being*, London: Vision (n.d.)., p. 305.

realizations of the letting-be of things in the sense of unveiling the Being within be-ings. Only as such does it reclaim the truth of Being, which is what poets and philoso-phers—when true to their mission—represent:

> To 'dwell poetically' means: to stand in the presence of the gods and to be involved in the proximity of the essence of the things. Existence is 'poetical' in its fundamental aspect—which means at the same time: in so far as it is established (founded), it is not a recommence but a gift.[17]

It is not only that morally there is no difference between authentic and unauthentic life. An authentic decision to realize human freedom which uncovers what normality is veiled and abandoned is ultimately revealed as one of the manifestations of the veil-ing/unveiling games of Being which in itself manifests the infinity of nothingness, its aimlessness and *meaninglessness*. This is so even when the human is transcended into authentic life and "dwells poetically" as an ecstatic creator. In this sense in Heidegger's philosophy there is no redemption.

Freedom manifests itself here as a transcending power: as a binding call to the hu-man mission as the shepherd of Being and as a Dionysian response to *the call of Be-ing—which ultimately is revealed as the call of his own lonely, finite, conscious*. As such it cannot but reveal the illusions and the abyss of untruth—as part of the a priori struc-ture of the essence of truth. But mostly the human subject is far from authenticity and from the kind of openness that makes possible transcendence, self-creation, and unveiling the truth of Being. She is deprived of sensibility and power for responding to her mission and to her own conscious.[18]

The normalized subject is swallowed by the meaninglessness of the "Them"; she for-gets herself as a finite openness towards infinity, exiled from the possibility of living in the nearness of Being. This is the starting point of transcendence: from unauthenticity towards authenticity, when the human subject faces nothingness as the only gate to the endless struggle for worthy life, for true, frightening, religious existence. The tra-ditional category of God is here replaced by nothingness and the traditional concept of love of God as the ultimate manifestation of religiosity is here substituted by true transcendence into authentic life. It is of vital importance, however, to acknowledge that ontologically, for Heidegger, transcendence, alone, does not offer a positive Uto-pia into truth as something positively attainable and as a gate for rest or nirvana. The various versions of unauthentic life and their concerns offer transcendence too; but only as an *escape* from the anxiety of facing nothingness and the infinity of empty freedom. It is an escape from endless, never-guaranteed, struggle for fulfilling the responsibility which does not offer a new Garden of Heaven in the form of dogma or a formed "way of life".

The historical fascinating success of normalizing education is offered a grounded explanation by Heidegger's philosophy: *the possibility of unauthentic concern and un-*

17   *Ibid.*, p. 306.
18   Martin Heidegger, *Being and Time*, p. 269.

authentic transcendence opens the gate for the human subject to flee from herself, from her responsibility, and from freedom as a danger. This is in the form of retreats into the "Them", into the Other not before he was deprived of his otherness. The "Them" replaces the Being-there as part of the possibilities of being-there.

In contrast to authentic dialogue with the Other normalizing education offers escape from loneliness and from the anxiety of ecstatic presence of the exile of the truth of Being. The "poetic dwelling" is represented by poets such as Hoelderlin, whose poetry targets the essence of language, the exile of the gods, and the possibility of being "*between*" "the gods" and "the people"[19] as manifestation of "this conversation, which we are".[20] The surrendering of the subject to the manifestations of normalizing education is not to be reduced to mere power- relations and manipulations as suggested by critical pedagogy or the post-colonial, multicultural, and feminist pedagogies of the day. In their rush for optimistic critique, "solutions", and languages of "possibilities" these alternatives ignore what Heiddeger's thought teaches us: that the abandonment of the subject contains much more than a mere self-neglecting enhanced by "exterior" manipulations. It is one of the ways by which Being reveals itself. Only as such does it represent an existential tiredness. And as such it constitutes the human's eternal companion. Like other modes of being-towards-death, this one too makes possible concern for the given realities as an escape. An escape from the human's mission to face the exile of the gods and the omnipotence of meaninglessness (from which accepted truths, meanings, values, yardsticks, perspectives, and identities spring).

This *escape* is responsible for creating objective validity, justifications for the "realities" and the calculative logic of control, production and representation in science, technology, and society. The rationality and efficient, functionalist, objective, justifications of the "They", or of normalizing education, to which the subject flees in his Fall (*Verfall*), is not "false". In the present order of things it "really" offers more efficient understanding of humans' life and constitutes an unproblematic promise of redemption, security, truth, justice, pleasure, or success, compared with the "unrealistic" reflective, transcendental impulse as it is galvanized in counter-education. The "Fall" expresses not an historical "mistake" or an outcome of unfortunate conditions to be optimistically replaced or corrected by efficient political struggle and emancipatory education. "Falling" here expresses the essential ontological structure of Dasein itself: "Dasein evades its very self".[21] This "Fall" is manifested in modern science and technology and indeed in the very possibility of genuine thinking, learning and teaching.

According to Heidegger, modern science and technology are instrumental-oriented. We may even use the word "oppressive", even if he does not, since he tries to avoid dichotomies such as oppressive-emancipatory. Modern science and technology challenge truly human possibilities and demolish the uniqueness of the things in the world which might have culminate into a call to the human to Life within which

---

19   Martin Heidegger, "Hoelderlin and the essence of poetry", in *Existence and Being*, p. 312.
20   Martin Heidegger, *ibid.*, p. 303.
21   Martin Heidegger, *Being and Time*, p. 179.

human's freedom is realized in truth.. In its essence technology is a central element of openness towards life and a flourishing of non-standardized life possibilities:

> Technology is a mode of revealing. Technology comes to presence in the realm where revealing and unconcealment take place, where *aletheia*, truth, happens".[22] Technology is no mere means. Quite the opposite. In its origin, in its essence, technology is *techne*, which for the Greeks did not refer only to the activities and skills of the craftsman but also to the arts of the mind and the fine arts. "*Techne* belongs to bringing-forth, to *poiesis*; it is something poetic.[23]

Modern technology and modern science also display—but in an essentially different way, namely in an instrumental, calculating, and subordinate manner—a diminishing of the otherness, the uniqueness of the object. "Everywhere everything is ordered to stand by, to be immediately on hand, indeed to stand there just so that it may be on call for a further ordering... We call it the standing-reserve (*Bestand*)".[24] Within this process modern science and technology transform man himself into a standing-reserve. Enframing and unconcealment as roads to realizing human freedom are blocked in a manner that does not enable the human to acknowledge and challenge it. Modern education is part of this process of dismantling the possibilities for self-constitution, of life as unconcealment. Instead life becomes a concern and a response to the call of instrumental, calculated thinking and its fabrications. This is where education can celebrate its victory over the possibilities for counter-education.

> When thinking comes to an end by slipping out of its element it replaces this loss by procuring a validity for itself as *techne*, as an instrument of education and therefore as a classroom matter and later a cultural concern.[25]

As we can see, Heidegger makes no effort to contribute to normalizing education or to scientific thinking and its successful reduction to the progress of technology, elevation of "the standard of living", propagating "joy", or enhancing "success". Nor can he contribute, as some scholars would suggest, to the improvement of schooling and the elevation of teacher-pupil relations. He is interested in something very different: in *Life*. This is where his conception of transcendence is anchored.

Within the outline of his attraction to thinking as a mode of transcendence but never as means, medium, or instrument, he offers an important alternative to normalized human relations and to the kind of schooling and teacher-pupil relations which

22   Martin Heidegger, "The question concerning technology", in: *Basic Writings*, p. 319.
23   *Ibid.*, p. 318.
24   *Ibid.*, p. 322.
25   Martin Heidegger, "Letter on humanism", p. 221.

are only too common and so well known to us. This is exemplified in special clearly in his "What calls for thinking?"

The situateness of the human determines his possibilities for reflection[26] and the kind of resistance she will put up to the closure of "her" horizons. In modern *Ge-stell*, in the human's being framed in modernity as advanced by modern science and technology, human situateness ensures the oblivion of the mission of the human, of life as something more than mere life. But for Heidegger, framing has deeper roots, and is not to be reduced to a specific historical situation. It springs from the very fact of situateness of human life, of always living enframed. In this sense there is not much truth in the rhetoric of emancipation and the promises of all positive utopias. Thinking itself is actually exiled while alternatives such as science celebrate their triumph. "Science does not think".[27] But if there is no air left for thinking for the modern human subject, how might true learning and teaching be experienced? In what sense is authentic transcendence possible?

According to Heidegger, who does not make the differentiation between a teacher and an educator, "*to learn means to make everything we do answer to whatever addresses itself to us as essential*".[28] We can, however, struggle for possibilities for learning, even in the face of the exile of thinking. In a certain respect it is exactly the absence of thinking that makes learning, thinking, and transcendence possible. But this is possible insofar as we start by radically unlearning what thinking has been traditionally. Heidegger's anti-functionalist, anti-positivist, and anti-instrumentalist attitudes are manifested here too. Genuine teaching is not a successful transmission of knowledge. "What teaching calls for is this: to let learn".[29] This is also the reason why teaching is more difficult than learning. The teacher is ahead of his apprentices in this alone, that he has still far more to learn than they—he has to learn to let them learn. This is also why he has to be far less sure of his material than those who learn are of theirs. This conception of teaching is very close of Heidegger's concept of unconcealing, which opens free relations between the human and beings in their openness, or of relating to the open-being. Since this kind of teacher is not instrumental and does not transmit information "his conduct, therefore, often produces the impression that we really learn nothing from him".[30]

So even in face of the success of modern science and technology, even in face of the present situateness, even in face of the absence of thinking—transcendence into learning to think is still an open human possibility. The presence of the absence of thinking does not halt genuine learning—and unlearning: it is its starting point.

---

26 Ilan Gur-Ze'ev, Jan Masschelein, Nigel Blake, "Reflectivity, reflection and counter-education", *Studies in Philosophy and Education* (2001), 20:2, 93–106. .
27 Martin Heidegger, "What calls for thinking?" in: *Basic Writings*, p. 373.
28 *Ibid.*
29 *Ibid.*, p. 380.
30 *Ibid.*

> Once we are so related and drawn to what withdraws, we are drawing
> into what withdraws, into the enigmatic and therefore mutable near-
> ness of its appeal. Whenever man is properly drawing that way, he is
> thinking—even though he may still be far away from what withdraws,
> even though the withdrawal may remain as veiled as ever.[31]

But in what sense is that which calls us to think preferable to concealment, framing,
and unauthentic life? For Heidegger there is no way to justify the one rather than
the other. In this sense, on Heideggerian grounds there is no way to favor this kind
of learning over the conventional kind. The two ways represent opposing versions of
concern.

The reception of Heidegger's ideas in the field of philosophy of education and within different pedagogies varies. Some scholars claim that it has no relevance whatsoever,
or at least that he never really had a great deal to say about education.[32] Some see
Heidegger's educational implications as nothing but "nonsense".[33] Others are basically
critical of his "abstractness" and still others propose various means to "implement",
instrumenatalize, or domesticate Heidegger's philosophy and make it "relevant" to
actual teaching in schools.[34] For all their differences, these responses to Heidegger's
thought are united in considering his thought in respect of schooling and normalizing
education. Even at their best, when following Heidegger, they refer to teaching as an
artistic-non-instrumental process.[35]

Normalizing education, as was shown, guarantees not only security, prosperity, cooperation and reproduction: it offers even concern and transcendence. This kind of
concern, however, represents an *abandonment* of another kind of concern, an authentic one, which does not satisfy itself by successful imposition on the things in
the world; it does not fulfill itself as technological success or social cooperation and
solidarity.

This other kind of concern makes another kind of transcendence possible. Here
truth as letting-be the otherness of beings realizes human freedom. It is transcendence not as "progress" or self-oblivion but as an outcome of the worthy suffering of

---

31 *Ibid.* p. 381–382.
32 George H. Douglas, "Heidegger on the education of poets and philosophers", *Educational Theory*
    (Fall 1972), 22, p. 449. Frank Margolis, "Heidegger and curriculum", *Philosophy of Education* (1986),
    42, p. 101.
33 William Bruening, "Heidegger on teaching", *Philosophy of Education* 37 (1981), p. 238.
34 Angelo A. Giugliano, "Heidegger, authenticity and education: the move from existentialism to phe-
    nomenology", *Philosophy of Education* (1988) 44, pp. 150–156. Helen Khoobyar, "Educational im-
    port of Heidegger's notion of truth as 'letting-be'", *Philosophy of Education* 30 (1974), pp. 47–58.
    Michael Dwyer, "The educational implications of Heidegger's authenticity", *Philosophy of Education*,
    (1988), 44, pp. 146. Ignacio L. Goetz, "Heidegger and the art of teaching", *Educational Theory*
    (1983), 33, 1, p. 8. Donald Vandenberg, *Being and Education: An Essay in Existential Phenomenology*,
    Englewood Cliffs, NJ: Prentice-Hall 1971.
35 Ignacio L. Goetz, "Heidegger and the art of teaching", *Educational Theory* (Winter 1983) 33, 1, p.
    7.

facing meaninglessness and living-towards-death. As such, transcendence faces the infinity of nothingness and makes the absent freedom and truth present. It becomes what Heidegger never speaks of: *worthy suffering*. It sheds light on the futility of the mere thingness in the beings which have been stripped of their uniqueness by human instrumentalism. Worthy suffering makes possible a kind of transcendence, which allows reflection on the production of meanings, identities, and quests. It even reflects on the representation apparatuses and their manipulations.[36] But can it also offer transcendence from pain/pleasure into the worthy suffering/happiness of facing the truth of Being/nothingness as transcendence into a worthier way of life? Into the terrain of truths which are not fabricated by successful violent manipulations? Is there a way of transcending metaphysical violence itself in the form of the closure/arbitrariness of enframing (*Ge-stell*), of human beings as standing-reserve (*Bestand*), of the limits of language and the effects of the essence of Being as ontological exile?

The kind of counter-education to which Heidegger's concepts of "unlearning", unconcealment", and "transcendence" are not foreign is still voiceless. It cannot become institutionalized or avoid becoming a dogmatic positive Utopia. It should avoid the quest for "authentic authority" and the acceptance of mundane violence as a tool for overcoming metaphysical violence as it is invested in normalizing education. When counter-education is not true to itself, in the name of authenticity and transcendence it will speak, with Heidegger, the vulgar language of National Socialism and other positive Utopias, and create a rhetoric of this kind:

> The knowledge of true scholarship does not differ in its tradition from the knowledge of farmers, lumberjacks, miners and craftsman. For knowledge means being at home in the world in which we live as individuals and as part of a community. Knowledge means growth of resolve and action in the performance of a task that has been given us...Knowledge means being in the place where we are put.[37]

From here the way easily leads to the conception of "we are but following the glorious will of our *Fuehrer*".[38] Every historical collectivistic-oriented situateness or normalization process has its *Fuehrer*: even the process of McDonaldization of reality or the infantilization processes in cyberspace as a totalistic pleasure machine.

But counter-education can find in Heidegger's philosophy a different kind of the concept of transcendence. In it transcendence is conditioned by overcoming authority, any authority, especially that of the one who "knows"[39] or sets the standards, quests or telos. Here it is impossible to differentiate between self-overcoming as "let-learn" and unconcealment as let-things-be what they already are in their essence. In both,

36   Ilan Gur-Ze'ev, Jan Masschelein, Nigel Blake, "Reflectivity, reflection, and counter-education".
37   Martin Heidegger, "Follow the Fuerher", in *German Existentialism*, translated by Dagobert D. Runes, New York: Wisdom Library 1965, p. 40.
38   *Ibid.*, p. 42.
39   Heidegger, "What calls for thinking?" p. 380.

thinking manifests itself, and the presence of the exile of Being allows authentic transcendence, or a kind of religiosity, in which redemption as a relevant pole of existence is saved. Transcendence into thinking, which is normally absent, is transformed into a special existential "moment". Facing the presence of its absence is already thinking:

> And what withdraws in such a manner keeps and develops its own incomparable nearness. Once we are so related and drawn to what withdraws, we are drawing into what withdraws, into the enigmatic and therefore mutable nearness of its appeal. Whenever man is properly drawing that way, he is thinking—even though he may still be far away from what withdraws, even though the withdrawal may remain as veiled as ever.[40]

But even here, when it is not the *Fuehrer* who calls for transcendence into thinking—but that to which the *Fuehrer's* voice responds or that call which he betrays, it is always "the call" which *chooses* us. It is always "the call" which selects us, challenges us in a way which, while it gives itself to the human, swallows the not-yet-really-human as an act of its creation. The transcendence from contingent human power-relations and the contextualized imposed production of truths, values, identities, consciousness, and representation apparatuses in its turn offers another kind of arbitrariness. It manifests the other face of metaphysical violence:

> And what it gives us to think about, the gift it gives to us, is nothing less than itself—itself, which calls on us to enter into thinking. The question "What calls for thinking?" asks for what wants to be thought about in the preeminent sense: it does not just give us something to think about, nor only itself, but it first gives thought and thinking to us, it entrusts thought to us as our essential destiny, and thus first joins and appropriates us to thought.[41]

Here, as a danger, counter-education unveils its essence and makes human transcendence possible—with no security, no promised "success", consensus or pleasure. And this is only the first step in the long way of counter-education, which should at the same time address the most concrete and banal manifestations of reality and the politics of the distribution of evils.

40 *Ibid.*, p. 382.
41 *Ibid., p. 391.*

CHAPTER 8

BEYOND POSTMODERN FEMINIST CRITICAL PEDAGOGY
TOWARD A DIASPORIC PHILOSOPHY OF
COUNTER-EDUCATION

Whose violence is it that *talks itself through* the "authentic I" to us Whose voice is it that summons "us", that alerts "me", that deceives-creates the "you" as hell, as a potential lover, as an infinite abyss? What stands behind the back of the endless possibility/unrestrained obligation to ask "who" or "what" is the implicit "I" who raise the question? Is it possible that the struggle over the essence of feminism, the mission of Judaism, and the possibility of counter-education meet here? These questions are here to be elaborated within the framework of postmodern feminist critical pedagogy.

Let's begin with the bottom line: as a sophisticated version of normalizing education, *postmodern feminist critical pedagogy fails to present an alternative to normalizing education*.[1] And yet, what it would have liked to say is of utmost importance for the possibility of counter-education which will make possible worthy suffering and a kind of homelessness within which meaninglessness, injustice and self-forgetfulness will not have the last word. Even against its explicit assertions it might contain remnants of an important saying, striving, need, which has not received the space and the power genuinely to express its essence. The truth of its essence remains always beyond the horizons of "its" rhetoric. This wordless truth as *readiness*, as a special telos and as Love, however, might guide us. It might guide us to Love: to an ecstatic solidarian, creative-dancing refusal of Thanatus as a quest for power as our home. It might point us to a Diasporic being-in the-world as *becoming*, within which we, yes, you and I, and especially "they" will face *the call* to responsibility and to the creative potentials of Life, which ultimately is beyond immanence and transcendence. This is the essence of Judaism, when it is not conceived within an ethnocentrist framework.

Is it possibly worth trying to climb beyond postmodern feminist critical pedagogy as a way of transcending normalizing education itself? But where is this homelessness? And of what is made such a Diasporic climber? How do we overcome normalizing education as a productive symbolic violence,[2] which creates the *"not-I" as "I am"* who is at once the overwhelmed victim and the most faithful agent of normalizing education, and its violences? Maybe we should go to a space where the violence of normalizing education is most subtle, where critical education has seemingly progressed most,

---

1   Ilan Gur-Ze'ev, *Destroying the Other's Collective Memory*, New York: Peter Lang Pub., 2003, p. 24.
2   *Ibid.*

in order to address these challenges? What is, however, this "normalizing education", in which postmodern feminist critical pedagogy is supposed to be—or is actually— the overcoming realization of its concealed exile?

Normalizing education is one of the manifestations of the creative power of meta- physical violence.[3] Normalizing education is realized in the process of subjectification as a process of fabricating the "I" as a productive fiction. At the same time it is an on- tological sign. It is concealed as a contextualized undeciphered power-game and rep- resented as a historical or as a material dimension, which becomes "real" and visible within the context of today's Western rhetoric and practices. Western philosophical foundations, modern technology, and current capitalist practices are the precondi- tions for its *concealment* as visible, detectable, promising "reality". These conditions are responsible for humans' forgetfulness of their forgetfulness as it receives a name and becomes a sign whose existence, effects, creation, and destruction are acknowl- edged. The given gaze and the legitimate listening as a matrix conceal not only open possibilities for getting close to the essence of the truth of becoming, they conceal the very possibility of the genuine possibility itself, by the way in which it represents openness, creation, and growth.

Central to the self-forgetfulness and misconception of possibility and improvisa- tion here is the concept and the psychological constitution of an *instrumental-oriented dwelling-in-reality*. This kind of dwelling is realized also in Western philosophy itself. This concept of philosophy, which was dominated by the Platonic quest for light and love of truth, is far from being at peace with itself and is currently embarrassed; it feels guilty at the present historical moment.[4] Maybe Judaism may help us here to liberate ourselves from the cave of Western philosophy and existence and help us to overcome Monotheism and save the worthier parts of feminist pedagogy in the way toward that which is symbolized by the feminine and Judaism when they are on the Diasporic road toward a rich, creative, improvised, self-overcoming, in light of love of Life.

Levinas does not explicitly say it but he implies that actually a resemblance exists between the quest for the Platonic light and the violence which governs/constitutes Western reality. Post-colonialist thinkers implement this concept of Levinas and Derr- ida to re-read the direct and symbolic violence and counter-violence between Western colonialism and its marginalized cultures in the third world and within the Western realm itself.[5]

The division between truth and violence yields the unification of peace and truth, wor- thy education, and love. In parallel it yields a conception of the essence of the human being and an appropriate ethics. The philosophies of Foucault, Lyotard, and Deleuze are a serious challenge to this project. According to Foucault

---

3   Gur-Ze'ev, I. 2001. "Philosophy of peace education in a postmodern era". *Educational Theory* 51: 3,
     pp. 315–336.
4   Emmanuel Levinas, *Emmanuel Levinas: Basic Philosophical Writings*, Bloomington: Indiana Univer-
     sity Press, 1996, p. 163.
5   Iain Chambers, "Waiting on the end of the world?" in: Morley, David and Chen, Kuan-Hsing (eds.),
     Stuart Hall: Critical Dialogues in Cultural Studies, London: Routledge, 1996, p. 209.

...one's point of reference should not be to the great model of language and signs, but to that of war and battle. The history, which bears and determines us, has the form of war rather than that of language: relations of power, not relations of meaning .[6]

Within the Foucaultian project the various versions of education do not differ in their central "essence" as normalizing power, and the educational regime does not differ from any other regime of truth which produces subjects, knowledge, and values within a history which has no "meaning". Like all others, this regime too should be subject to analysis not in accordance with good intentions, "truth", and a natural or sacred "faith in the human" or God, but

in accordance with the intelligibility of struggles, of strategies and tactics" without "evading the always open and hazardous reality of conflict", without "avoiding its violent, bloody and lethal character by reducing it to the calm Platonic form of language and dialogue.[7]

Foucault emphasizes *the productivity of power* and represents the subject—be it a "victim" or a "victimizer"—as one of the manifestations of contingent, meaningless, aimless, power-relations. In contrast to the traditional Western concepts of violence, now truth itself "isn't outside power".[8]

Foucault deconstructs the *quests* and the *concepts* that allow optimism about transcendent, orchestrated, essential change by human autonomy or reason. Traditionally the very possibility of transcendence made reflection possible. It also allowed a concept of a difference, which makes a difference of the kind that makes possible "peace" as the opposite of "war". He considers naive people who refuse to accept the omnipotence of epistemic violence. They are naive as long as they to not address the truth about truth: that *there is no difference that makes a difference*.[9]

In a human's life ontological violence is realized in various dimensions and levels: as symbolic violence, as structural violence, and as direct violence which becomes visible and threatens directly the self or the Other as "criminal acts", "military operations", and so forth. Here there is no room for love, for transcendence, for counter-education, yet there is much room for manipulating and misrepresenting the quest for love and the need for transcendence under very different flags, such as "love of

---

6   Michel Foucault, *Power/Knowledge: Selected Interviews and Other Writings 1972–1977*, translated by Colin Gordon, New York: Pantheon, 1980, p. 114.

7   *Ibid.*, p. 115.

8   *Ibid.*, p. 131.

9   Michel Foucault, *The Archeology of Knowledge*, translated by Sheridan, A. Smith, London: Tavistock Publications, 1995, pp. 210–211.

the motherland", "the voice of God", "the imperatives of reason", "critical theory", or "emancipatory postcolonialism".

In all its versions, normalizing education is responsible for constituting the "I" as a "not-I", namely constructing the "I" as some-thing and not as some-one—as a particle of the collective or as the humble slave of "the truth", "justice", or "beauty". The "I" becomes an object of manipulations, the locus of violent body politics, of symbolic and social reproduction and a site of camouflaging the manners by which the system hides its violent reproduction of the hegemonic order of things and the governing realm of self-evidence[10]

In other words, under these conditions *the human subject is an effect*, a construct, an echo, and sometime the veil that conceals the logic of the system of which it is a part. The subject is being constructed and is dragged into or allowed *a position* (even when re-positioning herself). At the same time the subject is *a function* in the discourse which has always contextual, historical, and material preconditions and realizations. As such, the human subject is both the victim of the system and its most devoted agent.

The human subject, however, as a potential, is infinitely *more* than that. The human subject is infinitely *different* from what she is determined to become by contingent power-relations, by individual and collective drives, imperatives of the historical moment, and the creative reactions to the possibilities imposed by Fortuna.

Love enables transcendence as *becoming*. It presumes the otherness and the truth of the mission so that one can genuinely reply "I am!" when called. The very possibility of the serious response to a genuine call which addresses me is what makes the difference. So, from the perspective of Diasporic philosophy, and as counter-educationalists, we can say: "Yes, there is a difference that makes a difference".

> Once we are so related and drawn to what withdraws, we are drawing into what withdraws, into the enigmatic and therefore mutable nearness of its appeal. Whenever man is properly drawing that way, he is thinking—even though he may still be away from what withdraws, even though the withdrawal may remain as veiled as ever".[11]

And only in this love of the truth, love of the otherness of the Other and self, does Love open a gate for Life as responsibility and improvisation—and genuine *learning* becomes possible. Learning to listen, properly to prepare oneself for seriousness and respond-ability of the kind we lost begins, paralleling *unlearning* and

> mak[ing] everything we do answer to whatever addresses itself to us as essential.[12]

---

10   Ilan Gur-Ze'ev, *Destroying the Other's Collective Memory*.
11   Martin Heidegger, *Basic Writings*, London: Routledge, 1996, pp. 381–382.
12   *Ibid.*, p. 373.

Such a possibility is never given, is always beyond factuality. As such it is an open possibility. Its possibility signifies the possibility of transcending normalizing education and "learning" as dogma; overcoming ethnocentrism, and resisting the fear of the infinite otherness of the Other and the beginning of genuine improvisation and creation. It signifies the potential of becoming a human subject, a creative love.

This potential of *becoming* a human subject signifies the potential burst of **the totally other**, of transcendence from the seeming omnipotence of the given "facts", "pre-conditions and the syntax of the discourse"; namely, it signifies the possibility of overcoming what Benjamin calls "now-time" in response to "Messianic time".

In Benjamin's thought, as in traditional Judaism, "Messianic time"[13] bursts into "now-time."[14] It momentarily penetrates the continuity of the vain progress of catastrophic time and creates in it a special extra-temporal point, at which time ceases to flow and a redeemed space of time is constituted, wherein it is possible to try to call things by their true name and to fight the "evil'" celebrating its victory. The struggle for knowledge is not value-indifferent; it turns out to be a moral struggle for the good life by an isolated, Diasporic, individual, who at most can hope to break the *continuum* which in principle is always victorious, and to which historical "progress" has been handed over ever since **the original sin**.

The tension between these two poles is the gate to the abyss of human destiny. Only as such does it open the gate for a *Diasporic existence*, which acknowledges homelessness, affirms meaningless, and does not try to escape fear, pain, hatred and responsibility.

All these are not challenged by the various versions of radical education, and even the hegemonic version of critical pedagogy fails here. Why is this so? It is because critical pedagogy too refuses Diasporic philosophy and calls for "home-returning" or for the erection of a new "home"—in the form of a worthy "we" of the victims-elected-ones, as an ethnocentristic-oriented existence, or as a close dogma. Emancipatory-critical pedagogy refuses existential, philosophical, and political homelessness and improvisation; homelessness which, at the same time, resists actual injustice, devotes itself to gazing at that which makes possible transcendence of the *ethical I*,[15] at the truth, and at *Diasporic Messianism-without-a-Messiah*.

For all their importance, the critical pedagogies of Paulo Freire, Ira Shor, Kathleen Weiler, Henry Giroux, Peter McLaren, Douglas Kellner, and bell hooks are not exceptional in this matter. What is the secret of the seeming omnipotence of normalizing education, which enables it to govern critical pedagogy, postmodern critical pedagogy, and even postmodern feminist critical pedagogy in its most advanced forms (some of which become post-critical and post-feminist)?

Here we have to consider the function of normalizing education, and we cannot avoid reconstructing its content within specific contexts; since what is of utmost im-

---

13 Walter Benjamin, *Gesammelte Schriften*, Frankfurt a. Main: Suhrkamp, 1974, p. 703.
14 *Ibid.*, p. 701.
15 Emmanuel Levinas, *Collected Philosophical Papers*, translated by Lingis, Alphonso, Leuven: Martinus Nijhoff Publishers, 1987, pp. 185–186.

portance here is *the creativity of its violence*, even in terms of openness, difference, drives, aesthetics, responsibility, and rationality.

Normalizing education is not content solely with the introduction of a certain set of values as worthy and relevant. It naturalizes their contingent representations as worthy, relevant, and valid as well as the untruth, danger, or irrelevancy of their Others. Normalizing education, however, does more than that in *introducing the yardstick to evaluate oppositional sets of values and conflicting evaluation apparatuses* as self-evident, as part of the subjectification of the subject. Namely, as part of the production of the self-identity of the human subject as self-evident, as a center for reflection and moral judgments for the "not-I", as a realization of the "I".

Normalizing education must integrate and naturalize a specific conceptual apparatus into a specific set of values.[16] Concepts such as "equality" and values such as "freedom" are not natural, authentic, or original—they are fabricated under specific dynamic conditions. They are produced at a specific historical moment in a concrete material and symbolic setting, which they serve and represent. The veil of Being is woven every moment anew. Its eternal repetition is made possible even by the effort to overcome the gap between the human needs-potentials and the Western mission of philosophy: the world is being deciphered, interpreted, manipulated, and re-represented—never without the agency of concepts. Within almighty dynamic symbolic creation, concepts, rules, and relations, which are enforced by normalizing education, create/decipher "reality" or "representations" into a Maya curtain or a matrix. The self-evidence, not only the horizons of critical reason, moral coexistence, and estrangement from nature, veils the possibility of facing the violence, which establishes unsatisfied drives, concepts, and values such as "freedom". It establishes specific concepts and not others as relevant, true, or possible. This introduction, centering, or enforcement, of a specific set of concepts—without revealing its blind interests and pre-constituted games—is one of the manifestations of metaphysical violence. Here it is realized as epistemic violence. Normalizing education is possible only as a result of its gigantic, creative, success.[17]

Epistemic violence[18] is a precondition for the explicit, unmediated use of violence, which as such is granted a name and is addressed as a "conflict" or as "violence". It is realized in the formation of conceptual apparatuses, knowledge, consciousness, ideological orientations, and consensus or self-evidence. It establishes the "we", the "they", and the relevant ideology of redeeming/educating/exiling/destroying/re-educating the Other so that there will be no room for *the otherness of the Other* and the Otherness of the "I" as potentially different from what she is directed to become.

---

16   Ilan Gur-Ze'ev, *Destroying the Other's Collective Memory*, p.8.

17   Gur-Ze'ev, Ilan, "Knowledge, violence, and education", 1999, "http://construct.haifa.ac.il/~ilangz/ new/" and see in: Ilan Gur-Ze'ev, "Postmodernism, values and value education in Israel", in: Yaakov Iram, Samuel Shkolnikov and Eli Shechter (eds.), *Crossroads: Values and Education in Israeli Society*, Jerusalem: The Ministry of Education Press, 2001, pp. 91–155 (in Hebrew).

18   Michel Foucault*Madness and Civilization: A History of Insanity in the Age of Reason*, translated by Richard Howard. New York: Tavistock, 1965, pp. 261–262.

Normalizing education is responsible not solely for constituting the "subject". It realizes itself also in introducing to the subject certain bodies of knowledge and representing others as irrelevant and illegitimate. Still others are lost, destroyed, or swallowed by the new system. It also expels certain "dangerous"/"foreign" sets of values, making others forgotten, irrelevant, or illegitimate in a process which at the same time imposes a certain *evaluation apparatus* that is immanent to the hegemonic order. The stability of the hegemonic realm of self-evidence and the identification with the system are very much dependent on this evaluation apparatus.

Only in face of the given horizons and the given scares, pains, codes, and pleasures—as well as in face of their silenced alternatives and transformations—does one evaluate one's own values. It is also the *never totally controlled arena* where she evaluates the values of the Other, and where the faith of alternative knowledge is predestined even in a supposedly free and critical pedagogy dialogues. The self-evidence of the apparatus which evaluates the values of the "we" and the values of the Other, as well as alternative concepts of knowledge, and not solely a certain tradition or knowledge, ensures the hegemonic order of things. It vaccinates the hegemonic reality against a potential critique that will decipher its violences and its aimlessness, and will undermine the justifications, inevitability, and self-evidence of the present order of things.

As the historical estrangement/enrichment between the tradition of objective reason and instrumental rationality draws to a close with the total victory of instrumental rationality, *rationality itself becomes irrational omnipotence*, a fierce enemy of human multi-dimensional edification. "Critique" itself becomes part and parcel of the order it is supposed to challenge.[19] This process is part of a larger process within which the logic of the hegemonic actuality is produced, represented, distributed, consumed, and re-produced. Today it is realized in the process of the shift from modernization to globalization and actualized in the productivity of the post-Fordist forms of production, distribution, representation, and consumption.

This process cannot be separated from the process of the subjectification of the subject. Here "the subject" is fabricated as a productive fiction that conceives itself as an agent that genuinely deciphers, controls, and transforms the world. The subjectivity is produced as part of *the Same*, as a thing, as part of the continuum of the reality governed in this historical moment by instrumental rationality.

Normalizing education realizes here its mission to de-humanize the subject and produce her as an object of productive manipulations.[20] It cannot avoid working to ensure her *self-forgetfulness*; by that it exposes itself to human *awakening* and to the challenge of counter-education. Within this process the subject is deprived of her otherness, she forgets her potential readiness to be called upon, and instead is granted the possibility to develop "her" subjectivity. She is constructed in a manner which will conceal from her that "her" subjectivity is nothing more than another manifestation of the logic of the system within which she is produced, nourished, controlled, and

---

19   Max Horkheimer, *Gesammelte Schriften* VII, Frankfurt a. Main: Fischer Taschenbuch Verlag, 1985, p. 511.

20   Ilan Gur-Ze'ev, *Destroying the Other's Collective Memory*, p. 2.

robbed of her otherness, of her potential to become other than what she is directed to become.

Normalizing education, in this sense, dehumanizes the human so that she will become an aspect, an echo, a product of the context, which produces her both as a victim and as an enthusiastic agent of the process of her victimization/de-humanization. Only in such a world is there room for love, worthy suffering, and critique. Only in such a world do preconditions of awakening exist and make Diasporic counter-education possible.

The critique of postmodern feminist critical pedagogy unveils, with special clarity, the secret of normalizing education as concealment, and the uncovering of this secret as another veil whose unveiling might open the question of the Diasporic human destiny.

Current postmodern feminist critical pedagogy is at a crossroads. Its embarrassment is only a fraction of the more general crisis of current postmodern feminist pedagogy, which in turn is but an aspect of the more general problematic of today's feminist theory and practice in an era facing a grand historical shift and disorientation.

Given the complexity of this crisis, "feminist teaching and pedagogy are, likewise, interpreted in many different ways by those who name themselves as feminist educators".[21] In such a reality we are faced with an opportunity to search for possible articulations of a Diasporic philosophy of education, which will give birth to a creative counter-education that will address the challenges of the present historical moment.

One major force, which has an important impact on today's postmodern feminist critical pedagogy, is the post-colonialist ideology, which is influenced heavily by various postmodern discourses.[22] The various versions of critical pedagogy, which insist (in different ways and degrees) on the centrality of the critical pedagogy theory of the Frankfurt School, will be very careful with the kind and degree of post-colonialist dimensions that they introduce into their concepts of critical pedagogy. According to Giroux, however, "Paulo Freire's efforts must be read as a postcolonial text".[23] And Giroux only represents here the general attitude in the non-German critical educational discourse. Others will receive "harder" versions of postmodern philosophy, and accordingly their post-colonialism will be differently integrated into their critical pedagogy. Still others will treat differently the post-colonialist ideology and "postmodern philosophy", and will try not only to go beyond current postmodernism but even to transcend critical pedagogy itself. Already at this stage it is important to note that in its radical versions *the post-colonialist influence draws critical pedagogy into an ethnocentric foundationalist emancipatory commitment*, while using post-colonial ideologies, which at the same time are committed to negate ethnocentrism, essentialism, foun-

---

21   Andrey Dentith, "Critical voyages: Postmodern feminist pedagogies as liberatory practice", *Teaching Education*, 12: 2 (2001), pp. 165–176.

22   Ilan Gur-Ze'ev, *Edward Said as an Educator* (forthcoming).

23   Henry Giroux, Henry, *Disturbing Pleasures—Learning Popular Culture*, New York and London: Routledge, 1994, p. 142.

dationalism, and any sort of universalism. These various receptions of post-colonial ideology exert a major impact on postmodern feminist critical pedagogy.

A different force directs feminist postmodern critical pedagogy in the opposite direction: to save some of the Enlightenment's ideals while criticizing some central elements of the present-day postmodern discourse and paying tribute to others. This trend manifests a weaker ethnocentrism than the other, yet it is not entirely free of ethnocentrism or from dogmatic anti-"Eurocentrism" or dogmatic anti-"whiteness". In some aspects it is theoretically weaker than the essentialist and "strong" ethnocentric version of postmodern feminist critical pedagogy, which negates altogether the humanist emancipatory commitment and stands on the border of negating critical pedagogy itself, even in its hegemonic version. It is manifested so clearly in the Ellsworth-Giroux debate.[24]

It seems that bell hooks, like Carmen Luke and Jennifer Gore, stands at both poles of this trend, while Ellsworth and Lather stand with the "harder" postmodern version of this kind of feminist critical pedagogy. Other postmodern feminist voices explicitly resist, or deconstruct, the emancipatory project altogether, as one can see in the works of Donna Haraway, Sadie Plant, and Zoe Sofoulis.[25]

Within the framework of cyberfeminism we are faced with a promising development of the post-colonialist feminist critique: *a post-feminist messianic project*. Its positive utopian educational vision demands our attention, since it offers a serious philosophical, existential, and political challenge to the critical concepts of violence, drives, agency, meaning, creation, and emancipation.

Still other voices are searching for new theoretical, educational, and political beginnings in light of what they see as the apparent failure of modern as well as "postmodern" alternatives to "traditional" drives, concepts, and acts of oppression and emancipation in the works of Deleuze and Lacan. It is a single line stretching from Freire to Deleuze, from neo-Marxist critical pedagogy to post-critique and post-feminism.

Some of these trends become anti-intellectual and some de-politicize theoretical educational discourse, while others offer an explicit, instrumental anti-humanistic-oriented political agenda. Very vivid here is the absence of *the presence of a comprehensive critical theory* or the absence of a serious philosophical framework[26] that will protect all these trends from being drawn into a strategic-instrumentalist orientation, within which there is room for neither poiesis nor a modified "homecoming" presence of objective reason, which synthesizes the Dionysian and the Apollonian dimensions of human creativity. In the absence of vital anti-instrumentalist responsibility, and in face of the implicit or explicit abandoning of critical theory's dialogical, solidarian, and transcendental dimensions, all these trends, for all their differences, are in danger

---

24 Patti Lather, "Post-critical pedagogies: A feminist reading", in Luke, Carmen and Gore, Jennifer (eds.), *Feminisms and Critical Pedagogy*, New York and London: Routledge, 1992, pp. 124–126.

25 Ilan Gur-Ze'ev, "Cyberfeminism and education in the era of the exile of spirit", *Educational Theory* 49: 4 (1999), pp. 437–456.

26 bell hooks, *Teaching to Transgress—Education as the Practice of Freedom*, New York and London: Routledge, 1994, p. 69.

of becoming a precious ornamentation of the sublime violence of the postmodern condition.[27]

Postmodern feminist critical pedagogy, however, does have many critical and potentially emancipatory elements. It is a genuine political and philosophical challenge to Western hegemonic educational ideologies. It questions educational praxis as well as the educator's philosophical, psychological, and gender contexts. The differences between the various feminist philosophies have, however, left their mark on the various feminist pedagogies, their challenges, and their disagreements and rivalries. Basically, these differences spring from the different postmodern versions they are committed to. We can categorize them as "hard" and "soft" postmodernisms.

"Hard" and "soft" postmodern positions give birth to feminist and post-feminist pedagogies, on the one hand, and to different versions of postmodern feminist critical and post-critical pedagogy, on the other. Both versions, however, fail to offer a worthy counter-education within which the truth of the essence of feminism and the telos of the critical Spirit will be addressed. Ultimately, both of them are part and parcel of normalizing education. According to Kathleen Weiler

> Feminist theory, like other contemporary approaches, validates differences, challenges universal claims to truth, and seeks to create social transformation in a world of shifting and uncertain meanings. In education, these profound shifts are evident on two levels: first, at the level of practice, as excluded and formerly silenced groups challenge dominant approaches of learning and definitions of knowledge; and second, at the level of theory, as modernist claims to universal truth are called into question. (Weiler 1991, 449–450) [28]

According to bell hooks

> Feminist and critical pedagogy are two alternative paradigms for teaching which have really emphasized the issue of coming to voice. That focus emerged as central, precisely because it was so evident that race, sex, and class privilege empower some students more then others, granting 'authority' to some voices more than others.[29]

She asserts that postmodern feminist critical pedagogy employs pedagogical strategies that "create ruptures in the established order, that promote modes of learning which challenge bourgeois hegemony";[30] here she explicitly insists that there is no genuine conflict between critical pedagogy and feminist philosophy and pedagogy. As we shall

---

27   Ilan Gur-Ze'ev, "Cyberfeminism and education in the era of the exile of spirit", p. 451.
28   Kathleen Weiler, "Freire and a Feminist Pedagogy of difference", *Harvard Educational Review* 61: 4 (November 1991), pp. 449–474.
29   bell hooks, *op.cit.*
30   *Ibid.*, p. 185.

see later, this is quite a problematic and controversial issue for other postmodern feminist thinkers.

Jeanne Brady and Audrey Dentith define critical postmodern feminism as a theory of pedagogy that provides the needed space to embrace the multiple positions required for democratic participation. They write:

> We purposely use a critical pedagogy discourse to safeguard the political intentions of feminism which can be compromised by an emphasis on postmodernism....It represents a politics of social change in which people participate in the shaping of the theories and practices of liberation.[31]

This postmodern alternative to the emancipatory critical pedagogy tradition is not to be seen solely in explicit postmodern feminist and post-feminist alternatives such as that of Haraway and Ellsworth: it is even manifested in some of the attempts to integrate postmodern and Enlightened emancipatory potentials, like in the project of Carmen Luke and Jennifer Gore, in their *Feminisms and Critical pedagogy*,[32] which is explicitly aimed at constructing "a politics of emancipation through resistance to all "phallocentric knowledge".[33]

As Patti Lather notes,[34] postmodern feminist critical pedagogy, or maybe we should call it "post-critical feminist pedagogy", tries to present itself as a radical emancipatory element within the current realm of self-evidence. Such an approach, however, might become a serious challenge as it offers us an alternative to the Frankfurt School critical theory, or an alternative to present-day comprehensive critical theory, which will address key concepts such as "education" and "violence" and will address the powers that produce, control, and challenge this totality. It is in great need of an articulated orientation to relate to the aims, preconditions, context, and practices of intersubjectivity whereby the feminist movement, in all its versions, runs away from a general critical theory and from these challenges.

The refusal/failure to offer a comprehensive critical theory is very significant for today's feminist critical pedagogy. This is not so much because it identifies "phallocentrism" with the colonialist violence of grand narratives, and universally valid values with foundationalism, essentialism and the quest to control justice and truth. It is much more in light of the following philosophical challenge: whither can we proceed from the rich tension between the celebrated postmodern nomadism and a genuine Diasporic philosophy? How can we overcome the gap between a positive Utopia, even when camouflaged as "hybrid, kaleidoscopic creative amalgamation be-

---

31 Andrey Dentith, "Critical voyages: Postmodern feminist pedagogies as libratory practice", p. 166.

32 Carmen Luke and Jennifer Gore (eds.), "Introduction", *Feminisms and Critical Pedagogy*, New York and London: Routledge, 1992.

33 Carmen Luke, "Feminist pedagogy theory: Reflections on power and authority", *Educational Theory* 46: 3, (1996), p. 283.

34 Patti Lather, "Post-critical pedagogies: A feminist reading", p. 132.

tween/through differences" and the Messianic impulse of negative utopia? What can
we do for enhancing the kind of religiousness which might be given birth from the
depth of the *abyss* which exists between the *ethical I*—who is pre-rational and exterior
to the political dimensions of life– and the *moral I*—who has to decide among various
alternatives and desires in the kingdom of scarce and conflicting political obligations?
Even here, confronting the crucial part of the theoretical, existential, and political
chain of postmodern feminist critical pedagogy, we are not faced with "the reply" to
this challenge. This should not surprise or discourage the Diasporic educators among
us. But should we accept that even the courage, the responsibility, and the eros which
will address this challenge are still beyond our horizons? The feminist response to
the violence of normalizing education and to the possibility of counter-education is
a critical question. It relates to the possibility of *critique as transcendence* and to the
possibility of going *beyond* the omnipotence of the abyss between the immanence of
"the system" and the "transcendence" of the subject, who is currently so embarrassed
in face of its unveiled subjectification.

Today's feminism is embarrassed theoretically and politically by questions such as
"Who/what talks itself through 'me'?" "What enables me to respond 'I am' when
called upon?" Or, "How do I critically address the issue of being a mere echo of the
order of things, which normalizes me, and constitutes even the yardsticks by which
I will evaluate and reflect on 'my' and 'foreign' values, codes, and apparatuses, which
determine the horizons even of my resistance, refusal, and destruction?"

According to Luke and Gore, the aim of feminist critical pedagogy is to constitute
daily pedagogical situations that empower students, to demystify canonical knowledge, and to show the ways in which relations of domination oppress the subjects in
terms of gender, race, class, and many other characteristics of their difference.[35]

According to Weiler, critical pedagogy in general, and Freire's version in particular,
are based on a vision of social transformation. Feminist pedagogy is presented within
this framework, and it also shares the assumptions about oppression and the possibilities of historical change. Implicitly negating Marx's theory on the relations between
base and superstructure, Weiler claims that the two pedagogies share an assumption
that human existence, in specific material conditions, is framed within repressive conditions, which are part of consciousness; both pedagogies understand consciousness as
something which is more than the sum of dominant discourses. Both view consciousness as having a critical potential, and both conceive human beings as subjects and
as functioning within historical horizons. At the same time, both are committed to
a vision of emancipatory possibilities, to a better world where justice prevails in the
end.[36]

Within the framework of feminist pedagogy, some emphasize the differences between feminist pedagogy and critical pedagogy to the point of complete detachment,

---

35   Carmen Luke and Jennifer Gore (eds.), "Introduction", *Feminisms and Critical Pedagogy*, New York
     and London: Routledge, 1992, p. 1.
36   Kathlen Weiler, "Freire and a Feminist Pedagogy of difference", *Harvard Educational Review* 61: 4
     (November 1991), p. 450.

and some try to maintain some common ground even within the framework of post-modern feminist critical pedagogy.

The critique of critical theory and "paternalistic" critical pedagogy takes place on two levels, the political and the philosophical. Oppositional stands on the political level largely incubate and obscure basic agreement with the philosophical conceptions of critical theory. By contrast, relatively minor disagreements on the political level sometimes hide commitments to basically different philosophical projects.

Elizabeth Ellsworth, a central figure of postmodern feminist pedagogy, started her project from within critical education.[37] Today she criticizes critical pedagogy with a postmodern rhetoric and negates critical theory and the "arrogance" of the Enlighten-ment's entire emancipatory project. Ellsworth's negation of metaphysics, foundation-alism, and metanarratives amounts to *anti-intellectualism* and abandonment of every speculative, comprehensive, or even holistic theory. In this she represents postmod-ern feminist critical pedagogy's abandonment of the critical pedagogy spirit and its struggle for human emancipation. No wonder Ellsworth founds her critique on her "private experience".

Here "private experience", "personal-ness" or "subjectivity" and its drives become an alternative spring to the reflective mind. But what kind of "experience" we are faced with here, when addressing the questions of the "not-I" constituting itself as the matrix of the postmodern "I" who "experiences"-"creates"-"deconstructs"-"plays" "her" self? Is it a Dionysian **will to power** that experiences and activates its generous creative powers? Or is it an echo of a very different kind, which represent an opposite movement, away from *Life* into another flat, mechanistic, anti-vitalist dynamism, whose *Danse Macabre* is activated by the music of Thanatus, namely decadence, while poeticizing the words of the quasi-erotic pleasure-machine and unlimited crea-tion/deconstruction? There is no renaissance here for the Nietzschean tension of self-creativity and destiny, on the one hand, or for the issues of subjectification and the omnipotence of the symbolic dynamics which govern the discourse, on the other.

To my mind, Ellsworth pretends to liberate the feminist educational project not from a defined theoretical stand but from theory per se—in favor of fashionable post-modern and postcolonialist rhetoric, in other words, in favor of fashion as such. This *liberation of feminist pedagogy from critical theory and from theory per se* inevitably transforms-enslaves the emancipatory spirit to dogmatic essentialist symbolic con-tingencies in two wings: to solipsism on the one hand, and to ethnocentrism on the other. She dismisses any theory that is rationally dependable. She refuses any assertion that is to be exposed as a "Western, modern patriarchalism" constructed as "elitist Western knowledge"; there is no room in her pedagogy for knowledge which was manifested, tested, or realized "violently" within the Western idealist framework. And so, central concepts of critical pedagogy such as class, human nature/needs, emanci-pation, or even "critique" become groundless, ridiculed, indefensible, or completely impossible. This postmodern feminist critique, however, also refers to the horizons,

---

37   Elizabeth Ellsworth, "Educational films against critical pedagogy", *Journal of Education,* 169: 3, (1987), p. 33.

orientations, and foundations of technological and scientific developments. It is of much relevance to the elaboration of the concept of "critique" and it is of vital importance for understanding the stance of critical pedagogy. But it acts in a way which is philosophically wrong and politically dangerous.

Ellsworth attacks the naivety of critical pedagogy's concept of dialogue. She emphasizes its *repressive-paternalistic* dimensions, as manifested in the critical pedagogies of Freire, McLaren, Shor, and Giroux. She forgets that as regards the Enlightenment's ideals and their effect on the orchestration of critical pedagogies they are influenced by the Frankfurt School's critical theory in its *first stage* of development. At that early stage of their intellectual development the Frankfurt School thinkers were still committed to positive utopianism, and were thus optimistic about the possibilities open for emancipation and their work was potentially repressive. Ellsworth criticizes in this light, for example, Giroux's concept of dialogue in the classroom, where students are supposed to manifest "trust, partnership and commitment to develop human conditions".[38]

An important element in Giroux's thesis is that the specific assertions of his positive utopianism are not predetermined. However, even in his thesis the partners to the dialogue must be able to agree on the purpose, limits, and regulations for change and for constituting a consensus concerning the dialogue. According to his scheme, *all* relevant voices and all actual differences are united in their efforts to form a worthy dialogical existence and to challenge certain moments of human suffering. As such they are also obliged to overcome the conditions that reproduce this kind of suffering.[39]

Ellsworth denounces the illusion of such a utopian dialogue. She challenges *the oppressive potential of the "we"* that is supposed to be a precondition for the dialogic revolt of the oppressed, as characterized by Giroux and the other patriarchs of critical pedagogy who follow the steps of critical theory of the Frankfurt School thinkers.[40] Following Judith Butler, Ellsworth emphasizes the omnipotence of social and cultural manipulations of the consciousness, and the effects of its theories about the world and about the self. Here her critique is of special value. However, if the subject is *totally* constructed,[41] there is no way for the human subject genuinely to escape manipulations, criticize and refuse injustice, or even partially constitute her identity; and certainly, under these conditions, it is impossible genuinely to change the rules/codes/telos/effects of the discourse or social reality for the better. Even the moderate ideal of *resistance as a manifestation of potential freedom* becomes impossible under such pre-conditions. What are the value and the telos of feminist pedagogy within such a theoretical framework?

---

38   Henry Giroux, "Literacy, the pedagogy of voice and political empowerment", *Educational Theory* 38, (1988), p. 72.
39   *Ibid.*
40   Elizabeth Ellsworth, "Why doesn't it feel empowering? Working through the repressive myths of Critical pedagogy". *Harvard Educational Review* 59: 3, (1989), p. 315.
41   Judith Butler, *Bodies that Matter: On the Discursive Limits of "Sex"*, New York and London: Routledge 1993, p. 124.

This is where this trend, represented by Ellsworth's postmodernism, differs from the other trend represented by Weiler, who shares with Freire and other critical pedagogy thinkers the Enlightenment's concept of the autonomy and reflective potential of men and women in their communities:

> Thus, like Freirean pedagogy, feminist pedagogy is grounded in the vision of social change. And like Freirean pedagogy, feminist pedagogy rests on truth claims of the primacy of experience and consciousness that are grounded in historically situated social change movements. [42]

The important issue here, however, is that within the postmodern setting of both trends in present-day feminist pedagogy there is no way of challenging the "experience" of the subjectified "subject" within the omnipotence of the discourse, and the tyranny of all-penetrating power-relations/games in the "world" as a metaphor for intersubjectivity in given conditions that have to be critically reconstructed, developed, and rationally changed as part of an ongoing creative dialogue. This is a positive and abstract Utopia. It is negated by Life every moment anew in a capitalist society. The capitalist moment, however, only signals the concealment of Being.

The retreat into the rhetoric of the omnipotence of the matrix, or into celebrating being drawn into *the pleasure machine* or into simplistic "resistance" and "transformation", is part of this veil.

The flight from existential, theoretical, and political acknowledgement, and from a Diasporic nomadic existence in always broken manifestations of the totality of Being, is not a way of saving individuality but the opposite; it surrenders the eros, the quest, and actualization of the human potential for autonomy, responsibility, and happiness in face of worthy suffering as a Diasporic coming-into-being. In doing so, this project abandons human need and the human potential for non-violent edifying intersubjectivity and for transcending the self-evidence, which is also the omnipotent matrix. As such it opposes the essence of feminism when it is true to itself.

Like many other radical feminists of the last decade, following Michel Foucault, Ellsworth tries to avoid being committed to a project that is determined "to control justice and truth", as part of a non-hierarchical feminist alternative to the elitism and the immanent violence of the modern *Western* patriarchal rationalistic emancipatory project which unavoidably leads to colonialism, racism, and ethnocentrism.

As a realization of this alternative, Ellsworth's feminist pedagogy suggests "a politics of partial narratives",[43] and it is of vital importance for her to separate her feminist pedagogy from critical pedagogy,[44] as a manifestation of Western cultural colonialism. Even critical pedagogy's attempt to proceed from Marcuse's ontological and episte-

---

42   Kathleen Weiler "Freire and a Feminist Pedagogy of difference", *Harvard Educational Review* 61: 4 (November 1991), 456.

43   Elizabeth Ellsworth, "Why doesn't it feel empowering? Working through the repressive myths of critical pedagogy", p. 303.

44   *Ibid.*, p. 116.

mological universal assumptions and obligations to more modest assumptions, like
Habermas's ambition to develop the critical discursive abilities of the speech community,[45] as pedagogically presented in the critical pedagogy of Stanley Aronowitz and
Wolfgang Klafki, is denounced and negated. Habermas's aim is to synthesize subjectivity and intersubjectivity, *Zwekrationalitaet* and *Vertrationalitaet*, which brings him
to the point of representing himself as the one to develop and correct the "old critical
theory".[46] Perhaps this is the reason for blaming him for offering a project which is
committed to silencing the different "voices" of the students,[47] which come from different cultural, gender, or racial backgrounds.

However, Ellsworth's attempt to escape what she conceives as the immanent violence of every "theory", and her attempt to find rescue in the safe haven of her personal "experience", the self-evidence of the oppressed, or impotent nihilism, are far from
offering anti-elitism or any genuine new vitalist spiritual power. On the contrary, this
stand is to be understood as the manifestation of the power dynamics and the conceptual limitations of the system against which this postmodern feminist pedagogy is
supposed to rebel. Such a politically correct response to celebrated postmodern rhetoric does not represent a new *spirit*. It does not open a space for a new hermeneutics
of the individual or the collective. Nor does it offer a new, courageous, beginning for
the struggle against the mystifications of the hegemonic power-relations in the present
realm of self-evidence. Ellsworth's alternative has no room for struggle for more equality, justice, freedom, and understanding. Love, beauty, justice, and happiness become
unreachable, as irrelevant insofar as they do not constitute space for anti-collectivism
and for the free human spirit. Nor does her alternative offer the impetus and the guidance for *transcendence* from a too comfortable human dwelling in the meaninglessness
of the established matrix as "home sweet home". It does not seek human solidarity or
other dimensions of negative utopianism that condition the type of dialogue representing the "heavenly eros" of Plato or the "negative imagination" of Adorno and the
humanist tradition at its best. And it certainly does not prepare its students to face the
culture war or *the coalition between postcolonialism and the world of Jihad*. It does not
invite students to insist on cosmopolitanism and nomadism in an era when capitalism
is ready (in the name of rationality within the framework of post-Fordism) to crush
every challenge—while losing all traditional orientations; this is also an era when the
enemies of democracy are ready to destroy all humanity and to redeem themselves as
courageous *shahid*s or as genuine-merciless representatives of the free market. For this
tradition, universalism, emancipation, and comprehensive theory were unsupported
by individualism within non-repressive intersubjectivity that constitutes, and constantly reformulates and transcends, the individuals' potentialities and realities.

The negative impulse of the dialogue is part of *ontological homelessness* which makes
possible a Diasporic existence, creation, and improvisation. It offers a non-ethno-

---

45   Juergen Habermas, *Theorie des Kommunikativen Handels*, Frankfurt a. Main: Suhrkamp, 1981.
46   *Ibid.*, p. 462.
47   Elizabeth Ellsworth, "Why doesn't it feel empowering? Working through the repressive myths of
      Critical pedagogy", *Harvard Educational Review*, 59: 3, (1989), p. 304.

centric-oriented human solidarity, and as such it refuses violence, even in the form of postcolonialist counter-violence. It acquires meaning only by realizing itself reflectively, aesthetically, ethically, physically, and pragmatically. Foucault, Lyotard, Guattari, and Deleuze, whose influence on postmodern feminist pedagogy is of vital importance, themselves represent a position which to an untrained ear might recite fairly similar poems.

According to Deleuze

> We had no taste for abstractions, Unity, Totality, Reason, Subject. We set ourselves the task of analyzing mixed forms, arrangements, what Foucault called apparatuses… We weren't looking for origins, even lost or deleted ones, but setting out to catch things where they were at work, in the middle.[48]

Post-critical pedagogy abandons the critical pedagogy impulse, with its denunciation of intellectualism, universalism, and "metaphysics". This trend is brilliantly advocated by Patti Lather.

In face of recent attempts to re-articulate critical pedagogy, to which *Educational Theory* has devoted a special issue, Lather offers the "hard" postmodern rhetoric on the ground that such attempts are "a boy thing". When she refers specifically to the two oppositional attempts to reconstruct critical pedagogy she explains that

> this is due not so much to the two lead authors being male as it is to the way in which both essays exhibit the masculinist voice of abstraction and universalism, assuming the rhetorical position of 'the one who knows', what Ellsworth calls 'the One with the 'Right' Story'".[49]

Lather offers an alternative, namely to

> salvage praxis in a post-Marxist time… Rather than the 'one right story,' what I propose in Jones's subversive repetition of the ruins of critical pedagogy is a knowing with/in our doing, what Derrida terms 'to do and to make come about, as well as to let come (about)'.[50]

It is difficult to draw a sharp distinction between this feminist pedagogy and other feminist pedagogies that conceive themselves as being within the framework of critical pedagogy. They too are trying to develop an anti-elitist anti-Western-colonialist-pedagogical-practice, founded on the "voice" and the self-evident knowledge of the op-

---

48 Gilles Deleuze, *Negotiations: 1972–1990*, translated by Joughin, M. New York, Columbia University Press, 1995, p, 86.

49 Patti Lather, "Critical pedagogy and its complicities: A praxis of struck places", *Educational Theory* 48: 4, pp. (1988), p. 488.

50 *Ibid.*, p. 494.

pressed collectives, emphasizing their ethnic, cultural, race, class, and sexual uniqueness as a source for worthier interests, superior perspectives, and preferable strivings
and codes which collide with those of the colonialist-oriented West. The silenced
voice that is here conceived as deserving legitimacy and empowerment is uncritically
assumed to evolve into a manifestation of legitimate alternative life possibilities. As
such it contains genuine anti-Diasporic emancipatory dimensions—even in the form
of rhetoric manipulations, authoritative education, militaristic values, suicide bombers, and other manifestations of justified "counter-violence" of the oppressed. It is not
so much that these do not emancipate effectively. It is the kind of "emancipation"
that is realized within this postcolonialist agenda. This kind of emancipating might
really offer the oppressed a sense of regaining honor, meaning, and hope. This victory,
however, is a triumph of anti-Diasporic education. Postmodern feminist education,
regretfully, is part and parcel of this triumph. But its victory over counter-education
and the potential Diasporic existence is never complete.

It is not very surprising that within the framework of postmodern feminist critical
pedagogy this potential is not realized. This is because in this version of postmodernism the emancipatory impulse is drawn into an automatic resistance to genuine
reflection and self-critique.

Feminist critical pedagogy, however, is intellectually restless on this point. As critical theory's rebellious pupils, these thinkers are explicitly still committed to reflection and to critique, and as postmodernists they are bona fide elitists. This raises the
problematic of *the position of the intellectual* and her *authority* within the framework
of feminist pedagogy. While paying tribute to the personal experience and to the
knowledge of the oppressed it reassures the supremacy of the (feminist) intellectual
as an arch-educator:

> Feminist educators like Fischer and Bunch accept their authority as
> intellectuals and theorists, but they consciously attempt to construct
> their pedagogy to recognize and encourage the capacity of their stu-
> dents to theorize and to recognize their own power.[51]

In this sense there is no difference between the "paternalistic"/"authoritative" dimensions of Freire's critical pedagogy and those of feminist critical pedagogy. The foundation of the authority claimed here is nothing other than *the good intentions and
the wisdom of the feminist intellectual*. What a problematic justification! Other feminists question this position as "simply a patriarchal mode of gaining and maintaining
power, a way of negating women's everyday experience, a means of separating some
women from the rest…".[52]

The political resemblance between this feminist critical pedagogy and the rhetoric
of postmodern post-critical feminist pedagogy enables the latter, as in the case of
Ellsworth, to take advantage of the former. The important educational work of femi-

51   Kathleen Weiler, "Freire and a Feminist Pedagogy of difference", p. 462.
52   Bernice Fischer, "Guilt and shame in Women's Movement", *Feminist Studies*, 10, (1984), p. 202.

nist critical pedagogy, which is represented by women like Gore, Kohli, Luke, and Weiler (that is, explicitly anti-elitist and non-academic), is ultimately forced to serve the academic success of the feminist elitism that Ellsworth represents. In representing an elitist alternative, Ellsworth does not offer an alternative to naive positive utopianism or any alternative educational theory.[53]

Ellsworth suggests a feminist-oriented post-colonialism that demands/envisions the peaceful coexistence of different communities and identities which are committed to and constituted by different knowledge, criteria to judge knowledge, interests, and goals. Within her proposed framework the different bodies of knowledge and the different conceptions about knowledge are all conceived as legitimate and incommensurable, and there is no way to evaluate one or some of them as better, valid, or invalid. The aim of education, according to Ellsworth, should be the nurturing of competence for cooperation across differences that will constitute temporary, local, and partial agreements for the sake of "the common good".

On the one hand the postcolonialist vision of dialogue within/across/between cultural differences falls ultimately into *a reversed ethnocentrism* enhanced by the marginalized. The discourse of "difference" becomes a safe haven for an automatic justification of its "internal" and "external" symbolic and direct violences. It is so common to hear from these postcolonialist educators "understanding" and justifications for Hizbullah, Hamas, Al-Qaida and other representatives of the world of Jihad and the promise of suicide bombers. It is actually but another version of normalizing education. On the other hand, dialogue, transcendence, and love are abandoned in favor of the deconstructed subjectivity and fluid exchange/recycling of "identities" which are but manifestations of the laws and dynamics of the various normalizing apparatuses. On both fronts this ideology does not challenge the logic or the actual practices of capitalism and ethnocentrism. This is since it is but one of the products and manifestations of the current capitalist mode of cultural production itself.

Ellsworth's project signifies a reality that cannot guarantee the success of deconstructing universals as long as suffering, meaninglessness, and the capitalist presence are determining discourses, existential possibilities, and material realities. At the same time, the celebrated praise of the local, partial, and temporary can only be victorious in the form of dissolving the very categories of "woman", "emancipation", "meaning", and "love".

Within the framework of this project, "woman" as a category and as a specific and concrete identity might disintegrate into innumerable identities, interests, and bodies of knowledge that will strive fully to realize themselves. They might be objects for endless deconstruction and border-crossings of identities that are never within themselves, never have a "self", never are a concrete "identity" or subject.

Linda Alcoff admits this danger of extreme deconstruction of essences and identities for unrepressed feminism, and she looks for a Foucaultian philosophical and

53   Nicholas Burbules and Susane Rice, "Dialogue across differences: continuing the conversation" *Harvard Educational Theory*, 61: 4, (1991), p. 399.

political solution within the framework of "cultural feminism",[54] which has important educational potential and which should have attracted more attention within
postmodern feminist pedagogy. As Seyla Benhabib observes, the "strong" postmodernist version of the "Death of the Subject" is not compatible even with the goals
of feminism.[55] Benhabib's claim is valid against postmodern feminism as reflected
in Ellsworth's postmodern post-critical feminist pedagogy when she asserts-asks: "if
this view of the self is adopted, is there any possibility of changing those 'expressions'
which constitute us?"[56] Therefore she negates postmodern feminism's understanding
of subjectivity as mere extensions of our histories on the one hand, and postmodern
essentialism in its multicultural and solipsist versions on the other. While accepting
parts of the postmodern critique of humanist universalism,[57] as a woman committed to feminist and human emancipation in general Benhabib resists the attempts to
abandon the Enlightenment's Utopia of human emancipation.[58]

This trend is shared by Carmen Luke, after a period of high hopes for the enrichment of critical pedagogy by postmodernist philosophies as an alternative to the phallocentrism of critical pedagogy itself.

> Feminist pedagogy [she writes in retrospect] conceptualized as (mater-
> nal) nurture and distanced from claims of pedagogical authority and
> institutional power, leaves itself wide open to the theoretical impos-
> sibility of having a 'foundation' from which to arbitrate knowledge,
> student voices and experiences, and the teacher's own epistemological
> position. I argue, therefore, that the theoretical turn to and celebration
> of difference in all feminisms, including feminist pedagogy, raises cru-
> cial epistemological and political questions about normativity which,
> in turn, call into question the theoretical validity and political agenda
> of feminism's 'truth claims'.[59]

This stand is a starting-point also for criticizing postmodern feminist post-critical pedagogy and post-feminist critical pedagogy feminisms. At the same time, these
trends might be included as radical versions of postmodern feminist critical pedagogy
or as their worthy transformation. Cyberfeminism might be a good example.

According to Plant,

---

54   Linda Alcoff, "Cultural feminism versus post-structuralism: the identity crisis in feminist theory",
     Journal of Women in Culture and Society 13: 3, (1988), p. 406.
55   Seyla Benhabib, *Feminist Contentions: A Philosophical Exchange*, New York : Routledge, 1995, p. 20.
56   *Ibid.*, p. 21.
57   Seyla Benhabib, *Situating the Self: Gender, Community and Postmodernism in Contemporary Ethics*,
     Oxford: Blackwell, 1992, p. 3.
58   *Ibid.*, p. 30.
59   Carmen Luke, "Feminist pedagogy theory: reflections on power and authority", *Educational Theory*,
     46: 3, (1996), p. 284.

cyberfeminism is an insurrection on the part of the gods and materials
of the patriarchal world, a dispersed, distributed emergence composed
of links between women, women and computers, computers and communication links, connections and connectionist Nets.[60]

Zoe Sofoulis, another representative of "hard" postmodernism in cyberfeminism, celebrates the post-phallic conjunction of women's art and high-tech.[61] It is a strong
promising illusion: Western culture, which in modern technology reaches the peak
of the perverse realization of the Greek concept of *techne*,[62] overcomes its immanent
instrumentalism and reificationist-orientation in cyberspace. Cyberfeminism, within
this concrete Utopia, is a prima facie postmodern arena where *the essence of femininity and art replaces masculinity* and the essence of Western "internal" and "external"
colonialism and its commitment to truth-light-victory-efficiency-death. The logic of
the Net is conceived as manifesting the truth of femininity: it is symbolized by the
clitoris inheriting the Thanatus-oriented masculine drive for truth and victory as symbolized by the phallus. Cyberfeminism, however, includes a rich range of views on
these matters.

Representatives of the "soft" postmodern influences on cyberfeminism have explicit
feminist emancipatory perspectives and they refuse to see themselves as post-feminists
or as post-human. Cyberfeminism is one of many realizations of cyberoptimism,[63]
which contains both "hard" and "soft" postmodern perspectives and contains some
(transformed) elements of the emancipatory project.

According to the cyberoptimists, cyberspace has no room for traditional Western
metaphysical and actual violence. *The identification of the immanent colonialist-oriented violence of Western normalizing education and the critique of phallocentrism and
patriarchalism meet here* in a manner that leaves unchallenged oppressive non-Western
and anti-Western educational violences in all their forms, as long as they are ecstatically "radical" and offer a new, "postcolonialist", racism that challenges "whiteness",
"Western canon" or "Israeli-American colonialism". The fruits of this attitude will be
the sophistication of violent normalizing education and the enrichment of electronic
normalizing education.

Of vital importance for cyberfeminism is the "overcoming" of "masculine" or "phallocentristic"-oriented claims for universality, eternity, objectivity, transcendence, and
a priori validity judgment claims, which parallels its abandonment of traditional immanent Western commitment to violate the otherness of the Other. According to
Plant

---

60 Sadie Plant, "On the matrix: cyberfeminist simulations", in: Shields, Rob. *Cultures of the Internet:
    Virtual Spaces, Real Histories, Living Bodies*, London: Farber and Farber 1996, p. 162.

61 Zeo Sofoulis, "Slime in the matrix: post-phallic formations in women's art in the new media", in: Jill
    Julius Matthews (ed.), *Jane Gallop Seminar Papers*, Canberra 1994.

62 Heidegger, *op. cit.*, pp. 307–342

63 Ilan Gur-Ze'ev, "Cyberfeminism and education in the era of the exile of spirit", *Educational Theory*
    49: 4, (1999), pp. 437–456.

The phallus and the eye stand in for each other, giving priority to light, sight, and flight from the dark matters of the feminine. The phallic eye has functioned to endow them with the connection to what has variously been defined as God, the good, the one, the ideal form or transcendence.[64]

In contrast to Western phallocentristic-oriented knowledge and patriarchal-dominated existence, *in computer-mediated communication as a nomadic postcolonialist space the order is supposed to be feminine* and connectionist, associative, and kaleidoscopic and open—not linear, hierarchical, and closed. According to Steffensen, the phallus, linear thinking, hierarchy, transcendence, and domination are replaced by the female clitoris, which is conceived as "a direct line to the matrix".[65]

Donna Haraway posits a post-feminist "hard" postmodern Messianism, in which

The dichotomies between mind and body, animal and human, organism and machine, public and private, nature and culture, men and women, primitive and civilized are all in question ideologically.[66]

This is a new kind of Messianism, which presents itself as dystopia, yet it is a new, postcolonialist *positive Utopia*, committed to feminize the world[67] in a manner that will not make possible transcendence or a quest for redemption, meaning, or Diasporic Life. **The totally other** is here totally *realized* as a matrix or realm of self-evidence. The subject and her autonomy/oppression become here radically transformed, and the Enlightenment's ideal of the self-creating dialogical subject is overtaken by the postmodern cyborg.[68]

The implicit philosophy of education in Haraway's texts proceeds from the concepts accepted in postmodern feminist critical pedagogy to a new horizon. She opens a complete alternative, beyond transcendence and immanence, beyond relativism, temporality, and partiality, in a world of total contingency and *incommensurability as an improved Garden of Eden*. This positive utopia contains a rich educational philosophy even if it refrains from presenting itself as such. It neither presents an alternative "homecoming" project for transcendence or redemption nor does it offer an alternative concept of worthy exile. Alternatively, *she offers a quasi-Diasporic dwelling in the deconstructed totality as worthy "home"*, beyond "good and evil", "truth and fiction", "beautiful-ugly", "transcendence-immanence" or even "Diasporic-anti-Di-

---

64   Plant, *op. cit.*, p. 172.
65   Jyanni Steffensen, "Slimy metaphors for technology: 'the clitoris is a direct line to the matrix'", http://ensemle.va.co.au/array/steff_01.html, p. 1.
66   Dona Haraway, *Simias, Cyborgs, and Women: The Reinvention of Nature*, New York: Routledge 1991, p. 150.
67   Plant, *op. cit.*, p. 1.
68   *Ibid.*, p. 149.

asporic". This philosophy is consistently developed to its logical conclusions within the postmodern feminist critical pedagogy of Ellsworth and Lather, which perhaps for political reasons pertains to a pedagogical rhetoric which their philosophical pre-assumption and their articulations fail to support, justify, or edify.

This *quasi-Diasporic* that is actually anti-Diasporic philosophy is further developed by "hard" postmodern feminists and by post-feminist authors who try to open new educational-philosophical-political-existential horizons. Here the work of Deleuze plays a special role. As such it can serve best postcolonialists such as Homy Bhabha and "hard" post-feminists, as well as the postmodern-post-critical pedagogy educational thinkers such as Lather and Ellsworth.

Deleuze's work is relevant to postmodern feminist critical pedagogy in the sense that it further develops and justifies the abandonment of the ideal of emancipation, the desertion of responsibility for the otherness of the Other, the centrality of the cultivation and edification of the (potentially) autonomous subject, and the possibility of reflection or ideology-critique which will make possible not solely meaning and aim but also creative bettering of the world.

Deleuze is against philosophy as transcendence. What he defines as radical empiricism, or transcendental empiricism, is actually an *anti-transcendental philosophy* in a way that will guarantee the deconstruction of the subject and the doing away with any meaning. Deleuze is committed to philosophy as a project of destroying "generality and particularity, Man and the man, but also Woman and the woman".[69] To do away with the subject is to do away with any ground or home or thought. This is the essence of "becoming-woman" for Deleuze and Guattari. It is not that the category of woman or the emancipation of woman, or understanding/resisting women's oppression, is here the telos of the project.

Does postmodern feminist enthusiasm represent a deep understanding of Deleuze? Or is it more of a regrettable misunderstanding of his philosophy, when they celebrate post-critical pedagogy imperatives? One such imperative is that offered by Deleuzian Messianism, when he says with Guattari:

> If becoming-woman is the first quantum, or molecular segment, with the becoming-animal that link up with it coming next, what are they all rushing towards? Without a doubt, toward a becoming-imperceptible. The imperceptible is the immanent end of becoming, its cosmic formula.[70]

He calls us to overcome, or abandon, dichotomies, criteria, or "conflicts"; they are not to be reconstructed, resisted, enhanced, or developed into understandings and

---

69   Ian Buchanan, *Deleuzism—A Commentary*, Edinburgh: Edinburgh University Press, 2000, p. 193.
70   Gilles Deleuze, and Felix Guattari, *A Thousand Plateaus—Capitalism and Schizophrenia*, translated by Mussumi, Brian. Minneapolis: University of Minnesota press 1987, p. 279.

solutions of the modern kind, since underneath a "conflict" there is never more than "the play of differences".[71]

If cyberfeminism strives to affirm Thanatus by being swallowed by the pleasure machine within which there is room only for the cyborg in the run to meaninglessness and nothingness, for Deleuze the road invites us to struggle imperceptibility with no transcendence, emancipation or redemption. The Deluezian telos is that of an all-becoming which is synonymous with a cosmic perception, in other words, with the total disappearance of the subject.[72] Following Mainlaender and the other most radical figures of philosophical pessimism,[73] for him the totality as nothingness is the ultimate aim of all becoming. Within this framework he articulates the category of "becoming-woman" which has attracted so much enthusiasm in postmodern feminism and among postmodern feminist philosophers of education.[74] Following Ellsworth and Lather, these trends celebrate a Deleuzian *"responsibility for 'non-mastery'" out of the "ordeal of the undividable".*[75]

The Deleuzian category of "rhizome" is very much at the center of some current postmodern feminist critical pedagogy projects that I see as post-feminist and post-critical pedagogy. Here the "hard" postmodern trends within postmodern feminist critical pedagogy develop to their logical conclusion. The concepts of nomadism and *rhizomatics* for Deleuze have much in common with the kind of "*connectedness*" that Haraway and other cyberoptimists make use of in their postmodern Utopia.

> The line-system (or block-system) of becoming is opposed to the point-system of memory. Becoming is the movement by which the line frees itself from the point, and renders points indiscernible: the rhizome, the opposite of arborescence, a break away from arborescence. Becoming is an antimemory.[76]

Rhizomatic existence, however, is far from a vision of an unlimited and unpredicted internal and external creation/becoming. What Deleuze tries to overcome is not solely the Oedipal molar constructs as opposed to the nomadic Body Without Or-

---

71   Gilles Deleuze, *Difference and Repetition*, translated by Joughin, M. New York: Columbia University Press, 1994, p. 51.

72   Gilles Deleuze, *Essays Critical and Clinical*, translated by Smith, D. and Greco, M. Minneapolis: University of Minnesota Press, 1997, p. 25.

73   Gur-Ze'ev, *Frankfurt School and The History of Pessimism*, 1996.

74   Inna Semtesky, "Continuities: Dewey, Deleuze and the possibility of spiritual education", *Philosophy of Education Society of Great Britain Annual Conference*, New College, Oxford, 2000, pp. 377–385.
Inna Semtesky, "Deleuze's new image of thought, or Dewey revisited", *Educational Philosophy and Theory*, 35: 1. (1993), pp. 17–28.
Zelia Gregoriou, "Performing pedagogy with Deleuze: the rhizomatics of 'the theory of education'", *Philosophy of Education Society of Great Britain Annual Conference*, New College, Oxford, 2002, pp. 227–237.

75   Gregoriou, *Ibid.*, p. 235.

76   Gilles Deleuze and Felix Guattari, *op.cit.*, p. 294.

gans. *Nomadism here is conceived as part of overcoming subject/object dichotomies*, as well as man-woman, or true-false dichotomies. It is not that "either-or" dichotomies are abandoned; it is that the very "existence" or "meaning" is abandoned in favor of concept-creation. Within this philosophical framework it is not an autonomous moral subject who is creating. It is not a dialogical self-edifying *human* who is in the center: ultimately, it is mere *relations* that present themselves and realize themselves as constitutive, as giving birth, as Life. In such a world there is room for rhizomatic creation but no room for meaningful suffering, responsibility, hope and hugging, love or resistance to evil, and surely no hope for non-violent transcendence as a moment of "difference" where we respond to the call of **the totally other**. Counter-violence is central to Deleuze, as he envisions a new "war machine" that will challenge the "state apparatuses".[77] The apparent similarities between the Diasporic philosophy of Adorno and the Deleuzian vision of nomadic life in rhizomatic spaces is exposed as a successful deception, realized by nothing but *the cannibalism of the postmodern pleasure machine* (which presents itself as "beyond postmodernism"). Once you overcome the deconstructionist carnivalist suggestion you see that these are actually two opposing utopian projects.

In this sense *we should acknowledge that the pleasure machine has the upper hand*. It is not only that the sole serious challenge to the McDonaldization of the post-Fordist world is offered by the world of Jihad. It is also that the post-colonialist critique is bonded in the Jihad's alternative and the postmodern promise anchors its postcolonialist and anti-phallocentrist hopes to the most advanced post-critical agenda of "hard" postmodernism. And so Gregoriou tells us that she finds Deleuze a worthy source for advancing current philosophy of education and pedagogical practices, as an alternative to pedagogy of the postmodern, which "has failed to legitimate itself in the eyes of the students".[78]

Not only has part of postmodern feminist critical pedagogy become post-critical. At the present moment of its development it deserts not only critical pedagogy but also feminism, and ultimately "soft" postmodernism itself. The more it becomes open to "harder" postmodern influences, the more it becomes politically neutralized and philosophically pessimistic-oriented. Its importance, nevertheless, is not to be underestimated.

Post-critical feminist pedagogy is in many respects an echo of postmodern rhetoric. It is so in two versions that are theoretically incompatible but politically and rhetorically often amalgamated.

Within the first, feminism tries, in vain, to retreat from speculative theory, human solidarity, and transcendence into the safe haven of the "self". Here the "self" is supposed to be at once the impetus to and an affect of "creativity" and "resistance". It is at once an omnipotent gaze, or a unique "listening" and "responding", which ultimately reveals itself as nothing more than a manifestation of meaninglessness: passions and effects of the codes of the discourse, which cannot be genuinely deciphered or tran-

77   *Ibid.*, p. 24.
78   Gregoriou, *op. cit.*, 236.

scendent. Almighty immanence is uncompromisingly "flat". Within this philosophy all de-territorializations, re-positionings, deconstructions, and creative effects can manifest and realize nothing but *contingent violent discourses*, powers, and structures. But we should ask: If the "self" is nothing but their echo how can she genuinely "resist" it or offer interests and conclusions other than the contingency they are effects of? And in what sense is she its victim? And what justifies the acknowledgement of her being an agent or its "echo"? All these questions are to be asked even before we ask: "In what sense is 'she' as some-thing, and not some-one, actually different from me, who voice her as a victim/agent of the system?" Here the abandoning of critical pedagogy's Utopia of dialogue, solidarity, and rational change of reality is negated, devoid of Nietzschean joyfulness, pre-Socratic naivety about experience, and the positivistic-sophistication of 20th-century logical positivism.

Today's decadent sophistication is more of a fashionable rhetoric with no promise of Life or even of a tragic end to this part of the human odyssey. It has lost even the sense of serious nihilism or of *tragic heroism*, which were so dear to Spengler's rejection of the Enlightenment's concept of progress in the previous *fin de siècle*.[79] These thinkers even refrain from rearticulating the essence of the humanist project, which insists that the human is after all more than, and infinitely different from, the power structures that influence her within the framework of normalizing education.

The second version, which negates critical theory and critical pedagogy's humanistic universalism, retreats into the realm of *self-evidence of the marginalized*, the silenced, the oppressed, and the misrepresented. It abandons humanistic universalism and its Utopia. It introduces, instead, an unreflective optimism and functionalist instrumentalism.

Lather presents postmodern feminist pedagogy as an *alternative* to "philosophies of presence, which assume the historical role of self-conscious human agency and the vanguard role of critical intellectuals"[80] while reserving a future role for critical pedagogy.[81] All this, however, occurs while going beyond the tradition of critical philosophy itself, not solely beyond critical pedagogy:

> Perhaps the need to look beyond old critical premises and toward continuing revision might be more palatable if displayed under the sign of (post)critical.... In translating critical theory into pedagogical agenda, (post)critical foregrounds movement beyond the sedimented discursive configurations of essentialized, romanticized subjects with authentic needs and real identities, who require generalized emancipation from generalized social oppression via the mediations of liberatory

---

79   Gur-Ze'ev, *op. cit.*, pp. 30–31.
80   Patti Lather, "Post-critical pedagogies: A feminist reading", in Luke, Carmen and Gore, Jennifer (eds.), *Feminisms and Critical Pedagogy*, New York and London: Routledge, 1992, p. 131.,
81   Patti Lather, "Critical pedagogy and its complicities: A praxis of struck places", *Educational Theory*, 48: 4, (1998), p. 497.

pedagogues capable of exposing the 'real' to those caught up in the distorting meaning systems of late capitalism. [82]

According to Weiler, the source of the chief problems of critical pedagogy is the modernistic conceptualizations of the critical pedagogy thinkers, who use concepts such as "class", while the context of many of them, as in the case of Freire, contradicts the background and the possibilities of critical theory and critical pedagogy, as the ones possible in technologically advanced countries. Weiler rightly claims that even the dichotomy between oppressors and oppressed is too brutal and should be problematized in critical pedagogy.[83] Another important element in this critique challenges the sexist attitude of critical pedagogy. Even if one can find some traces of it in Freire's work, it is wrong to blame Shor, McLaren, and Giroux for it. This is politically oriented rhetoric founded on a common philosophical ground, such as that concerned with the concept of human beings held by Carmen Luke, Jennifer Gore, Kathleen Weiler, and Henry Giroux.

Weiler, in opposition to Lather and Ellsworth, aims at *saving critical pedagogy's emancipatory project* via feminist pedagogy.[84] She combines sensitivity to differences and personal experience as a founding element of knowledge[85] with the commitment to universal emancipation. However, in keeping with the fashionable rhetoric in postmodern and radical feminism, she negates "essentialism" and a comprehensive critical theory, so the concept of a certain "identity" that has to be emancipated becomes abstract. She is on the verge of an antithesis to the philosophical grounds of the emancipatory project.

Luke properly seeks the source of critical pedagogy's problematic in its relations to critical theory. In our technological, social, and cultural context, asks Luke, what value can the critical theory of Adorno, Horkheimer, and Marcuse have?[86] She shares post-critical feminist pedagogy's critique of the pedagogical actualization of critical theory as leading to or based on androgynous essentialism and naive realism. Such an education leads to the quest to *control the masses* and to activate them in a unified collective manner that will make "liberation" possible. She criticizes this stand as detached from real history and from the acknowledgment of real power-relations and actual discourse.[87]

However, at the same time she tries to avoid the kind of relativism into which Ellsworth and Lather are drawn. She does not totally abandon her modernist theoretical commitment to the power of grand narratives for reconstruction and creation. But

---

82   Lather, "Post-critical pedagogies: a feminist reading", p. 131.
83   Kathleen Weiler, "Freire and a Feminist Pedagogy of difference", *Harvard Educational Review*, 61: 4 (November 1991), p. 452.
84   *Ibid.*, p. 455.
85   *Ibid.*, pp. 463, 466.
86   Carmen Luke, "Feminist politics in radical pedagogy", *Feminisms and Critical pedagogy*, New York and London: Routledge 1992, p. 45.
87   *Ibid.*

in what sense do these two versions of postmodern feminist critical pedagogy really challenge the Frankfurt School's critical theory?

Critical Theory's concept of reason is very *different* from the one challenged by postmodern feminist critical pedagogy thinkers. Actually, they attack a straw man, and unfortunately they are too far from challenging the genuine problematic of the Frankfurt School concept of reason. In some respects critical theory as an implicit Diasporic philosophy is much closer to the concepts of reason held by Martin Heidegger, Michel Foucault, Gilles Deleuze, and Jean Lyotard than to the ones held by Juergen Habermas, Jennifer Gore, Kathleen Weiler, and Carmen Luke. This problematic is manifested brilliantly in the mature parts of the Frankfurt School critical theory, which beginning with *The Dialectics of Enlightenment* was overlooked or forgotten by critical pedagogy's friends and foes alike.

Late Adorno and Horkheimer occupied themselves in reconstructing the historical development and the concrete social and cultural circumstances of the instrumentalization of reason as *a non-reversible development* in the present historical moment.[88] Within the Western historical framework of critical theory, they conclude that unless an unpredictable interference occurs, no good intentions and progressive talent of educators devoted to radical education will be of much help in countering these developments. On the historical level, the instrumentalization of rationality is reconstructed as representing and serving the imperatives of technological progress and economic development, which have become the dominant cultural ruling logic of the McWorld. Already for Horkheimer fifty years ago instrumental rationality becomes "a magic essence", and it is right to describe it as *the triumphant return home of mythos,*[89] which leaves no room for the kind of critical human subject that the Enlightenment was committed to edify.[90]

According to the Frankfurt School's critical theory in its second stage of development, such a reality leaves no room for an alternative positive utopianism or for a positive critical pedagogy (like the one vainly attacked by feminist pedagogy today), which will challenge the present order, its apparatuses, and powers.[91] There is actually a predestined harmony between "the system" and "the victim". The human subject has become today what fascism strove to reduce her to, which is a natural human existence.[92]

The constitution of an order that represents extreme and unchallenged rationality in such a context is *irrational* from the viewpoint of traditional objective reason. This rationality is realized by almost complete control of the psychic structure and the conscious of individuals and collectives. However, this does not mean that under

---

88   Max Horkheimer, *Gesammelte Schriften*, XIV, Frankfurt a. Main: Fischer Taschenbuch Verlag, 1988, p. 141.

89   Max Horkheimer, *Eclipse of Reason*, New York: The Seabury Press, 1974, p. 96.

90   Max Horkheimer, *Gesammelte Schriften*, VII., Frankfurt a. Main: Fischer Taschenbuch Verlag, 1985, p. 26.

91   Max Horkheimer, *Eclipse of Reason*, p. 26.

92   Max Horkheimer, *Horkheimer archive* VI. 1a, pp. 26–27

such conditions there is no room *for "pluralism", namely, for false forming of the various, conflicting, modes of false critical conscious.* Such a false critical conscious can be manifested in the naive emancipatory project of "paternalist" critical pedagogy, as well as in its postmodern feminist alternatives, which are committed to positive utopianism.

The historical reconstruction of critical theory's understanding of instrumental rationality's victory, however, is complemented by a reconstruction of an *ontological* dimension which is of vital importance for the possibilities of grounding the hermeneutics of the self and the possibilities of a new educational dialogue grounded in the sensitivity and understanding of "difference".

Right from its first stage, the ontological dimension was central to the critical theory of the Frankfurt School thinkers in terms of the possibilities of emancipation and the success of counter-education in a reality where instrumental rationality celebrated its victory over the tradition of objective reason. It is manifested, for example, in Walter Benjamin's *To the Critique of Violence*,[93] in which political violence is elaborated in the historical context where there is no room for redemption but where, at the same time, the facts of actuality do not have the last word. Reality is conceived within a framework in which history is just one of its moments. The Diasporic gaze overcomes the dichotomy between transcendence and immanence. The Diasporic gaze manifests the *otherness*. Otherness is also the telos of a unique, Diasporic, kind of listening, which is both ahistorical and historical, individual and universal. Diasporic gaze and Diasporic listening relate also to the power-games of the historical moment, yet they are never to be reduced to the productivity of the governing manipulations.

Diasporic existence is never a true citizen in the Augustinian "earthly city", yet it rejects any kind of "heavenly city" or dogma to dwell in. It avoids all utopian kinds of "homecoming" and nomadism that avoids responsibility, improvisation, genuine creativity, anti-dogmatic religiosity and love of Life. In this respect, metaphorically, it is "Jewish". As such its very Diasporic existence is threatened from "within"—to become "Zionized"—and from everything "outside"—*to be either extinguished, or morally executed, as the victim who became the arch-victimizer*, the Nazi of the present day, as so many of our postcolonialist friends would claim.

To the fully developed Frankfurt School critical theory, the triumphant return of the myth within the framework of instrumental rationality is even worse today than its ancient versions. This is because of its more efficient penetrating possibilities.[94] In this context, the erosion of the possibilities for the very existence of an autonomous subject is totally neglected by most current critical thinkers. This does not mean that Benjamin, Adorno, and Horkheimer abandoned Utopia, or that from here one should ignore the educational meanings, some of which are quite close to some central conceptions and sensitivities of current postmodernism. However, one should not ignore the fact that such a critical theory repudiates the optimistic pre-assumptions

---

93   Walter Benjamin, *Zur Kritik der Gewalt und Andere Aufsaetze*, Frankfurt a.Main: Suhrkamp Taschenbuch Verlag, 1974.
94   Adorno and Horkheimer, *Op. Cit.*, p. 9.

and the positive Utopia of the dominant versions of critical pedagogy and their various alternatives.

In postmodern feminist critical pedagogy the claim for liberation is grounded in a dialectical acceptance of the *equality* of different discourses, strivings, pains, interests, identities and cultures. The very possibility of defending and developing the category of "feminism" or "woman" becomes impossible. As a result, the commitment to solidarity, as an imperative and possibility of developing and defending feminine identity and knowledge, is to be decided by the *efficiency of the violence* of symbolic dynamism and power-games which rule the social space. This version of critical pedagogy, like other major trends in current critical pedagogy, has not succeeded in synthesizing the problematic of essentialism, foundationalism, and transcendence, or the recognition of the Other's suffering, rights, and potentialities with the preconditions and claims of a philosophy that insists on human reflection, transcendence and love from the framework of philosophical pessimism.

Fully developed Frankfurt School critical theory understood the realization of Enlightenment in our era as *a mass deception* within the framework of the culture industry, in which the subject too is transformed into a commodity, including critical pedagogy's educational knowledge. The rationalization of all levels and dimensions of life and the progress of instruments and possibilities of controlling the subjects by the system[95] brought to its peak the use of the subject as a totally committed agent of reproduction of the realm of self-evidence. Under such conditions it is impossible to escape the omnipotence of the system.[96]

The historical reconstruction of dynamics suitable for the demolition of the ideal of the free rational subject and its concrete possibilities is realized here on one level. On the other, theoretical, level, according to Adorno and Horkheimer, from the very beginning "the individual" is nothing but an illusion that normally serves the strengthening of the control over people's consciousness and the construction of life possibilities that will make possible the maximization of their productivity in the service of the system in which they are activated.[97] This productivity is conditioned by the degree of their normalization, and that is the real aim of education. This subject-reason two-level concept of Adorno and Horkheimer follows Benjamin's two-level concept of time, revolution, and redemption, which they forcefully rejected in the first stage of the development of their thought in light of their Marxist positivism; but later they were so happy to abandon it only in order to embrace—and develop—Benjamin's negative utopia. This abandonment is not only a *loss*. It is also to be considered a sign of the transformation of critical theory into an explicit Diasporic philosophy which opens an alternative door to the presence of loss, worthy suffering, human edification and creativity. Of vital importance here is the Jewish concept of *hope*, which refuses a positive concept of redemption.

---

95 Mark Poster, *Critical Pedagogy Theory and Poststructuralism: In Research of a Context*, Ithaca and London: Cornell University Press, 1989, p. 67.
96 Max Horkheimer, *Eclipse of Reason*, p. 96.
97 *Ibid.*, p. 141.

Hope which emanates from theology is a central element in this concept of critical knowledge:

> Theology is—and I consciously phrase it carefully—the hope that injustice, which is typical of the world, will not have the last say… a yearning that in the end the hand of the killer will not remain on top of the innocent victim.[98]

In this sense Horkheimer's concept of hope is close to Multmann's *spero, ut intelligam*: I hope therefore I understand.[99] This is the touchstone for Benjamin's and Horkheimer's negative utopianism, which is so important for the possibility of current counter-education: the possibility of saving the purpose of the struggle for the self-constitution of a free, solidarian, Diasporic, individual; a struggle for the clarification of moral causes via social involvement, via political praxis. According to Horkheimer, "the good" may shine in spite of everything, not within a positive utopia, but in a stubborn struggle "against the ruling power",[100] a struggle with no arrogance, and lacking optimism. And this is his route for clarifying the "truth" as "the thought that rejects injustice".[101] For Horkheimer, as earlier for Benjamin, "the path is the truth".[102] This is an endless, path, whose homelessness is Diaspora, yet in a certain sense it is everywhere at home.

In opposition to the Enlightenment's vision of the common good, truth, beauty, or universal human rights, desires, and potentialities as a utopia that should be struggled for and should empower the critique of its actual negation, post-critical feminist pedagogy represents the self-evidence, the false-conciseness, and the impotence of the marginalized as foundations or "truth" to be empowered and directed against the self-evidence of the hegemonic ideology.

From this perspective, the consensus reached by the reflective subject taking part in the dialogue offered by postmodern feminist critical pedagogy represents *a misleading positive Utopia*. This is so especially in light of its declared anti-intellectualism on the one hand, and its pronounced glorification of "feelings", "experience", and self-evident knowledge of the marginalized collectives on the other.

Postmodern feminist critical pedagogy, in its different versions, claims to overcome the foundationalism and transcendentalism of Enlightenment's emancipatory and ethnocentric arrogance, as exemplified by ideology critique, psychoanalysis, or traditional metaphysics. Marginalized feminist knowledge, like the marginalized, neglected, and ridiculed knowledge of the Brazilian farmers, as presented by Freire, be-

---

98   Max Horkheimer, *Gesammelte Schriften*, VII., Frankfurt a. Main: Fischer Taschenbuch Verlag, 1985, p. 26.
99   Heinz Zahnt, *Die Sache mit Gott*, Muenchen, 1966, p. 254.
100   Adorno and Horkheimer, *op. cit.*, p. 230.
101   *Ibid.*
102   Max Horkheimer, *Dawn & Decline*, translated by Shaw, Michael. New York: Seabury Press, 1978, p. 212.

comes a model for legitimate and relevant knowledge. This knowledge is represented as the foundation for an alternative to hegemonic education, and as an alternative to the knowledge it represents as relevant, legitimate, and superior.

However, neither the truth value of the marginalized collective memory nor knowledge is cardinal here. *"Truth" as resistance to injustice is replaced here by knowledge, whose supreme criterion is the power of self-evidence*, in other words, the potential productivity of the creative violent apparatuses which put it into operation and into "being". These are the apparatuses which represent and serve the same order of things, which fabricate the human subject and her evaluation and judgment possibilities, which all function under the command of the return of the myth as an omnipotent postmodern pleasure machine. The dialogue in which adorers of "difference" take part is actually a desired production of this same pleasure machine.

From a Diasporic point of view which is true to itself, *marginalized and oppressed self-evident knowledge has no advantage over the self-evident knowledge of the oppressors.* This is also true from a consistent critical attitude.[103] Reliance on the knowledge of the controlled and marginalized collectives, on their memory, hate, and prejudices, on their conscious interests and their commitment to become hegemonic and control justice and truth, is wrong and dangerous no less than reliance on hegemonic knowledge.

Postmodern feminist pedagogies are far from courageous enough to face the promise of *worthy suffering* and to address *meaninglessness* as an ontological transcending sign of exiled meaning. For all the importance of the postmodern feminist educational critiques, and especially in light of their critique on the critical tradition, they have failed to approach the essence of the truth of educational violence. One of the main reasons for the failure of this project is its insistence on a positive utopia, on the one hand, and its rejection of a Diasporic existence on the other. It insists on *conquering the arena* and making it a safe, familiar, earthly Garden of Eden. **The fall**, it insists, must be overcome, redeemed, deconstructed, or totally ridiculed, to be redeemed and become our comfortable "home".

In all its versions, postmodern feminist critical pedagogy does not try to go beyond the transcendent-immanent dichotomies and "solutions". It is so close to doing so, yet it never makes the "tiger's leap", the concluding move, into an attempt to articulate a Diasporic philosophy of counter-education. The mature work of the Frankfurt School of Adorno and Horkheimer, which Horkheimer represented as a development of Jewish negative theology,[104] might offer us a worthy guide to such a Diasporic philosophy, which some feminist philosophers of education have sought, in the work of Deleuze and in the promise of cyberfeminism.

---

103 Ilan Gur-Ze'ev, "Toward a nonrepressive critical pedagogy", *Educational Theory*, 48: 4, (1988), p. 480.

104 Max Horkheimer, *Gesammelte Schriften*, VII, Frankfurt a. Main: Fischer Taschenbuch Verlag, 1985, pp. 386–390. See also:

Max Horkheimer, *Gesammelte Schriften*, XVIII., Frankfurt a. Main: Fischer Taschenbuch Verlag 1985, p. 183.

Here, on the edge of the creativity of Eros and Thanatus, in face of the fabrication/ deconstruction of the gap of disparity between immanence and transcendence, post-modern feminist critical pedagogy fulfills and consumes itself at its best. It is where it is so close to unveiling the absence of true Diasporic philosophy in the critical and postmodern feminist critical feminisms.

A Diasporic philosophy that is true to itself cannot become relevant to counter-education through mere intellectual *performance* or as an act of pure *will to power*. The becoming, the becoming-emancipated in face of the utopian **not-yet,** meets the nearness to the truth of Being in the Diasporic philosophy—*or it does not.* Diasporic philosophy is not created or revealed, it is not solely immanent, and it is not merely a transcendent element. It is philo-sophia as a mode of ecstatic, eternally foreign and not fully satisfied existence in the nearness of Being.

As a religious *becoming*, it is a concrete utopia, which is present in this world, in reality, within material conditions at a specific historical moment. It becomes present as that which is referred to by drives, shortage, suffering, and absence—but also by non-mechanistic creation, happiness, and love that knows how to give birth.

As Horkheimer conceived Judaism, a Diasporic philosophy is a religious commit-ment to negativism. "Judaism", according to Horkheimer, is unique in its rejection of a conception of God as a positive absolute. This is the reason for its concentration on the human and not in the essence of God. Its Utopia is negative. Judaism was never a strong state—it was *hope* for justice.[105] It is "a non-positivistic religion".[106]

If a Diasporic philosophy is to be articulated today, its "Jewish" heritage should transcend ethnocentrism, overcome Judaism and even Monotheism itself, and be-come *universalistic.*

Its universalism must be manifested in its bodily, existential, aesthetic, moral, and intellectual dimensions. And its contexts should be bodily, historic, cultural, social, and political realities. As a way-of-homeless-life, Diasporic philosophy represents *im-provisation* of a unique kind in the capitalist hegemonic realm of self-evidence: it is "feminine" and "Jewish" in face of the complicated globalizing process of standardiza-tion and hysteric deconstruction-reconstruction within hyper productivity-consump-tion of the McWorld.

As "feminine" improvisation it gives birth to life. It gives birth to life as responsi-bility for Life as more than mere life; without surrendering to instrumental-oriented "masculinity", to "patriarchalism", dogmatism, hierarchicalism, and to all the other manifestations of violence. It realizes the essence of feminism as endless self-creation and giving-birth in which the self transcends selfhood by responding to **the totally other.** It is a respond-ability which makes possible responsibility and which reveals an *impetus.* This is an impetus that gives birth to the Other as the most intimate fellow-human and to the worthiest togetherness. It is affluent and as such it is not impotent,

105 Max Horkheimer, *Dawn & Decline*, translated by Shaw, Michael. New York: Seabury Press, 1978, p. 206.
106 Max Horkheimer, *Gesammelte Schriften*, XIV. Frankfurt a. Main: Fischer Taschenbuch Verlag, p. 332.

yet it commits itself to creative love of Life. While it can never be content with itself it is closer to its mission when its affluence gives birth to hope, to bodily and spiritual realities. It offers to the world and to itself love and Diasporic acceptance of the totality, never fanaticism and hatred. It presents human new beginnings, as the most serious improvisation with the given "facts" into a never one-dimensional Life, where the Other in his otherness is indispensable. It is the diametrical opposite of patriarchalism exactly when it complements true masculinity.

Such a kind of improvisation meets the essence of Judaism when it relates much more to the all-presence yet non-linearity and non-hierarchical presence of providence as a dialectical opposition to God. As such it offers the negation to normalizing education and to the omnipotence of the "facts", existing "power-relations", "codes" of "our" (potentially) victorious discourse, and to the imperatives of the "historical moment". As a *religious impetus* it actualizes what postmodern feminist critical education strives for in vain: it realizes counter-education without being swallowed into counter-violence.

What we are faced with here is a moment of ontological Diaspora. Diaspora, here, is much more than an edge whither an uprooted collective is being exiled, or wherein it lives, while in quest of "homecoming". Ontological Diaspora is made possible only by the Diasporic stance of Being itself, namely as the exile of nothingness. We do not have to go into theological articulations as to the stance of God the creator as exiled, or into God's evil, suffering, and impotence,[107] to be able to see creation itself, Life itself, as a Diasporic ontological dimension. Accordingly, as in Judaism, human Diasporic existence is an ecstatic Messianic existence, which has no "transcendent" or "immanent" truth, interest, Messiah, or "home". It is the way of life of an eternal loving wanderer who in a certain sense can be everywhere at home, where there is space for non-hierarchical, non-dogmatic love of Life, improvised creativity, and an effort at becoming different from educated for.

Counter-education is determined by such homelessness. Like the Jews (before Zionism damaged so severely the essence of Judaism) it represents a negative utopia as a concrete utopia to live by, not to live in. The gap between the two is made possible by the same "material" which makes possible the abyss between the (pre-rational) *ethical I* and the (rational, politically contextualized) *moral I*. The meeting of the essence of "Judaism" and the essence of "feminism" facilitates a struggle over the possibility of counter-education, which is prima facie a Utopia, never a reality. It is a negative Utopia, which is not to be disconnected from the tradition of negative theology. As such it calls for humans to be prepared to be addressed in an un-instrumental irruption of the unexpected, of the newly-born, of Genesis. Here humans are *called* to be challenged in a way which will awake/create the *ethical I*.

It is a possible awakening, never a guaranteed one. And as such it is actualized morally and pragmatically in history, in and against a concrete discourse, collective, country or "home". Here the human's genuine home is every moment anew thrown beyond the existing horizons of the world of power-games and successful violence. It

107 Feuerbach 1975, p. 13

is represented by hope. Hope is here actualized by poetic-ethical acknowledgement of *the absence of the Messiah*, by a constant responsibility for Diasporic awakening. This awakening is not abstract; it is tested and actualized by improvised action in the world; by doing the good, by doing the good which makes possible truth as resistance to injustice, and by giving birth ??in the reality as the realization of the uniqueness of Genesis every moment anew.

As such, counter-education rejects all versions of collectivism and claims for the true, the good, or the beautiful as a realization of the "we", "ours" or any dogma. It insists on "universalism" in the sense that is determined by suffering and promised by hope for happiness. As a "feminine"-"Judaist" rejection of violence it insists on *Life*. Here "the good" is not "good" because it has the upper hand, but because it continues to give birth to an improvised resistance to the victory of violence.[108]

Women and Jews are the ultimate manifestations of evil. Jews and women throughout the history of culture faced the most intimate, creative-redeeming, ecstatic discrimination, and the refusal to be acknowledged or respected in their otherness. And yet, like the Jews throughout history, in face of infinite evil[109] counter-education that takes seriously the essence of the history of women should insist today on its Diasporic, non-violent, responsibility for that which is beyond mere life as the purpose of life. And even this commitment of counter-education should be introduced within the framework of a Diasporic philosophy. It is accepted in an improvised, creative, non-dogmatic manner: *Diasporic philosophy tells counter-education clearly that the demand for justice might be realized only at the cost of its transformation into its negative.* It cannot become triumphant unless it becomes another manifestation of normalizing education.

This is what postmodern feminist critical pedagogy refuses to acknowledge even when it defends the better parts of the dominant critical pedagogy. Here, on the other hand, the essence of postmodern feminist critical pedagogy contradicts its adorers' ideology and meets its destiny: it becomes a genuine counter-education. As such it is never at home, never genuinely true to itself, always in the state of "becoming-a-woman".

---

108 Max Horkheimer, *Dawn & Decline*, translated by Shaw, Michael. New York: Seabury Press, 1978, p. 207.
109 *Ibid.*, 206.

CHAPTER 9

CYBERFEMINISM AND EDUCATION IN THE
ERA OF THE EXILE OF SPIRIT

Today many important critical theorists of various orientations discern the promise of radical democracy and of a more symmetrical production, distribution, and consumption of knowledge and commodities. Thinkers as diverse as Lyotard, Ellsworth, Landow, Burbules, Standish, and Haraway are united in seeing *new possibilities for the individual* as an autonomous initiator and participator, a reality which enhances fresh opportunities for all people who share the Net. "Authority as we have known it will change drastically",[1] says one; radical democracy is about to be realized in the Web, claims another.[2]

In the feminist movement there are many and diverse voices criticizing while favoring the new technological developments, others who are skeptical, and still others who enthusiastically welcome the current developments in cyberspace. Here we treat only the most favorite of the feminist receptions of the new development: "cyberfeminism".

The participants of cyberfeminism in its narrower sense all share "hard" postmodern philosophical assumptions, while some of the participants of the cyberfeminism in its more general sense are committed to "soft" postmodern philosophical rhetorics. The former are committed to incommensurability, to seeing the subject as a mere position in language games, and to the abandonment of "meaning", "dialogue", and "emancipation" while the latter are committed to dialogue (contextual), an emancipated subject, and the legitimation of claims for emancipation, democracy, and self-constitution. It should come as no surprise that some of the participants move back and forth from "soft" postmodernism to "hard".

Our aim here is to critically reconstruct the critique and the utopia of cyberfeminism. We argue that for all the importance of this critique the bottom line is that *cyberfeminism does not advance feminist emancipation* and is far from contributing to the elevation of counter-education, which will challenge the violence of the hegemonic order of things and its educational manipulations. Cyberfeminism, we assert, is

1 Mark Poster, "Cyberdemocracy: internet and the public sphere", p. 11. http://www.hnet.uci.edu./mposter/writings/democ.html
2 Mark Poster, "CyberDemocracy: internet and the public sphere",http://www.hnet.uci.edu/mposter/writings/democ.html

part of the system that has to be overcome and not a radical alternative to the present actuality and to its normalizing education.

CYBERFEMINISM: "SOFT" AND "HARD" POSTMODERN INFLUENCES

Within cyberfeminism the adorers of cyberspace are united in their optimism about the prospects of educational emancipatory elements in cyberspace. They share a broader *cyberoptimism* which envisions cyberspace as an arena where "all voices are equal", marginal groups raise their "voice" and participate in a *radical democratic environment*. It is a space where "power becomes imaginary"[3] since "in simcult the essential is nothing and nothing is essential",[4] and "*the death of the political*"[5] finally comes about. Within this process

> women do become more important… as machines get more autonomous, so do women. I think women—once they start to make the connection—feel more comfortable with the technology. And really the notion that it is masculine is a convenient myth sustained by the present power structures. This myth is increasingly irrelevant and is an untrue picture of what's occurring.[6]

This particular feminist version takes part in a more general critique of the entire Western culture and its social asymmetrical organization. It explains the patriarchal social hierarchies by its *phallocentrism*; it attacks Western centering of privileged knowledge, its conception of objective reason, its binary rational dichotomies, and its abstractions which permitted, justified, and developed an oppressive intersubjectictivity in which women were subordinated in all dimensions and levels of life. According to Sherry Turkle, cyberspace opens an alternative to traditional Western symbolic and material, individual and collective oppression,[7] which is phallocentrist in its essence.

The "hard" postmodern influences are manifested in cyberfeminism as conceived by some as post-feminist self-constitution[8] and as post-human by others.[9] According to Plant

> Cyberfeminism is an insurrection on the part of the goods and materials of the patriarchal world, a dispersed, distributed emergence com-

---

3   Mark C. Taylor and Esa Saarinen, *Imagologies: Media Philosophy*, New York, 1994, p. 4.
4   *Ibid.*, p. 7.
5   *Ibid.* (no page number).
6   Sadie Plant, Interview, p. 1.
7   Sherry Turkle, *Life on the Screen: Identity in the Age of the Internet*, New York and London 1993, p. 9.
8   Sadie Plant, "Vorshung durch Technik", http://www.thing.de/blau/blau19/plant.htm, p. 1.
9   Janni Steffensen, "Slimy metaphors for technology: 'the clitoris is a direct line in the matrix'", http://ensemble.va.com.au/array/steff_01.html, p. 1.

posed of links between women, women and computers, computers and communication links, connections and connectionist nets.[10]

Zeo Sofoulis, another representative of "hard" postmodernism in cyberfeminism, celebrates the post-phallic conjunction of women's art and high-tech.[11] Representatives of the "soft" postmodern influences of cyberfeminism have explicit feminist emancipatory perspectives and they refuse to see themselves as post-feminists or as post-human Under the title "cyberfeminism" Kira Hall reconciles two conflicting feminist responses to computer-mediated communication, liberal cyberfeminism and radical cyberfeminism.

> The first, influenced by postmodern discussions on gender fluidity by feminist and queer theorists, images the computer as liberating utopia that does not recognize the social dichotomies of male/female and heterosexual/homosexual.... The opposing perspective... has resulted in the separatist development of numerous lists and bulletin board systems which self-identify as 'women only'".[12] For Faith Wilding, cyberfeminism is more than a chance to create new formulations of feminist theory and practice: it addresses the complex new social conditions created by global technologies—"it is a browser through which to see life.[13]

CYBERSPACE: NEW PROSPECTS

Whiting within cyberoptimism—of which cyberfeminism is only an element – cyberspace is presented as a space where digital information is freely transmitted electronically, without the theoretical, emotional, existential, and political preconditions of traditional Western culture. It is an arena where knowledge is decentered[14] and *authority is overcome* in a new Nietzscheian gay science.[15] Here the truth or falsity of this information is not a constitutive element. Accordingly, within cyberspace it is a function, not a potential true (or false), redeeming (or damning), correcting (or misleading), or transcending element. It is freed of claim of universal validity and it is not committed to force itself on the Other who manifests his or her dangerous potential by not agreeing, not being part of the "we", the "just" or the "truth". In cyberspace, as a non-transcendental decentralized communication system, questions of origin, au-

10   Sadie Plant, "On the matrix". P. 182.
11   Zeo Sofoulis, "Slime in the matrix: post-phallic formations in women's art in the new media", in: Jill Julius Matthews (ed.), *Jane Gallop Seminar Papers*, Canberra 1994.
12   Kira Hall, "Cyberfeminism", in Susan C. Herring (ed.), *Computer Mediated Communication: Linguistic, Social and Cross-Cultural Perspectives*, Amsterdam/Philadelphia 1996, p. 148.
13   Faith Wilding, "Where is feminism in the cyberspace?" http://www.studioxx.org/xwords/cyber-femme.html, p. 10.
14   George Landow, Hypertext: *The Convergence of Contemporary Critical Theory and Technology*, Baltimore and London: John Hopkins Press 1992, p. 77.
15   *Ibid.*, p. 74.

thenticity, or true knowledge becomes irrelevant.[16] There is no room for the claim for authority within this framework, which also deconstructs the claim for (patriarchal-oriented) transcendence of the author[17] or the legitimate interpreter, which normally serves to subvert women and other Others while speaking on their behalf.[18] Truth as a constitutive idea, as an assumption, or as an erotic quest, is foreign to cyberspace and its dwellers. Yet cyberspace, according to the cyberfeminists, opens new possibilities and frees the traditional religious, intellectual, theoretical, and philosophical discourses of many aspects of their traditional immanent violence.

According to the cyberoptimists, within cyberspace there is no room for traditional Western metaphysical and actual violence. Traditionally, Western violence springs from Western knowledge's commitment to *universal validity* and from its immanent commitment to protect the wall that separates the true from the false, those who have valid criteria from those who have invalid ones, the sage from the savage. Within "cyberculture" there is room for "cyberpunk", in which sublegitimate, alternative, and oppositional subcultures, often framed by a radical body of politics, have their say at the center.[19] As a term applied to a broad range of representational media and cultural practices (e.g. films, comic books, role-playing games, hacking, and computer crime) the cyberpunk is very much connected to cyberfeminism. Within this framework it is conceived as a "critique of the masculinist techno-cultural discourses".[20] Cyberfeminists find great interest in cyberpunk as a manifestation of a "post-human" condition, which opens new emancipatory possibilities. Of special importance here is the issue of anti-phallocentrism and the quest for a feminine total alternative in the form of connectionism. Here the overcoming of male-oriented knowledge, intersubjectivity, and control of nature is articulated within a *post-human utopia* which reflects the influences of "hard" postmodernism: "cybernetics and genetic engineering combine to denaturalize the category of the 'human' along with its grounding in the physical body".[21] According to the cyberoptimists, cyberspace contains various and conflicting logics, interests, and possibilities. It contains not only *freedom* for all different bodies of knowledge such as fluid, contingent, and hybrid, and sacks of claims, propositions, and beliefs; it opens its gates to symmetrical representation of different narratives, assumptions, claims, and yardsticks about knowledge, not solely to different narratives and bodies of knowledge. It permits

16   Mark Poster, "Cyberdemocracy: internet and the public sphere, p. 3, http://www.hnet.ici.edu/poster/writings/democ.html
17   Tuomas Nevanlinna, "The critique of the author-figure", http://www.designmedia.net.nevanlinnadead2_kuva.html
18   Rosi Braidotti, "Cyberfeminism with a difference", p. 12. http://www.let.ruu.nl/womens_studies/rosi/cyberfem.htm; Tuomas Nevanlinna, "The critique of the author-figure", p. 1, http://www.designmedia.net/nevanlinnadead2_kuva.html
19   Mark Dery, "Flame wars", in Mark Dery, (ed), *Flame Wars: The Discourse of Cyberculture*, Duke University Press, 1994, p. 8.
20   Jyanni Steffensen, "Slimy metaphors for technology: <the clitoris is a direct line to the matrix'", http://ensemle.va.co.au/array/steff_01.html, p. 1.
21   *Ibid.*

non-ethnocentrist dialogues among differences, according to this line of argument, yet it also encourages multiperspective receptions[22] of the various dialogues. This is a very important educational element of cyberspace and it opens new possibilities for the constitution, representation, and acceptance of silenced women's narratives. Within cyberfeminism the abandonment of the "masculine" claims for universality, eternity, objectivity, transcendence, and a priori validity of judgment claims and values is of vital importance. Parallel to it is the abandonment of traditional Western immanent commitment to violate the otherness of the Other and his/her alternative truths. In this sense cyberspace is a new human environment, a virtual space that is determined by its immanent openness. This generates a new kind of intersubjectivity, which Langdon Winner calls "cyberlibertarianism".[23] This is due to the nature of cyberspace as a Net, as a chaotic non-hierarchical interchange among various sets of information, values, identities, and interests, which is always partial, temporal, and local, and not linear. Here the constitution of knowledge and the relation to it are less harsh, compulsory, linear, abstract, and merciless, and it is much more open, sensitive, caring, instinctive, play-like, or "feminine". For this reason, while it is open to everyone's participation it does not have universalistic pretensions; nor does it have claims about the eternity of its truths or about objective or eternal validity of its foundations, yardsticks, agreed conclusions, and goals. In this sense it is an alternative to Western masculine, instrumental or phallocentric-oriented concept of knowledge and to hierarchical intersubjectivity. In this sense it is part and parcel of the postcolonialist agenda and its emancipatory educational utopia. And as such it is far from being a "post political alternative" and one has to ask even about its contribution to the constitution of the coalition between the McWorld, the world of Jihad and the new racism.

One of the manifestations of Western phallocentrism, according to this line of argument, is to be seen in meta-narratives and in their role in the formation of the Western mind and human coexistence. Within this context a special role is reserved for hegemonic written cannons, formal curricula, and books, and their operation in the general process of authoritarian normalizing education. This applies especially in the school arena,[24] where the book (or truth), the teacher, and the hegemonic cultural and social hierarchies are presupposed, justified, and reinforced. By contrast, within the framework of cyberspace "the center of Western culture…the fixed, authoritative, canonical text, simply explodes into the ether".[25]

22   Anne Balsamo, "Feminism for the incurably informed", in Mark Dery (ed.), *Flame Wars: The Discourse of Cyberculture*, p. 127.

23   Langdon Winner, "Cyberlibertarian myths and the prospects for community", http://www.rpi.edu/~winner/cyberlib2.html

24   Colin Lankshear, Michael Peters, and Michel Knobel, "Critical pedagogy and cyberspace", in: Henry Giroux, Colin Lanksheare, and others, *Counternarratives: Cultural Studies and Critical Pedagogies in Postmodern Spaces*, New York 1996, p. 154.

25   Richard A Lanham, The Electronic World: Democracy, Technology, and the Arts, Chicago and London 1993, p. 31.

Within cyberfeminism, cyberspace is conceived as a *totalistic alternative* to the historical masculine role which is symbolized by the phallus. According to Plant

> the phallus and the eye stand in for each other, giving priority to light,
> sight, and flight from the dark matters of the feminine. The phallic
> eye has functioned to endow them with the connection to what has
> variously been defined as God, the good, the one, the ideal form or
> transcendent truth.[26]

For Plant, while the phallus guarantees man's identity and his relation to transcendence and truth "it is also this which cuts him off from the abstract machinery of a world he thinks he owns".[27] In contrast to Western phallocentristic knowledge and communication, which is hierarchical, linear, and violent to the Other or to the irrational/false/unproductive, within the computer and in computer-mediated communication the order is feminine and connectionist, not hierarchical. Information in cyberspace is not centered, but is "inherent everywhere".[28] The phallus, linear thinking, hierarchy, transcendence, and domination are replaced by the female clitoris, which is conceived as "a direct line to the matrix".[29] This destopia is based on *the feminization of the world*.[30] It is founded on the female "hole that is neither something nor nothing",[31] in which the fertility of the Net, of connectionism, intuitionism, improvisation and simulation opens new horizons for life. Life now is understood in terms of "a perverse alliance between women and machines". The transcendent authorization of interpretation is lost, and with it the ontology grounding Western epistemology and its quest for power. As so common in traditional cults, cyberfeminists try to articulate a cyberfeminist mythology in which computer technology from its beginning already entailed the telos of the overcoming of the masculine inner logic and its hierarchical order. As a postmodern mythology, here the emancipation is not of the human subject, not even of "the woman", but of *machines and women who liberate themselves* together from the male-dominated world. Sadie Plant invests much effort to show that the important programmers of the computer were women whose role has been forgotten. She uses mythical language to elaborate an alternative grand narrative to the masculine one. She starts with creation, life in the Garden of Eden, and *the Fall*, reconstructs the establishment of male-dominated human history, and finishes with cosmic connectionism; here, within cyberfeminism, as before the

---

26   Sadie Plant, "On the matrix: cyberfeminist simulations", in Rob Shields, *Cultures of the Internet: Virtual Spaces, Real Histories*, Living Bodies, London 1996, p. 172.
27   *Ibid.*
28   Sherry Turkle, Life on the Screen: Identity in the Age of the Internet, London 1996, p. 132.
29   Jyanni Steffensen, "Slimy metaphors for technology: <the clitoris is a direct line to the matrix", http://ensemble.va.com.au/array/steff_01.html
30   Sadie Plant, Geekgirl no. 1, an interview with Sadie Plant, http://www.geekgirl.com.au/geekgirl/001stick/sadie.html, p. 1.
31   Plant, "On the Matrix", p. 180.

Fall, everything binds together with everything else and the lost intimacy is restored. In this Utopia there is no room for the human being as manifested in the masculine history of domination, suffering, and quest for truth.

Cyberfeminism tries to show that cyberspace is feminine in its essence. Within this effort it conflicts with general postmodern anti-essentialism. This is where feminine and masculine essence and telos are compared historically and conceptually in order to constitute a teleological explanation starting from Adam and Eve and concluding in cyberspace as a feminine totality, or as an improved version of the Garden of Eden. Following the mythization of the female and in line with the post-human women in cyberpunk, in the mythology that Plant introduces it is only natural that women gave birth to "the first programming language for an abstract machine yet to be built". Her reconstruction of the invention of the proto-computer Turing machine is supported by poor historical work. This encompasses the resurrection of the (post-Garden of Eden) "Apple", "poison", and the "feminizing hormone estrogen...which gave rise to a powerful set of mathematical ideas, one of which is known as a Turing machine".[32] The constitution of cyberspace is represented as *the final victory of the feminine over the masculine* essence and its philosophical and political manifestations.

Cyberspace has a feminist "essence" for Plant, and this is why it is a "natural" space for women. This is because they, in contrast to men, were always unconsciously living and preparing themselves for the historic moment of the construction of cyberspace. They did so by "always" living connected, according to the model of the Net, in their traditional marginalized gossip locations, in their communal work at the fields, in the kitchens, in their work as telephone operators or secretaries, and in many other locations and venues.[33] Plant maintains that the new arena is unique in that the stance of productive knowledge, the needs of technological development, and the powers that are dissolving the traditional male-dominated world are irresistibly forcing feminine connectionism. Within what we see as her teleological reconstruction under the feminized/computerized context, the "order-emerging-out-of-massive-connections approach defines intelligence as no longer monopolized, imposed, given by some eternal, transcendent and superior power, but instead evolves as an emergent process, engineering itself from the bottom up".[34] In Plant's reconstruction the historical development of computer technology brings about a post-human, and in a way post-feminist, or "real feminine" totality which is in conflict with the inner logic of the phallus that guarantees man's identity and relation to transcendence and truth—and cuts him off from the abstract machinery such as computers. Within the phallocentric culture men were traditionally identified with the truth or the quest for truth and transcendence, while women were identified with "simulation, imitation, lies, and intrigues"—and this is exactly what makes cyberspace "feminine".[35] This feminist utopian representa-

---

32 *Ibid.*

33 Sadie Plant, "Das Netz ist weiblich" (the Net is feminine),

34 Sadie Plant "The virtual complexity of culture", in: George Robertson (ed.), FutureNatural Nature/Science/Culture, London and New York 1996, p. 204.

35 Sadie Plant, "Das Netz ist weiblich", p. 3.

tion of cyberspace as an emancipated arena, as a non-violent emancipation from the quest for originality, truth, and transcendence in cyberspace,[36] has to be addressed.

ADDRESSING "SOFT" CYBERFEMINISM AND ITS UTOPIA

Against the utopian presentation of the cyberspace as women's *Eldorado* we should place the studies of Susan Herring, Kathleen Michel, and others, who challenge the representation of the Internet as a feminist environment where non-phallocentric knowledge has the upper hand.[37] There is plenty of evidence to show that men dominate the Internet and that actually it is quite a violent environment even in its more feminine aspects. As Leslie Regan Shade shows, in many respects even in academe, "cyberspace is not a gender-free space".[38] The contingency of information gathered by the "link" system and the plurality of windows with no center, hierarchy, transcendence potential, or a priori validity claims, was not followed by a non-violent, "feminine", trend or by a new non-aggressive intersubjectivity. Counter-educational potentials for equality and respect for the Other are certainly not realized towards women and among women in this arena. Needless to say, the question of being human and the internalization of oppression by the oppressed women, highlighted in their cooperation with the evil industry of the male world's normality and in their resistance to it, are here totally ignored. We will argue that the reasons for the importance of the de-humanization or for the efficient normalization of the post-modern feminist emancipatory project within the framework of cyberspace lie in the inner logic of the system.

On the second level, we should challenge the optimism of the cyberfeminists, who present the Net as a terra where "soft" post-modernism is realized in actual "feminized" intersubjectivity. Our claim (which will be developed later on) is that the dwellers of the cyberspace do not avoid and do not overcome social manipulations which constitute, guide, develop, and destroy their potential autonomy as human subjects in "normal" power-games. Actually they internalize the logic of oppression while transforming it. They identify themselves with it, and realize it, while abandoning their otherness, their potential uniqueness as well as their responsibility to the otherness of the Other and the imperative of the dialogue which they are. The Internet is not an arena where alienation is overcome. Instead, alienation is forgotten and is not addressed. It is part of the *abandoning of human Life as a Diasporic mission*. This abandonment is part of an advanced, anti-Diasporic de-humanization process, which ironically is conscious to itself—but from the standpoint of the (victimizing) system, as its (victimized) agent while claiming to be beyond the victim-victimizer dialectics. This is why for the cyberfeminists, as for so many other cyberoptimists, the successful de-humanization process and the tyranny of an apparently aimless technological advance are conceived as something to celebrate.

---

36 *Ibid*, p. 4.
37 Leslie Regan Shade, "Gender issues in computer networking", p. 5.
38 *Ibid.*, p. 6.

Our claim is that there is nothing new in the normalization process as such, yet this kind of normalization opens a new stage in the anti-Diasporic history. All normalizing education processes are targeted against the human potentials of the subject. The uniqueness of cyberspace is in its sophistication, effectiveness and its new kind of deconstruction/connectionism. In contrast to the cyberoptimists' claim, we claim that *cyberspace is not a politically and economically neutral sphere*: it is rather one of the most sophisticated manifestations of current global capitalism and its culture industry. As Paul Standish shows,[39] it reflects a new stage in the distancing of *techne* from its original meaning and from human destiny, which according to Heidegger are inseparable. Contrary to many cyberoptimists, we argue that the supposed "anarchy" and freedom of exchange of knowledge and representations of silenced "voices" are very problematic, and they are so in the two following senses.

   A. While actually allowing silenced "voices" to be heard, they are open to sophisticated psychological, economic, technical, and ideological manipulations and distortions. Unidentified intruders or any participants can enter the dialogue, distort massages, and pretend they are committed to an open dialogue while actually working to subvert or destroy the conference, misusing the free participation in discussion groups. The concept of cyberspace as an ideal speech situation or as a manifestation of free multicultural dialogue is highly problematic. This is because of the absence in cyberspace of what Levinas calls "the face"[40] of the Other, because of the disregard of the otherness, the shedding of responsibility by the *ethical I* within a transcending dialogue which actualizes counter-education. In cyberspace as an arena of constant fluid information, identities, passions, and fashions there is no room not only for responsibility and love but for critical distance also. The *absence of critical distance* does not allow alienation, dialectics, and challenging the self-evidence or the hegemonic consensus. It is problematic also because of the postmodern concept of indeterminability within constant border crossing, and absence of acknowledged norms and standards. Contingency and fluidity are problematic here not only concerning the context but also concerning the identity, the consciousness, or the self of the subject. Here there is room for resistance and change but there is no room for (the absence of) freedom, reflection, and struggle for non-contingent change, no room for eros and dialogue.

   B. The concept of feminist emancipation in cyberspace represents a new stage in the development of technology and of globalization of capitalism, in what one may call virtual capitalism which while pretending to realize the idea of nomadism is anti-Diasporic in its essence. Far from being an anarchist, neutral, arena where authority, hierarchies, and manipulations are dissolved, the Internet, as a manifestation of virtual capitalism, is a worldwide profit-making system, which struggles mightily to serve a will to nothingness. Here there is less room for reflection, transcendence, and dialogue, and no room for the uncontrolled, anarchic domains which are propagated by the "soft" post-modern cyberoptimists who are still faithful to the suggestive pow-

---

39   Paul Standish, "Only connect: computer literacy from Heidegger to cyberfeminism", p. 2.
40   Emmanuel Levinas, "Is ontology fundamental?", in: *Basic Philosophical Writings*, Indiana 1996, p. 8.

ers of positive utopias such as the free subject, non-violent dialogue, and solidarian intersubjectivity. Surely there is here no room for a genuine Diasporic existence.

We claim that the proclaimed new possibilities for free choices of individuals, their self-constitution, and uncontrolled "Diasporic" intersubjectivity is an illusion. This illusion serves the current normalizing education. This illusion and others, such as fluid identities of the fragmented subjects, are important as parts of the new stage of *subjectification*. This is a process of production of the postmodern I who is detached from her otherness, and ultimately does not represent her potential autonomy, self-constitution, or responsibility, for the Other and for herself, and her potential dialogical transcendence/self-constitution.[41] This "subject" is a construct of a subjectificated self: it is not an *ethical I* who manifests the human dialogical potential and the Diasporic mission.

SUBJECTIFICATION, NORMALIZING EDUCATION, AND THE *ETHICAL I* IN THE CYBERSPACE

Education is a positive movement of making the subject into a "subject" who will act as an object of normalization, construction, education, and destruction. As such, he or she is supposed to be an agent of the system, ensuring the realm of self-evidence which he or she reflects and perpetuates and the social order of which he or she is a construct. Education is always committed to educate in light of a positive utopia or a relevant distopia. Counter-education is utopian too, yet it is committed to a negative utopia, challenging the success of normalizing education and the current order of things. Education, in all its versions, as a movement of reducing the subject to a "subject", committed to ensuring that human beings will not be able to activate reflection.[42] Reflection is not to be reduced to a cognitive activity. Primarily it is an ethical stance and it precedes reason, morality, and politics. Reflection manifests the human dimension in the subject as some one who refuses to become some thing. In reflection she or he manifests responsibility for transcendence. Transcendence over the given, over the self-evident, over the normalized I which was constructed and manipulated by the system. Responsibility for reflection and transcendence is not to be detached from responsibility for the totally Other. Here the Other is not an object for manipulation, control, education, or destruction but a precondition for a subject as an *ethical I*, a precondition for the struggle of refusing to be a "subject" who functions as an object of "its" system. By normalizing the subject, education causes her forgetfulness of her Diasporic responsibility and potential, ensuring its pleasure, self-forgetfulness and productivity. It turns the imperative for reflection on and the responsibility for the internal and external Other into its opposition, onto reflectivity, for a commitment for the self-evident, the secure, and the pleasurable. Normalizing education makes the subject a fiction, a naive and/or dangerous positive utopia or distopia. From its abso-

---

41   Ilan Gur-Ze'ev, "Counter-education in the era of the exile of the Spirit", in: Philosophy, Politics and Education in Israel, Haifa: Haifa University Press 1999 (in Hebrew).

42   Ilan Gur-Ze'ev, Jan Masschelein, Nigel Blake, "Reflectivity, reflection and counter-education, *Studies in Philosophy and Education, 20* (Fall 2001).

lute responsibility for the totally Other the *ethical I* confronts the meaninglessness of the world she has been thrown into and the realm of self-evidence in which it is being normalized. The *ethical I* confronts the chasm between the ethical and the reasonable, the private and the public and does not try to escape a dangerous life. For the *ethical I* mere life is not the aim of life. The *ethical I* is responsible for the otherness of the Other, for **the not-yet**, for the infinity.

The ethical I has nothing to do with a utopian or positive utopian reproduction of the given reality. Negative utopia of overcoming all self-evidence and facing mean- inglessness (in the form of contingency, contextualism or the gulf between ethics and reason) is realized in dialogical life in which the otherness of the Other—not her sameness—is a precondition for reflection and transcendence. The *ethical I* struggles to be a subject—always within a dialogical movement—with the Other. However, we have to remember that the subject is not given, is not a fact; autonomy is a potential, a mission, and the Other when not destroyed or "educated" contains her otherness, alienation, and danger, and only as such is *love* possible. From the perspective of Di- asporic philosophy dialogue, reflection, and transcendence are not given either; they are not to be realized as part of the given world, as the "soft" cyberfeminists want us to believe. However it is a concrete utopia, which can be struggled for and realized, even if only in microscopic settings.

Within Diasporic counter-education, reflection and transcendence can be realized for an instant, and then they disappear again, making room for normalizing edu- cation and the hegemonic order of things—but also for indeterminability, conflict, dialectics, and openness to diversity. Its negativity, its absence is what makes utopia an open possibility. It makes possible the "subject" struggling to become a subject and it makes possible Diasporic *readiness to be called upon* by **the totally Other**. When chal- lenging normalizing education, Diasporic counter-education cannot have the upper hand; this is because it is a negative utopia. The moment it has the upper hand it is no more Diasporic: it will become part and parcel of normalizing education. As such she struggles to realize the utopia of the Diasporic subject, resisting the present given reality in all its guises: as "facts", "deconstruction", and fragmentation.

Counter-education in this sense cannot join the party of the cyberoptimists in any of its versions. What the cyberoptimists are celebrating, even in the "soft" postmod- ern version, is the abandoning of the Diasporic promise: disappearance of negative utopia, the demolition of reflection, and the abandonment of transcendence as part of overcoming traditional metaphysics. The moderate cyberoptimists pretend to herald emancipation from the arrogance of libertarianism and from what we call normalizing education. We claim, however, that factuality in the present historical moment is not the end of normalizing education but its sophistication. The cyberoptimists praise cyberspace for overcoming centralist education, censorship, hegemonic interests, and metaphysical claims for truth, universal validity, and transcendentalism in all its forms. Only under these conditions are women freed, according to "soft" cyberfemi- nism. We think, however, that *as long as there is no room for the Diasporic ethical I, for reflection and for transcendence in cyberspace—as we become part of the system or become identified with the system itself ("we are the Net")—we are more effectively enslaved*, not liberated, like the prisoners in the Platonic cave. The individual who is praised by the cyberoptimists is a "subject" not a subject—the manifestation of the power of the system to mystify reality, produce and control the self and its strivings, conceptual apparatus, interests, and competence. The Diasporic struggle to become a subject and to realize the responsibility of the *ethical I* in a dialogue in which there is room for reflection and transcendence represents the erotic resistance to Thanatus. Cyberspace as the framework for the most sophisticated myths is fertilized by the nihilistic quest for nothingness and represents the triumph of Thanatus; the quest for abandoning responsibility for Diasporic life as more than mere life, throwing itself to the endless temptations of virtual capitalism and quasi-improvisation where quasi-ecstatic life and quasi-creativity enable total identification with the system and with pleasurable meaninglessness and self-forgetfulness as the aim of Life. Pleasure and efficiency replace Love of Life, poiesis and genuine creativity.

Within this process the privatization of the subjectified-normalized self, its reification and its quest for un-oriented symbol exchange and pleasure-producing illusions are essential. Self-forgetfulness has the upper hand and Diasporic existence and negative utopia are abandoned. In this sense the assumed Web's contingency, improvisation, chaotic and "dialogical" (ex)change of ideas, identities and subjectivities, are misleading. This is because their productivity, improvisation and chaotic richness is actually determined by their normalizing-domesticating-anti-religious *effectiveness* in camouflaging the process by which this false subjectivity, its will, and its Thanatus-oriented quests are produced as an agency of capitalistic expansion and of normalization processes which it has neither the will nor competence to unveil, resist and transform. One of the best manifestations of the presence of capitalistic organization of the choices and realization of the reified and controlled "free will" is the way the "links" operate in the Net.

As Nicholas Burbules shows, the key element in the hypertextual structure in cyberspace is the link.[43] The cyberoptimists regard links as matters of quasi-religious spontaneity, preference, and uncontrolled creative connections. Burbules warns, however, that

> the act of a link is not simply to associate two givens… links change the way in which material will be read and understood: partly by virtue of the mere juxtaposition of the two related texts…and partly by the implied connection that a link expresses…this involves the reader making connections within and across texts, sometimes in ways that are structured by the designer/author…In on-line texts, links define a fixed set of relations given to the reader, among which the reader may choose, but beyond which most readers will never go. Moreover, links do not only express semic relations but also, significantly, establish pathways of possible

---

43   Nicholas Burbules, "Rhetorics of the web: hyperreading and critical literacy", http://www.edu.uiuc.edu/facstaff/burbules/ncb/papers/rhetorics.html, p. 1.

movement within the space; they suggest relations, but also control access to information.[44]

As Suzanne Rice and Burbules rightly claim, the use of the link and reflection on the strategic interests and personal limitations of its designers ultimately rely on values, communicative virtues, patience, and sensitivity to the context.[45] These, however, are made possible by critical education of the kind that cyberfeminism is committed to destroy. But we would like to go farther than Burbules and Rice. The disregard of the call of **the totally Other**, the unattainability of the quest to be a Diasporic subject, the unrealizability of reflection and transcendence—in other words, the absence of the messianic moment in cyberspace, all ensure the reproduction of the "subject" as an object for the system's manipulations which are at once contingent and rational, necessary and meaningless.

Postmodern conditions ensure feminist educational emancipatory rhetoric as a productive element within cyberspace as a violent, efficient, productive anti-Diasporic system of subjectification; a deceiving, quasi-ecstatic anti-humanist *pleasure machine*. It does not allow responsibility for the suffering of the Other, challenging the mysteries of the self-evident and the trivial, or a struggle that realizes a moral commitment to change reality. In this sense, not only is cyberspace far from being the lost feminist post-alienated Garden of Eden, it is in fact the most advanced challenge to the emancipatory project and to the emancipation of women. The tension between the normalizing educational powers and counter-education is even sharper in "hard" cyberfeminism, where the subject is supposed to be altogether absent, an obsolete thing of the modern world which was successfully drawn into the chaos of complete contingency, hybridity, fluidity, and meaninglessness.

ADDRESSING "HARD" CYBERFEMINISM AND ITS DISTOPIA

"Hard" postmodern feminists conceive cyberspace as a new distopian environment. Within this framework Elizabeth Lane Lawley claims that the definitions of "woman" and "man" are shifting within cyberspace. She argues that "we cannot fix a single center from which the experiences of women with computer and communication systems can be viewed".[46] In explicit opposition to the critics of instrumental rationality and its immanence in current information technologies, she sees in cyberspace an educational promise for women's liberation that will enable them to overcome the subject-object, man-woman, nature-culture dichotomies within which they have been traditionally oppressed. This is where Lawley, following Donna Haraway, finds the cyborg

---

44 Nicholas Burbules, *ibid.*, p. 3.
45 Suzanne Rice and Nicholas Burbules, "Communicative virtues and educational relations", http://www.edu.uiuc.edu/pes/92_docs/rice_burbules.HTM, p. 6.
46 Elizabeth Lane Lawley, "Computers and the communication of gender", http://www.itcs.com/elawley/gender.html, p. 2.

ideal so important. Lawley describes *a post-gender world* as the environment where the hope for woman's liberation can finally come true as her final elimination.

The anti-essentialism of "hard" postmodernism becomes an "emancipatory" element by the defeat of gender differences.[47] The possibility of unlimited re-inscription and change of the body in cyberspace fascinate Lawley. Actually it is a vision of *overcoming the bodiness but not the thingness of men and women*. It is a vision of eliminating the body as different from the mind, consciousness, or myth. She is fascinated by the possibility of entering an environment where it is impossible to divide the appearance from its construction, the subject from its creations, the representation apparatus from "reality"; she aims at overcoming the historical categories of "women", "other", or "object".[48] The hybridity and fluidity of women's identity promises, according to this vision, women's emancipation. This is in a world where "we may be forced to deal with shattered categories and shifting identities".[49]

Lawley does not care that the cyborg not only transforms "woman" and "man" but also the very relevance of the subject and the possibility of meaning, Love and creation. The celebration of contingency, hybridity, constant change, and emancipation from the challenges of reality is seen here a "solution" to the challenge of love of life in eternal Diaspora; as emancipation of women in a very special manner: by eliminating the woman or the feminine. Here women and computers rebel against the phallocentrist world and create a new, holistic *anti-Diasporic space were the cyborg is at home*, where there is no room for the subject and for the messianic moment, where the utopia of dialogical creation and self-overcoming are abandoned.

The fluidity and contingency of endless identities, passions, and myths, accompanied by the end of authenticity, ensure, according to Plant, the end of male domination and actually of domination as such.[50] This does not hinder some of the other "hard" cyberfeminists, such as Verena Kuni, from speaking of *the future world as a feminized arena*.[51] Yet by dissolving the category of the subject and her Otherness, we argue, it will be even harder for men and women to challenge the apparatuses of creation, representation, and distribution of normalizing education. In face of the exile of spirit, the jargon of emancipation and radicalism is still kept alive, but in a cynical manner. The "hard" postmodern cyberfeminists make use of the language of emancipation and dissent while abandoning the ideals of the subject, dialogue reflection, transcendence, and responsibility. These ideals and quests are abandoned here for the sake of their being more easily swallowed by the system and adjusted to the Net, the Web, virtual reality, MUDs, or other manifestations of system. This point is still clearer in the case of Donna Haraway.

---

47   *Ibid.*, p. 5.
48   *Ibid.*, p. 6.
49   *Ibid.*, p. 8.
50   Sadie Plant, Das Netz ist weiblich", p. 4.
51   Verena Kuni, "Future is female: some thoughts on the aesthetics and politics of cyberfeminism", http://www.kunst.uni-mainz.de/~kuni/abs-cf1.htm, p. 1.

Haraway's departure point is traditional Western male-dominant culture and her work exemplified with special clarity the intimate link between the postmodern feminist critique of phallocentrism, postcolonialism and the new-racism. According to Haraway, Western culture is a racist, colonialist culture, which includes progress and appropriation of nature as the resource for the production of culture.[52] She sees in the postmodern conditions[53] new emancipatory potentials for women: technological and social evolution have brought about a situation where "the dichotomies between mind and body, animal and human, organism and machine, public and private, nature and culture, men and women, primitive and civilized are all in question ideologically".[54] Haraway maintains that within the new conditions the world becomes a problem of coding and resistance to instrumental control. Note that in contrast to the "soft" postmodernists, Haraway does not refer to a feminist emancipation in light of the new constellation as an arena where the patriarchal world is becoming feminized, alienation reduced, and more equality, respect for the Other, and solidarity realized. She sees the postmodern condition as an arena where the issue of the subject, her life, and her possible emancipation is becoming radically transformed, and the Enlightenment's ideal of the subject is being overtaken by the postmodern cyborg.

As one of the manifestations of the postmodern condition the cyborg "is a cybernetic organism, a hybrid of machine and organism, a creature of social reality as well as creature of fiction".[55] Haraway does not look for more equality between men and women, between cultures and classes; she is not in quest of a solution to the traditional problems of philosophy and society. Instead she opens a complete alternative, beyond relativism, temporality, and partiality, as suggested by the various educational trends in the "soft" postmodern feminism. "Soft" postmodernism has abandoned the search for perfect harmony. Its educational alternatives are optimistic about the prospects of overcoming asymmetrical relations, inequalities, and oppression in postmodern conditions, especially in cyberspace. Haraway goes in another direction, where there is no quest for free dialogue and more symmetrical relations among different identities, interests, cultures, races, sexes, and classes.

For Haraway, the incommensurability of differences and the radical conception of contingency make possible the formulation of a new totality. Here coding and decoding symbols parallel creation and re-creation of the cyborg as some thing that is supposed to overcome traditional Western conceptions of the human subject. In our mind this idea is as the opposite of the object as some one who struggles against the pressure to reduce her into some thing, trying to become someone. For Haraway, as for Plant and other "hard" cyberfeminists, in the sense that it is a creature in a postgendered world[56] the cyborg overcomes the psychological, social, and philosophical

---

52 Donna Haraway, Simias, *Cyboooorgs and Women: The Reinvention of Nature*, New York 1991, p. 150.
53 *Ibid.*, p. 161.
54 *Ibid.*, p. 163.
55 *Ibid.*, p. 149.
56 *Ibid.*, p. 150.

problems traditionally connected to the male-dominated world, and as such it is a manifestation of the telos of Western culture.

Haraway introduces the world of the cyborg as an improved Garden of Eden,[57] in which totality is constituted not by homogeneity, eternity, stability, and absolute truths realized in a perfect manner. The cyborg lives while "committed to partiality, irony, intimacy, and perversity. It is oppositional, utopian, and completely without innocence".[58] Here "the difference between the human body and machines on the one hand and nature on the other is a thing of the past".[59] Haraway presents a utopia where the world as a dialectical arena of antagonistic and binary identities, interests, and human powers is overcome. She presents a totality of endless, groundless, aimless, meaningless coding and decoding. The world and the self intermarry, and there is no room for a Diasporic *ethical I*, who struggles to realize her potential autonomy by insisting on being at home everywhere while refusing any dogma as a "home", on critical reflection and on dialogical transcendence, which reformulate the self and the world. Haraway's utopia mystifies not only the self and the world but even the utopia, and makes it part of the current realm of self-evidence. She presents a totality "not of a common language, but of a powerful infidel heteroglossia", which curiously she still defines as "feminist". It educates to being drawn into a world where Haraway can prefer being a cyborg to being a goddess.[60] It is a world which has regained its intimacy to the totality, as the cyborg is in a spiritless world, without any alienated Other, an object, or a *not-I*, a world that has to be deciphered, transcended, or overcome.

The post-modern cyborg who is swallowed up by electronic technology is not the modern alienated, suffering subject, who is confronted by the dilemma of destroying the Other or being destroyed, dominating or being dominated. In Haraway's words, "it was not born in a garden", and therefore it is not committed to return to the Garden of Eden by redemption which is determined by one, absolute, holy truth; nor is it committed to a revolution or realizing the Enlightenment's (or another) secular emancipatory project which is committed to the realization of a positive utopia. In this manner *the human being as some thing*, as a cyborg, is relieved of the obligations of the kind of modern Western education which was committed to truth and to binary concepts such as evil-pious, true-false, beautiful-ugly, oppressive-emancipatory. "The machine is not to be animated, worshipped, and dominated. The machine is us, our processes, a aspect of our embodiment".[61] Within this project education is entirely mystified and veiled. It becomes part and parcel of the self-evident and the present order of things. To the extent that it is still identifiable, it can only aim at improving the productivity or the pleasures of the cyborg and eliminating all surviving manifestations of the modern world: differences between men and women (and the oppression

57   *Ibid.*, p. 151.
58   *Ibid.*
59   *Ibid.*, p. 163.
60   *Ibid,* p. 181.
61   *Ibid.*, p. 180.

which is traditionally attached to them), culture and nature, humans and machines, good and evil, true and false, reality and fantasy. From the partialities, differences, and temporalities which have nothing in common, on the one hand, and the quest for nothingness which determines them, on the other, Haraway is committed to building a new Garden of Eden, a new totality where the self-evident and the present order will not be able to be threatened by anything or anyone.

This is an improved version of the human situation in the Garden of Eden, where Adam and Eve were already potentially in conflict with God's imperative or with the temptation of the serpent. They already had a choice, namely in a way they were *free* to choose, even before eating of the tree of knowledge of good and evil. It was a fragile totality, containing the seeds of its destruction. The educational problems of getting the knowledge of the good, distributing the true knowledge, and living accordingly are but a consequence of the imperfect Garden of Eden.

The postmodern condition, as shown by Plant, Haraway, and the other "hard" cyberfeminists, can offer a perfect totality where the Sisyphean effort of education and its violence will come to an end. What they offer is an arena where there is no room for life as struggle and for human responsibility. The world of the cyborg or the realization of *connectionism*, where everything amalgamates with everything and everything is connected to everything else in an endless, borderless, and meaningless fluidity, is not an alternative to the logic of control which they identify with Western phallocentrism and colonialism in the psychological, philosophical and political levels of existence.

Within this version of connectionism, in the absence of the Diasporic *ethical I* or the utopia of the subject, there is neither room for the grand refusal nor to genuine creativity and religiosity; there is no philosophical air to breath for the negative utopia of solidarity and love or for the struggle against the untrue and the unjust. In other words, there are no pre-conditions for struggling against normalizing education. This is because factuality as successful violence was first internalized and then fragmented into endless "differences", where no difference really makes a difference, where there is no room for the Other and her otherness. This kind of connectionism may be realized in the future—and the development of biological computers may contribute to further develop this new totality. We see it, however, as *a quest for nothingness*, a Tanatus drive that uses a domesticated eros to run away from life as a problem and as a burden, as openness, and a call for the totally Other.

Life as an easygoing optimism or "irony" here replaces a dangerous Diasporic mission. It is a quasi-nomadic celebrated elimination of self, swallowed by the system and its pleasure machines. Here there is no room, no quest, and no potentials for negative utopianism and counter-education. This attitude is also present in MUDs and in virtual reality technologies.

In its ideal, the technology of virtual reality promises a technique that will allow the creation on the screen of a view totally manipulated by a "subject" who will sense virtual reality as perfect reality. She will be able to have anything she imagines on the screen, and by the same token to feel as if virtual reality is perfectly "real" and to react accordingly, physically and emotionally. In the creation of virtual pain and virtual pleasure, totality, infinity, and eternity are reachable. In the case of the perfect virtual-reality machine, which realizes pleasure or suffering, as in the case of the perfected cyborg, is there a possibility to "plug out"? This stage of realized "hard" postmodernism raises hard questions: who here is the subject, and what or who here is the object? What is the meaning of "free decision" or of "creation", in the sense of who or what manipulates what, who or what is sovereign here? Here we are confronted with a potential pleasure (or infernal) machine in which the challenge of education and that of emancipatory feminist education has no meaning and no purpose. The problematic of insisting on refusing to return to the thingness, to be part of the Same, of Diasporic responsibility to worthy suffering, love, mystery, or hope for transcendence becomes irrelevant, meaningless; because when nothing is any longer meaningful or meaningless, worthy or unworthy, true or false, real or unreal there is no Diasporic alternative and nomadism becomes a manifestation of self-forgetfulness—not of Diasporic creativity, love and alternative togetherness.

According to Sherry Turkle,

> MUDs put you in virtual spaces in which you are able to navigate, conserve and build... MUDs are new kind of virtual parlor game and a new form of community. In addition, text-based MUDs are a new form of collaboratively written literature. MUD players are MUD authors, the creators as well as consumers of media content... As players participate, they become authors not only of text but also of themselves, constructing new selves through social interaction... On MUDs, one's body is represented by one's own textual description, so the obese can be slender, the beautiful plain, the "nerdy" sophisticated... MUDs make possible the creation of an identity so fluid and multiple that it strains the limits of the notion.[62]

Turkle is very optimistic about the feminist emancipatory potential of MUDs since it is an arena where construction and reconstruction of identity take place as a new form of life; life as a *play* in which one creates and re-creates identities, and the border between "real life" and a "play" is transcended, or at least reformulated for men and women. Turkle emphasizes that "for some this play has become as real as what we conventionally think of as their lives, although for them this is no longer a valid distinction".[63]

Cyberspace as a manifestation of the "hard" postmodern world is a world where there is neither room for *responsibility* for the Other nor for one's owns self. Ultimately there is no room for education since there is no human subject and the kingdom of necessity has disappeared. Ultimately there is no room for counter-education. At last education is not threatened by any rival. It constitutes a totality, which recalls the Gar-

62   Sherry Turkle, *Life on the Screen: Identity in the Age of the Internet*, New York and London 1995, pp. 11–12.

63   *Ibid.*, p. 14.

den of Eden or Marcuse's vision of future society, where the conflicts between nature and culture, subject and object, the pleasure principle and the reality principle, and even the principle of individuation[64] are overcome.

COUNTER-EDUCATION FACING CYBERFEMINISM

The "hard" and the "soft" versions of postmodern cyberfeminism that have been reconstructed here are united in supporting and reflecting the present postmodern condition and its capitalistic subculture. Paul Standish has done a good job in showing the relations among hegemonic economic powers, social inequalities, and the prosperity of cyberspace in schools and in the educational arena at large.[65] Standish, however, is siding (not without some doubts) with the anti-instrumentalism of Cyberfeminism, and thinks that "Cyberfeminism explores the possibility of the recovery of something of those different ways of thinking that might counterbalance or infiltrate a more calculative rationality".[66]

Standish follows Heidegger's critique of Western instrumental rationality, and sees in the computer a technological manifestation of instrumental rationality. He accepts that computers are most efficient at handling, exchanging, and making available large amounts of information, and that today Western society cannot do without them. For Standish "the problem is that the ease with which we then access and pass on this information displaces other ways of knowing and understanding and being in the world".[67] However, when referring to recent developments in cyberspace, where the male-oriented characteristics of the computer are being developed, along other multi-media potentials, into a "masculine" technology, Standish is less satisfied with Heidegger's position, and he sides with the optimism of cyberfeminism. According to Standish, "in identifying the seductive ease and harmlessness of the masculine calculative thinking Heidegger may have failed to anticipate fully the way this transmutes in the physical experience of new technology. He may also not fully have realized the extent to which the technology itself is transformed where hierarchical structures of organization are replaced by the modal formations of the Web".[68]

We accept the central aspects of the critique of Standish and the cyberfeminists on the instrumentalism of the current technological advance, but we do not share their understanding of the "feminine" characteristics of cyberspace; nor can we share their optimism and Heideggerianism.

---

64   Herbert Marcuse, "Culture and revolution", Herbert Marcuse Archive 406.00, 4 in: Ilan Gur-Ze'ev, *The Frankfurt School and the History of Pessimism*, Jerusalem 1996, p. 111 (in Hebrew).
65   Paul Standish, "Only connect: computer literacy from Heidegger to cyberfeminism", *Educational Theory*, (Fall 1999). 49: 4 pp. 417-435.
66   *Ibid.*
67   *Ibid.*
68   *Ibid.*

Standish does not do justice to Heidegger in the sense that when he refers to the Web he does not ask the question of the inner logic of cyberspace technology or the question of the subject in total disengagement, Geworfenheit. When he refers to the "feminine" character of the Web he forgets to question this reality in face of the question of *Dasein* in the Heideggerian sense which he praises. For Heidegger "*das Dasein ist Seiendes, dem es in seinem Sein um dieses Sein Selbst geht*": the subject is unique in the sense that the Dasein is, by its being committed to the question of being. Contrary to Standish we think that, following Heidegger, Adorno, and Levinas, we should develop the critique of instrumental rationality by raising the issue of the concrete possibilities and limitations of human life within cyberspace.

Today's counter-education should emphasize the difference between information and knowledge, dialogue and information interchange, change of identity and transcendence in face of the Other as a representation of infinity. Counter-education should also address the questions of cyberspace and the strengthening of capitalism, and why its moral toll and its manifestations in the Culture Industry are not being problematized by current philosophies of education.

When cyberfeminism and its optimism are problematized within this framework in light of Diasporic philosophy, there will be much less room for positive utopianism and more for resistance, reflection, and responsibility towards the Other as a human being, as a girl or a boy, a women or a man, and not as a cyborg or a contingent, aimless, careless manifestation of the system in virtual reality, or in MUDs.

In the face of current reality it is of vital importance to raise the possibility of Diasporic counter-education. Within counter-education the possibility of refusing to be swallowed by thingness and become part of the *Same*, the question of the subject, the possibility of reflection, and the meaning of the struggle for dialogical transcendence are re-evaluated, transformed, and striven for. Here the (potential) autonomy of the subject is vital, and it is realized always within dialogical relations with Others whose otherness is acknowledged as legitimate and relevant for human life. The struggle for such a potential dialogue necessarily entails challenging the realm of self-evidence and the current order, which includes the present self, its interests, knowledge, consciousness, and passions, as enforced by the systematic normalization of the subject.

The present aim of Diasporic counter-education should be to insist on religiosity and to advance critical philosophy of education beyond the concept and strives of modernism-postmodernism, and of monotheism in all its forms. This is part of its struggle over the possibility of Diasporic love within the present process of sophisticated de-humanization by normalization processes like those realized in cyberspace. There the victim of the system becomes its devoted agent by self-discipline, adjustment to the rules of the game, abandonment of responsibility, and commitment to life for the not-yet and the totally Other.

Even if cyberspace is a one-dimensional system, iasporic counter-education can make much use of the tension among the pre-modern, the modern, and the postmodern over cyberspace. The real oppression of women and the actual suffering outside cyberspace and its apparatuses of representation, as well as new possibilities within cyberspace, allow the presence of hope and the very possibility of refusing the suggestive power of Thanatus and its educational efficiency. One of the first steps, however, should be a critique of the various optimistic versions of current cyberfeminism, and getting ready for *the call* of the philosophical Eros and Diasporic ethical responsibility.

CHAPTER 10

SPORTS EDUCATION FACING GLOBALIZING CAPITALISM

The present historical shift and the social and cultural changes that are carving out their way to the future do not today enhance theological tension, intellectual vitality, or revolutionary consciousness, nor practices of resistance of the kind that character-ized the class struggle of the 19th and the first half of the 20th century. The constitu-tion of the MacWorld that is the arena of "the risk society"[1] is taking place in face of its victims, who are at the same time also its strongest and most devoted agents. The change in the function, representation, and consumption of sport, sports education, and physical education faces little, if any, resistance. This should not be understood as a failure of physical educators or of the active and passive participants in sports in the present globalizing process. Consumers and producers alike, whether armchair TV supporters of Real Madrid football club, media "experts", or interviewers, do not as a rule resist or offer any critical alternative. By and large they enthusiastically support, cooperate with, and even idolizing this development. What we face here is the instrumentalization of sports education and the reification of sport as part of hu-man life deteriorating into its natural, mythical, and objective dimensions; human life becomes part of a mechanical-"natural" continuum. A moment of *the Same*. The human subject betrays its otherness and is about to be swallowed by thingness. This historical triumphant cannibalism of the object consuming the subject is paralleled and enhanced by rapid erosion in the western master signifiers and ideals of control and order, of certainty and security, which were so central to modernity. A new world order, a new economy, and a new kind of capitalism are being formed,[2] and the ap-paratuses of representation and cultural production are, accordingly, offering a new kind of sport and a new kind of sports education.

According to the supporters of globalizing capitalism, these developments open new horizons for creativity, multiculturalism, and tolerance.[3] The present function of sport and sports education within this framework is assumed to be part of the open-ing of new possibilities for creative life for the individual and part of supplying more pleasure to the public through free, individual choice. This reality is presented as part of a development of which another dimension is the demolition of traditional hier-archies, objectivist yardsticks, authorities, exclusivity in representation of "the truth" and of education in line of the hegemonic class, ideology, ruler, or tradition.

---

1   Ulrich Beck, *World Risk Society*, Cambridge: Polity Press, 1999.
2   Ulrich Beck, *World Risk Society*, p. 2.
3   *Ibid.*, p. 3.

According to the supporters of the ideology of globalizing capitalism these new developments represent the establishment of a new world order. This new world order offers us a new kind of cosmopolitanism, a new international morality,[4] a new kind of world memory,[5] of post-national communitarianism that is founded on global risk[6] and global pleasures in the form of activities and symbolic participation that enhance consumption of cultural products and competitive, healthy self-realization. In a way, life becomes a totalistic realization of "sport"; sport, in this particular realization, becomes a symbolic manifestation of the truth of the present historical moment.

More than offering a new agenda I try to locate the horizons of the present perversion of sport. This text is not neutral. It does not make do with critical reconstruction. It explicitly strives to identify potential possibilities for transcending the present borders of the cultural politics of "sport". In this sense it is of vital importance for us to differentiate between the mission of sport—and that which is referred to by this telos, and the reality of "sport", its practices, production, representation, and consumption in present-day globalizing capitalism. Globalizing capitalism and its culture industry are the actual arena where both theories and practices of "physical education" take place, parallel to the education for and consumption of competitive sport, as well as the philosophical frameworks which make possible the conceptual field for these theories and practices.

In this sense philosophy of sports education will be presented here in its historical-social-cultural contexts, to enable us to reach the gates of the fundamental problematic of the philosophy of sports education in its wider sense. If we follow this road we may perhaps come closer to the possibility of challenging philosophy of sports education's abandonment of its mission. Such an Odyssey cannot avoid storming the closed gate on which these questions are inscribed: What is the mission of sport, if at all it has such an aim? What are the manipulations for ensuring the forgetfulness of the essence of the mission of sports education? What are the practices which ensure the trivialization, banalization, and ridiculousness of these questions? And what are the powers, interests, dynamics, and ontological signs which they serve, hide, and unveil?

Even when trying harder and harder, philosophy of sport will not succeed in totally disconnecting the ties between its response to the call of the question of the mission of sports education and the enigma of the aim of human Life in a post-modern era. But does the human have any "aim" at all? And even if human Life has a purpose and meaning—is there any open way to reach it, and even to explicitly articulate it in a public sphere? Is it perhaps the essence of human Life that its mission not be given, nor offer itself articulated, nor be theoretically accessible? Is it possible that when true to itself it will offer mere silence or its negation? As self-negation and absence, could the meaning of Life also be revealed as an anchor of freedom, calling humans to face bravely indeterminacy, endless openness, and alienation? Is it possible that at

4   Ulrich Beck, *What is Globalization?* Cambridge: Polity Press 2003, p. 86.
5   Daniel Levy and Natan Szneider, "The institutionalization of cosmopolitan morality", *Journal of Human Rights*, 3: 2 (2004), pp. 143–157.
6   Beck, *ibid.*, pp. 16–17.

the same time it is also an abyss between the regimes of production and consumption of representations of the given facts—and worthy life? From the viewpoint of Diasporic philosophy[7] we can ask: is it possible that a Messianic moment will appear, in which, or, from which, the question of the aim of Life will burst in, or at least the presence of the closing horizons and the forgetfulness of the question of Life's aim and meaning will rise, again, in the form of a young, vital readiness for a call to be ecstatically responded to? Is it possible that at a certain historical moment a renewed human vitality will become a reality in face of questions such as, "Do humans still have a mission, yardsticks, and meaningful imperatives? Is it possible that within a Diasporic perspective the closure of the truths of globalizing capitalism, as manifested in reified sport, will be challenged?" And more specifically: "Is it possible that instead of struggling to reclaim its former place as an important moment in preparing the human's readiness to face the question of her destiny, sport will contribute to a nomadic, Diasporic, existence, that will enhance a more mature humanity?" This question is not disconnected from the possibilities of overcoming normalizing education and opening the gate for counter-education. Here I will try to probe the possibility that it is imperative that the philosophy of sports counter-education become part of this Diasporic transcendence. Modest as our aim in this elaboration might be, it still represents a commitment to worthy life, love, creativity, and solidarity. But in face of globalizing capitalism and its culture industry we should explicitly ask this: Is there still openness and meaning in post-modern conditions for genuine Diasporic life, for counter-education, and for Love of Life?

Responding to these challenges precedes, yet does not cancel, the questions which attract sports theoreticians who are so busy today meeting the demands of globalizing capitalism and ask —mostly within an instrumentalist orientation: "what are the best ways for improving physical fitness of young and older producers-consumers in technologically highly advanced Western societies?" Sometimes they are attracted even to philosophical questions whose instrumental orientation is less evident. Here they ask: "why is it important to raise the standards of fitness?" Or "where should western society concentrate its care and efforts and in light of what principles?" "What is the proper education needed for advancing the decision makers in the field of sport?" Or even "what kind of education is needed to produce a more just and/or rational distribution of efforts and funds in sports, which today confronts the imperatives of globalizing capitalism and the truths of the symbols and passions of the post-modern 'spirit'?" Another important set of questions is of the kind of legitimacy of approval/disapproval of drug-use in sports, or in diverting efforts and capital in favor of sports activities which, while less popular or commercially successful, contain unique manifestations of the sporting spirit. From time to time even fundamental questions for the philosophy of sport, such as "What is fairness in a post-modern era?" Or even "Is there today a sports 'achievement' that is justifiable in itself and for itself, regardless of its rating or of the bottom line in the bank account?" Still, even on the rare occasions

---

7   Ilan Gur-Ze'ev, *Toward Diasporic Education*, Tel Aviv: Resling, 2004 (in Hebrew).

when such questions are raised they are disconnected from the eternal questions of the philosophy, meaning and aim of Life, as well as from actual social realities.

To my mind, it is of vital importance to address these challenges in the most concrete manner, but without disconnecting them from the possibilities/limitations of the utopian quest and mission of sports counter-education.

The ridiculing, banalizing, perverting, or abandoning of the central questions of sports education—as is so common in today's philosophy of sport—is not a mere coincidence. It has an economic value and makes an important contribution to collectivism and other forms of de-humanization. This is the synthesis between the central drives of the world of Jihad and the MacWorld.[8] Counter-philosophy of sport should offer not a gateway to joining this coalition but a gate to Diasporic life in face of its apparent triumph. This Diasporic alternative does not necessarily search for a theoretical "home-coming", for the constitution of a social earthly Garden of Eden, or for the pleasurable quasi-creative deconstruction of solidarities, values and calls for edifying self-constitution. As a Diasporic human existential, philosophical, and political alternative[9] it does not necessarily retreat into relativism, cynicism, or anti-solidarian de-teritorialization of the self. As suggested by the example of sports counter-education, it can also offer new kinds of solidarity, intersubjectivity, responsibility to the body and to the cosmos, and new possibilities for the spirit.

Today it is impossible to seriously challenge the post-modern globalizing condition, unless as part of a general struggle for change in existential, cultural, and political realities. Such a struggle is a *Utopia*.. As a utopia it opposes present realms of self-evidence, which form the current existential, conceptual, political, and aesthetic horizons. But, who is the one who is today mighty enough to dispute present rational manifestations of globalizing capitalism, or fight the imperatives of post-modern technological advancement? Nevertheless, I claim, even in the era of "the end of philosophy", and even if deconstructed or transformed, these questions are not completely castrated by the system. The struggle for transcendence, I insist, is still possible, even if only in a negative, nomadic, manner—and this should be the great mission of Diasporic-oriented sports counter-education in the post-modern era.

Sports counter-education has today a special challenge, in face of the culture clash between Western and non-Western civilizations, embedded with the divisions imposed by capitalistic globalization (which do not fit the above dichotomy). Capitalistic globalization itself is woven and differentiated by local processes, and their contingent, hybrid and temporary collective and individual realities.

At the same time, for the MacWorld, for the Jihad world, as well as for their coalitions, most of the veiled violences that facilitate and reproduce the post-industrial order of things remain unproblematized. This is so even when it is woven, like in the 2001 UN conference in Durban (South Africa), with religious violence, ethnocentric policies, racial, cultural, and other discriminations and counter-discriminations. These form the "I" and on a certain level the conditions, representations, and threats

---

8   Slavoj Zizek, *Welcome to the Desert of the Real*, Tel Aviv: Resling, 2002, p. 158 (in Hebrew).
9   Ilan Gur-Ze'ev, *Toward Diasporic Education*, p. 14 .

of "nature" of which the human soul and body are parts. They constitute the human body as a political site, and capitalize the powers of the spirit and the body for further mystification of Life, while hiding ecological threats to the earth, health risks for the human body, and reified human relations as precondition for today's self-perception and re-positioning of men and women who compete for "success", power, pleasure, and recognition. The counter-violence of the Third World's victims, when articulated in queer, feminist, anti-globalizing, post-colonialist, Islamic fundamentalist, and other rhetoric, challenge this order, while being part and parcel of the post-modern condition. Paradoxically, they contribute to the strengthening of unrestrained market-oriented policies on the one hand, and empower the invisibility of normalizing violences on the other. The sublimation and de-sublimation of the MacWorld and the Jihad world parallels (as Adorno already understood) a perverse pact between the superego and the id at the expense of the reflective "I". The fruits of these violences produce and reproduce the unreflective representations of human "fitness" and adaptability, within the de-humanized consciousness and body. As such they present the true nature of normalizing education and serve ecological, moral, and other threats to the very existence of the human world in a global scale.

In globalizing capitalism these violences ensure the construction of the human as a successful producer/consumer; even as a post-colonialist anti-globalizing, feminist, or "green" activist. It prepares humanity for its supreme sporting realization: "successful" adaptation and eating the fruits of "fitness" in the market as a perfect producer-consumer.[10] It prepares, represents, justifies and offers an ornamentalization of a totalistic arena, which inherits past religious ecstatic experiences and promises quasi-transcendence and a deceiving telos. Fundamentalist religious alternatives will challenge this direction and offer an alternative totalistic "spiritual" dehumanization. Central to the framework of this alternative is overcoming or destroying the body of one's self. Sometimes, as in the case of Iranian Khomeinism, it will accept and integrate the world's sports industry. In other cases, such as the Jewish ultra-orthodox community, any compromise with the secular world is flatly refused. Yet disciplining the body and mind in accordance with the imperatives of normalizing education will always unite the various conflicting fundamentalist alternatives. In Western and non-Western societies, which were completely overwhelmed by the logic of the capitalist production and consumption, traditional sports activity and its symbols were overtaken by this logic; a process of incorporation, which includes physical education and education for competitive sport, and its rational consumption. The relevant theories concerning today's sport are recruited to veil the transformation of sport as sacred work into "sport", and to ensure the furthering reification and virtualization of *Love of Life* and its immanent freedom. By functioning efficiently on this level they contribute in a most sophisticated manner to the transformation of "sport" into an unproblematic, reified, part of current capitalist culture industry, within which body, nature, and creativity become mere instrument, function, or commodity. The human body and spirit abandon their connections to nature on the one hand, and to the

---

10   Ilan Gur-Ze'ev, *Destroying the Other's Collective Memory*, New York: Peter Lang, 2003, p. 143.

telos of spiritual edification on the other. The virtual reality of the advanced capitalist human conditions offers a victory of the abstract, dehumanized, "home-returning" project over the Diasporic alternative, while presenting a quasi-nomadic "alternative" in which post-modern Life, in all its spheres, becomes a totalistic realization of the idea of sport.

The Olympic Games, which, according to tradition, began in 776 BC, testifies to the presence in the classical Greek world of the essence of the ideal of sport. It is a religious essence in a pre-institutionalized sense. The religious essence of the sports ideal and its transcendental mission were realized also in a formed, symbolic manner, as a formal declaration of the Olympic Games as a practice in honor of the Olympic Zeus. The first of the five days of the Olympic Games, as organized in 472 BC, was wholly devoted to sacrificing and other sacred practices. The competitions were meant to call the spirit. They were intended to manifest the human spirit in its directedness to the excellent, to the superb, to the holy. Sport was, for the Greeks, a *sacred* practice. This is why only after the competitors took their vow and pledged allegiance to the supreme ideals of this human-Olympic event could they participate in the various competitions, which officially began on the second day. The last of the Olympic days was again devoted to sacrifices, to declaring the winners and crowning them with garlands of olive branches. In the Platonic state, gymnastics and life in light of the ideal of sport are preconditions for the edification of the philosopher-king and for the constitution of the ideal state.

In other words, the essence of sport, prior to its transformation into a commodity, is transcendental. When true to itself, the transcendental dimension of sport is individualistic-oriented while reuniting the human with other humans and with the cosmos in all its richness, diversity, and infinite openness. It can, of course, betray its telos and abandon both its individualistic and cosmic dimensions, while offering a deceiving individualistic agenda (in the form of sports "stars" as a commodity where the "stars" themselves act in their personal life as a fabrication of their public representation). It can, in parallel, also offer a deceiving cosmopolitan ideal in the form of a symbol, a representation, which is a mere sign in the commodity market that has lost its relation to nature and to genuine human interests, potential, and glory.

When true to its essence and telos, sport represents the impetus of Love of Life. As Love of Life it raises the human from lower levels of existence to her supreme goal within the forms of constant *self-elevation.*. This kind of self-elevation is actualized as a self-overcoming that is also a form of self-constitution. Self-overcoming, we should bear in mind, for the Greeks was unimaginable to actualize within the closeness of one's self; it was conceived as determined by responding a heavenly *call*. This call was conceived as differing substantially from the drives, calls, and reactions of the self: it is a *transcendental call*, to which the proper response is the human's worthiest practice in a cosmos in which he becomes a citizen in his home. But while it was institutionalized and conceived as potentially important for civil life within the framework of the hegemonic order, sport, like philosophy, carried also a Diasporic potential. It was a potential estrangement from the world of facts. It contained the potential for a refusal to see contingent order and the limits of the body and spirits as having the last word:

it incubated the imperative of overcoming the governing facts and the limits of the body and spirits in the name of a transcendental call, a potential which contained an immanent Utopian massage and an alternative to the telos set by hegemonic normalized education.

Facing this ultimate-potentially Diasporic and autonomous essence of sport, Christianity, which conquered Latin Europe during the early middle ages, had to overcome, restrain, or transform the Love of Life, non-religious happiness, and the practice and ideal of sport. Naturally, therefore, Emperor Theodosius I cancelled the Olympic Games in AD 393.

Imitatio Christi and the ideal of being a genuine diviner were supposed to dictate the only legitimate Diasporic way to worthy life and transcendence. It refused to tolerate any educational competition. However, all the prohibitions, restrictions and control did not succeed in completely blocking the manifestations of the essence of the ideal of sport, even if only in restricted, partial, or sublimated ways: it survived even when the human body and earthly life in general where conceived as a jail for the God-loving spirit or as an invitation to hubris, or to devoting oneself to the lower manifestations of life in this world.

The practices realized in the courts of earls, dukes, and kings, however, opened new gates to aesthetization of knightly ideals and to both physical and sports education, which became legitimate as it was integrated into the Christian tradition. Religious myths and well institutionalized traditions brought it to the level of a convincing illusion of an ethical ideal, a synthesis which in the renaissance reached its peak. For example, Juan Louis Vivas, a Spanish scholar who was a distinguished teacher in many of Western cultural centers in the 16th century, understood that his quest for a *Christian peace* and for spiritual elevation must find a proper legitimate space for sport too. It was not to be solely preparatory practice for military achievements, but an important stage in the spiritual elevation of the human. He even constructed a philosophical-ethical framework for private practice.[11] It is important, however, not to confuse the Church's willingness to accept some sports practices, as part of a process of their being swallowed by Christian-oriented politics, with its *principal rejection of the essence of the ideal of sport*. The Church was not mistaken in identifying a dangerous competition here for the soul and telos of the spirit of the human being.

According to Saint Augustine one should sharply distinguish between the human body, which has not only a living soul but also "a life-giving spirit", and the "animal bodies", which "are not souls".[12] The human being, according to this conception, is essentially a heavenly creature, not because of but in spite of his earth-made body. According to this doctrine

---

11   Juan Luis Vives, "Linguae latinae exercitation", in: Peter McIntoch, *Fair Play—Ethics in Sport and Education*, London: Heinemann 1979, p. 21.

12   St. Augustine, *The City of God Against the Pagans*, translated by Henry Bettenson, London: Penguin Books, 1984, p. 356.

The first man, was 'of the earth, earthly', and he was made as a 'living
soul', not a 'life-living spirit'; that condition was reversed for him after
he had merited it by obedience.[13]

After *the Fall* the life-giving spirit which raised Christ from the dead ensures also that
it "'will bring to life your mortal bodies also, through the indwelling of his Spirit in
you.' The body will thus be related to the life-giving spirit as it is now to the living
soul".[14] The very possibility of this appearance, living in light of the possibility of
resurrection, opens the gate to happiness and joy within the horizons of spiritual life,
true religious life, which separate humans from other creatures. It is the mission of the
Church to guide humans to this dimension of human life; to overcome earthly joy and
happiness, pleasure and bodily strivings, which turn the human body and soul to be
drawn into the vanity of daily life and its infinite meaninglessness.. This is why it was
so important for this striving in Christianity to overcome what it conceived as quasi-
love and quasi-spirituality, which were considered especially dangerous enemies.

Modernity positioned human subjectivity and the ideal of being a citizen of this
world in the center—in secular philosophical and political terms. Accordingly, treatment of the ideal of the sport again changed dramatically. In modernity, sport as an
experience of the body, the soul, and the spirit was conceived as containing potential
joy, solidarity, and "healthy" love. As such it reflected and contributed to the historical
loss of ground by the Church in terms of its spiritual capital and its relevance to daily
life, compared with its former hegemony over the interpretation and realization of the
worthy way of life towards true love, happiness, and transcendence.

Modernity, however, initiated a dynamic that ultimately challenged its own foundations and telos. On many fronts of the innovations, such as capitalism, in individualistic-oriented humanistic education, criticism, and sports, it deconstructed not only
the dogmatic institutionalization of spirit, but *exiled Spirit itself.* It dissolved not only
the possibilities of the kind of transcendence it wanted to overcome: it eliminated the
very quest for transcendence and the possibilities for overcoming mere thingness and
pleasurable meaninglessness as a human "home". This fate did not spare the transcendental dimension of sport itself; a dimension which was part and parcel of the ideal
of sport in the classical era, during the middle ages, and in the renaissance, preceding
its transformation into "sport" and before its gaining popular fame; before arresting
the creative and solidarian potentials of sport as Love of Life and as a unification
of improvisation and training, self-constitution and attunement to the richness of
the cosmos, of the body and spirit, of the unification of aesthetic form, the roots of
natural life strivings, moral imperatives and cultural standards. But even if the birth
of "sport" signifies the exile of the edifying idea of sport, its end does not end its existence and does not terminate its immanent self-negation.

The ideal of sport, which is centered in modern sport as an important human involvement, values highly its psychic and even spiritual aspects, and certainly is not

13   *Ibid.*, pp. 536–537.
14   *Ibid.*, pp. 537.

content with its physical manifestations. As such it still realizes a quest for transcendence. But in modernity the soul, the *anima*, inherits the former preeminence of the Spirit. The telos of progress which is cherished by modernity is no longer conditioned or sanctioned in or by obedience to the gods or love of God, but rather in seriousness towards the ideal of healthy humanity and the love of human life and its telos in this world. The glory of humanity in this world as its "home" is conceived here as a value and humanity as a reality in light of which sports education in its broader sense is undecided between emphasizing physical fitness in its popular contexts and the devotion to education towards success in competitive sports and its consumption, which fertilizes "stars" as a commodity, displayed by sportsmen, media heroes, businessmen and politicians.

Modernity spreads the ideal of sport with great generosity across all fields of the public arena as a relevant guide for a model-behavior, and its educational functioning is similar to that of the knight and the monk in the middle ages. It was accepted in many abundant ways in modern realities of public life as a relevant manifestation of the good conduct, *arete*. An expression such as "in this manner be a sport, still contains the commitment to overcome instrumentalism or egoism and mere purposeness. And as such it retains a relation to high-flying or *self-overcoming*, which a modern human should realize. "Be a gentleman!" or "Be a sport!" further develops and cherishes its roots in the classic ideal of human elevation as manifested in the Socratic concept of *arete* or Machiavelli's concept of *virtu*. It departs from the Christian ideal of *imitatio Christi* and the chivalrous ideal of total commitment to honor and justice by emphasizing, instead, human solidarity and love of Life as a realization of absolute love overcoming the displays of **the Pleasure Principle**. This historical shift reflects the modern centrality of the anti-Diasporic humanistic-oriented ideal of universal emancipation. This project is anchored in the concept of "the human spirit", as manifested in the Olympic Games. Here people from as many as possible different countries, classes, races, sexes, and cultures ideally (and at times actually) overcome that which divides them and is unique to them, and reestablish, together, the world as an earthly Garden of Eden. This anti-Diasporic concept of human life, creativity, and solidarian self-constitution is realized also in the charter of the Olympic Movement.

The first article in this charter states:

> Olympism is a philosophy of life, exalting and combining in a balanced whole the qualities of body, will and mind. Blending sport with culture and education, Olympism seeks to create a way of life based on the joy of the effort, the educational value of good example and respect for universal fundamental ethical principles".[15] The second article states: "The goal of Olympism is to place sport at the service of the harmonious development of man, with a view to promoting a peaceful society concerned with the preservation of human dignity.[16]

15   "The *Olympic* Charter", http://multimedia.olympic.org/pdf/en_report_122.pdf (3.11.2004, p. 10).
16   *Ibid.*

The common essence as exemplified in the modernistic orientation of sport education stems from the notion that humanity has a "spirit" or manifests a unique "spirit"
or "essence". One of its better manifestations is the ideal of sport, along with other
displays such as art and science, and sacred rights such as freedom. As one can clearly
see in the charter of the Olympic Movement, the philosophical foundation of modern
sports education in its broader sense represents the anti-Diasporic nature of Enlightenment. It represents identification with the pre-assumptions of modern science and
with a positive Utopia that frames Enlightenment's social philosophy: homocentric-
rationalized Life might and should become a worthy "home" for the humans. It might
and it should realize this telos while overcoming the horizons set by tradition and
the abyss, dangers, and myths imposed by religious redemptive-Diasporic calls for
transcending this world and its pleasures/temptations/pain. Overcoming the monotheistic "home-returning" project was here of vital importance philosophically. This
was so in the sense of establishing universal human reason as an alternative to the
omnipotence and infinite goodness and wisdom of God; in the sense of constituting
an existential alternative to the love of God as a guiding telos for the human in its way
of transcending his bodily and earthly needs, aspirations, and limitations; and in the
sense of overcoming the monotheistic promise of a redemptive relation between the
human's exile in this world of flesh, meaninglessness, loneliness, violence, and suffering, and total, universal, as well as individual salvation. This monotheistic tradition offered a Diasporic perspective that made possible education for a redemptive existence
within the framework of the "home-returning" project. By offering the homocentric
project Enlightenment was anti-Diasporic and critical in its essence. As such, it offered an alternative, earthly, positive alternative, by educating for the humanization
of the world and its constitution as a worthy, stable, secured, beautiful, rational, just
"home". It never challenged the philosophical, existential and political assumptions of
"home", truth, or the quest for truth and worthy, aesthetic, life.

The anti-Diasporic philosophical assumptions of modern sport as represented by
the Olympic Charter represent its Enlightened commitment to the religion of humanity, as manifested in the positivistic religion of the kind of Saint-Simon or Au-
guste Comte, Karl Marx, and V.I. Lenin, a religion which secularizes and further
develops traditional religious myths that Christianity reproduced so successfully until
modernity.

As an ideal, sport worked its way even in medieval times. It was accepted after being domesticated and instrumentalized by Christian communities and theologies—as
well as other, non-Christian ones. Still, the main trend insisted on emphasizing the
dangers immanent in sports education. They did all in their power to expose it as an
agent of the body and of the natural life forces, endangering the "home-returning"
project that promised salvation via transcendence by overcoming the natural dimensions of Life and Love of Life. *Love of God* and edification promised an alternative
"home" to that promised by the ideal of sport, of science, and of rationalized, worldly
pleasures. The religious relations between being exiled in this world and redemption
allowed meaningful Life and love that offered happiness and meaning even in face of
pain, aporia, and solitude. The monotheistic "home-returning" project was commit-

ted to suppress and overcome these anti-Diasporic dimensions of Life, such as those propagated by the sports ideal: human self-love and earthly ideals, such as freedom, creativity, joyous effort, and fairness. Secular ideals, including the ideal of the essence of sport, were rightly conceived by the guardians of Christian dogma or Jewish tradition as a challenge to traditional Godly supremacy and a threat to the "home-returning" project. Philosophy of sport, from this point of view, constitutes a special kind of negation of the quest for truth and surrendering to true love; and as such, sport is a hindrance to true happiness in humans' realization of their spiritual dimension since it is a specially dangerous form of humans' self-love and domestication in a sinful, spiritless, world.

The sports experience and the earthly joy it offers attain the summit of the human's self-idolization instead of surrendering to the true God. In many respects they are worse even than adultery. The main challenge to the modern ideal of sport, however, did not come from a religious revival. It came from a very different source, and its influence was internalized and realized within sports activity itself. It represented a different source of energy: the quest for domestication of the earth, the body and soul, and even mystery, danger, beauty, and the quest for truth. Establishing home-centric Life as a secularized, earthly, Garden of Eden is very different from the "home-returning" project, which insisted on transcending the body and mind in light of love of God and his imperatives. It is, however, closer to this project than to the negative utopia or the anti-monotheistic, "Gnostic", Diasporic philosophy that overcomes all promises of truth, valid values, moral education, positive creativity and peaceful, comforting, guiding, consensus.

Modern nationalism found rich and diverse ways to secure the surrendering of not only sports activity but even of sports ideals themselves. Here I do not refer mainly to "political influences on the sportive activity and the Olympic movement", as some do.[17] I shall bypass central issues such as the politics of sport—for all their importance—and I restrict myself to the representation of *the essence of the ideals of sport* as part of the modernization process; I shall refer, if only briefly, to nation-building, to the culmination of ethnocentric creativity, and to the culmination of national militarism. At times as a rival, but normally as a partner to the same process, the logic of capitalism co-opted sports activity. The army, industry, school, and the media integrated the sports ideal and activity to ensure that they be incorporated in the national project. Sport became of special importance for strengthening the system and for veiling and internalizing its violences in ever more sophisticated ways, along with chauvinism, local folklore, and pride/frustration within the various developments of capitalist glocalization. How does sport function today, as a part of globalizing capitalism?

According to Ulrich Beck,

---

17 Winnifrith Tom, "Playing the game: morality versus leisure", in: *The Philosophy of Leisure*, New York: St. Martin's Press 1989, pp. 149–150.

The peculiarity of the present, and future, globalization process lies in the empirically ascertainable scale, destiny and stability of regional-global relationship networks and their self-definition through the mass media, as well as of social spaces and the image-flows at a cultural, political, economic and military level…

What is new is not only the everyday life and interaction across national frontiers, in dense networks with a high degree of mutual dependence and obligation. New too, is the self-perception of this transnationality (in the mass media, consumption or tourism); new is the 'placeless' of community, labor and capital; new are the awareness of global economic dangers and the corresponding areas of action.[18]

Glocalization is another part of the same development, in which the local identities, folklore, ethnocentrism, traditions, and modes of creativity and self-definition are integrated into the same process. Glocalization manifests more clearly also the loss, the "must", and the inequalities that are rationalized and imposed by globalization as an unavoidable world-wide restratification. Within this development, sport is presented globally and it is celebrated by universal rules, standards, strivings, and ways of consumption.

At the same time, however, sport as a global commodity is manufactured and consumed locally, serving and representing both ethnocentrism and false universalism in the form of globalization. It is of vital importance for sport's success as a worldwide commodity to function in the service of local passions and as a manifestation of the negation of the otherness of the Other. Without local rivalries, hate, and chauvinism, the worldwide reception and production of sport would not have been so successful. The glocalization of the production and consumption of sport makes possible the hidden educational agenda that sport serves so well, namely the successful activating and veiling of the violences of normalization; of controlling the hegemonic representation and consumption apparatuses, interests, powers and philosophical pre-assumptions of advancing capitalism. As such it strengthens the relevance and the vitality of self-inflicted dehumanization processes, while uniting the powers of the deepest instincts and strivings of the individual with the collective consciousness and standardized behavior: the human becomes part of the local crowed, the lonely consumer with his TV set that is connected to the universal "we", and to the forgetfulness of his responsibility to constitute his own aims, standards and creativity. He or she becomes a mere producer-consumer in a world where deconstruction, irrelevance, or exile is the faith of modern master signifiers and ideals, on the one hand, and authentic solidarity, creativity and love become co-opted and transformed by the system, on the other.

The betrayal of its own Enlightened ideals is not new to sports education. From its very beginning sports activity became—already within the framework of the modern nation-building project, establishing national ethos, and constituting effective colonization of the Other—a central element of the effort of the modern system to create,

18   Ulrich Beck, *What is Globalization?* Oxford: Blackwell, 2003, p. 12.

represent, and consume the modern body and soul and to create the healthy-conquering national "we". The development of eugenics, and the wide-scale jailing, castrating, and killing of mentally-ill, handicapped, and "just" poor all over the West, not solely in Nazi Germany, at the end of the 19th and in the first half of the 20th century, were part and parcel of the process that facilitated the centrality of domesticated sport in current culture industry. However, sports ideals such as readiness for and joy in prolonged effort, self-overcoming, and the quest for a "record" were not solely important in dramatic collective and sometimes militaristic contexts. They were even more important in forming the capitalistic normality—in its democratic and totalitarian contexts alike.

Within this process, ideals such as fairness, joy and happiness, which are bounded to the modern concept of sporting solidarity, are limited to the borders of the collective. Its vitality is directed to the Other as chauvinism, and to the frustrated, unfulfilled, standardized, and normalized self as self-hate and hero worship; being content in drawing one's self in the "fan", celebrating one's *pater familias*, or "stars". Note, however, that these practices dialectically clash with other, humanist-oriented practices that are realized in modern sport. This dialectical praxis reflects the philosophical origins of port.

Modern sports education is founded on a philosophical ground that has been destructed in the post-modern era, by developments that globalizing capitalism and today's sports education manifest in such a dramatic manner. The modern era made possible the relevance of universalistic-oriented non-instrumental philosophical categories that were supposed to be realized by sports education, enhancing free play, peaceful competition, equality, fairness, and Love of Life, serving no higher values and no ultra-human telos. Even if within the horizons of the politics of sports, this philosophy actually was used as a cover for legitimizing violence and colonization.

At the same time, it is true that sports education in its wider sense *actually* opened the gates to solidarity among individuals from diverse economic, social, religious, and racial backgrounds. Within the framework of modern sport and its educational ideals, from time to time men and women devoted to running away from themselves by realizing the modern ideal of sport actually in a mechanical, abstract manner mete as equals. They do so regardless of, and at times in conscious opposition to "their" asymmetrical backgrounds in terms of ethnicity, nationality, culture, religion, race, and gender. This is part of modern Western reality in different respects and levels, both as athletes and as "fans".

Nevertheless, in both cases this happened as a fragile, temporary, threatened, manipulated, exceptional moment, only to serve, ultimately, the interests of big business, militarism, and the self-disciplined human; the kind of human that will become the agent and the victim of global capitalism which is the supreme articulation of **the purpose principle**, that can flourish solely on the fertile ground of the human's self-forgetfulness and in her being swallowed by disciplinary powers of activization that pre-set the human's telos in the service of the totality of the aimless immanence. Normally, this quasi-realization of the sports ideal served the competition drive and the violent manifestations of **the purpose-principle**, namely the negation of **the plea-**

sure principle. In the service of this sublimation of the inner violence in the service of greater exterior instrumentalization of life, under the umbrella of modern sports education men and women were driven to ever greater identification with "their" heroes and ethnocentric-oriented collectives, while being part of a reification process that further de-humanized and strengthened the achievements of other normalizing educational apparatuses. One of them is the promise of empowering marginalized collectives and individuals who have not many other sources for pride, hope, visibility, acknowledgement and empowerment. But at the same time, popular physical education also contributes to modern democratization of the society and has functioned as an important element in the transformation of modern societies and cultures. We may ask, however, what is the role of sport in this process, and where does it lead modern societies before their entrance into the era of globalizing capitalism?

The process of *sport's serving for the standardization and productivization of modern societies* was part of a more general effort of forming the modern human and her strengthening not against, but rather for the empowering of manipulating social behavior in accordance with the needs of instrumental reason, the industrial revolution, and the nation state. It made a special contribution to changing military requirements, which emphasized the need for ever more individual innovation, improvisation, enterprise, cooperation, and total devotion to "the aim" pre-set by "the rules of the game" in all spheres of life. This is because the advancement of modern military techniques could no longer be accomplished by past blind, sheer obedience.

In its explicit and implicit versions modern sports education was central to both the advancement of industry and the sophistication of national ethnocentrist violences. It was instrumental for developing and empowering character, and skills such as punctuality, productivity, endurance, and self-commitment.[19] It promoted treating not only the natural world and the social sphere but even the inner nature and the otherness of Being as an object of manipulation. Every manifestation of Life, and even the body itself, was consumed in the service of the advancement of the rationalization and instrumentalization of the world. Vividness itself was called to realize itself in a reductionist manner that demolished its uniqueness and its otherness. Everything was supposed to be reduced to a mere function. Sport was no exception.

At the same time, however, central ideals and values of modern philosophy of sports education, such as freedom, universal solidarity and self-edification, were dialectically, even if only potentially, also subversive and oppositional. This is due to their erotic dimension, a potential transcendence, and universalism, which being unavoidable was oppositional to the world of facts and the specific manipulations in the historical settings where they were realized.

Even in face of manipulative modern national standardization, and in face of the near omnipotence of the capitalist logic realized in all levels and dimensions of life (and sometime a bitter strife enhances the two), modern philosophy of sports education still maintained its relation with the humanist tradition and the mission of

19   Max Horkheimer, "Neue soziale Verhaltungsmuster [Zur Soziologie des Sports]", in *Gesammelte Schriften* VIII., Fankfurt a. Main: Fischer 1985, p. 222.

edifying humanity in a solidarian, universalistic manner that dialectically was still connected to the Love of Life, erotic play of the self with nature and with the not-yet-oppressed human potentials; edification of the deepest strivings in their infinite connections to the richness of nature in an ethical yet ecstatic relation to the moment and to the infinity of the Other.. In this sense modern philosophy of sport offers transcendence *in*—*not from*—the immanence of Being. It negates in the most concrete manner the pre-assumptions and the ideals of the redemptive-Diasporic religious project of "home-returning" by overcoming nature, body, earthly love and sublunary creative pleasure of the kind offered by modern philosophy of sport.

This is what grounds modern solidarity among people sharing a common sports activity. Their solidarity, ultimately, symbolizes *total commitment to this world* as a worthy, pleasurable "home", where play, competition, and togetherness de-territorialize human existence into a renewed intimacy with worldly Life, the collective, and the consensual dogmas and standards. The walls of this "home" are ideally not made of bricks, which were made of a violent molding that prevents transcending critique and subversion. The powers of this "home" ensure the protection and reproduction of the self-evidence as well as the impotence of criticizing the representation apparatuses and the other violences that make possible the borders between "we" and "they", good and bad, relevant and irrelevant, true and false.[20] Only after the constitution and the securing of these *walls* is it possible for these violences to establish the self-evidence and the promise of a humanist-oriented pleasurable, playful and harmonious coexistence of the body and soul in their balanced relations with themselves, with the Other, and with the world. This is the modern ideal gate to equality, freedom, and solidarity among all humanity. As such, modern sport becomes an important philosophical and existential element for any peace education which takes its mission seriously.[21]

Such a practice has specific and concrete existential, philosophical, and political manifestations, as one could see in 1936 Berlin Olympic Games on the eve of the Second World War. A humanist philosophy of sports education, with a strong commitment to world peace and anti-ethnocentrism, could not at the same time also work for anti-dogmatism and for subverting human self-forgetfulness. Such an orientation is a constant threat and a serious challenge both to ethnocentric trends and to the capitalist logic that made modern sport possible from the very beginning. Historically it turned out that both ethnocentrism and advanced capitalism managed successfully to swallow and control both the subversive potentials and genuine humanizing aspirations of modern sport.

Historically, it turned out that modern philosophy of sports education found itself powerless or irrelevant in its engagement with these challenges. How are we to explain this impotency in the best case, and joining its rival in the worst? Before we try to offer an answer maybe we should ask: *Why is it that modern sport did not even come close to the achievements of traditional religion or modern art in terms of resisting the modern*

---

20 Ilan Gur-Ze'ev, *Destroying the Other's Collective Memory*, p. 16.
21 Ilan Gur-Ze'ev, "Philosophy of peace education in a postmodern era", *Educational Theory*, 51: 3 (Summer 2001), pp. 315–336.

world of facts and passions of which it is at the same time a part? Why did sport, along with music, become a modern religion of the masses, a "home" that offers standardization, domestication, and human self-forgetfulness in the level of passions, morality, consciousness, aesthetic, politics and economics in their deepest forms of realization?

Modern philosophy of sports education did not come to grips with the role of sport in modern capitalistic and totalitarian realities. It did not problematize its essence. It did not study the relations between sport and time. It did not question the relation between sport and imagination on the one hand, and sport and internalized violence on the other. And it certainly did not search for the critical, subvertive, and anti-hegemonic transcending dimensions of a sports counter-education, or for an alternative to what the West called for so many centuries "sport".

Modern sports education forgot its mission to transcend itself and to overcome the world of facts, fears, and consensus, and it betrayed the dialectics of its own existence: it did not try to understand that its mission is to offer a kind of sports education that will challenge normalizing physical education on the one hand, and education for competitive (individual and collective) sport and its representation, distribution, and consumption on the other. It did not meet the historic expectation/possibility of modernity: to offer humanity a kind of education that will contain more than sports ideals and practices in the limited sense, but also conceptions and practices of reflection, resistance, creative improvisation and self-discipline, as well as challenging the existing social-cultural context within which sports activity is situated. It did not critically reconstruct the relation between sports activity, the politics of the representation apparatuses, and the general historical-social-cultural context. In short, it did not offer sports counter-education.

The political dimension of sport within the framework of a genuine counter-education, however, requires *consciousness* and *praxis* which will challenge the hegemonic politics of representation and the power structure that it serves and reflects. What we are faced with here is the need for resistance to sports activity and theorizing sport as an object for manipulation in the service of abandoning eros, creativity, and genuine relation to the human depths and the "exterior" nature and making mere life the aim of Life.

In other words, it means nothing less than a challenge to the abyss that Western thought since Plato, and surely since Descartes, constituted between the human subject and the world of objects, between the body and mind, between the intellect and the passions, between voice and movement, between praxis and imagination, between the moment and eternity. Reestablishing a non-naive intimacy to the body and to the cosmos, without being swallowed by it or sinking into nirvana, calls for a Diasporic alternative not solely towards one's self-consciousness and its theories, symbols and forms but towards one's abysses and bodily pre-formulated forms of existence.

Actually, it means a non-instrumental, playful philosophy of holistic life that reconnects humanity to the truths of the Gnosis; an erotic seriousness and creative bodily poiesis turned into intersubjectivity which is in a sense Diasporic in this world: which is in the deepest sense a representation of *the totally other*. And as such itchallenges not only the quest for truth and the values of traditional societies and normalizing education. It also overcomes, in a playful, creative, loving, manner, the modern process of instrumentalization of the relation towards the Other, treating her as some-thing and not as some-one.

As such sports education is so much connected through *play* and *creativity* to Love of Life. It is a concrete negative Utopia. Against all the facts of modern reality and the techno-scientific world, in opposition to the self-evidence of reified life and instrumentalized eros, it is committed to offer not only a bodily-poetic negation of these facts but also a concrete alternative to the modern transformation of love, imagination, time, and pleasure.

As a negative Utopia it is Messianism without a Messiah. Yet historically, modern sport did not realize its potentials as a negative utopia and became part and parcel of a modern positive Utopia. It did not respond to the challenge of dialectically realizing a possible erotic, Dionysian, Diasporic, stand towards life as an abyss, as a danger, as a nomadic endless de-territorialization and transformation. The Diasporic philosophy has many negative aspects and realizations, but as a dialectical theory and human existence it has also "positive" aspects of which sport, when true to itself, is one of its supreme manifestations. It offers playful, anti-violent competitive edification of body-spirit relations. It signifies refusal to be swallowed by the call for nirvana on the one hand and for *the victory of the Same*, of the given facts, consensus and violent "victories" of the self-satisfied conqueror on the other. Modern sports education, however, did not insist on its otherness in face of the new forms of standardization and "spiritualization" which this abandonment facilitated in terms of mythical-rational-fashioned consumption of pleasures in a process within which human relations themselves, not only the cultural representations, are being totally reified. It is a development within which *the instrumentalization of knowledge, the reification of human relations, and the new forms of consumption of cultural products become essential parts of a process of standardization of life* and their return to the continuum of the thingness, of the Same. Why did modern philosophy of sports education fail to be true to its Diasporic mission?[22]

It failed because it cannot be true to itself (regardless of its "success") unless it becomes philosophically independent and politically antagonistic to its context—alienation that it feared to develop. Surely it did not develop alienation into a negative utopia within the framework of counter-education that will offer Diasporic sports counter-education. Its becoming sports counter-education, and developing its moral and political implications, would transform "sport" on the spot.

Still today, the moment sports education neglects its oppositional politics it becomes instantly and everywhere overwhelmed by totalitarianism, capitalism, and ethnocentric national ideologies. It becomes their loyal servant, even when maintaining a deceitful mirage of political neutrality or internationalism.

Critical thinkers such as Max Horkheimer already noticed the actual role of sports in the middle of the 20th century.[23] Its social function is to enhance the de-politiciza-

---

22   Ilan Gur-Ze'ev, *Toward Diasporic Education*, pp. 139–150.
23   Horkheimer, op. cit., pp. 221–234.

tion of the individual in the public sphere; to contribute to the exile of spirit and the possibilities for transcendence; to improve the function of those involved in the production and consumption, and to enhance the efficiency, of promised and realized pleasure as a dormitory drug for the populous. A special contribution is here reserved to the media.

The media represent and distribute "sport" and the promised pleasure arising from this ecstatic orgy. In a certain sense it is the media which produce or make possible "sport" as part of the same process that produces the customers and the fashions of the consumption of sport. The media is a vital part of a culture industry which domesticates-infantilizes-amuses its customers/producers and ensures a productive anti-eroticism. This anti-eroticism, which is made possible by the *pleasure machine* of which modern sport is part, allows the illusion of nearness to the essence of Love of Life and the delusion of transformation of capitalist factuality into real possibilities for solidarity, joy, and a happy attitude to the body, to nature, and to creative togetherness that will overcome "sport".

It is especially clear in competitive sport and in the education for the unreflective popular consumption of the ideal of *mere (pleasurable) life as the aim of life* where drawning in the empty "I" is enabled. It ensures disregard of the otherness of the Other[24] and blindness to the totally otherness of Life as danger and as a challenge. It enhances the constitution of a post-modern human who is completely drawn into the subjective pleasure of humans deprived of their individuality, which celebrates a false ecstatic catharsis. It sinks into the abstract "I" that functions as an agent of the "we". After being emptied of messianic rhythm, and fully committed to disregard transcendence, the quasi-erotic or fully standardized human is swallowed by the Same; it becomes part of a meaningless continuum. Within this surrender to immanence and abandonment of the transcending utopian axis of Love of Life, the human crumbles into *thingness*.[25] It retreats to become part of the immanence as if the world has became its "home"; not as a retreat to a pre-cultural unity with the cosmos. It is much more a flight into the heart of the "progress" of the techno-scientific world; a retreat into the psychological, philosophical, cultural, and social "home" that instrumental reason establishes as a sophistication of the anti-human progress of the anti-Diasporic project of establishing a earthly Garden of Eden. Globalism today is further developing and glorifying this historical project.

In this anti-transcendentalism, sport becomes a form of mere satisfaction of pre-socially organized drives, which are in opposition to the quest for happiness, which traditionally within the framework of Diasporic philosophy were called upon in light of the absence of truth: an invitation to Love of Life. The logic of capitalism in the age of globalism is committed to anti-Diasporic normalizing education. It realizes its

---

24   Emmanuel Levinas, "Is ontology fundamental?", in: Adrian T. Peperzk, Simon Chritchley and Robert Bernasconi (eds.), *Immanuel Levinas: Basic Philosophical Writings*, Bloomington and Indianapolis: Indiana University Press, 1996, p. 9.

25   Emmanuel Levinas, *Collected Philosophical Papers*, translated by Alphonso Lingis, Dordrecht: Maetinus Nijhoff Publishers 1987, p. 51.

anti-Diasporic commitment in glorifying and enriching the quasi-ecstatic immanence and deconstructing or ridiculing transcendence. And so it works efficiently for the standardization of each and every sports "experience" as a poiesis—and its function is mere commodified "experience", favoring "diversity" and catharsis while exiling the otherness of individuals, things, and the not-yet instrumentalized erotic and poetic manifestations of Being.

The sports "experience" in the form of physical education and as education for the consumption of competitive sport transforms happiness into "pleasure". It connects the id with the normalized dimensions of the super-ego. Happiness, play, creativity, improvisation, and love are stripped of their otherness, of their subversive, Diasporic, horizons, that allow the call for transcendence; they are repositioned as a recycled part of the immanence of globalizing capitalism and its logic. Eros is repositioned in all its glory in this historical moment—after its domestication, in the service of Thanatus.

Under the rule of the logic of capitalism and the philosophical and existential horizons of the immanence it enforces, Love is replaced by wonder and astonishment; and it is the astonished "I", not solely her admired "star", who becomes an *object*, a mere thing, a sign that functions with no telos, will, or truth in the immanence of the system.

As a particle of the abstracted humans who become "fans" or as a market-made/represented athlete, the "I" functions as a mere symbol. A symbol, which has been totally commodified.. The otherness of the "I" is forgotten, abandoned, or ridiculed in a manner that ensures its insignificance exactly at the moment when it works as a false signifier. The "I" is constituted and initiated by the representation apparatuses, and functions as a reaction. Even in the most intimate experiences at best in order to find herself she imitates her celebrated public representations. In the absence of the ideal of the autonomous subject, grand individuals are celebrated, actualizing the absence of a genuine public sphere. How ironic it is that this reality is so close to the Utopia of Gilles Deleuze, who, in the name of nomadism and rhizomatic existence, offers us the telos of an *all-becoming*. An all-becoming which is synonymous with a cosmic perception, or with the total disappearance of the subject. Following Mainlaender and the other most radical figures of philosophical pessimism, for Deleuze this is the ultimate aim of all becoming.

The insistence on "flexibility", "hybridists", "nomadism", and endless identities to be purchased, consumed, replaced, and recycled celebrates "the individual free choice" on the ruins of genuine freedom and of the true autonomous human subject. There is neither freedom in the immanence nor gates to transcendence. Only as such can globalizing capitalism give life the possibilities of "authentic" "experience" for the football fans of Real Madrid; not before extracting each of the individuals from her individuality, from her otherness, from her Diasporic orientation. Today, here, and only here, within this process there is a kind of nomadism that makes possible hope and emotional compensation for otherwise insignificant, standardized, de-humanized consumers of the sports industry; reified humans who are led to find in their consumption of "sport" the only or one of the only routs for their true self. This is how normalizing education works. Of special importance here is the process of *sub-jectification.*[26]

Modern sports industry acts as an apparatus of normalizing education in the sense that it produces the self-evidence as poiesis and facilitates the productivization and standardization of the energies of a false individuality; as part of a development which creates, preserves and enhances collective celebrated self-forgetfulness. Fashions, standards, commodities, producers and consumers are fabricated within the same process and are all leveled down to mere manifestations of the Same.

A vital element of the immanence of the present historical moment is *the need for a false, deceiving, impression of a Dionysian outburst, ecstatic creativity, and cathartic con-sumption of cultural products as a purifying excitement.* Here sport plays a special role in the production of this illusion of dynamism within the framework of a totalistic immanence. The sports industry as a vital part of present-day normalizing education contributes to ensuring the success of the present *unchallenged negation of Life*, the exile of creativity, and the subversion of Love. This, in settling for the present order; identifies with the governing facts. In the form of sports fans, humans are willingly being swallowed by the system—taking up a predetermined position in a dynamic, complex field of power-relations within which the possibilities of function, reaction, learning, and change are pre-set and impose temptations, rewards, and sanctions. Within the horizons of global capitalism it means that the process of subjectifica-tion of the subject is actualized by the subject's own becoming a devoted consumer of sports, even if only in a fragmented islet of freedom and joy in front of her TV set, throwing herself into self-forgetfulness; becoming a total consumer, while en-joying freedom of choice, and actualizing herself in realizing her identification with the "stars" or the "achievement", or "beautiful play", even if only for a fraction of a second; imposing a halt on the continuum of routine, oppression, and meaningless-ness; yet never unconditionally: only as a devoted agent of the same system and as its self-negating, entertained, victim.[27]

In advanced capitalist societies sports education (in its broader sense) offers a seem-ingly "different", "individual", and "free" attention, listening, and gaze; *a playful, plea-surable celebration of creativity*, pleasure and togetherness are being celebrated. This illusion of the "free", "different", "individual" gaze and listening is also connected to another important illusion: the illusion of a different sphere of events, a freer existence within the present order of things. This *illusion*, which sport helps to enhance, plays a central role and makes a special contribution to the negation of Love of Life while en-suring the pleasurable, quasi-transcending, forgetfulness of this negation. Here sport takes part in a comprehensive effort to eradicate and abandon the memory of Love of Life by enhancing of the devotion to the logic of the present order and empowering the efficiency of the apparatuses which are structurally committed to veil the violences of the hegemonic system. It is done by advancing new forms of collectivism, further

---

26   Gilles Deleuze, Negotiations—1972–1990, translated by Martin Joughhin, New York: Columbia University Press 1995, p. 113.
27   Neil Postman, *Amusing Ourselves to Death*, London: Methuen, 1987.

developing the subjectification processes and cultivating the pleasures which it offers its victims in ever more direct, sublimated, and "democratic" forms of satisfaction.

Modern sport, at the same time, is obliged to hide its true mission: it hides its role in the modern transformation of Love of Life and exchange of the erotic or religious quest for happiness for the drive for ever more pleasurable standardized satisfaction in the form of a quasi-ecstatic sports violence. Self-forgetfulness plays the part of individual erotic transcendence or of collective catharsis. In other words, its quasi-transcendental and false-edifying dimensions serve to hide its role in deconstructing genuine transcendence and Diasporic religiosity. But what is it that makes sports education (in its broadest sense) philosophically, existentially, and politically so relevant and effective? The resemblance to Love of Life. The resemblance of reified joy to happiness. It is exactly the physicality, the immediacy and the "authenticity" of the enthusiastic sporting experience in all its forms that makes sport so suitable and effective in ensuring the invisibility of the violences of the normality of the present order of things. The quasi-Dionysian energies enhanced by "sport" and "the sporting experience" make a most valuable contribution to the forgetting of the exile of Spirit and the invisibility of its forgetting. Each new "authentic" burst of hysteria contributes substantially to this capitalist-organized perverted catharsis.

As part of modern culture industry, sports education in its broader sense is not centered on schools or sport organizations; nor is it activated by the sportsmen, experts, media stars, and so forth. Far more, it is made possible by the cultural logic of capitalism, which makes possible, constitutes, and manipulates these "stars", "events" and "experiences" by its control of reality and its representation apparatuses. The logic of present-day capitalism constitutes an implicit, informal, philosophy of sports education, which is in direct conflict with the formal, acknowledged, and hallowed ideals and values of modern philosophy of education, as articulated in texts such as the constitutive charter of the Olympic Movement.

Today it is wrong to separate this informal philosophy of sports education—which is extremely relevant and effective—from the education propagated in the other channels of normalizing education such as MTV, McDonalds, CNN, and the Internet.

And yet, within and against these borders, a subversive-critical potential is still preserved in the explicit philosophy of sports education. The locus of this subversive and critical potential is the current reality of modern sports organizations. Note that this critical potential of modern philosophy of sports education is immanent in the essence of sport. This is precisely because sport, in its essence, contains self-negation: while part of the given physical, social, and cultural reality, it also represents a concrete actualized relation to the promise of emancipation from the given facts; a promise of love of bodily, natural connections to not-yet controlled and manipulated human experiences; a promise of Life as overcoming the present horizons; a promise for joy and happiness that is simultaneously connected to the spontaneous, improvised and physical—and to the disciplined will, responsibility and creativity. It is so close to the poetic attitude to Life.

The human potential for solidarity is here realized within the framework of self-constitution and elevation which unites the body and the soul, the human and the cosmic, the cultural and the natural, the spontaneous and the disciplined self, in a creative synthesis that offers transcendence.. This kind of promise for transcendence is modern, enlightened, and anti-Diasporic too, in the sense that it offers humanistic horizons within which it is possible to struggle for the constitution of social and cultural life as an earthly Garden of Eden. Here, ultimately, systematic efforts of individuals and collectives are to establish non-mechanistic and non-purely intellectual creation, self-constitution, joy, and peaceful intersubjectivity. It is important, however, to note that already here, in this refusal of the "home-returning" projects, the concept of "home" and its philosophical pre-assumptions are preserved. For all the importance of critique and social transformation, this project is still connected to the promise of a *positive Utopia* of peace education, humanist-oriented civil and democratic education, and the quest for an alternative to God or universal reason that was deconstructed by late modernity and globalizing capitalism.

In the field of sports, counter-education in the age of global capitalism should proceed from the tradition of critical theory and humanist-oriented sport and peace-education potentials towards Diasporic philosophy as a worthy tradition for today's counter-education. If true to itself this project cannot but be part of a more general project which challenges the essence and various aspects of normalizing education; an effort which is not to be separated from a concrete action: existential, philosophical, and political involvement to change reality. It is a struggle. A struggle which cannot be reduced to challenging the productivity of present representation and reproduction apparatuses.

A Diasporic-oriented counter-education in the field of sports will treat seriously the humanistic transition and the critical potentials of sports education. Special attention will be given here to the edifying elements of critique of the hegemonic sports industry. At the same time, however, the alternative of solidarity, joy, and non-instrumental efforts of the body and soul, of the individual and the partners, actualizes the utopian struggle as an opposition to hegemonic standards, ideals and practices. Of special importance is here the revisiting of *joyous playfulness* of the body-soul toward the richness of the cosmos the Other and the otherness of the "I" as against the ideal of competition and conquest. And yet, Diasporic-oriented counter-education in the field of sports cannot be content with such aims and achievements.

If true to itself, it should struggle to overcome this positive utopia of a humanist alternative and offer a serious response to the possibility of a negative utopia. The Diasporic negative utopia of sports counter-education has also "positive" dimensions and it shares humanist-oriented critical sports education. At the same time, however, it negates the optimistic vision of a humanizing sports education within the framework of a positive utopia of enforcing a worthier sports education.

The Diasporic refusal to see the historical moment and its hegemonic power relations and factual tendencies as a "home" to be domesticated, or as a de-territorialized "home" to be inhabited in light of a worthier positive Utopia, differs substantially from the alternative view of sports education that critical pedagogy might offer us in its best moments. Counter-education, when true to itself must be Diasporic. This is because counter-education must challenge any theoretical, ideological, or political "home", any master signifier, dogma, or ethnocentrism as manifestations of the Same, of the thingness of Being, which human beings are called to guard and transcend.[28]

> Counter-education, in this sense, must be at once Messianic and nega-
> tive at any cost. This means that it cannot satisfy itself even with iden-
> tification with the negation of self-evident, with the resistance to the
> ethnocentrism of the oppressed, and it cannot identify itself with the
> 'worthier' violences they actualize against their own 'internal' and 'ex-
> ternal' Others.[29]

Diasporic philosophy offers present-day counter-education a radical alternative to he-gemonic concepts of Life, transcendence, subjectivity, inter-subjectivity, and agency, and to praxis. It also offers an alternative view of the relations between nature and culture, mind and body, the individual and society.

Sports counter-education here should simultaneously offer a dialectical view of transcending the present horizons that are imposed by global capitalism; dialectics here should present radical negation that is not abstract; a negative Utopia that does not abandon Love. As such it is a sign for the possibility of a radical change in relation to the cosmos, to the body, and to consciousness as a normalizing "home".

The move from abstract, mechanistic, and dogmatic "critique" into Diasporic exist-ence and Diasporic-oriented sports counter-education might become a manifestation of Love of Life; a celebration of the body, of play, of improvisation, and a togetherness with the otherness of the Other, while edifying the nomadic way of existence.

Global capitalism is not a mere closure. It does not exhaust itself in fabricating false images of universalism, individualism, improvisation, and free choice: *it also opens new possibilities* for a Diasporic existence that need not become a mere intel-lectual message. In the form of counter-education, the relevance of today's Diasporic philosophy calls for concrete and specific fields of becoming, of self-constitution, of transcendence, and of Love of Life and togetherness. As such it challenges both the traditional philosophical and existential dichotomy between the subject and the ob-ject, the body and the mind, exile and redemption; it challenges also the post-modern "solution" as manifested in current global capitalism.

Sports counter-education might become one of the fields of manifesting Diasporic exis-tence in the most concrete manner. It might offer a creation that is not merely an intel-lectual project. Nor is it mere bodily experience. It is a creation that does not satisfy itself in an individualized, de-politicized self-edification. A creation that unites body and soul, the individual, the community and the cosmos, the passions and the con-scious, and that transcends the abyss of subject-object dichotomies without abandon-ing dialectical thought, imagination and creation. Sports counter-education might

---

28   Martin Heidegger, *Being and Time*, Oxford: Basil Blackwell, 1962, p. 234.
29   Ilan Gur-Ze'ev, "Critical theory, critical pedagogy, and the possibility of counter-education", in: Michael Peters, Colin Lankshear, Mark Olssen (eds.), *Critical Theory and the Human Condition*, New York, Peter Lang, 2003, p. 34.

signify a possibility for a creation that transcends "critique" into a rich, nomadic, Diasporic existence. Diasporic existence is not of the kind of the "home-returning" projects within the monotheistic religions (and secularized political theologies) that promised solutions and salvation. Counter-education here offers an alternative Diasporic philosophy, which opens the gate to a possible alternative existence: Diasporic existence while insisting on utopian negation also rearticulates intimacy between the aesthetic, ethic, intellectual and political dimensions of life as a manifestation of creative Love. Diasporic Love is of the kind Plato refers to in the Symposium:

> On the birthday of Aphrodite there was a feast of the gods...When the feast was over, Penia or Poverty, as the manner is on such occasions, came about the doors to beg. Now Plenty, who was the worse for nectar...went into the garden of Zeus and fell into a heavy sleep; and Poverty considering her own straitened circumstances, plotted to have a child by him, and accordingly they lay down at his side and conceived love... And as his parentage is, so also are his fortunes. In the first place he is always poor, and anything but tender and fair, as the many imagine him; and he is rough and squalid, and has no shoes, nor a house to dwell in; on the bare earth exposed he lies under the open heaven, in the streets, or at the doors of houses, taking his rest; and like his mother he is always in distress. Like his father...he is always plotting against the fair and good; he is bold, enterprising, strong, a mighty hunter, always weaving some intrigue or other, keen in the pursuit of wisdom, fertile in resources; a philosopher at all times... He is by nature neither mortal nor immortal, but alive and flourishing at one moment when he is in plenty, and dead at another moment, and again alive by reason of his father's nature.[30]

---

30   Plato, "Symposium", in *The Works of Plato*, translated by Benjamin Jowett, New York, 1927, p. 162.

CHAPTER 11

DRIVING AS A MANIFESTATION OF THE ESSENCE OF THE CURRENT HISTORICAL MOMENT

A mighty silence accompanies "traffic accidents," which are conceived in the public sphere[1] as an unavoidable and sometimes even as holy sacrifice of human victims to the Moloch of the current historical moment: the imperative of our day's flight from the burdens and openness of the abyss of existence into the affluent, pleasurable *quest for "home"*.[2] Within this quest for "home" forgetfulness itself becomes kitsch, is banalized, and reintroduced by the culture industry as instrumental. The instrumentalization of the screaming of the victims within the framework of the productivization of their silencing and representation take part in the process of camouflaging the exile of Spirit.[3]

Camouflaging *the exile of Spirit* veils the possibilities of living transcending, vivid, nomadic, Diasporic, life, in the present historical moment, within and against the recycled, closed, realities of the present realm of self-evidence.[4] And yet, driving becomes an important alternative to the possibility of transcending Diasporic life, while it is one of the most successful apparatuses of silencing such elements as the quest for love, freedom, creativity, improvisation, transcendence and self-positioning, rudiments that Diasporic philosophy can offer today's counter-education.

An intensive active life and rich rhetorical suggestions constitute this silencing that is so effective in the current world of motorized driving. The cost of this success is the avoidance of the struggle for genuine transcendence since it helps to establish the truth that transcendence should not be struggled for; as it is already actualized in the present reality. In today's order of things, as manifested in the arena of normalized driving, freedom, creativity, improvisation, and transcendence are enabled only in terms of efficiency and further instrumentalization of Life, and human life itself, even when it presents itself in regard to the loss intimacy or even the quest for nearness to the essence of Life and to seriousness in respect of its absence. *The loss* never appears

1   Juergen Habermas, The Structural Transformation of the Public Sphere, Cambridge: MIT Press, 1992.

2   Ilan Gur-Ze'ev, Toward Diasporic Education, Tel Aviv: Resling, 2004 (in Hebrew).

3   Ilan Gur-Ze'ev, "Counter-education and globalization", in: Yifaat Weiss (ed.), *Memory and Amnesia—The Holocaust in Germany*, Tel Aviv: Hakibutz Hameuchad, pp. 419–428.

4   Ilan Gur-Ze'ev, *The Frankfurt School and The History of Pessimism*, Jerusalem: The Magnes Press, 1996 (in Hebrew).

in our day in terms of avoidance of facing Life, meaninglessness, or aimlessness, or in terms of the possibilities of happiness and creativity in Diasporic life. In fact, the loss in the arena of driving is currently activated only in instrumental contexts such as demanding a reduction in the number of victims sacrificed, aided by "technical means" like "stronger enforcement of traffic regulations", "more investments in the sub-structure", and "traffic safety education". The essence of issues such as the institutionalization of traffic accidents and the rationalization of the "mistakes" that allow/produce them is systematically unaddressed.

In the standard discourse of traffic and road-safety, the enslaving myths of "the inspiring car", "heavenly driving", and "speed" are systematically ignored too, and with good reason. They function dialectically as regulative false emancipatory ideas ("liberating-creative driving") and at the same time as a vital part of the current worldwide de-humanization process of global capitalism and its culture industry. The sacrifice is not limited to technological progress. It is also an imperative of its ideals and symbols and it is presented in terms of inevitability: an imperative that, from an impersonal point of view, is rational and desirable. It is not viewed as being non-advantageous, an imperative of Fortuna, or as a manifestation of the all-mighty Moira; it is certainly not reviled as part of the toll of the present "progress". Nor is it represented as quasi-transcendence that makes possible the forgetfulness of facing Life with a Diasporic existence and homelessness with love, creativity, and improvised responsibility toward the suffering and the pleasurable domestication of the Other.

Since the loss is conceived in terms of the instrumental way of life, driving as a liberating experience and its victims both become part and parcel of the same victimizing reality. Traffic "accident" victims are viewed as a necessary and even a desirable means of protecting current consumerism and presenting it as emancipation. The current representation of driving experiences and the present celebration of its quests and their realizations support and enable the edification of this false consciousness by technological progress and the improvement of "the quality of life" and its pleasures, which have became an aim in themselves. This "quality" of reified life is the essence of Life at the current historical moment. In this epoch the "quality" of Life is nothing but standing stock, an instrument and crystallization of economic and technological "progress" as a manifestation of a unique successful quasi-spiritual "homecoming" to the pleasurable replacement of the Garden of Eden and the quest for redemption. Driving becomes an erotic, quasi-religious, experience; it makes possible the forgetfulness or the successful ridiculing of a Diasporic consciousness and the quest for transcendence.

This quasi-religiousness perpetuates the forgetfulness of humans that was traditionally facilitated by dogmatic and collective religious and secular "homecoming" projects. Today it offers a unique vivid alternative to improvisation, creativity, and happiness, and to the affirmation of Life by the Dionysian eros so that the Dionysian eros is gaily swallowed by the system and integrated into the present order. It is being castrated, transformed, domesticated, and only then does it reappear as part and parcel of the immanence of the totality of the present order of things, which nothing of worth is exterior to or "above."

In the present order that is governed by *forgetfulness* of the creative quest for the aim of human Life, human beings sink into ever more intensive recycled meaninglessness, Being is forgotten, and the Dionysian/religious "life" of thingness, of meaninglessness, is glorified and idolized as a "heavenly inspiring new Mercedes". The symbols themselves are reified and no longer refer to the transcendent. Within the framework of the present order *reification becomes "spiritual" and the world becomes, again, inviting "home"*, or, at least an arena from which narcissistic-oriented "homecoming" projects become meaningful within the framework of current realization and productivization of global capitalism and instrumental reason.

Within the framework of this retreat from Life as an abyss and openness into the closure of thingness and the Same, it is the car as a living symbol that is endowed with a life of its own; its life is adored and its mythological representations are religiously sanctified. This glory masks the conditions that make it possible. The car, the motorcycle, the speedboat, and the plane are depicted as "strong", "inspiring", "loyal", "admirable", "beautiful", and "lovable". They become objects of passion and they are even perceived as "divine". They do not unveil the powers and the passions that are committed to ensure and hide/banalize the exile of Spirit, but rather indicate its *intimacy with the death drive*.

As current driving unveils, in the present order of things Eros is enslaved in the service of Thanatos. The "speed", "performance", and "charm" of the motor vehicles, which slay the attendants to the uncontrollable, to the quest for the transcendence and authenticity of the human, are the adorable, the admired and the divine—not despite, but rather because they are assigned to death. Death is the nothingness of the driver's "unsuccessful" life on the one hand, and simultaneously the essence of the aimless "success" within the order of things that today's glorified driver manifests on the other. It is not the human that is triumphant in the productions of today's politics of representation—it is its negation that is celebrated in such exciting, inviting and quasi-edifying manners in the present order.

The traffic "accident" takes the form of the meaningless end of "successful" life. It is conceived as a *void* bereft of any collective "meaning", value, or transcendental dimension. This is to be attributed to the accomplishments of camouflaging the politics of luck that is so vital for veiling the essence of the current historical moment and relevant perspectives, sensibilities, yardsticks, values, knowledge and passions. Under these conditions, death is represented as personal, as an active form of the presence of (private) "bad luck" which, psychologically, is totally unexpected. At the same time, however, this private bad "luck" is inevitable, an uncompromised requirement, carefully calculated and immensely productive from the economic-rational point of view. The issue of the unexpected, in the sense of the Roman's Fortuna, has its role both in the modern totally administered society and in the post-modern "flexible" self-regulated systems. This issue, however, normally does not get the attention it deserve, and for good reason. From where is it possible in the present order to question its constitutive strives, its ruling practices, its meanings, its evils, and its aims? Not only is there no longer such an Archimedean or utopian point of view: the very passion, drive, quest for questioning the aim of Life and its meaningless has become irrelevant, and the language for its articulation exiled, while new master signifies have not yet replaced the exiled ones. Diasporic philosophy is not halted by such a reality, yet currently it is marginalized by its alternative that current driving manifests and realizes so powerfully. But this success exacts its toll and the victims are so many and so silenced.

The de-humanization processes in the present order produce victims whose suffering does not get a name; in the present public sphere, the traffic victims do not receive a name, a place, or a "voice" that will reclaim their humanity and challenge their systematic victimization even after death. They are voiceless, rationalized, instrumentalized deaths which, by contributing to the public horizon as commodities and statistical data, lead to encouraging reproduction and enhancing successful advancement of the present order. As such it prevents the unveiling of its truth and the possibilities for counter-education that will develop edifying Diasporic ways of life and encourage creative love of Life within and against the present reality.

Within the present horizons, "death in a traffic accident" is just one of the representations of the normal technological functioning of the system. It can be controlled to a large degree, statistically, by rational strategies and known manipulations at a cost that is rationally evaluated and justified in determining the life-and-death balance on the roads in a productive way. This balance between suffering and efficiency has a double function: it is proof of the system's effectiveness on the one hand, while it is the apparent inspiring presence of danger, openness, creativity and freedom in this world on the other. In both ways it establishes the stability and the validity of the given reality as a genuine "home".

The present reality, and the false consciousness it allocates, symbolize the continued triumph of the closure of the present realm of self-evidence to which human beings are attached and by which they are produced. Within its horizons, present human "normality" and its potentialities are attached to, and reproduced by, instrumental reason's control and its reproduction activities. They produce, present, advance, and reproduce human beings and their normality.

In the present order, normality, in the play of the production and reproduction of its self-evidence and regulative principles, *needs* "traffic accidents." It needs the "accident" and the ("bad") "luck" as a productive symbolic energy for the rational organization of subjects, passions, meanings, and borders to be crossed and overcome in an abstract, individual manner that will not challenge the fundamentals of the present order.

The organization, control, distribution, and consummating of current normality needs, in the requirement of its being as self-evidence, to be veiled. It is of vital importance that its essential qualities not be questioned, identified, or challenged from a Diasporic point of view. The importance of its being veiled lies in its need to maintain itself without being perceived as anti-transcendental.

In challenging the current historical moment from a Diasporic unveiling effort one should acknowledge that in a certain respect there is truth in the popular expression that "only total abolition of transportation will prevent traffic accidents". That kind of "accident", as the category of "accident" pinpoints, is not to be totally eliminated, since it is not the intervention of Moira here, not a transcendental intervention against the rational constitution of the order of things. It is, on the contrary, the face of this order itself and its inner logic that appears when encountering death and suffering in traffic "accidents". This logic is especially crystallized in the logic of motor transportation, which has peculiarities and localities in its ontology that are not to be reduced to mere crystallization of a stronger power. Yet the current realm of self-evidence and its knowledge networks, dynamics and power-relations is the only framework within which the logic of motor traffic and its "accidents" are possible. It is not just one of its manifestations.

Motorized traffic realizes a certain logic that can be criticized from a Diasporic perspective in face of the absence of conscious alienation of the kind on whose actuality Karl Marx or even Herbert Marcuse could still establish the quest for a qualitative change in human existence. The Diasporic perspective that is here presented is even more radical in the sense that it cannot satisfy itself in any ideological, political, or existential "home", and its negativity can be preserved even in the absence of conscious alienation and in face of the dawn of philosophical, educational and political projects of emancipation.

It cannot be defeated by failure or ineffectiveness, or even by the apparent triumph of post-modern manifestations of meaninglessness. Here we have to differentiate between the various utopian humanist-oriented "homecoming" projects that were defeated or overcome by their national or fundamentalist-oriented religious rivals and the Diasporic tradition of refusing to be swallowed by nihilism, on the one hand, and the positive utopias that offer nirvana, justice or truth in one of the rival "homecoming" projects on the other. Today the humanistic-oriented "homecoming" project (or the project of establishing on earth the genuine Garden of Eden) is not defeated: in fact it is almost completely manipulated, reintroduced and domesticated as a possible individual reified pleasure. The current capitalistic-oriented utopia is conditioned, constituted and justified by a reality that contains a system of codes of behavior and offers transcendence and quasi-meanings, passions, interests, fears, and dreams of which motorized road interaction is one of the supreme manifestations.

Traffic in the current historical moment universally, across different cultures and rival societies, realizes subjects, objects, and truths that are united in their anti-Diasporic productive commitment. This commitment is addressed by and realized in the practices of certain institutions. These institutions reveal a power that is beyond their specific and concrete manifestations when they institutionally/legally/expertly deal with traffic "accidents". Such institutions include the police, hospitals, centers for psychological treatment, car factories, traffic media and experts, the fashion industry, public relations experts, teachers, and many more. Without death on the roads, without "accidents", practically and logically, there is no life for these institutions, intervention theories, practices, and experts. Their well being, and even their very life and purpose, progress, and satisfaction in their professional life, are conditioned by the death rate on the roads. Outside or without the existence of those regulations, theories, practices, and institutions there cannot be a successful *forgetfulness of human forgetfulness* of its non-instrumental mission. In the absence of a Diasporic questioning, critique, and alternative creation the essence of the current de-humanizing way of being is hidden, affirmed and reproduced by its own victims.

The forgetfulness of human homelessness is assured by the historical establishment of indistinctness between the human life, in all its dimensions and levels, and the realization of the logic of techno-economic efficiency, which actualizes **the purpose principle**. In the field of transportation it offers total instrumental rationalization of life, even when it maintains and reassures the present balance of traffic injuries and suffering by avoiding "unproductive" or "unreasonable" investments in symbolic, financial, and political changes necessary for saving human lives. For the living, on the whole, the victims produce values lower than those who were saved—by not changing the situation that led to their suffering or death in "accidents".

Money and conflicting social interests alone do not determine the balance of evils that people suffer in the present order in the field of transportation. Western societies today are willing to suffer many hardships that have nothing to do with monetary gains: what is at stake here is *the productivity of striving and hopes*, the identification with the untruth of our historical moment and its universality and omnipotence that is guaranteed and reproduced by symbolic capital, and conflicting utopian calls to which the attention and passions are surrendered—much more than by financial capital. While being distinct, these conflicting utopian calls, or promises for emancipation and *self-fulfillment as surrender*, are integrated in different networks of power/emotions/knowledge-relations.

These historically based syntheses determine the balance of evils in the present order of things. In other words, the dynamics of symbolic and financial capital, in their changing context, determine the "good" or "bad" "luck" statistics and the exact range and scope of traffic "accidents" needed to preserve and develop the present order. By that I do not mean that a change in the rate of traffic deaths and injuries is not possible. I am only showing the procedures and powers determining the chances and the directions of such a possible change. Here one should distinguish between subjective sufferings and evils and the very existence, as individual, temporary, and conscious being, of human beings in current inter-subjective contexts; that is, existence as evil and existence within and as part of an objective will and power that manifests itself in subjective wills and power-relations in changing contexts.

The objective justification of traffic "accidents" also has a subjective dimension, ranging from the maintenance of present and promised commodities to those motorized participants who have not yet been hit.

In line with what Heidegger called Ge-stell, the current technological one-dimensional order of things hides the possibility of rescuing the uncontrolled potentialities, both in the compromising settlement in the present order and in the revolt against it. Within this existentia it is not just that spirit is in exile; even the reason of protest[5] and revolt has been conquered and is possible only as a *Diasporic existence* that is not confirmed, reassured, nor gratified and reworded by the current world of facts.

---

5   Herbert Marcuse, *One-Dimensional Man*, London: Routledge, 1964, pp. 123–143.

Within this order human beings are manipulated, activated, and destroyed in a productive manner in all dimensions and levels of their private and public existence, and *the illusion of liberation* is one of its most needed symbolic energy focuses. This mirage is not an illusion that activates people; rather it is a material dynamic in the network and appears objectively as a commodity that is manufactured, distributed, marketed, purchased, and consumed. It even has its market price, and what can be more "real" and objective than that?

What is at stake here is the transformation of human beings and their relative autonomy, the deconstruction of their dialogic essence and their reflective capabilities, and the industrialized destruction of their bodies. On the roads, specifically, it is realized in two seemingly antagonistic manners: on the one hand, participation in the traffic flow, privately and publicly enjoying its fruits, while on the other hand, suffering its evils and limitations to the degree of threatening public prosperity and destroying the individual.

It is worth pointing out the destructive element of the productive dimension of motorized traffic and emphasizing the overall rationality and productivity of the human's destruction, which is deciphered, in the case of traffic "accidents", as one aspect of a complex process. Here a greater integration between the public and the private spheres is provided, to the degree of the complete elimination of the private sphere. In other words, it annihilates a potentially spiritual and emotional autonomous realm in which the human's dialogic nature and uniqueness of being enable him or her to reflect on the conditions of the negation of the conditions for realizing his or her essence. What is at stake here is not his or her self-realization but the prevention of his or her struggle to reflect on the conditions determining his or her limitations, possibilities, and orientations. Diasporic existence is prevented by ensuring or at least enhancing the illusion that the current world is the human's world in which he or she is to make every effort to prepare himself or herself to be swallowed by the regulations and pleasures of *the pleasure machine* that is our day's actual Garden of Eden.

It is facing, not avoiding, the abyss of meaninglessness, namely, facing courageously, in a mature, Diasporic manner, the modes of production of meanings, quests, and ways for satisfaction and escapism/liberation making Diasporic existence possible as a concrete refusal to human integration in thingness, in the present reality. Love of Life, responsible nomadism, creativity, worthy suffering, reflection, and transcendence are vital elements of Diasporic existence even in the current post-modern moment. Existentially, economically, technologically and philosophically it is still an open possibility. The current global sophisticated sterilization of transcendence, on the other hand, protects the constitution of a one-dimensional immanence and one-dimensional life possibilities in a realm in which, ideally, everything would be automatized and rationalized with no "external" threat, with no transcendental axis that would challenge the self-evidence and the factual of the given reality. Under such circumstances the Diasporic energies of love, happiness, reflection, transcendence, creativity, and transformation are reconstructed and transformed into productive elements improving the efficiency of the present system. The current "homecoming" safeguards the unproblematic retreat of alienation into integrated myth, of the disintegration of the abyss of Life into unified thingness, of the transformation and integration of the human subject into an object in an omnipotent, closed, wholeness in and within whose immanence dwells the gay forgetfulness of the reified, post-modern, human. The return of the immanence of myth exiles the possibilities of the presence of **the totally other**, of transcendence, namely, of Diasporic existence.

The omnipotence of the immanence of myth is established today within ever-greater rationalization and rapid greater efficiency of the reproduction of the current reality. It happens while propagating the "individualistic" elements of the system and the possibilities for competition, self-decision, and change as an open option for every normal human being in *the learning society*. An ideal closed Platonic cave is constituted in an anti-humanistic and ultra-instrumentalist era: motorized vehicles, especially the fast models, glorify "individualistic" values in a special context. Within this context, unlimited mobility, total privacy, and "individualistic" control of life and fate are praised as part of their actual destruction.[6]

Within the framework of the current capitalist globalization, technological developments, and the representations of the culture industry is there less room for counter-education, which strives for reflection, struggles for dialogue and transcendence, and offers resistance to the present order of things? The present conditions effectively reduce the social, cultural, conceptual, and existential potential for genuine dialogue and true solidarity. Under these conditions there is less room for the individual's struggle to become Diasporic, to become some-one rather than some-thing—to become an ethical I, who not only reflects but also commits herself to transcendence in relation to the Other as part of a responsibility toward the otherness, toward Life. The current world order reproduces itself by reducing the human being into some-thing, a mere agent, a efficient producer/consumer. As such, she accepts the present realm of self-evidence, identifies with it, and abandons the Diasporic love of Life as an actualized preparation for and response to the sudden possible appearance of **the totally other**. Immanent to the current world order is that there is neither room for dialogue nor for solidarian self-positioning, and self-constitution.

Diasporic philosophy allows the otherwise irrelevant question: why should we, within this order, challenge the present reality through counter-education? *Why should we search for our otherness, for our humanity by searching for alternative, microscopic and general realities*: concepts, experiences, and actions of which can ultimately change the system and its cultural, social, gender, and ethnic formations? The reduction of the subject into a "subject" and the development of a contingent, multicultural, fluid, local and temporal identity, lead to knowledge and value forms that are part of the general reification of the current globalization of capitalism. Within the present culture industry that represents and serves this order, "the individual" is hailed purely in terms of her status as a consumer/producer. Free choice and democracy are expressions that find themselves celebrated purely within a rhetoric that serves the reproduction of this anti-humanist order.

6   Mary Tiles and Hans Oberdiek, *Living in a Technological Culture*, London and New York: Routledge, 1995, p. 130.

According to the concept presented here, the current social and cultural conditions erode the possibility of struggling for self-reflection, radical cultural critique of the existing system, and its rational transformation in the Kantian sense. It includes reducing the possibility of reasoned and solidarian acts of changing the system and its cultural, social, gender, and ethnic formation. As part of this circular dynamic, the hegemonic system effectively distributes a liberation consciousness that serves as an agency to improve its own reproduction. In light of its deprivation of human dialogue and reflection potentialities, it might be called false consciousness.

The Diasporic quest for transcendence and the advancement of reflective power represent a movement that is well suited to the metaphor of vertical creative movement: a movement that is essentially a potentiality and is aimed by Love of Life toward the not-yet-realized, to the absent, and that is not content with any "homecoming" project or any nirvana. Traditionally, this kind of movement was not conditioned by, but was rather attached to different kinds of movement that actualized the Diasporic consciousness within rival projects of "homecoming." Traditional movement possibilities were dialectical, while the Diasporic, reflective, potential manifested "vertical" ("platonic") movement and openness to the eternal and the absolute. It was cyclical and part of the eternal movement of the universe that gave dialogue its transcendental possibilities. At the same time, it was based on the recognition of the human limitations of the horizontal movement possible within the framework of "the realm of necessity". Still, an alternative concept of Diaspora and an alternative quest for movement that was beyond the dichotomy between immanence and transcendentalism, which offered a Diasporic consciousness against and not as part of "homecoming" projects, were always a challenging human possibility. This eternal nomadic existence is even today relevant and opens new possibilities for current counter-education.

In Plato's Phaedrus, "the being which really is" is in a "region" "above the heavens," and real human existence is to be realized only by *transcending* the human being from the given "up" into it, "winged" as it were:

> The natural property of the wing is to carry what is heavy upwards, lifting it aloft to the region where the race of the gods resides, and in a way, of all the things belonging to the sphere of the body, it has the greatest share in the divine, the divine being noble, good, and everything which is of that kind.[7]

The present possibilities of movement are different. Today's fast traffic is taking place in a context in which "vertical" movement, transcendent, religious, movement of the homeless creative individual toward the veiled mysterious, has become irrelevant and has actually disappeared, while "horizontal" movement within the immanence of the one-dimensional framework of "the same" is no longer looked upon as limited, hard, and slow. Motorized traffic does not represent a mere technological change. It represents a totally different metaphysics of movement and different human possibilities.

---

7   Plato, "Phaedrus", translated by C. J. Rowe, Warminister: Aris and Phillips, 1986, p. 61.

> Speeding is precisely elimination of expectation and duration...Shift-
> ing the soul this time from the brain to the motor will free man from
> apprehension about a future that no longer has any raison d'etre, since
> everything is already there, here and now, present and over at once, in
> the instantaneous apocalypse of messages and images, in the great old
> joke at the end of the world![8]

Motorized traffic is necessarily a movement of a new kind, a kind that is presum-
ably unlimited and borderless. The (inevitable) absence of limits to this movement
has a twofold manifestation: in speeding ability and in the ability to drive anywhere
while disregarding the challenges of purpose and meaning, and establishing a promise for *immanent transcendence* within the given reality not as its overcoming but as
its realization. The ability of getting anywhere overthrows the traditional concept of
movement, a concept that received its meaning in light of its purpose according to
and within physical hardships and limitations as well as practical ambient factors
and the slow moving nature of locomotion prior to technological acceleration. The
new speedy mobility is unique by being represented and conceived as an expression
of privacy and independence; here drivers are supposed to drive their vehicles as a
perfect expression of their free will, unbounded by external limitations with a feeling
of no control or direction whatsoever. *The realization of free will, creativity, determination in care for the self, and the ability to change and improvise are conceived, or at least
are supposed to be conceived, as an expression of privacy and autonomy in the world as a
rewording "home".* At any given moment such privacy might direct itself upon others
as an inescapable disaster or it may come about in the form of understanding and cooperation with them, as a way of demonstrating that they are in control of motorized
vehicles, namely that they control Life itself. The Garden of Eden is instrumentally
regained.

Traditional traffic mobilized men and women and their assets in a linear axis within
a recognition of its limits and its passion for an erotic movement which is essentially
different from that characterizing the daily round of life where "everything is the
same." The essential movement in pre-motorized traffic was driven by an erotic power
for transcending man from daily life, from the limited and the defective toward the
good, the beautiful, and the right, the real and the eternal.

The essence of today's traffic lies in the absence of erotic silence, an absence that
reproduces the continuum of the totality of "thingness." In the present realm of self-
evidence, the phenomenon of "the same all the time" is recruited into the dialectic
between and within horizontal movement in the realm of space (speed) in which
speed inherits the realm of time (eternity)—a dialectic that characterized the quest
for (vertical) transcendence. Historically, the narcissistic being enclosed within the
car with the illusion of overcoming time and of control of external space, and the
motorized vehicle as a locus of "excitement", not only replace religious ecstasy, the

---

8   Paul Virilio, *The Art of the Motor*, translated by Julie Rose, Minneapolis: University of Minnesota
     Press, 1995, p. 92.

traditional quest for eternity, and the Enlightenment's devotion to autonomy and reflective capacities: even more, they almost ensure the very possibility of Diasporic nomadism and the quest for genuine transcendence. *The illusion of controlling a human-made machine in a completely self-created and self-controlled environment is today's Tower of Babel.* It is far different from controlling an animal in the service of human needs. It avoids the question of God, his laws, and the problem of not being a God or being exiled from God, truth, meaning, aim, and Diaspora. But the realm of human creative fulfillment that the original Tower of Babel builders tried to construct was a religious act of refusing all projects of "homecoming"; it was an alternative to the heavenly enterprise, indeed its foundation, and it was Diasporic in the sense from which today's counter-education should learn much when it articulates its refusal to be integrated in today's world order of things.

The *illusion* suggested by the automobile represents an alternative to previous stages in the history of Western civilization. It also represents an alternative to the cultural stage of commitment to an ideal of a free public sphere, where reason and free men and women were supposed to flourish within a dialogue that dwells in concrete social conditions. This transition from one realm of self-evidence to another is technologically very productive. It also defines productive self-reproduction possibilities of the system that utilizes human beings as drivers and travelers—who are transformed into a *commodity* and are treated as objects. They become "flexible parts of the market" for car dealers, doctors, policemen, teachers, and advertisers. In parallel, they become *objects* in the sense of a flexible, dispensable, workforce in which, "practically" and rationally, it is useless to make a division between the driver, the car, the movement of the car, and the movements of production/consumption dynamics. That is not to say that motorized traffic has to manifest itself in the same ways in any possible world. It is argued that in a different realm of self-evidence a different set of passions, myths, procedures, and criteria would be in operation. Another metaphysics would be at work in it also, in which traffic behavior would no longer represent the quest for avoiding Diasporic homelessness and the striving for its replacement with domesticated passions for "homecoming" that represent surrendering to fear, to "God", to the governing manipulations of the "home".

An enlightened Judeo-Christian Utopian quest strives to create such a reality that would be a better, more humane reality. In the meantime, the productivity of present anti-metaphysics secures the scientific and technological progress within which the myth returns as the sole ruler in science's and (instrumental) rationality's name. This reality manifests a false consciousness that reproduces and advances it within the framework of technological progress where it is useless logically to make any distinction or separation between the accident and the mistake. This is so since the accident manifests a personal mistake that is logically necessary and socially productive, according to the system's inner logic. The new myths that determine the causes of traffic "accidents" are scientifically accurate, socially necessary, and technologically productive. In a sense, it is so in such a way that the highest conscious expressions of individuality have become nothing less than the expressions of the demolition of the subject's autonomy. This reduction represents the destruction of a kind of ideal commitment to a negation of power fields in which the hegemonic discourses produce a consensus that constitutes an ever-evolving realm of understanding in which subjects recognize other subjects and collectives as solidarian partners for a common movement toward Utopia.

False nomadism produces total identification with the world as a an infinite, diverse "home" by ensuring false libertarian consciousness. Here, driving functions as a myth that enables one to see the road networks and the regulation dynamics of present society as the antithesis to the penetrating forces of the system in the private sphere. The driver functions as a eunuch, protecting the public and the private spheres from being penetrated by new, vivid, and young myths on the one hand, and from the Diasporic alternatives on the other. The current world order is defended this way against the rough winds of a new realm of common self-evidence that is about to overrun and conquer the aging, dissolved realm of self-evidence that is under pressure. The *castration of the erotic essence of movement* in a world where motorized traffic was unknown and instrumental rationality did not rule might be seen as productive. It is productive from the point of view of the capitalistic commodities market.

Under these conditions, there is much need for *Life as an abstraction*, for virtual creativity, and for false nomadism. Within this framework the "normal" or "average" driver is born. Every insurance company realizes this possibility. This "normal" driver who identifies with the fast driving myth is the one who surrenders himself to the systematic castration that the present capitalistic society imposes on its followers. The struggle for genuine freedom and transcendence has no place. There is no room for a struggle for freedom and transcendence in a reality where man conceives of himself as one who might be with himself as a driver, as one who "controls the business", and as someone who "acts in a right manner", according to rules which he cannot avoid, even for a moment, with no danger of capital punishment.

In ages when instrumental reason did not reign as sole monarch driving had a different character. It was a manifestation of the gap between the ideal and the present situation, from the viewpoint of the exiled person from the absolute, truth, or God. It was conceived as mobilizing and instructing in a Diasporic reality that is essentially transcendent. See, for example, Ecclesiastes 2: 3, "My heart conducting itself with wisdom, how yet to lay hold on folly", or Lamentations 3: 2, "He hath led me and caused me to walk in darkness but not into light". Today, when traffic and transportation are viewed with an anti-ontological and non-dialectical eye, traffic is conceived as self-regulated movement in an alternative unlimited reality that is self-sufficient, an aim in itself within the framework of an omnipotent immanence only within which is there room for transcendence. The philosophy of Gilles Deleuze and Felix Guattari is one of its best manifestations.[9]

The Deleuzian concepts of nomadism, life as a dynamic work of art, and transcendence are vital for any current reflection on today's driving and surely for understanding its relation to other modes of anti-Diasporic movement, such as that which cy-

---

9   Gilles Deleuze and Felix Guattari, *What is Philosophy?* translated by Hugh Tomlinson and Graham Burchell, New York: Columbia University Press, 1994.

berspace is offering for cyber feminism and cyberpunk. This is because in its ultimate anti-humanistic axis Life becomes "the active force of thought", and thought becomes "the affirmative power of life". "Thinking would then mean discovering, inventing, new possibilities of life".[10]

The comprehension in fashionable conventions and in dominating and repressive administrative procedures of automatic movement that present-day traffic represents is taking the place of the erotic quest for absolute truth that traditional forms of transportation have represented since the collapse of the Tower of Babel. Even the Enlightenment's vision of the human being in the world, traveling within this framework, still held on to some essential elements of the Judeo-Christian realm of self-evidence. In traffic and in the present context, and especially in the "excitement" of driving at high speed (e.g., like that possible in a "powerful" BMW) and so forth, the driver can reassure himself that he has autonomy over reality and sovereignty over time in the public sphere—overcoming its non-narcissistic regulations, and drive back home, within and into the endless horizons of his narcissistic-totally-constructed-manipulated self. Giving the driver the private sphere within the public sphere hides the disappearance of both dimensions. It presents neither an accident nor good or bad luck, but expresses the efficiency of the system's own realization by reducing human beings to drivers or passengers. The matrix manifests itself through agents and dynamics as exemplified by drivers and passengers in traffic, and there is no other reality or absolute idea outside it, as there is no reality to systems outside the realms of self-evidence.

Diasporic philosophy does not claim that human beings are mere representations and agencies of the systems that create, activate, imprison, and control them. In light of Diasporic philosophy a dialectic between ontological and historical dimensions is unveiled. Historically, there are various symbolic and extra-symbolic opportunities and limitations for human beings to transcend the system and its limited horizons. Ontologically, it is important to emphasize the forgetfulness of the wholeness of Being and its openness to the not-yet-realized, the dimension of potentiality, of **the totally other** as represented in the **principle of hope**. However, even within the framework of Diasporic philosophy, the transcendence and the overcoming of limitations and hegemonic strategic attitudes, symbolic, and extra-symbolic dynamics, are concrete, specific, and historically and locally contextualized. That is why the anti-humanistic and anti-Diasporic-oriented tendencies in the relatively prosperous West are so effective, as can be seen in the traffic arena.

The world of fast traffic is a place where Diasporic humanistic potentials have no environment in which to be realized and developed. The constant noise of the engine, the density of the traffic, and the impossibility of a certain, determined attitude to the environment—that is both spiritually and ecologically balanced—contribute to the constitution of the dynamic and the *speedy intersubjectivity* that are an arguably logical and political imperative. Psychologically, the speeding and the quest for speed can be characterized as a "quest for danger" and sometimes as a healthy "stress backing". I

---

10   Gilles Deleuze, *Nietzsche and Philosophy*, translated by Hugh Tomlinson, Minneapolis: University of Minnesota Press, 1983, p. 115.

am searching it for an ontological sign of the success of Ge-stell within it, which hides the uncontrollable. We must search for the unobservable that traditional Western art and *tekhne*, in the Greek sense of the word, brought into the light of everyday reality out of the realm of mystery, as something that is autonomous in this daily reality and not as part of it. Under such circumstances, human possibilities and limitations were different from the ones confronting the new man of today. Today's exciting driving as a mystic experience, as *poiesis* in the sense of seeking the limits of the (im)possible, rather than as an expression of the manipulation possibilities of the present system, is a manifestation of stolen freedom and false revolt within a totality where there is no relevance to the concepts of estrangement and repression. Such an earth has no room for trying to rebuild the Diasporic humanist enterprise, as exemplified in the projects of the builders of the Tower of Babel, Socrates, Buddha, Moses, Erasmus, Schopenhauer, Kierkegaard, Nietzsche, Benjamin, and Adorno.

Within the horizons of the false public sphere, it seems inevitable that on the public level rational men and women will contribute their share to decisions on issues such as reducing traffic speed, prohibiting driving under the influence of drugs or alcohol, and other regulations of that sort. At the same time, *on the private level* they are driven both to demand their stolen freedom by the negation of instrumental rationality's demands and to preserve the well-being of the system and their own safety as agents of that system and its current dynamics and horizons. In practice, whenever possible the new man will rebel against the conditions that constitute him, his possibilities, his pleasures, and his miseries at the earliest opportunity. The taboo that Ge-stell constituted will be destroyed with extreme joy, real joy, whenever possible, sometimes at all costs. This rebellion is punitive and useless and does not represent nomadism and Diasporic existence. In fact it represents its diametrical opposition, fear and forgetfulness. This forgetfulness of the quest for creativity and transcendence is realized in the irony of the current world order that calculated such a reaction and that has called for it under its secret educational agenda.

In conformity with the present order of things, a person realizes the forgetfulness of Diasporic existence[11] as a driver. The driver leaps the abyss between immanence and transcendence in the new totality that becomes "home" and enforces irrelevance on all philosophical and social impasses. According to the degree of "success" of his relative effectiveness in representing himself as one who is "successful"; to a large extent the driver is recognized as a persona according to the car that he has or does not have. He drives a vehicle that simultaneously enables him both to manifest "success" and to rebel against his stolen uniqueness and freedom in the ocean of rules, regulations, and control apparatuses that manifest and hide the essence of the logic of the present world order. From the "outside" a reaction will be identified on a scale ranging from "dangerous driving" to "madness". There are studies emphasizing the incommensurability of the subjective and the objective dimensions in motorized driving.[12]

---

11   Ilan Gur-Ze'ev, *Toward Diasporic Education*, p. 114.
12   Lester and Charles Lave, "Barriers to increasing highway safety", in: Peter Rothe (ed.), *Challenging the Old Order; Toward New Directions in Traffic Safety Theory*, New Brunswick and London: Transaction Publishers, 1990, p. 78.

I do not see in it an incommensurability manifestation, but rather one of the many representations of *normality* in the present mythic one-dimensional realm of self-evidence. This is a false rebellion because it is planned and controlled by the system, constituted on the private and collective repression and guilt consciousness of a supposed primordial sin[13] practiced daily in the earthly hell of normality.

This normality is produced and reproduced by the different elements and dynamics of symbolic energies which allow the destruction even of the mere potential of reflection on knowledge, post-modern de-humanization, and global capitalistic forgetfulness; the possibility of a utopian glance at the possible non-repressive, non-instrumental attitude that could have represented a comprehensive alternative to a totally different concept of movement and traffic is completely obfuscated.

Within such a utopian alternative there is a room for a different self-motion and intersubjective mobility where there are no rational, calculated, institutionalized traffic "accidents". The self-driven movement is never independent. It is always contextualized and materialistic, but it can struggle to overcome limitations by deconstructing the realm of self-evidence that is enclosed within its horizons. It can try to transcend itself by revealing coded social manipulations and truths, validity parameters, and consciousness production operations; by deciphering these codes and by denoting their political meaning. In this sense the alternative universality and the alternative individualism here represented in these terms create a potential for a liberation that is met by dangerous alternatives to humanist tradition and whatever liberalism has realized in the present political, social, and cultural systems that we have at present in Western societies. A spiritual alternative to the present order might create an alternative realm of self-evidence that would be less problematic and more terrible, in light of Enlightenment ideals, humanist values, and liberal social regulations to which present Western societies are committed. The history of motorized transportation reveals Western culture's openness to, if not quest for this alternative; where there is no place for autonomous subjects, solitary intersubjectivity, reflective discourse, or dialogical attitudes to society's challenges.[14]

In modern times the road networks have become an arena of knowledge that contains its specifications and uniqueness, but have basically reflected, tested, and reassured the rationality of each driver and of the entire system. The logic of the present realm of self-evidence is built within the collective consciousness, in the symbolic and commodity distribution and consumption practices. They are present in the education of each person to behave within the given horizons of reified procedures, rhetoric, and practices that are both universalistic and one-dimensional. The roads and the behavior on them reveal an educational enterprise and examination process of the universality of the symbolic violence of the present normalizing education.

---

13 Sigmund Freud, "Totem and Tabu", in: *The Standard Edition of the Complete Psychological Works of Sigmund Freud*, Vol. 18, translated by James Strachey, London: 1971.
14 Ilan Gur-Ze'ev, Jan Masschelein and Nigel Blake, "Reflectivity, Reflection, and Counter-education", in: *Studies in Philosophy and Education*, (2001), 20: 2, 93–106.

It has become an arena in which human rationality is tested, realized, and reassured daily by each driver in each second of her driving experience. Too much independence, nonconformism, ignorance, or luck of practical experience in this field is sanctioned or rewarded not by a personal teacher, ruler, class or interest group, but by the logic of the present order, a network in which they themselves function simultaneously as its agents, rebels, and victims. Driving in the traffic network becomes a manifestation of the creativity and totality of the immanence, within which "transcendence" is possible after all, while reducing the human to a driver, an affect, a mere reaction to another reaction, an echo to the omnipotence of meaninglessness in which there is no "exterior", redemption or possible Diasporic, creative, existence.

Traffic today represents an important site of instrumental rationality and its anti-Diasporic successes. These successes are manifested everywhere. However, the success of instrumental rationality is not totally without problems, as can be seen in ecology, medicine, or transportation. These *cracks* in the present order open possibilities for hope and for the actualization of Diasporic life. On the roads, failures of the present order are of tremendous magnitude: exactly where it is most vital, traffic becomes ever more intense, costly, and inefficient, as can be seen in traffic jams in the big cities around the globe. Yet as in other fields, instrumental reason's failure is normally recognized solely according to its own standards, and so are the suggested solutions. This proves to what degree a realm of self-evidence is omnipotent—until its downfall. Traditionally, a realm of self-evidence could be destroyed from the outside or stagnate and disintegrate from within, since it includes or could include antagonistic spiritual elements. The uniqueness of the present Western realm of self-evidence is the absence of spiritually antagonistic elements. Therefore, dramatic antinomies that represent instrumental reason's total control do not endanger its systems or its perpetual advancement—at all costs, total catastrophe included.

The traffic that in the West is more or less available to all levels of society represents the erosion of reification, repression, and revolt against it. The dynamics of regulations, their realization, and their changing conditions, from both the system's and the users' point of view, are not to be divided. The system is sophisticated, flexible, diverse, and at the same time one-dimensional and universalistic. There is no repressive group interest or conception to be revolutionized or challenged. To survive as a driver one must adjust to the system and contribute one's share to its well-being. The driver is a manifestation of the commodity exchange in which even death in a traffic accident is a rational requirement of the market, a technological advance, and the continuation of "raising the standard of living" among the surviving drivers. These ideals and requirements have evolved out of modernity, but they negate its Enlightenment utopia and its concrete social and cultural potentialities.

The world of traffic is only a fragment of a complicated totality; however, it is a major junction between different networks. Here is a perfect manifestation of the almost absolute validity of the universality of the master signifiers of the present order, as understood and performed by the representatives of the different sources. This is not to ignore that in present post-modern conditions, more than ever people can simultaneously participate in different and sometimes conflicting constellations which may be political, conceptual or psychological, modern, post-modern, and/or pre-modern. The acknowledged pluralism is promoted essentially as a one-dimensional phenomenon, facilitated by an irresistible universalistic logic that there is no public way to resist it or to revolt against it with no immediate punishment. This argument can be seen in the present conditions and rules of traffic and road "accidents". The "accident" is thought to be one of two things: either misunderstanding by those involved in the traffic or "bad luck". The second possibility might take the form of a kind of institutionalized neglect of road conditions that cause the "accident", which is systematically represented as a personal issue, or "bad luck", as if it were a heavenly punishment. Such is the attitude of many of the cases of the first category, when "bad luck" or "mere coincidence" are manifested in the form of a drunken or "bad" driver approaching from the opposite direction.

Diasporic philosophy offers us an alternative to Foucault's thesis concerning the clinic or the jail. In respect of traffic space it offers us a reflection on driving as one of the best normalization and disciplining sites. It unveils the forgetfulness and the normalization process not as a Foucaultian closed site that determines the limits of normality, but as a meeting point between the different networks that are united in their anti-Diasporic commitment. This synthesizing process is the one leading to the production, stimulation, and transformation of the various networks and sites as the production of their aim—which is localized by the realm of self-evidence and the dynamics and borders that are possible within it as its concrete and specific realization.

The closure as reconstructed in road traffic is not the space and disciplinary one that Foucault examines. The closure/stability of the realm of self-evidence is the one that determines the quantities and the conditions of the openness of networks, their pluralism and permitted difference. It is also that the one which determines the construction and de-construction possibilities of passions, codes, concepts, and practices. As motorized traffic has shown on the roads, there is not an alternative spiritual foundation or social bearer for the renewal of concepts or the rebirth of ideals, nor for the appearance of a new relevant critique on the current reality and its systems. Within the framework of the current realm of self-evidence such understanding has become irrelevant, or even a sign of illness or undeniable weakness. Basically, the function and the possibility of experiencing estrangement from the current cultural problem is supplied by the erosion of the antagonistic manifestations between the rationality of capitalistic symbolic and commodity production and the humanist ideals of the Enlightenment, which have been completely integrated into the prevailing realm of self-evidence and its systems.

Filippo Tomaso Marinetti understood that *speed is a new spirituality*, a religion, that "will master time and space", that gives rise to "a new morality"[15] and

> A new beauty; the beauty of speed. A racing car whose hood is adorned
> with great pipes, like serpents of explosive breath—a roaring car that

---

15 Filipo Tomaso Marinetti, "The new religion-morality of speed", in: R. W. Flint (ed.), *Marinetti; Selected Writings*, London: Secker & Warburg 1972, p. 94.

seems to ride on grapeshot—is more beautiful than the Victory of
Samothrace.[16]

A similar yet very different myth from the one about which Marinetti dreamed on
was realized to the degree of mastering the current order of things. Some of Marinetti's ideas have a place in this order. Yet the dream has been de-contextualized, transformed, and takes place in a new realm of self-evidence, where the status of concepts
and myths is totally changed.

In the second half of the 20th century a new realm of self-evidence started to form,
and humans therein were reduced to a function as mere producers/consumers. This
reduction was provided by the same dynamics that led to the constitution of emancipatory humanist utopias in the Enlightenment era. Intensified and transformed, these
dynamics changed the modern realm of self-evidence into a new realm in which the
conceptual possibilities and the ideals, values, dialogue, and possibilities for struggle
that were opened in modernity were systematically closed and eroded. If in modernity the human subject was conceived potentially as a site of reflection, dialogue,
and solidarity, and as a focus of emancipatory social action, in the second half of the
20th century, this ideal has been transformed into a mere sign of a function. Man
has become *a sign of a function* in the context of his producer/consumer abilities:
and only as such is he relevant to the self-reproduction of post-industrial society and
the development of its symbolic world. This is the context of the flourishing rhetoric
about preserving and protecting human life and the awakening of sensitivity regarding the fatality of traffic accidents in an era of their indisputable decrease if we look
at percentages of casualties.

At the same time, the vitality of traffic "accidents" has become increasingly more
important for the system. The mass production of commodities has become committed to a vast interchange that has led to the rapid devaluation of goods through
the promotion of new fashions and technologies and the wearing out of goods. This
eliminates ineffective producers and well as problematic consumers or socially unproductive groups. Their destruction has many modes and, as the system becomes
more sophisticated, it is less direct, vulgar, and explicit and ever more efficient. This
destruction ensures the continuing production and consumption of new fashions that
increase the exchange of commodities and the system's reproduction. It protects the
workplaces of men and women—though not the people themselves, who become
owners of cars, motivated by passions and dreams shaped by the automobile as an
agent and as an ideal.

It has become unprofitable to produce cars that will last for long. Their rapid replacement is built into the system. The intensified dynamics has been transformed
from the means of the present order to an end in itself. The movement of commodities, increased and revolutionized in many ways by modernity, has become, in the
new realm of self-evidence, a vital element in stabilizing its systems and protecting its
horizons. Just as human beings have to reflect and advance the present order of things

16   Filipo Tomaso Marinetti, "The founding and manifesto of Futurism", *ibid.*, p. 41.

by being agents of increasing dynamism, so are they also caught up in the same matrix of disposability and themselves are in constant change and increasingly worn out, rapidly and totally. From the capitalist, i.e., rational, point of view, traffic accidents are a necessity, a matter of life or death. Yet this is but a manifestation of a deeper development, of progress within the framework of Thanatos, of hiding from God, without the possibility of utopia and without anything mysterious or uncontrollable at their disposal in which they might engage. A real solution to the traffic problem and a dramatic reduction in the number of victims and the attitude to them is a serious *threat* to the current order of exchange and the current symbolic understanding of space, as well as the mental constitution and the attitude of the drivers.

It is worthwhile, in this context, to note the connection between a reduction in speed and a reduction in accidents and causalities. "All the empirical data prove that whenever and wherever a speed limit had been introduced, the number of accidents decreased", argues Hans-Georg Retzco.[17] There are exact details showing the dramatic link between the decrease in the number of accidents, especially in deaths and serious injuries, and the decrease in traffic speed.[18]

Spolander argues that the reduction in traffic speed will result in a significant drop in the number of causalities in accidents, which will remain at a ratio of 4:3,even in the case of a minimal reduction in the speed limit.[19]

Accidents are to be understood within the context of interpreting the *essence* of traffic and the new status of movement in the current realm of self-evidence. This is the starting-point for understanding the link between the mistake and the accident, the personal and the public spheres. This is the current status of the realm of understanding and communication possibilities as they are manifested in an era when the traffic space is a communicative network. It is where the functions of the newest false human subjectivity are produced and operate, and are represented, destroyed, and reproduced. Men and women become relevant—are alive—as reproducers of motorized movement and as the victims of the symbolic reproduction of the extinction of their human essence. It is a process carried out by the very same subjects who are the agents of their systems and manifestations.

On a more political level, why and how is it that there is no agreement on reducing the speed limit, investing more resources in infrastructure, improving the safety dimensions of cars and implementing regulations that will lead to a significant drop in the number of victims? My argument is that philosophically and politically, the present level of suffering in casualties and the continuation of road accidents and deaths represents a *rational equilibrium*, from the point of view of the existing order. Traffic safety education is of special importance because it has the quickest and the largest rhetorical impact while being politically the least expensive and, philosophically, the least problematic. In the Israeli arena, this might be exemplified by Eliahu

---

17 Hans-Georg Retzko, "Speed and accidents in German motorways", in: *International Proceedings Conference on New Ways and Means for Improved Safety*, Tel Aviv February 20–23, 1989, p. 6.

18 Krister Spolander, "How to reduce speeding", *ibid.*, p. 73.

19 *Ibid.*

Richter, a traffic researcher, who says that "the myth that there is a need to increase safety education and drivers' preparation education in order to decrease the slaughter on the roads by higher awareness has been proven wrong again and again".[20]

Another Israeli researcher, Irit Uchmann, presents a similar argument. She maintains that while the National Israeli Institution for Driving Preparation gives courses for about 90,000 drivers annually, the usefulness of these courses is never actually checked. The director of the Israeli National Institution for Safe Driving declared frankly, "Most of the course is directed toward re-studying traffic regulations… It is nothing but a waste of time, and even a terrible waste of money and energy".[21]

The American economists, Lester and Charles Law, calculated that the cost of saving one person's life from a traffic "accident" is worth 850,000 hours of extra driving time. And since the average life of an American is equal to 600,000 hours, they have "proved" that it is irrational to save a person's life at the cost required under present conditions. Saving one victim under such conditions is described (somewhat un-scientifically?) scientifically as a lousy deal.[22]

They also state, explicitly, that society is clearly not prepared to increase traffic safety by decreasing people's mobility and comfort. Society is unwilling to deprive poor people from the right to drive unsafe cars if the alternative is that they would not be car owners at all.[23]

According to these researchers, this is the reason for the lack of investments in a sub-structure that would drastically lower the number of victims. I do agree with their conclusion that a substantial decrease in the number of traffic victims is possible. To a certain degree, I even share their conclusion that "society" is not interested in reducing the number of causalities. True, as things stand today, the demand for lowering the injury ratio is completely irrational. However, in contrast to these researchers, I do not think that we should see this issue as a manifestation of society's free will, or as a manifestation of genuine social and cultural progress.

By claiming that a substantial reduction in the number of traffic victims is irrational from the system's point of view I do not mean that such a reduction is in itself irrational. The current system does not value life and has no regard for the victim's life since it does not consider the life of the victim as anything that exists per se, nor does it view the victim's life as something that is valuable in itself. My point refers to the economic and symbolic energy that the system has to invest in order to change the present balance. The symbolic energy and economic cost of creating social, cultural, and physical conditions that will substantially reduce the number of traffic victims is irrational under the current system. The level of rational control is such that in light of the experts' data the conditions of society would have changed already if such a

20   Eliahu Richter, "A national or a scientific failure?" in: Universita, Jerusalem 1993, p. 9 (in Hebrew).
21   Irit Uchman, "A rational approach toward traffic accidents", Tnua Vetachbura, 27, 1990, p. 21 (in Hebrew).
22   Lester B. and Charles A. Lave, "Barriers to increasing highway safety", in: Peter Rothe (Ed.), *Challenging the Old Order*, p. 89.
23   *Ibid.*, p. 23.

change were not merely irrational, which apparently it is in to the present order of things. Normally, hegemonic rhetoric masks this imperative of the current system, but sometimes the functionalist symbolic exchange reveals its truth. To avail of the private rhetoric of researchers working for insurance companies, transport, and road works might be of some use, but even their public declarations are sometimes good enough for this purpose.

A. D. Reynolds and R. F. Dawson's rhetoric might demonstrate instrumental reason in action, in their devotion to an "objectivist", "neutral", and functionalist attitude. Already in the 1970s they were occupied in calculating the rationally justified investment in preventing car accidents and their victims. In their report they treated the problem in such terms as "the cost of a death is not less than the loss of the output which the deceased person would have produced" if he or she had not been killed in the accident.[24]

The experts question the economic worth of the life and death of a car accident's victim, and in these reports they say that "it is sometimes argued that if society loses an accident victim's output, it also gains the consumption that he will no longer need". The calculation of the economic value of one person's life is very precise in such reports; they even differentiate between the value of women's and men's lives. Dawson, for example, found that the British economy lost £4360 in each fatal accident in which a man is the victim, but gained £1120 in the case of the victim being a woman: "Since the work done by housewives was given a low value in the calculations, society could be said to gain on average…when women are killed in road accidents".[25]

Norbert Elias is one of the few thinkers that have set the traffic issue in a non-marginal place in their social and cultural critique. In the spirit of Aristotle and Kant, Norbert Elias presents an essentialist concept, according to which human essence is manifested in self-control and self-regulation. For Elias this is realized within the framework of present reality, with the traditions and regulations shaping its formations and dynamics. Unlike Aristotle and Kant, however, he identifies self-control and regulation with technical control. More specifically, self-control is realized and tested functionally on motorized road traffic: "Controlling the car (which includes its maintenance) is nothing but an extension of the driver's self-control or self-regulation".[26]

For Elias, cultural development is a universal educational process of humanity. One of the major forces of education, according to Elias, is the progress of technization of a given society. Here he places technization—the historical process of transportation—in a special position. The supreme trial of every culture is its ability to develop an ever-higher degree of self-control, and this is manifested in the issue of traffic in general and accidents in particular. As in the thesis presented here, Elias also argues

24   C. H. Sharp, *Transport Economics*, Amsterdam: Harwood Academic Pub., 1973, p. 67.
25   *Ibid.*
26   Norbert Elias, "Technization and Civilization", *Theory, Culture & Society*, 12 (1995), p. 25.

that it is wrong to make a division between traffic accidents and the status of knowledge and the dynamics constructing the present shape of society.[27]

Elias maintains that not only are the victims of traffic accidents in the developed culture of Western societies inevitable; they are a true indication of how far Western culture has gone in making technological development one of its most important parameters. He sees a connection between further advancing the technization of traffic and improving self-control as indications of cultural progress. His findings identify a considerable gap between the rate of traffic accidents in Western societies and that in non-Western societies.[28]

Elias uses his data to defend the special stance of Western culture and the advantages that Western societies have over non-Western ones. The differences are substantial and noticeable in the effectiveness of social standards that concern self-control and regulation. The major cause of traffic accidents, according to Elias's thesis, is the driver, and the degree of the driver's self-control is an outcome of the level of his or her cultural development. The degree of cultural development is evident in the individual's self-control, a component responsible for causing the accidents and responsible for their victims.[29] I do agree with Elias that road accidents are not a matter of luck or chance, and in fact they are not "accidents".

Elias refers to the cultural progress of the West as a manifestation of the progress of rationality and the advancement toward a higher degree of integration. In that respect too *traffic accidents are a manifestation of rationality* (or the degree to which society has been rationalized) on the one hand, and a justified punishment or a pedagogically necessary treatment that non-Western societies have to suffer on the other. Although his thesis has to be rejected on a few grounds, it is still an important. It implicitly presents the road as an arena in which rationality is tested, as it were objectively, by manipulating the vehicles, drivers, and their communication abilities with other drivers in the context of their intersubjectivity. They are examined in parallel on their ability to know and understand agreed conventional codes and regulations, and on their realizing this ability by applying the required amount of self-control in equalizing the human with the car, or the airplane, or the speedboat.

I do not agree with Elias's conclusion that the degree of traffic efficiency reveals the degree of a culture. His studies are useful, however, for the deconstruction of the cultural context and philosophical essence of its potentials. More than that, I can make use of some of his findings as an illustration of my argument concerning the success of **the purpose principle** within the framework of advancing instrumental reason that develops vital elements of hegemonic forces in post-industrial society. This rationality has a special presence in interchange networks, transportation, and the representation of knowledge, its agents, and other commodities. The efficiency of the system is manifested by motorized traffic and not in the cultural and social stage, as Elias

---

27   Norbert Elias, "Technization and Civilization", *Theory, Culture & Society*, 12, 3 (August 1995), pp. 8–9.

28   *Ibid.*, pp. 23–34.

29   *Ibid.*, pp. 24–25.

tries to convince us. So the level of traffic accidents does not represent some punishment, or luck, or "accident", whose essential characteristics lie in its being an incident, an inevitable catastrophe. In contrast to Elias and other conservatives defending the present anti-humanistic Western order of things, I see in traffic "accidents" the logic of the system, the forces constructing its rationality and its self-presentation and manipulations. Since this rationality is instrumental in its essence, it is not determined by values and is attracted to the mission of the anti-transcendental being, an aim of self-reproduction and advancement of nothingness, of Thanatos. This concrete representation of instrumental reason has social, economic, and technological results in the public sphere and in the remains of what could have been the public sphere of the individual.

Therefore, the implementation of a policy that would lead to a real reduction of traffic "accidents" might clash with **the purpose principle**, which is indifferent to any value-oriented obligation. It would also be at odds with transcendental ideals, being the supremacy of preserving and developing human life and well-being, and preferring it to further technological advancement possibilities, as well as other elements of protecting the life of the control and repression potentialities of the system. Four possibilities are to be raised in referring to the limits of the rationality of a praxis that will substantially reduce the number of traffic "accidents" and their victims.

A. Further reduction will be needed in the speed of the traffic. In such a case, the *symbolic function of driving* might bring the driving and other related networks into total chaos. This should be understood in terms of a space where killing time and extrinsic controlled self-constitution have become central and productive educational and political dimensions of prolonging the life of the system.

B. Substantial changes will be needed in traffic organization, in car structuring, and especially in the representation of the producer/consumer as human-machine. In such a case, *the erotic passion between the driver and the car might be confused*, and a demand might come to constitute different social borders, relations, and dynamics in which an erotic state between human beings might be constituted. There is even the danger of lightening the educational contribution of a false erotica between human and motorized vehicles under the new cultural conditions. Such a critical light might reveal the part that modern speed driving plays a part in the self-forgetfulness of humans, in their refusal of transcendence, and in their forgetfulness of forgetfulness.

C. The dangers of the traffic routes as sites of knowledge exchange and realization. A reduction of the dangers involved in fast driving and an essential change in the ways in which the dangers on the roads are represented might damage its economic, social, and cultural production. *The productivity of the attitude to the danger* involved in speedy traffic is based on the dual structure of this kind of danger: as an enemy and as an object of strong passion. This danger is represented as something that has to be overcome. By the same token, it is represented as a dimension of *otherness* in the heart of a one-dimensional world that demands the release of surplus energy and frustration in such a way that in the final analysis it will secure present normalization strategies, power hierarchies, and dynamics. These are elements that protect, serve, and hide themselves as self-evidence. Life on the edge, like philosophy on the abyss, might be an erotic reflection of health, as Nietzsche proclaimed. However, at certain historical moments like ours, looking for the danger and running away from unplanned and uncontrolled life are two dimensions of one and the same trend: the Thanatos track of self-forgetfulness, which is also the forgetfulness of Being, the nothingness.

> And so everything rushes at man, man-target is assailed on all sides, and our only salvation now is to be found in illusion, in flight from the reality of the movement, from the loss of free will...[30]

D. The changes I envisage threaten the very possibility of struggling for the realization of human freedom, solidarity, and dialogue in history. This is the case because there is no way totally to ignore the essential difference between self and intersubjective understanding/realization and freedom, between Eros and Thanatos. Traffic is an arena where the possibility of dialogical, solidarity and alternative communication is tested daily. Today's roads provide the best manifestations of rationality, of "healthy" competition and cooperation between people as if there were a vivid dimension of a free and democratic public sphere. The aforementioned possible changes in the symbolic and traffic operation might crack the self-understandability of some apparatuses and strategies of the system, endangering other entities—that of traffic—thus endangering the entire order of things.

The forgetfulness of forgetfulness might be cracked too, and new possibilities for Diasporic readiness, gaze, and listening might become possible. Cracking vital self-evident dimensions might question the ways of production and reproduction of the conceptual apparatus, the hegemonic collective consciousness, normalization strategies, and educational manipulations responsible for reproduction of the necessary public attitude and criteria and so forth. Essentially, different forms evaluation, communication, and intervention approaches might penetrate radical alternative driving and traffic philosophy. As such, they might bring about an alternative, Diasporic, human condition. Such an order must represent a different intersubjective grammar and a different human attachment to Being and to human beings, technology, and ecology, as well as to the unspeakable or uncontrollable. The object of such a transformation is not to be identifiable within the borders of the current realm of self-evidence. Within the possibilities opened by such a seemingly Diasporic self-positioning, transcendence is both negative and positive, yet it must be of a utopian essence. Existentially and philosophically it must accept the primacy of (the possibility of the sudden appearance of) **the totally other**, of the potential over the actual: it must be politically aggressive or be smashed by the hegemonic educational dynamics of the system and its despair.

A radical examination of motorized traffic and the reconstruction of the accidents function, as well as a study of the possibility of alternative education for safe transportation, all demand a critique of instrumental rationality, its context, and its operation.

---

30   Paul Virilio, *The Art of the Motor*, translated by Julie Rose, Minneapolis: The university of Minnesota Press, 1995, p. 132.

A Diasporic philosophy for counter-education, however, must tell us the bitter truth, namely that what I am suggesting here engages only one dimension of the issue: the political dimension; and it is at odds with Diasporic philosophy that is true to itself. It is but another positive utopia, a new "homecoming" project that has to be transcended.

Motorized traffic and accidents are but one mode of Being's games of revealing and hiding: games and, as it were, its way of motivating humans into realizing themselves as "being toward death".[31]

It is within this questioning, I think, that we should try to understand the philosophical dimension of technological and transportational progress. Heidegger's ontological questioning, as well as the understanding of the procedures of the human body, soul, and truths according to Foucault, still enable room for Habermasian critical reconstruction and for Adorno's critique on instrumental rationality. These elements are vital for a future Diasporic philosophy and for counter-education that does not contradict itself. The invitation to Diasporic existence and to the reflection offered here is "pessimistic", but by the same token it is utopian. It understands the current advancement of transportation and education for safe transportation as manifestations of nothingness. At the same time, it treats the contingent historical stand of concrete networks as a real world. It is where happiness, falsity, possibilities of hope, and concrete opportunities are present and deserve protection in the struggle for their development, especially by the de-construction of the current realm of self-evidence to the greatest possible degree, though not by all means.

After all, education on the issue of safer transportation and the call for more careful behavior on the roads might become an important part of a struggle against the powers manifested in the slaughter on the roads, namely countering the logic of the current Western realm of self-evidence. Such counter-education, even under the present circumstances, might be aided by existing antagonistic sites in the system, or newly developed focuses that contain the potential of becoming vital elements of the coming realm of self-evidence. Specifically, I am referring to the destructive/educational potential of the tradition of the free public sphere in modern Western culture.

Essentially, this tradition is conservative in its self-understanding, but for our purposes here, a more central issue revolves around the very separation between the public and the private sphere. This rich tradition contains (and might reproduce) the explicit and implicit codes and parameters that guide behavior in the public sphere and the alternative possibilities of the human subject. Normally, this is the basis of producing and controlling the subject in accordance with hegemonic concepts and interests, or power balance in the system. At the same time, this power might be directed against the system, might serve as part of a *transformation* that would enable a more autonomous and less controllable subject and intersubjectivity. Human life might thus become richer and contain new possibilities, as part of an enterprise that opens new horizons and drives toward new dangerous normalization systems and opportunities for liberation.

31   Martin Heidegger, *Sein und Zeit*, Tuebingen: M. Niemeyer 1957, pp. 265–266.

Countering the present reproduction of traffic accidents, resisting the current ways of distribution and consumption of "the problem" and its suggested solutions, might become parts of such a utopian struggle. Such a struggle must become a radical political and philosophical praxis. It is important here to note some conservative elements and pinpoint the possibility of their transformation within this utopian struggle. After all, the alternative education for safety transportation is but one of its bearers and builders. Such an alternative education is impossible without maturity manifestations such as a new type of communicative action that is not under the control of the purpose principle, overcoming anti-narcissistic self-forgetfulness and the reestablishment of refinement in the public sphere of behavior.

However, all these elements and their attributes are impossible in the absence of dramatic change in concrete social and cultural conditions. I do not share Habermas's optimism and positive utopianism concerning the possibility of communicative action and scientifically based advancement toward the "ideal speech situation" that would constitute a solidarian partner in dialogue. Here I see more relevance in Jean Baudrillard's conception of a communication that sees no way out of our present situation. However, that is the end of Baudrillard's truth and the opening opportunities for an alternative communication/traffic education: it is a project that will target the realization of the new ways of driving—as a representation of transcending traditional kinds of solidarity within a new aesthetic motorized movement, as part of the entrance of challenging the exile of Spirit and its alternative power/knowledge relations.

The Hebrew term *derech eretz* (the way of respect) contains vital importance for any education in safe driving and for any alternative communicational praxis. It exceeds and completes the traffic issue. In Judaism there is a unique synthesis between Torah (the Jewish written law) and Torah Shebe'al-peh (the Jewish oral law) as a reflection of the dialectic of the earthly life and the heavenly world, nature and man. In Judaism the heavenly world does not reduce earthly life and material things such as the body to something of a lower degree. The written Torah proclaims the sanctity of the ways of this world and the sanctity of the human soul, the body and its passions and needs. That is why Judaism praises human worldly ways of conduct as an autonomous dimension that is not of a lower degree and is never totally separated from heaven, as in principle the written Torah and oral tradition—Torah Shebe'al-peh—cannot be separated. These worldly ways and man's conduct in earthly matters are not to be separated from God's imperative, from the truth of the Torah and its truth from heavenly eternity. In this sense, while having its history, different interpretations, educational and political manifestations,[32] *derech eretz* delineates a religious dimension. While representing the earthly dimension in human life, *derech eretz* manifests the redemptive aspects in our daily life. As such, it also represents the general utopian axis of humanity's enlightenment as developed by figures such as Schiller, Kant, Hegel, and Marx. They represented a mature conception of *derech eretz* in which acknowledging the absence of the traditional God does not negate utopia or the moral value of daily matters and the acknowledgment of different ways of life. As written in Talmud

32   Mordechai Broier (ed.), *Persons and Roads*, Tel Aviv 1987 (in Hebrew).

tractate *Derech Eretz Zuta*, 71, 2: *Kol derachecha yiheyu leshem shamayim* (Let all your ways be for the sake of heaven).[33]

I would like to develop this concept into a general humanistic educational attitude, as exemplified in the traffic issue. That is, alternative traffic education is connected to an alternative conception of movement and to an alternative, utopian conception of the public sphere.

The concept of *derech eretz* on the roads has two aspects: one of knowledge and one of action. Each is contained in two different contexts: private and public. In the public sphere, *derech eretz* is conditioned by the recognition of an epistemological system that is conceived as legitimate and makes possible knowledge concerning relevant codes and norms in the current public sphere.

Unlike mere politeness, behavior manifesting *derech eretz* is conditional not only on the act being conceived as polite, but on other men and women being trained to behave in accordance with it. This is because it is conditioned by knowledge; it is not a matter of making people behave "properly" (which would leave open the issue of repression) but of a real educational enterprise. Under this interpretation, *derech eretz* is not just an epistemological issue, and it cannot be realized only as a concrete moral, obligatory, conscious action. In this sense, *derech eretz* is not a mere epistemic function or a framework. It is conditioned by a special sort of knowledge, one that is morally oriented, namely courteous behavior shaped by acknowledgment of the other's identity, needs, rights, hopes, and limits, and ultimately directed to a common transcendence. From this perspective education in *derech eretz* on the roads might be realized only as the politics of overcoming **the purpose principle**, which constitutes the heart of instrumental reason and capitalist practice.[34]

Marx suggests the utopian movement in sexual relations between free men and women as a concrete criterion for true communism,[35] namely for overcoming **the purpose principle** that is the essence of both capitalism and vulgar communism. This kind of intersubjectivity, which is determined by recognition of the Other as another, as different, and as a partner for critical dialogue and solidarian creativity, is manifested in the Jewish category of *derech eretz*.

The *derech eretz* counter-education that Diasporic philosophy here offers us is but a revolt against the totality of the present reality and is directed at its being questioned and its deconstruction. In contrast to postmodern educational rhetoric, however, such a counter-education is committed to overcoming the driver as an ego with no essence, which realizes itself by negating the Other's otherness. As such counter-education has a utopian axis: a commitment to the revelation of the idea of a human being as a homeless person, as a *Diasporic lover of Life*, and as a guardian of Being even when defending a rational, open, and free public sphere. This humanistic renaissance avoids being just one more manifestation of the narcissistic power that is produced by the

---

33   Rabbi Asher Frizker, *Masechtot Derech Eretz*, Tel Aviv 1950, p. 19 (in Hebrew).

34   Karl Marx, "On the Jewish Question", in: *Early Texts*, translated by David McLellan, Oxford: B. Blackwell, 1971, p. 114.

35   *Ibid.*, p. 147.

current culture industry. This negative utopia connects, again, the private person to a public sphere, which is being constantly criticized and re-formulated by the individuals creating it. While insisting on their Diasporic existence and on their responsibilities, human beings might become social again, in the sense that the builders of the Tower of Babel exemplified, namely Diasporic, *refusniks* of Godly or other dogmatic "homecoming" projects, and as such building themselves and the entire cosmos as an unending transcendental "home." This Diasporic creativity is not motivated by fear or violently imposed discipline but by love of Life and responsibility that is eternally improvised with the Other. Only there is an alternative movement and self-positioning possible.

Today the very possibility of humans counter-educating themselves against the current trend to de-personalization and indifference in regard to the Other is conditioned by the effectiveness and strength of instrumental reason's manifestations. Listening to the possibilities of Diasporic *derech eretz* on the roads might bring humans into *Diasporic nomadism* that is not an abstract negation that forbids creating any ethnocentric "home": it resist dogmatic, closed, ethnocentric-oriented "homes", but not empathy with the Other as an improvised "home". It might offer a possibility of resisting the present order's hegemony, within which the human is reduced to mere statistical data and an almost totally controlled function.

This "almost" is of utmost importance for any possible counter-education today. Counter-education in *derech eretz* on the roads transcends the level of treating the issue of driving as a mere private, economic or "safety" matter, and re-articulates it as *a political, moral, philosophical, and existential movement toward the possibility of worthy Diasporic life*. Even as a negative utopian enterprise, this is impossible when one is deprived of any tradition. Diaspora-oriented counter-education, therefore, must be established via a hermeneutic approach to the tradition or traditions denoting the moral and spiritual dimensions of manners and making it possible to insist that *derech eretz* be realized.

In one sense, Diasporic counter-education here is very Jewish, in respect of its understanding the centrality of the presence of the absence of God, truth, and justice, and in its accepting the relations between the exile of God and the Diasporic essence of human existence. On the other hand *it must overcome Judaism as a "truth" and monotheism in all its manifestations*. It should denote and develop its multicultural yet universalist-humanist implications. Judaism might be interpreted in an anti-ethnocentric way, as part of a universal enterprise of edifying, transcending, and liberating the human as such. It can avoid ethnocentrism and cultural neo-colonialism by avoiding the mistakes of both current conservative universalistic and multiculturalist discourses. As a humanist alternative, it should cross the existing borders between classic critical theory and Foucault's project in suggesting the possibility of a new critical dialogue and political praxis. Reinterpreting concepts such as *derech eretz* and educating for an alternative transportational reality and traffic behavior, against its conservative understanding, on the one hand, and as part of a dialogue with other cultural concepts, on the other, might evolve into a meaningful defense of reason and a more human order of things.

Diasporic counter-education is very different from the prevailing critical pedagogy. If true to itself Diasporic counter-education must deconstruct the inner logic of the current realm of self-evidence and subject it to interrogation. It must be questioned, if there is still the possibility, today, of redeeming a sense of estrangement to the degree that it may become enlightened. If it is today still possible, it must challenge instrumental reason and ethnocentrism in order to reestablish humans' attachment to each other and to (negative) utopia through the opening up of a dialogue.

Deciphering the essence of "traffic accidents" must face the contingency of the formation of the realm of self-evidence and the systems reflecting it.[36]

A realm of self-evidence creates or is realized in local social-cultural systems that struggle and communicate with each other and that are violent in their nature. The present order of things is not to be identified with a national sovereignty. It crosses political borders and is much closer to cultural spaces, but it is not identified with them since it includes local social hierarchies, their financial and symbolic power struggles, and political praxis. Systems can change characters and borders, and the direct dynamics and limits within their subjects.

Negative utopia, if and when overcoming the present realm of self-evidence and deconstructing local systems and their power-relations, is always individualistic and cannot be delivered to collectives as the true dogma. Even then it is never secure or guaranteed, and it is "founded" on the void made possible by the promise of the principle of hope that is about to storm it every minute and every day. However, even for the individual, this concrete negative utopia cannot avoid relating to the present historical moment and the concrete capitalistic and nationalistic realities in order to challenge them by counter-education, such as *derech eretz* on the roads. Counter-education here cannot refer to an abstract individual as a contingent supreme standard. It speaks about the constitution of new values, new myths, and a new heroism of sacrifice for the totally different, the transcendent. In its nature, such a counter-education is opposed to "education for safe driving on the roads". Such an approach is determined to de-construct present reality and transcend itself. It aims to generate this Diasporic project without being non-humanistic, but with the determination to transcend humanism and to save it from the presence it wants to deconstruct. Such a determination requires challenging considering the institutionalized "accidents", their and production, selection, and designing apparatuses even on the roads.

Counter-education must rest on acknowledgment and on making use of interests and dynamics that currently shape the local systems. On one level, it has to use insurance companies and other interest focuses that are for the moment opposed to those of the car industry, importers, and the government. On another level, it can make use of the remains of the nation-building myth and Kantian moral conceptions in anti-conservative contexts, which can be directed toward concrete action against this aspect of the death industry known as "normal traffic conditions". The remnants of

36 Ilan Gur-Ze'ev, *The Frankfurt School and the History of Pessimism*, Jerusalem: Magnes Press, 1996, pp. 222–224 (in Hebrew).

national fanaticism may be of some use too, in a counter-educational action against the world of "traffic accidents".

Such an action is conditioned by the refusal to accept the forgetfulness of forgetfulness, against the refusal to rebel against the self-understood, and specifically against hegemony trends in the Israeli system. One might assume that such counter-education is really going to decrease the number of traffic victims. Such an instrumentalist might succeed, but only by acting in such a way that will ultimately advance and fortify the system in which a revolt functions in the form of actual or potential "traffic accidents", i.e., like any commodity. Counter-education is fed by **the hope principle** that has no power to reduce the number of casualties. In principle it cannot be "successful". It can only appear as a refusal of "success", normality, and self-understanding, as a negation of nothingness that the present reality manifests.

Even so, we have to aim and prepare ourselves for the possibility of counter-education that will offer a Diasporic negation of the current ways of the Western order and a total refusal of its self-evidence. Such a refusal must include acceptance of the liberation of the oppressed (intellectually, psychologically, and economically) potentialities. Realization of the demand for such an education is possible only if the entire social horizon can be changed and a real public sphere can flourish. In such a utopia, a new place for technology and for transportation will be provided by the new human being. There is the place for an essentially different kind of traffic, which has a different telos from the current one. There and only there will equal status be attained for all traffic victims. Even then, will they be victims of a way that is not theirs? And what will be the form of an alternative that we cannot positively describe? All that we can do is act against the negation of its possibility, and rebel against the evil industry that constitutes the one-dimensionality of the present reality as a worthy "home".

CHAPTER 12

COUNTER-EDUCATION IN FACE OF HOLOCAUST/NAKBAH
AS AN ISRAELI/PALESTINIAN HOMELAND

The quest for nirvana, nothingness, or homeland, even the reflection on the issue of homeland, is never at home with itself. The moment "homeland" as a constructed articulation or a reflected feeling enters the linguistic space and receives its "voice" is the brink of a great *loss*, of distance and of exile from what "homeland" refers too. Entering the language of homeland, quest for homeland, or overcoming being exiled from homeland as it is or as it should become, entails becoming a citizen of the platonic cave. Here a collective, a realm of self-evidence and the continuum of the *Same* are constituted, orchestrated, nourished, regenerated, created and destroyed. This platonic cave, whose borders are pushed ever farther from its existing horizons, is constituted by powers which are effective enough to secure the invisibility of their manipulations for the collective which it creates, activates, controls, represents and victimizes every moment anew. Precisely the depth of the evidence of selfhood, orientation, yardsticks and aims of the individuals who feel at home in "their" "homeland" manifests their effective displacement into exile from themselves as they might have been. As its history shows, the language of homeland, or Heimat, might also open new possibilities of unveiling the violences of the hegemonic system, and open possibilities for transcendence and counter-patriotic education.

Consciousness, or even an unconscious commitment to one's "homeland", is testimony to the violence of the process of individual and collective identity formation, representation and reconstruction. It calls for unveiling the human toll of normality, self-evidence, and effective thinking and being with one's self—of the efficiency of the hegemonic normalizing educational violence. At the same time, however, the longing for Heimat, or for returning to the "home-land", manifest an immanently alternative quest, antagonistic, alienated to the self-assuring hegemonic continuum, foreign to the creation of reality as a natural and eternal Same, of which the national homeland is but one, historically short-lived, example. This other, non-collectivist, never formed, and in no way given quest, makes possible the presence of **the totally other**, as a transcendental element. While never being at home with itself it makes possible a religious readiness for the *call* of **the totally other** beyond the horizons of the *Same* as home. As such it incubates a voiceless call for a struggle which is also a breakthrough, for overcoming the temptations of the platonic cave of homeland within the framework of dogma, fatherland, nirvana or refusal to improvisation and poiesis. Such a *call* is a challenge and a threat to the triumph of normalizing education and its actual or promised Heimat. This is since it invites actualizing respond-ability and responsibility for a proper addressing this call. As eternal-nomadism, as becoming, as improvisational response it endangers not only the relation to one's homeland in terms of identification and self-denial as a way for peace with one's self, patriotism, willingness for sacrifice or hate/fear of the Other. Much more than that, this possible transcendental call endangers being at home in all other manifestations of the Same, the continuum and the self-evidence, namely of the manifestations of *Thanatus*. A worthy response to this call is a great danger for the achievements of normalizing education and for domestication "resistance" of the kind offered to us by current post-colonialist theory. It includes suffering, albeit worthy suffering and transcendence, which have no determined "aim", "goal", "truth" or nirvana. This messianic moment is a religious element, which offers not an alternative concept of homeland or sweet Garden of Eden on earth—but an alternative presence of exile, homelessness. In this respect it is inseparable from the presence of the quest for love of homeland or the miseries of its loss.

The academic treatment of the issue of homeland is not irrelevant to our topic.

> Heimat is where one is born, where one receives an education, comes
> to consciousness of selfhood, adjusts oneself to family and society, or
> constructs a 'social entity'.[1]

Sociologists and social psychologists have explained Heimat as a basic human need, comparable to eating or sleeping.[2] According to Celia Applegate political scientists have also spoken of Heimat in terms of natural human tendencies, in particular tendencies to form political allegiances, whether on the local or on the national level.[3] According to this scholar Heimat is not only a source of security in the patria, fatherland, and motherland. It is much more than that: it is, as Karl Phillip Moritz and the romantic tradition understood, an image of "homey tranquility and happiness…"[4] Rolf Petri too emphasizes Heimat as a social stabilizing element.[5] He denotes the importance of Heimat as a relation and as a sense of place of origin, as familiar land, as the opposite of being faced with a strange place. Petri is right in emphasizing that the concept of Heimat as being at one with oneself (Bei-Sich-Sein) also had a meta-physical element which made possible and fertilized the feeling and the expressions relating to a semantic field which stretches from conceptions such as "Father Rhein" to conceptions such as "the German blood"[6] as unifying and elevating elements. Petri

---

1   Wilhelm Brepohl, "Heimat und Heimatgesinnung als soziologische Begriffe und Wirlichkeiten" in: *Das Recht auf die Heimat. Vortraege, Thesen, Kritik*, ed. Kurt Rabl, Munich 1965, p. 43.
2   Celia Applegate, *A Nation of Provincials—The German Idea of Heimat*, Berkeley, Los Angeles, Oxford, 1990, p. 5.
3   *Ibid.*
4   *Ibid.*, p. 7.
5   Rolf Petri, "Deutsche Heimat 1850–1950", p. 3.
6   *Ibid.*, p. 5.

advances the academic discussion on this issue by showing the instrumentalization of the Heimat feelings, conceptions and cultural activities within the framework of changing economic and national struggles.[7] At the same time, Petri argues Heimat also functions as a subjective space where a person who is not at one with herself can introspect and experience herself, meeting and reassuring her identity.[8]

I will try to make clear my conceptions of homeland and the role of the quest for homeland, as well as the human situation, in two different conceptions of homeland or Heimat by first reconstructing the role of normalizing education in establishing, representing and reproducing notions of homeland. After showing it in relation to homeland as a safe haven of familiarity I will try to elaborate on it in another version, from the point of view of the Exiled. This second version will be in the center of this elaboration while focusing on the case of the Israelis and the Palestinians.

The Israeli/Palestinian concepts of homeland and exile will be reflected with special attention to the function of the instrumentalization of the memories of the Holocaust and Nakbah as a manifestation of normalizing education. This from a counter-educational perspective does not offer a positive utopian concept of homeland but it does position itself in an alternative exile. It offers a Diasporic philosophy as a framework for a struggle for *overcoming* both Israeli and Palestinian, and actually all normalizing collectivist-oriented, concepts of homeland (and loss of homeland/striving to reestablish the lost homeland). This Diasporic alternative to the concept of victimhood will challenge the hegemonic concept of victimhood; it will offer a Diasporic alternative to other, related concepts such as loss, suffering and exile as generally shared by both rival collectives, overcoming the surrender to the *Same*, to which both collectives are subordinated.

A Diasporic concept of homelessness represents ecstatic readiness, thrilled sensitivity and a poetic quest for counter-education—not for the triumph of an alternative symbolic bombardment. This is the most we can do, and in this too we already represent normalizing education and the Same as our homeland. Addressing this contradiction might become an acknowledgement of the kind that opens gates to much greater dangers and possibilities such as nomadic self-articulation, love of the otherness of the Other's exile, and new, not-ethnocentristic, kinds of improvisation, creativity, responsibility and togetherness.

Normalizing education realizes itself in many ways, arenas and compositions. One of its central manifestations is in constructing collectives and individuals. "Home", here, is essential. The ability of normalizing education to reproduce itself while using its victims as its agents is determined by effectiveness in establishing a totality in which there is no alarming or awakening gap between the normalized individual and the normalizing system. The system produces realms of self-evidence in which the yardsticks to evaluate, the identifications, and the characterizations are self-assurance, of which the individual becomes a part, an agent, a function, a symbol. If the identification of the individual with the system ensures a safe closure and a comfortable

---

7   *Ibid.*, p. 35.
8   *Ibid.*

totality, he or she will not feel alienation from his or her normalizing space of manipulation and he or she will regard it as his or her "home". Concrete and specific contextual, historical, material, and symbolic conditions always determine the construction of such agents of the hegemonic realm of self-evidence.[9] It is always vulnerable, always on the edge of being colonized by another system and alternative ideologies, collectives, power relations, consciousness", interests and social formations.

The collective is a close grouping. It is a close grouping of normalized *individuals*—a manifestation of the efficient reproduction process of the hegemonic normalizing education. As such it is committed to internal and external *colonization* processes. Its *effective violence* is a precondition for its reproduction and enhancement. The ultimate victory of normalizing education over its alternatives is in its ability to *veil* efficiently its creative violence. Its effective violence is tested by its competence in ensuring an unproblematic identification of its victims with its violence, making it into a present or a promised "home". The space of this violent process of normalizing education becomes "home" when the violence is sufficiently efficient. It gives birth to and cultivates the safeguards of the horizons of its prisoners. One of the most efficient policing powers is the prisoners' love of this "home" or "home-land", their commitment to disregard, destroy or redeem their own and their Others' internal or external love of homeland. It is of vital importance in constituting peace, tranquility and love of the kind that will make possible the prosperity of the close, oppressed, victimizing "we". Fundamentally this means the safe reproduction of the hegemonic system and the impotence of its victims to unveil the violences which create and partially control their identity, their quests, their fears, their enemies and their love of their selves, their "we", their "homeland" and their "enemies".

Nationalism is but one of many possible manifestations of the production of collectives by the violence of competing narratives within the framework of normalizing education. The concept of homeland or Heimat and the love and devotion for one's homeland are a manifestation of a successful de-humanization of humans, by constructing not only their narrative, identity, love, fears and hatreds but also their identification with this process and committing themselves to it as its guardians and agents. Normally such systems and ideologies collide with their Others in a creative-violent meeting in which each side manifests its *love of homeland* by destroying the Other and colonizing its rivals as heroes, patriots, good citizens or devoted disciples. These clashes need not always break out into *explicit* violence, war, or conquest of physical spaces.

In different historical situations and social and cultural contexts it has different manifestations and is never fixed, stable and secure. The production and closure of collectives has many different versions. Some use the rhetoric of openness, radicalism, progressivism, pluralism, anti-dogmatism and kaleidoscopic, hybrid, contingent educational processes and so forth. This is manifested, for example, in cyberspace, in actualizing consumerism or activating the McDonaldization of intersubjectivity,

9   Ilan Gur-Ze'ev, "Introduction" in: Ilan Gur-Ze'ev (ed.), *Conflicting Philosophies of Education in Israel/ Palestine*, Dordrecht: Kluwer, 2000, pp. 1–7.

all which are manifestations of normalizing education which create collectives, their sense of homeland, their horizons and their Others.

The Israeli-Palestinian context manifests a clash between two narratives and normalizing educational systems, which produced and reproduce *two collectives who are committed to negate the otherness of the Other as a vital part of each one's self-constitution.* This self-constitution of the collective is actually the act of the negation of self-constitution of the individual human. It is an act of robbery by the system: robbery of the human potentials for overcoming collectivism while introducing false love and a deceitful attitude to Spirit; robbery of genuine creativity; robbery of the preconditions for a mature response to a *call* of **the totally other**. It demolishes the potentials for dialogical self-constitution. It is actually the self-realization of the aimless, meaningless immanence. In each different historical moment it uses the consciousness of self, identity, collective memory and quests for a freed homeland in each collective for self-reproduction which is committed to denying the concept of the homeland of the Other and "liberating" the geographical space as well as the symbolic arena as part of its normalizing education, which also has its explicit and sometime military violences. It is not the absence of a common discourse or bridge between the narratives of Israelis and Palestinians that is responsible for the successful veiling of the symbolic violence which is responsible for the visible violence between the two collectives. It is just the opposite: it is their concept of homeland and their concept of the collective and its Other which binds them together in a common narrative that conflicting normalizing education fertilizes daily.

Israelis and Palestinians represent a unique concept of homeland, distinct from the normal concepts of homeland, fatherland, motherland or Heimat as a safe, familiar, tranquil place, which constitutes the identity of the individual and the collective. In the Israeli-Palestinian case it is the *Diaspora* which is the constitutive element. Both for the Israelis and the Palestinians being exiled as a collective experience and consciousness is the central dimension of normalizing education. Its effects are essential in constituting the collective identity, the memories, the quest for home-land and the commitment to defend its borders, interests and imperatives against the Other.

The Israelis and the Palestinians are also united by another essential element: each of the rival collectives conceives the same space as its home-land and itself as the sole legitimate reflection of its identity and religious-metaphysical meaning, goals and imperatives. For all the differences, and they are of vital importance, the two collectives in this case share a commitment to destroy the Other; the rival normalizing education, its narrative and its commitment to struggle against what it conceives as criminally violent practices against the legitimate and original inhabitants of the country. The instrumentalization of the memories of the Holocaust and the Nakbah are essential for this discourse between the two normalization processes and narratives[10] to such a degree that both should be conceived also as one, united process, manifesting and

---

10   Ilan Gur-Ze'ev and Ilan Pappe, "Beyond the Destruction of the Other's Collective Memory: Blueprints for a Palestinian/Israeli Dialogue", *Theory Culture & Society*, 20:1, February (2003), pp. 93–108.

realizing the essence of normalizing education and the mechanism of constructing homeland or Heimat as "home" which has not only "land" but also its telos and Others, who are committed to colonizing it and turning the land into their "home" and mission as part of destroying the identity and all that is dear and worthy in the "we".

In Israel the memory of the Holocaust is not left to contingency. It is officially instrumentalized and institutionalizes by a special law. A unique governmental agency (*Mosad Yad Vashem*) was established to preserve and represent its memory and implications. The history of the changing representations of the Holocaust memory and the official educational "lessons" of the Holocaust are beyond the scope of this paper. The focus here is on the centrality of the memories of the Holocaust to the goals of Israeli normalizing education in general and in its relations to the concept of homeland in particular.

From the start, the Israeli instrumentalization of the Holocaust memory treated the memory of the Holocaust as part of the polemics with the Jewish non-Zionists and the rest of the world, aiming at establishing "the lessons of the Shoa" as an ultimate justification of the Zionist claim for establishing Palestine/Israel as a "national home" or as the realization of "home-returning" to Zion, both as the only way to secure the safety of the Jews and as the realization of the inner imperative of Jewish history.

The mainstream Zionist attitude to Israel/Palestine is to be understood as a secular political theology. It conceived an undividable connection between the true identity and telos of the *Land* of Israel and *the Children of Israel*. It saw Israel/Palestine as the "historical homeland" of the Jews, where the passage of time did not diminish their legitimate right to gather and live in it while building it, or "redeeming" it. Moreover,

> Since it is almost a desert, and almost unpopulated by others, and we, for our part never abandoned our hope to return to this land, as manifested by the 12th of the principles of our faith, all our prayers and all our history.[11]

A. D. Gordon, one of the greatest and most influential figures of the Zionist labor movement, was very clear about the connection of the secular Zionist claim to Israel/Palestine as a Jewish homeland with the Jewish essentialism of the Zionist project, even in its most radical secular forms. "Judaism", he asserted, "is one of the foundations of the 'I' of each one of us".[12] And as such he saw in the Bible the assurance of the right of the Jews to the land, as eternal evidence of its being the main source of legitimacy. He added the argument of work and creativity as manifesting/creating power of the identity of the land, constituting it into a "home":

> We have a historic right to the land, and this right remains ours as long as another, alternative, power of life and creativity do not purchase it

---

11   Moshe Lilenblum, "On the revival of Israel on the land of our ancestors", in: *M. L. Lilenblum; A selection of His Essays*, Tel Aviv (No date), p. 76.
12   A. D. Gordon, *The Nation and The Work*, 1916, p. 366.

entirely. Our land, which beforehand was 'the land of milk and honey' or, at any rate, gave birth to a high culture, became wasteland, the poorest, most distressed of all civilized countries, and almost empty. This is as a sign that the country awaits us, reassuring our right to the land.[13]

The justification of the religious-cultural-political "purification" of the homeland is actualized or quested from the safe distance of exile, suffering and vulnerability that conceives itself as a quest from exile to liberation. Diaspora is the locus of this symbolic responsibility for liberation from exile—even while located within the geographical borders of Israel/Palestine. This, in opposition to what we can find in other Heimat or homeland discussions. In the Israeli case this is where the call for fearless "creativity" and struggle comes from, as manifested in the mythization of Josef Trumpeldor and the *halutz* (pioneer) as creative, innocent, ethnocentrist, fearless, farmer-warrior. The national-religious and the secular nationalist trends in Zionism were united in their essentialism, conceiving the essence of Palestine to be Israel, or, Zion, where Zionism, if it succeeded, would realize *a renaissance of the nation* and its religion/spiritual-cultural creation.[14] One trend emphasized the spiritual-religious aspects, and saw in Israel/Palestine the revival of *Yavne* and the rabbinical-Halachic tradition. Its secular version was represented by Ahad Ha'am. He introduced a concept of homeland, which distinguished a spiritual homeland from a physical homeland. His project too was vitalistic and ethnocentric, demanding the recapturing the relation to the essence of Palestine/Israel by the Jews. This, however, was not in order to guarantee political domination: within this concept of homeland the imperative was to reestablish Israel/Palestine as a Jewish spiritual center, while most of the Jews could continue their physical lives in the Diaspora as their political, economic, and socially relevant context. The second trend saw in Israel/Palestine the revival of *Beitar* and the vitalistic-nationalistic tradition. The third trend looked at Israel/Palestine as an ancient home from a rationalist Eurocentristic orientation, according to the ideals and the self-image of Western bourgeoisie of the day. While conceiving Israel/Palestine as the historical homeland of the Jews Herzl was prepared to accept any refuge to solve the immediate threats to Jewish existence and security, and develop it into an independent Jewish state free of emotional, religious, mythological and other irrational bonds of a collective to its homeland. When the Zionist congress defeated his "Uganda program" and he vowed, "If I forget you, O Jerusalem... Let my tongue cleave to the roof of my mouth" (Psalms 137:5–6). While committing himself to struggle for re-making Zion into the homeland of the Jewish people as the ultimate goal of Zionism, his commitment was more of an internal political maneuver (to prevent the collapse of the Zionist movement) than a reflection of his deep sentiments for Israel/Palestine.

13   *Ibid.* p. 244.
14   Ze'ev Ya'avetz, "The unity", in: Y. Obsey, Hilel Bavly, M. Fiershtein and others, (eds.), *Becoming a Nation*, I., New York, 1938, p. 122.

Historically, the fourth trend emerged victorious in Zionist history, albeit affected by and containing elements of the other trends, of which the one represented by Ahad Ha'am was by far the least influential.

Both right and left wings of the hegemonic Zionist movement were committed to *an uncompromising negation of the Diaspora*. The negation of the Diaspora was founded on its being conceived as a perverted, unnatural way of Jewish life, not only dangerous.

Within the Zionist secularized political theology Jewish life had a universal and a national telos. The fulfillment of the historic-cosmic mission of the Jewish nation originating in the revelations and experiences of the founding fathers, and their birth through and with the religious significance of the sites and symbols of the space. Within the Jewish tradition and the Zionist narrative this telos of Israel was not concluded with the presenting to the world the book of books, not by giving birth to Christianity and Islam, and not by Jewish fertilizing of modern Western culture with some of its most important figures and ideas. Within the Zionist framework the imperative of the telos of the Jews was to negate the Diaspora and re-create *sovereign* national political and cultural life in their homeland. The realization of their telos within their universal and national utopia is formulated in modern Western revolutionary leftist or rightist articulations. Yet essentially it draws on and continues the ancient Jewish religious conception of the special role the Children of Israel have in this world, with its metaphysical foundations on the one hand and on its Messianic attitude to the future and its presence on the other. Moses Hess, Berdichevsky, Aba Achimeir, Borochov, Uri-Zvi Grinberg, Jabotinsky, Arlozorov, Ben-Gurion and Menahem Begin are all united in this secularized vitalistic political theology.

The conception of homeland here has three dimensions. **One** is of seeing *Palestine*, in its essence, as *Israel*, namely seeing its Palestinian identity as a historical stage, which manifests its decline, its downfall, paralleling the downfall of the Jewish people in the Diaspora. It is conceived as an "almost unpopulated land'" or as desolate land ("*Midbar shemama*") which calls for its flourishing, purification, and elevation by its returning owners, who are by no means immigrants, and certainly not colonizers. This project of the renewed connection between "the unpopulated land with the until-then homeless people (*Aretz lello am le-am lello aretz*")" is also a political project of literally conquering the land, establishing a Jewish majority, and enforcing a Zionist hegemony.

This project was conditioned by the success of Zionist education which was committed to giving birth to "the new Jew" as a pioneer, (*Halutz*), as Israeli-born (a *Sabra)*, or as a soldier. Zionist education had the mission of colonizing the soul of the individual and creating a new collective harmonious totality as a precondition for the success of the political and military struggle over colonizing physically, politically, militarily and culturally the space and establishing a Jewish hegemony which would reflect its essential identity and its Messianic mission. Here the concept of homeland as a future political struggle to create a nation and its homeland is inseparable from the metaphysical foundations of a concept of *revolution as homeland* on the one hand, and from the utopian axis or a positive utopian concept of homeland on the other.

In this sense the political-activist present-oriented trend in the Zionist movement is revealed as a movement which is inconceivable outside its orientation to the past and future. It is also to be understood only in its metaphysical foundations and spiritual mission. The violence of normalizing education and its manipulations are revealed here as a precondition for the struggle to realize this project of creating a new collective and a new country on the foundation of the Diaspora identity of the Jewish people and by overcoming the Palestinian identity of the land.

The purification of the Diaspora mentality and the purification of Palestine of its Palestinian manifestations and its transformation into Israel became part and parcel of the project of re-entering history and returning to the track of fulfilling the supra-political mission of Zionist politics. During the last 120 years the Zionist hegemonic normalizing education which created the Israelis and Israel could not create this collective and "its" space without the alterity of the otherness of the Diaspora mentality and the Diaspora's economic, social and cultural conditions on the one hand, and without the alterity of the otherness of the Palestinian identity on the other. This clash was a vital element for its self-constitution—as it was at the same time unavoidable for Palestinian normalizing education and its nation-building project.

For Israeli normalizing education it was of vital importance to establish a unified, coherent narrative of a collective memory. Its starting point was biblical Zion and its utopian axis was purified Israel. This narrative, which created the Zionist subject, was constructed by a sense of telos, which was founded on the logic of *megalut lege'ula* ("from exile to redemption").[15] After World War II this narrative placed as central the Holocaust and its lessons. The *migalut lege'ula* narrative was concretized and realized by the concept of *misho'a litkuma* ("from downfall to re-constitution").

In its various articulations this narrative was founded on a concept of the all-embracing presence of the *absence* of homeland on the one hand, and on the historical *presence* of violent injustice against the Jews on the other. Essential for this secularized political theology was the acknowledgement of the Jews as the ultimate victim of human history while being the subject of history and the agent of its telos. The metaphysical relation to the Land of Israel was essential to this narrative. Only the Bahai religion has such a unique relation to Israel.

At both of its poles—historical victims of unredeemed world and as the bearers of the claim for universal and national justice—the concept of home was essential. The Diaspora of the Jews and living as permanent victims of human history did not reflect solely the exile of the Jews from their country and their loss of sovereignty: it reflected also a general human condition of living in an unjust, unredeemed world. In this sense Zionism was only one manifestation of a more general and much richer Jewish utopian commitment, realized within various and conflicting revolutionary projects, ranging from anarchism and Marxism to scientific revolutions in modern Western culture and society.

---

15   Ilan Gur-Ze'ev, *Philosophy, politics and Education in Israel*, Haifa: University of Haifa Press 1999, pp. 64–65.

In the Zionist narrative the history of homelessness—as the history of overcoming the exile in human reality as a real home for all people—is inseparable from the issue of the presence of historical violence. Historical violence or the whole-presence of the conditions, which Marx called "pre-history", is conceived as manifested with special clarity and unavoidable toll in the evil done to the Jews throughout history. After the Holocaust this secularized political theology became a central challenge for Zionist normalizing education. It became instrumentalized in support of the Jewish claim to Israel as a sovereign Jewish state as well as against the Palestinian narrative and its concrete challenges to the realization of the Zionist narrative.

The concept of victimhood and the self-conception of the Jews as the paradigmatic victims of secular history were essential for the fabrication of the narratives of *megalut lege'ula* and *mesho'a litkuma*. Within the hegemonic Zionist narrative the concept of victimhood was historically paralleled to the period of Jewish life in the Diaspora. Normalizing Zionist education presented an equation between the conclusion of Jewish victimhood, the realization of the telos of the Land of Israel, and the self-emancipation from the Diaspora mentality (*galutiyut*) and from the "unnatural" Jewish life in the Diaspora by returning to the normality of power-games, security and sovereignty in "their" "homeland".

Within this perspective the land of Israel itself was presented as captive, perverted, or made into a spiritual and literal desert by strangers and primitive invaders. Even the keenest Zionist thinkers, who truly respected the Arabs and called for addressing seriously their presence, failed to overcome these Western perspectives and the limits of 19th-century Orientalism.[16] Today, when by now we can critically reconstruct and evaluate not only Orientalism but the postcolonialist critique itself, we should acknowledge the limitations but also the reason for the Zionist misunderstanding and underestimation of the presence of the Palestinians in he country in the late 19th and early 20th century: the country was economically, technologically and politically underdeveloped, with relatively very few people, many of whom lived as nomadic Bedouins with almost no urban life and no exclusive national identity; not a single high school, no universities, no industry, not even political parties to represent the Palestinian interests. When the Zionist founding fathers came here they did not see Palestinians but "a country without a people for a people without a country" not solely because they were captives of Orientalism and Western superiority: truly, in modern terms of nationhood, economy, transportation, culture or technology—*there was not much to see*, unless you were a fanatic postcolonialist or an incurable romantic who came in search of a biblical way of life.

Palestinian identity, however, was not late to follow the Israeli nation-building project; Zionist normalizing education and the Zionists had to respond to a conflicting reality—morally, politically and militarily. A special educational and political effort was made for *ge'ulat hakarka* ("redemption of the soil"). The homeland itself, the return to which was conceived as an emancipatory and purging factor. The land was conceived as captive, a prisoner in unnatural conditions, deserted and humiliated.

16   Edward Said, *Orientalism*, Harmondsworth: Penguin Books, 1995.

The grand mission of **the new Jew** was to redeem the soil and emancipate her/himself: to (re)build and be (re)constituted by the new-old "home". It was an ecstatic Messianic ethos of creation and self-elevation, which the Palestinians made so necessary then, and continue to do so to the present day. There was no way to separate the two, according to Zionist normalizing education. The memory of the Holocaust was instrumentalized to this goal, and the central claim of Zionism was presented as tragically and undisputedly manifested by history and *Amalek*, its agent.

The Zionist educators presented Amalek as a historic agent, which is responsible for Jewish victimhood. "Amalek", wrote Ben-Zion Dinnur, the central figure in the history of Israeli education, "is a constant (element) eternally present among the gentiles" (*Mida hamehalehet bein ha'umot*). The Holocaust was presented as one of the peaks in the continuum of the history of Jewish victimhood while living in the Diaspora. Hitler or Hitlerism was paralleled to the eternal essence that the historic Amalek represented. But while Hitler was presented as synonymous with Amalek the defeat of Nazism was presented as not synonymous with the defeat of Amalek.

Amalek, while presented as the agent responsible for the victimization of the Jews in the Diaspora, was also and still more presented as presence at home too, in Israel. The Palestinians became the present-day Amalek and the distorted reality of Israel as Palestine; a victim of the effort to reclaim, recapture and "redeem" it was presented as a martyr (*kadosh*) equaling the Palestinian martyr/ victim/victimizer (*shaheed*). The *kadosh*, however, was a victim who sacrificed himself or herself, and theologically was in tension with the concept of bravery in Judaism, which represents not bravery in military action but in self-overcoming in face of a religious call for spiritual elevation. The concept of the *shaheed*, by contrast, was constituted in relation to "*Din Muhamed biseif*" (the law of Muhammad is by the sword").

Victims of the refusal of the Zionist road to homeland and victims of the struggle for "the liberation of Israel" as the homeland of world Jewry were united by Zionist hegemonic education. Under slogans such as *Megalut lege'ula* the school curriculum reflected and fabricated a Zionist subject that did not question the foundations, the practices and the aims of this narrative, its rivals and its enemies. History textbooks, school rituals, memorial days, memorial books and special ceremonies, even art, the media and the museums were committed to the reproduction of the hegemonic narrative and helped to mobilize in a constructive manner daily symbolic and non-symbolic violence. All this was for the realization of the lessons and ideals of this narrative in face of and against "the Amalek of our generation", the Palestinians. One of its pedagogical manifestations is the day commemorating the Holocaust (*Yom Hasho'a)* very close to, almost united with, the day commemorating the fallen of Israeli solders in the wars of independence (*Yom Hazikaron Lehalelei Ma'arahot Israel*); the latter is followed, with no interval, by the beginning of the celebrations of Independence Day (*Yom Ha'atzema'ut)* of the Jewish state.

While rejecting the Jewish concept of Diaspora as an ontological sign and as a precondition for the fulfillment of the Jewish mission in the world, and as a manifestation of its being the chosen people, Zionism rejected exile; Zionism negated the philosophical foundations and the existential perspective of Diasporic eternal-impro-

viser as a potential transcending way of life. It refused this kind of overcoming monotheism, phalocentrism and colonialism and transgression in and from any "home" in
favor of endless cosmic as well as microscopic homes in the in between, in the infinite
life possibilities within the tension between the moment and eternity. The negation of
the *Gola* (Diaspora) as a mentality and as social-cultural historical context for Jewish
life was a precondition for the hegemonic Zionist movements struggling for a political, historical negation of the Diaspora and for the constitution and development of
Israel as the homeland and sovereign state of the Jews. This project could not be struggled for without a parallel negation, that of the legitimacy of the Palestinian narrative
and their claim for Palestine as the homeland of the Palestinians, and the negation of
their negation of the Zionist project. It is impossible to understand the Israeli-Palestinian explicit and visible struggle detached from the symbolic and visible violence.
The struggle about the names of sites such as Jerusalem/al Kuds or Ein Hod/Ein Hud
and their Israeli or Palestinian identity (and the kind of their "Palestinian" or "Israeli"
identity) are inseparable.

The refusal the acknowledge the legitimacy of the existence of the Other and/or the
legitimacy of its claim to Israel/Palestine as its homeland *unites* the two collectives in
a dialectics which simultaneously makes possible/enhances the visible and the nameless violence among the two hostile groups while constituting their very existence as
a collective. Each of the struggling collectives sees itself as the *sole legitimate owner*
of the place and accepts the Other as a threat or perversion of the authentic or ideal
identity of its homeland. Each of the rival narratives and of the parallel normalizing
educational systems accords a special place to the relations between the victim and
the victimizer.

For the Israelis as Jews, the remembrance of their history as a chain of victimizations
which manifest the evil in this world and the special goal, and the uniqueness of the
Jewish people in history, is not a mere religious imperative. It is also a constitutive
element of their traditional education and the formation of their traditional identity
as Jews; it became a formative element in the hegemonic Zionist education, until the
changes in the cultural and existential conditions that were inflicted by the MacWorld
the last generation. These new conditions hold for certain parts of society more then
for others, and in some situations differently then in others, and yet, they change
completely the socialization of the kind that traditional Zionist normalizing education was committed to and made possible by. As long as we refer to these, Fordist and
not to the post-Fordist conditions, or, in other words, as long as we refer to Zionism
as part of the world of Jihad and not as part of the MacWorld (which is partially still
true for many Israelis even today) we can say that here, *within the history of victimhood* the remembrance of the Holocaust became of vital importance for the Zionists.
Within this project the memory of the Holocaust was and is still instrumentalized and
reproduced in relation to four interconnected and sometime conflicting challenges:

1. Within the traditional strife with the Jewish non-Zionists and anti-Zionists, as
the ultimate "proof" of the fundamental claim of Zionism, its negation of the Diaspora and its call for a Jewish return to its homeland as the only guarantee of its
security as a collective of its return to normal national life.

2. The tension between the imperative of "back to national normality" and the self-conception of a unique nation with an unmatched history and human telos among the nations even within the secularized returning home. Not only the fathers of Zionism such as Hess, Borochov, Jabotinsy, Gordon and Arlozorov, but even post-independence leaders of the Zionist left and right such as Ben-Gurion and Begin, reproduced and further developed this secularized political theology. The issue of Jews as the ultimate victims in world history, and reestablishing a Jewish homeland and a *Sabra* mentality as opposed to the Diaspora mentality (*Galutiut*), demanded and justified the instrumentalization of the Holocaust memory.

3. The instrumentalization of the Holocaust memory and its ever greater role in the hegemonic Zionist narrative was enhanced in face of the Palestinian *Nakbah*, the constitution of a rival Palestinian narrative which challenged the Zionist narrative; also in face of the Palestinian violence and its negation of the Zionist instrumentalization of the Holocaust, its lessons, and its commitment to the establishment and strengthening of Israel as the Jewish homeland as the ultimate answer to the Holocaust. The Palestinians' transitional denial or minimization of the Holocaust, their denial of the right of Jews to return to Israel as their homeland, or for that matter their denial of the legitimacy of any Jewish existence in Israel, along with their violent resistance to the realization of the Zionist project, became unified. They became unified into a conceived reality of a new Holocaust not in the Diaspora but in Israel. The response to this existential and ideological threat was integrated into the refusal to acknowledge the suffering brought down on the Palestinians and the injustice done to them by the realization of the Zionist project.

Fear of a new Holocaust and fear of acknowledging responsibility for the *Nakbah* became inseparable. So was the denial of the otherness of the Other by National Socialism, the denial of the otherness of the Other, his/her suffering and aspirations of the Palestinians regarding the Jews as such, and as Israelis, and the denial of the otherness of the Other by Israelis regarding the Palestinians, their suffering and their aspirations.

Palestinians and Israelis were united by their refusal to acknowledge not only historical tragedies and suffering, but also the present suffering and aspiration for a homeland as a peaceful, secure Heimat. Both sides' refusal to recognize each other's right to a homeland became *a constitutive element* for collective identity formation and articulated an exiled point of reference for the conception of each collective's homeland. More and more Israelis are aware of this, within a process of the formation of a post-modern reality in which the constitutive myths of Zionism and its creative violences are rapidly being disintegrated, ridiculed or criticized. Within this process more and more Israelis recognize Israel as Palestine for the Palestinians, namely, acknowledge Palestine as the legitimate homeland of the Palestinians as well as the historical injustice done to them during the Nakbah, before that tragedy and after that to the present day. Parallel to that process fewer Israelis see Israel as the legitimate homeland of the Jews alone, and a growing minority no longer see it as the legitimate homeland (historically or presently) of the Jews. In face of this development, and as part of it, the mythization of the Holocaust memory has become more efficient than ever. Instrumentalization of the Holocaust memory within this process, however, was not realized so effectively by the hegemonic Zionist normalizing education, which has almost disintegrated completely and lost its manipulative potential for most of the Israeli middle class.

4. Within the post-modern conditions in the Israeli post-Fordist arena and its culture industry the Holocaust memory is not lost. It has become integrated into the system and is being produced, distributed and consumed like any other reified merchandize in the representation market. The McDonaldization of this arena makes "Holocaust experiences" and "Auschwitz trips" goods, which incubates a special value. Here not a modern conception of a given or promised homeland is being produced but its postmodern alternative. This process does not carry with it many potentials for Israelis' recognition of Palestinian suffering and responsibility for their toll, and even when it does it de-politicizes this recognition. More than that, it deconstructs the quest for homeland as well as sensitivity to homelessness. It not only dismantles the commitment to national solidarity and willingness for self-sacrifice for the realization of collective ideals and imperatives: at the same time it dissolves the ability for responsibility for the Other's being exiled, uprooted from the homeland, and the potentials for resisting injustice and struggling for a dialogue. Meaninglessness as a pleasure machine becomes an unlimited, omnipotent home.

Palestinian normalizing education parallels and corresponds to the Zionist one. Without being a mere reaction to the Zionist project it cannot be conceived without or outside the life-and-death struggle between the two. For the Palestinians too the formative collective experience is that of *exile*, of being a suffering, homeless people, even when not uprooted from their land.[17]

Edward Said is very clear on this point: "…There is no doubt that we do in fact form a community, if at heart a community built on suffering and exile".[18] The point is not that the Palestinians do not give up their identity in face of their tragedy and ongoing daily suffering. Much more than that it is the suffering, the loss of the homeland, which formulates their identity. Mahmud Darwish writes on this issue in his poem "The Palestinian wound":

> …We are discharged of remembering, the Carmel hills are within us,
> and on our eyelashes the grass of the Galilee, do not say: I wish we
> would run towards her like a river, do no say! We are in the flesh of our
> homeland…and she is within us![19]

The longing for the actual Palestine, for the land, becomes a formative element of the identity as represented by the normalizing apparatuses and its agents. The represen-

---

17   Glen Bowman, "'A country of words': Conceiving the Palestinian nation from the position of exile", in Eenesto Laclau (ed.), *The Making of Political Identities*, London and New York: Verso, 1994, p. 139.

18   Edward Said, *After the Last Sky*, London 1986, p. 5.

19   Mahmoud Darwish, *Dewan Mahmoud Darwish*, Beirut 1989, p. 342.

tation apparatus, the symbol and its agents as authentic "Palestinians", are united. Darwish himself proved partially aware of this in one of his interviews:

> This is an attempt at fixation of the land in the language and in the body. In the Palestinian case there is something specific and special, and this is that when the Palestinians went away and were exiled they took with them their keys. They were at pains to keep the keys in a safe place. Regardless of the fact that it was in exile or in a country to which they immigrated. In this sense the key itself took along the house. In this sense the house is attached to the one who left. Not only people left: the land itself departed with the Palestinian wherever the Palestinian went. Consciously and unconsciously he had the need to feel that he carried the place with him and the lost homeless one was both person and land. This is why I have many expressions of homeland as a suitcase. My homeland is simultaneously not a suitcase and a suitcase.[20]

This present experience of homeland is in tragic contradiction to a traditional un-formulated homeland as part of self-evidence and inner-self, which was destroyed in the *Nakbah* or whose destruction is articulated in the word *Nakbah*. It is to be seen in light of the absence of an Arabic equivalent for the word Heimat or homeland. In literary Arabic the closest word is *Mauten*. Another close term is *Muskat al-ras* (where I lay my head to rest) or the house of the grandfathers.[21] This conception of homeland as Mauten becomes much closer, yet very different in face of a direct experience:

> like the one experienced by the Jaffaites and all the others who immi-grated from the Palestinian towns and villages—then, the longing and the quest become *Mauten* or *Muskat al-ras*. The experience of the town or the neighborhood and the house in which one grew up, in which he tasted the first bits of happiness in his life, part of his inner life that is impossible to strip him from, becomes something much higher than a tangible thing. It becomes a symbol.[22]

Here the Jewish concept of homeland in exile and the Palestinian concept of home-land, as well as their concepts of loss, and victimhood become very close on the one hand (without losing their differences) and part of a dialectical unity, on the other.

The Jewish presence is conceived here as a *contamination* of the pure land of Pales-tine, and in many cases as a *daily rape* of the land and its innocence.[23] Homeland as

---

20 Mahmoud Darwish, "There is no holiness to the executioner", *El Carmel* 52 (Summer 1997), pp. 221.

21 Hisham Sharabi, *Jafa, an Aroma of a City*, Beirut: Dar el Fatah, 1991, p. 15.

22 *Ibid.*

23 *Ibid.*, p. 15–16.

the place of the most contaminated, distorted, and perverted, of rape by its unlawful violent conquerors, is shared by the Jews/Israelis and the Palestinians. Some Palestinian thinkers who acknowledge the similarity position the two conceptions within the framework of rival narratives struggling over hegemony in a symbolic fight, which is also a political and existential tragic struggle.[24] From the Palestinian view, however, there is no symmetry between the two claims for homeland and the two conception of the contamination or sacrilegious rape of the land, as there is no symmetry between the two concepts of Diaspora and home-returning.

The Palestinian narrative is not yet formed and there is much struggling over the construction and the legitimate presentation of the Palestinian identity. Still, all Palestinian political activists, most Palestinian intellectuals, and most of the Palestinian population are united in their conception of the *illegitimacy of the Jewish colonialist presence in Palestine*. They resist as "colonialist" the Israeli conception of Israel as a Jewish homeland and the relation of Jews to the Palestinians and their responsibility for the *Nakbah*.

The ethnocentric attitude of the Zionist hegemonic narrative is reflected in the Israeli Declaration of Independence. It is matched by the ethnocentrism of the Palestinian narrative and in its realization in its constitutive texts such as the National Charter (1964 and 1968) and the Declaration of Independence (November 1988).

According to paragraph 1 of the National Charter of 1968

> Palestine is the homeland of the Arab Nation and is an integral part of the great Arab homeland. The Palestinian stock is part of the Arab nation.

Paragraph 3 states that "The Arab Palestinian nation has a lawful right on his homeland" and in paragraph 4 *the Palestinian identity is articulated in relation to the land*: The Palestinian identity is an essential rooted character, which does not disappear. The sons inherit it from their fathers. The Zionist occupation and the disintegration of the Arab [Palestinian] nation, as a result of the Holocausts that it suffered, do not harm the personality of the Arab Palestinian people and ??its Palestinian belonging of the nation and do not negate them".

In the Palestinian Declaration of Independence this attitude of the relation between the land and the Palestinian identity is quite explicit. It says there: "On the land of God's ??usher to humanity, on the land of Palestine was born the Palestinian people, there it grew, developed and created its human and national existence which is an organic, inseparable relation between the nation, the land and history".

It is important to note, however, that all three official texts were written by Palestinians in the Diaspora. The view of the exile is present here with particular centrality when Palestinian identity is spoken of as a reflection of the identity of the land and as an essential dimension, not a historical, contingent construct. In the unofficial texts,

---

24   Edward Said, "Keynote essay", in Ghada Karmi (ed.), *Jerusalem Today; What Future for the Peace Process?* Berkshire 1996, p. 16.

in stories, poems, dramatic works and essays, the experience of the *Nakbah*, the exile and the daily experience of loss of the homeland and enrichment of remembrance is explicitly presented as the constitutive element in the formation of the Palestinian collective identity. Edward Said, who notes this constitutive element,[25] emphasizes also the constitutive function of the collective suffering and violence that was inflicted on the Palestinians,[26] paralleling the Zionist narrative of the Jews as the paradigmatic victim in human history also in this respect. The formative power of the loss of homeland is explicitly paralleled with the Jewish one but within an ideological framework, which presents the Zionists as mere colonizers.[27]

Many scholars, writers and poets emphasize this theme.[28] The loss of the homeland did not make it unreal or remote for the Palestinians, as for the Jews who prayed for it daily and committed themselves to being "next year in Jerusalem" wherever they were and in all central events of Jewish life. For the Palestinians this attitude to homeland might be represented by Mahmoud Darkish when he writes

> We have a country of words. Speak speak so I can put my road on the stone of a stone. We have a country of words. Speak speak so we may know the end of this travel.[29]

Palestinian existence is the experience of uprooted people from the land that is raped daily by its victimizer.[30] The Palestinian experience of exile, according to Said, manifests the "unhealable rift forced between a human being and a native place, between the self and its true home".[31] *Exile, victimhood (or the presence of the Nakbah) and suffering or Palestinian identity and Israeli colonialist victimization, become inseparable.* A central role in this Palestinian narrative is played by the resistance to the Israeli instrumentalization of the Holocaust memory as part of Israeli effort to justify, hide or marginalize the Palestinian tragedy as a terrible price they had to pay for the realization of the Jewish colonialist project.

The Palestinians did not only reject any Jewish claim to being the legitimate owners of the land or the Children of Israel. They rejected, and until this day continue to present *an uncompromising rejection of any relation between the Jews and Israel as their homeland*, not solely those Zionist and Jewish non-Zionist claims to be the sole legitimate owners of the land or the Children of Israel. The suffering of Jews in the Diaspora in itself was never a central Zionist argument for the justification of their right

---

25 Edward Said, *After the Last Sky*, p. 5.
26 *Ibid.*
27 *Ibid.*, p. 120.
28 Glen Bowman, "'A country of words'", p. 145.
29 Mahmoud Darwish, "We travel like other people", *Victims of a Map*, translated by Abdullah al-Udhri, London: Al Saqui Books 1984, p. 31.
30 Hisham Sharabi, *Ibid.*, p. 15–16.
31 in Janet L. Abu Lughod, "Palestinians: exiles at home and abroad", *Current Sociology*, 36: 2 (Summer 1988), p. 61.

on the country as a Jewish homeland yet suffering and victimhood were undeniably central to Jewish political theology. As a mirror picture of the Zionist narrative, the Palestinian national movement traditionally bound up its refusal to acknowledge and offer empathy to the historical victimization of the Jews with its refusal to acknowledge the special relation of the Jews to Israel. This attitude is manifested even in the negotiations of Israelis and Palestinians. Israel's offer of giving up its sovereignty over the site of the Jewish temple (*Har Habait*), which is also a Muslim mosque that was built on it and an important religious site (*Al Aaksa*) in exchange for official Palestinian recognition of the Jewish relationship with the site was unconditionally rejected by Yasser Arafat.

As is the "normal" case of narratives engaged in life-and-death battles, so in the Israeli-Palestinian case the struggle over the power to represent the space as *Israel* or as *Palestine*, the fight over political control of collective sovereignty between the two parties, the strife as to who is the victim and who is the victimizer, and as to the power to construct and represent the identity of the Israel/Palestine, have become inseparable. The philosophical and the political relations between the Holocaust and the *Nakbah* and who owns Israel/Palestine and whose homeland it is have become a unifying element for internal and external Israeli and Palestinian violence, which at the same time is also a fruitful constitutive element of reproducing ethnocentric collectivism of each of the warring sides. Within the framework of each collective the Other is a threat to the very existence of the collective and is perverting the homeland by its very existence, so that the land itself is victimized, not only its authentic owners. The Zionists changed the Palestinian names of the sites, renaming them according to their "authentic" Hebrew names or inventing new names, inseparable from uprooting the Palestinian dwellers or of changing the topography, the architecture or the demographic and political *arche* of spaces and sites in Palestine—from a Palestinian perspective. This is why when Palestinians counter this violence traditionally they do not center their counter-violence on the Israeli army or police. They target the civilian population on the one hand, and factories, traffic lights or post offices, and even forests on the other.

Setting forests alight normally does not receive much attention when Israeli/Palestinian violence is analyzed in light of the cost of these exchanges in terms of human life, property, and additional political barriers to dialogue. The arson, however, is an event worthy of much more attention than it usually receives.

The returning to Israel and the constitution of the New Jew was for the hegemonic Zionist narrative connected with the ideal of reentering into an intimate relation with the land, cultivating the soil it as a way of life, and hard labor as an ideal for the reconstitution of the individual and the nation. A. D. Gordon acknowledged already at the beginning of the twentieth century the presence of Arabs—not of Palestinians; he writes in 1909:

> The country is ours as long as the Jewish people is alive and does not forget its homeland. On the other hand, it is wrong to decide that the Arabs have no share in it. Who then has more rights? One thing is for

certain.... The country will belong to the side that is willing and able to suffer more, and to work harder for the land.... This is the imperative of reason, this is also the conclusion of justice—and it accords also with the nature of things.[32]

The "redemption" of the land was conceived and actualized by buying the land and farming it. Redemption of the soil and self-edification by hard work and creativity became inseparable in the Zionist project. Those who position Zionism as a colonialist movement fail to face not only the uniqueness of this colonization process, which involved *buying the land* from its owners *whatever the cost*, increasing the value of the Palestinian property, and creating a tragedy not only for Palestinian farmers who had to leave their homes and the land they had tilled, sometimes for centuries. Simultaneously it also created a huge immigration movement from the neighboring countries, which was to constitute most of today's Palestinian population, and competition by the Jewish immigrants on the labor market with the Palestinians. They fail to see the idealistic dimension of this process, which was a vital element in the construction of the new Israeli collective. They fail also to see the meaning of the conception of entering a desolate and neglected country, planting trees on its bare mountains, draining its swamps, and farming its valleys.

The draining of the swamps of Hadera, as an example set by the Jewish immigrants at the turn of the nineteenth century, became an important myth within the Zionist normalizing education at schools, literature, theater, and other apparatuses and trees are central figures here. In the play *The gathering of the boxes* by Andre Finkerfeld-Amir the desolation of the country is symbolized by the mosquitoes (which spread diseases around the areas of the swamps). In the draining of the swamps and the farming of the fertile land recovered at high cost in human life, the eucalyptus trees take part as central heroes. They are called "the heroes of Hadera", and together with trees from other redeemed lands they drive away the desolation.[33] Tree-planting in the country became not only a national celebration and a compulsive element of schooling; it became internalized in the collective psyche, joined with the traditional Jewish sense of the holiness of the country and the religious-mystic essence of trees and tree-planting.

This activity in the bare and neglected country, as the Jewish, modernist-oriented *Halutz* found it, became a symbol of the redemption of the country from its desolation, a focal point of the exile who returns home and of the homeland which is returned to him. In school rituals it was celebrated often in the form of symbolic marriage. At the same time it had a political dimension of controlling the space, manifesting the edifying presence and the power of the Zionist project, preventing Palestinian settlement, and empowering the violent colonization of the Jewish Diaspora mentality and replacing it with Israeli mentality, if not in reality at least as an ideal.

---

32   Gordon, *ibid.*, p. 96.
33   Yoram Bar-Gal, *An Agent of Zionist Propaganda; The Jewish National Fund 1924–1947*, Haifa 1999, p. 240.

The Palestinian resistance to the Zionist project had and has many forms, one of which is to burn the forests of Israel. In Israel/Palestine there are almost no natural forests, most of them having been planted as part of the Israeli settlement. This is conceived by the Palestinian intellectuals and politicians as a successful colonialist aggression, and the blooming or afforested land and its extensive tourist industry, and popularity among Arabs and Israelis, alike are conceived as *a daily rape of the home-land.* Accordingly, this kind of arson has a special meaning. The total negation of the Zionist project, its hegemonic narrative, its instrumentalization of Jewish victimization and suffering in Diaspora, and its claim for Israel/Palestine as its homeland are united in this action. Its point of reference can be referred to in other, more articulated positions and actions, such as the refusal to acknowledge to Holocaust or the minimization of its extent and moral implications, or the current official rejection of any Jewish relation to Jerusalem and to Temple Mount. Still, in such sporadic, individual, and yet consistent acts of setting fire to the "forests of the Jewish National Fund" which are committed as if pervert so successfully and joyfully the view of the Palestinian homeland, there is special manifestation of the Israeli-Palestinian struggle.

The forests are set on fire, like the beloved daughter whose blood, according to the Palestinian tradition, is liable if she has "offended the honor of the family". This tradition is so much alive to this very day in the Arab world. In Arabic the words for "land" and "family honor", though spelt differently sound somewhat alike—*ard.* Poets, writers, educators and politicians are fond of punning with the two words to mean *the land which gave itself, devoted itself to a degree of total surrender and even a love affair with Israelihood* and with the actualization of the ideal of enforcing/rediscovering the Jewish identity of the Land of Israel. An exile's attitude to the homeland, then, refers also to those who hold on and did not leave, against all the odds and difficulties inflicted by the Israeli presence. Hisham Sharabi's words are paradigmatic on this issue: "Man", he says

> does not really embrace his homeland unless he loses it. Immigration is essentially different. Facing the rape of my land and losing my home-land, my grandfather's house and the views of my childhood is a kind of assassination.[34]

This, while uprooting its Palestinian identity. Accepting this process means for the Palestinian intellectuals an acceptance and even siding with the rape of Palestine as homeland, offending a sacred marriage—and as such this deed has to be purified. And what is more purifying than blood and fire?

The Palestinian commitment to liberate Palestine is unconditional and uncompromising, as manifested by its intellectuals. It persists even when politically there is a will for a pragmatic settlement. However, even politicians such as Yasser Arafat, when they go deep into the foundations of the conflict and are faced with the principles

---

34   Hisham Sharabi, *ibid.*

of rival concepts of homeland, refuse to accept the Jewish right, even as a partial or a moderate right or even relation, to Israel/Palestine.

Traditionally this was the hegemonic attitude of the Zionist movement, yet from its very beginning it was accompanied by an active opposition which argued for the rights of the Palestinians, resisted the injustice that was inflicted upon them, and protested against it within the Zionist movement and as opposition to it. Both sides have changed their positions, to various degrees. Influences such as the empowerment of the Palestinian national movement in the shadow of the victory of the Zionist project by establishing a strong state in the economic, technological, military and cultural respects, as well as the presence of an ever stronger influence on Israeli society of instrumental rationality, global capitalism, and multi-cultural realities all had their influence. In Israeli society one important influence was the demolition of the Zionist ideology and its idealistic-collectivist concept of homeland, of which the exile was the locus of relating to and struggling for, at least for the secular part of the Israeli society.

These processes have deep and rich affects such as establishing strong individualism and McDonaldization of this advanced techno-scientific consumption-oriented society. In face of these developments the traditional Zionist-propagated concept of homeland has lost its vitality and much of its relevance. As part of this development growing parts of the Israeli society acknowledge not only the presence of the Palestinians as a nation but also their narrative and their legitimate rights, aspirations as well as their *Nakbah*. This process is paralleled by an ever stronger Palestinian negation of any justification of the Jewish claim not only to an equally justified legitimate narrative in which Israel is a homeland of the Jews, but even of a partial or lesser justified claim for its homeland. Today there is no Palestinian intellectual who will question Zionism as a mere violent Western colonizing movement, which uprooted and destroyed the Palestinian homeland and its peaceful normal life.

This asymmetry is particularly conspicuous when post-modern Palestinian intellectuals treat the issue of the Israeli-Palestinian conflict, its roots and future. While conceiving the Palestinian identity as historically developed and contingent (and therefore not "right" or "wrong"), "authentic" or "inauthentic" intellectuals such as Edward Said will reject the Israeli narrative as "violent" or "manipulative" and refuse to acknowledge any claim for legitimate Jewish conception of Israel as the homeland of the Jewish people.[35] The most advance move in this respect is the attempt to appropriate the Jewish narrative and introduce *the Palestinians as the true Jews of today*.

Edward Said joins Azmy Bishara and some other Arab intellectuals who call today for a halt to the traditional Arab denials of the Holocaust or even of the Arab attempts to minimize its scale and moral implications. At the same time, however, Said favors

---

35 Ilan Gur-Ze'ev, *Edward Said as an Educator* (forthcoming). See also: Ilan Gur-Ze'ev and Ilan Pappe, "Beyond the destruction of the Other's collective memory: blueprints for a Palestinian/Israeli dialogue", *Theory Culture & Society*, 20:1, (February 2003), pp. 93–108.

a Jewish-Palestinian dialogue much more than an Israeli-Palestinian dialogue[36] Said
sets a precondition for the dialogue: the one side—the Jew—will accept that it is the
colonialist victimizer and the other side is its victim.

> There is no symmetry in this conflict. I must say it and I deeply believe
> in it. Here there is one side who is guilty and another side, which is the
> victim. The Palestinians are victims.[37]

Said insists so much on acknowledging the Holocaust and Jewish suffering not solely
for the sake of empathy with Jewish suffering and life in exile of its homeland. He
does so within a dialectical argumentation within which the ultimate victims of Hitlerism in the Holocaust are not the Jews in the Holocaust but the Palestinians in the
Nakbah.[38] This is since the victims of the victims are the ultra victims. The struggle
about "whose homeland is Israel/Palestine?" Or "Does, in its essence, the space merit
the name Israel, Palestine, both, or neither?" becomes inseparable from the question
not of who suffered more but "Who is the ultimate victim in human history?" *It is
a life-and-death struggle over whose narrative is the right one and who is its perpetrator.*
Asked otherwise, *what control apparatus on the representation of the narrative is stronger
in destroying the rival narrative and hiding the violences which make possible a simplistic
justification of the "authentic", the "right", or the "justified" claim, interests, suffering and
"counter-violence" against its Other?*
   But Edward Said, like some other Palestinian intellectuals, want more than that.
He is not satisfied with negating the Jews' claim to Israel as their homeland and with
convicting them as victimizers. By the same token he, like so many other Palestinian
intellectuals, wants also to air their own Jewishness, and he proclaims himself as the
authentic Jew of today: Jewishness as an existence in a permanent exile, Jewishness as
homelessness.

Theodor Adorno said that in the twentieth century the idea of home is pushed
away. I guess that part of my critique of Zionism is based on its overestimation of
a home. It claims that we need an home, that we will do anything to appropriate a
home, even if it means to make others into homeless…I never understood the claim
that this place is mine and you get out. I dislike also the drive to one's roots, to the
pure origin. I believe that the grate intellectual and political disasters of the twentieth
century were actualized by condensing movements which attempted to simplify and
purify. They said that we have to build here the tenants or the *Kibbutzim* or our army
and start all over again. I would not like it even for myself, I do not believe in it. Even
if I had been a Jew I would struggle against it. And it will not last for long…believe
me…I am the last Jewish intellectual. You do not know anyone else like that. All the

36   Edward Said, "Keynote Essay", in Ghada Karmi (ed.), *Jerusalem Today: What Future for Peace Process?*
      Ithaca: Publishing for International Campaign for Jerusalem, 1996, p. 16.
37   Edward Said, "My right of return"—an interview, *Ha'aretz* 18 Aug. 2000, p. 22.
38   Edward Said, "The only alternative", p. 3.

other Jewish intellectuals are masters from the suburbs. From Amos Oz to those who live here in America, so that I am the last one, the authentic follower of Adorno. I will articulate it like this: I am a Jewish Palestinian.[39]

This trend is part of a wider one, which represents the Zionist, and very often any Jew, as a prima facie colonialist, or the Nazi of our times. It is a widespread phenomenon in the Arab world, from which Bishara and Said explicitly distance themselves. However, it is fair to ask if Said really does present an alternative to this trend. Or is he in fact offering a more sophisticated version of the same postcolonialist project?

Within the framework of Said's postcolonialism, in the first stage the Israelis are presented as the most brutal colonialists. In the second stage of this postcolonialist project, the Palestinian (namely, Said himself) inherits not only the victimhood of the Jew but also the historical moral mission of Judaism. Maybe we should relate here also to Said's admiration and jealos of Theodor Adorno and his intellectual homelessness as a gate to mature critical theory. This is on the personal level, but there is here still a much richer psychological level. Said tries to overcome the Adorno legacy (or the Diasporic ideal) as a prima facie Jewish moral and philosophical *vanguard* within the framework of his postcolonialist theory. In his effort to establish moral uniqueness for the Palestinians as superior to their Jewish victims/victimizers, Said has theoretical difficulty addressing their unique Diasporic moral stance in the world's monotheistic history.

The postcolonialist ethics of Said presents an infinite eternal inequality between the colonized victim and the colonialist victimizer's violence. This inequality is to be addressed by postcolonialist education and politics too make possible the salvation not of the Palestinians but of the Israelis and the colonialist world at large. The Israelis are doomed here to become the arch-colonialist playing the role of the ultimate victim becoming the ultimate victimizer, while the Palestinian people are presented as the supreme collective in, and the moral vanguard of, a postcolonialist world since they are the chief victim of the ultimate victim in the Holy Land. These conditions make possible self-decolonization in the form of self-imposed de-Zionization by the Jews and the position of granting refusal to grant forgiveness by the Palestinians. This, however, is an eternal process that establishes a postcolonialist dialogue on eternal moral inequality as a gate to a new, postcolonialist, reality.[40]

Victimization becomes the final fatherland for the Palestinian as the supreme deliverer of the postcolonialist ethics under the guidance of its arch-educator—Edward Said himself, of course. This is the framework for the establishment of the hegemony of the Palestinian narrative and sovereign homeland on a different level, the level of world politics and power relations.

While Said insists on a difference between the evil of the National Socialist regime and the Israeli injustice inflicted on the Palestinians he is more violent against the essence of Judaism, its moral historical mission, its Messianism, and its claim to Israel as

---

39   Edward Said "My right of return", *ibid.*
40   Ilan Gur-Ze'ev, *Edward Said as an Educator*, *ibid.*

the Jewish sacred homeland. This attempt of his to deny the Jews the right to consider themselves as a people (they are only a religion) and their more than two thousand years of connection to Israel integrates into a wider Palestinian trend of equalizing the Nakbah and the daily life conditions under Israeli rule to Auschwitz and to the moral implications of the Holocaust. This, even when explicitly rejecting this part of the Palestinian normalizing education. While accepting that the Holocaust had a tragic influence on present-day moral behavior of the Israelis[41] I disagree with Said's conclusions, with his aim, and with the agenda of his postcolonialist disciples.

Said contributes, in his special way, to the equation of the Holocaust and the Nakbah, or at least to the representation of the Nakbah as an outcome of the communization to Jewish victimization—at the expense of victimizing the Palestinians. This trend does not challenge the general Palestinian trend of presenting the Israelis as the present-day Nazis, as is reflected in a relative modest way in the poem of Ha al Matukhal:

> Many years ago you fell under the deeds of the butchers in Dachau/ Your father was slaughtered in the Warsaw Ghetto/ You cried in the face of your sister's rape in the hell of Auschwitz/ Have you forgotten? How did you dare to reestablish Auschwitz in the midst of the desert?/ How did you dare to uproot a nation from its homeland? How did you dare to burn the children/ Have you forgotten?[42]

Facing the Palestinian move into the next stage of declaring themselves as "the real Jews", as in the case of the Palestinian poet Kamal Bulta who declared "I feel that I am a Jew", Mahmud Darwish presents a fearful reaction:

> [it is a must] to warn the too-easy writers among the Arabs of the danger of these tempting metaphorical images, when all of a sudden the oppressed Arab Man sees himself as "the new Jew" in a moment of a difficult loneliness.[43]

For Darwish it is but another manifestation of the violence of Israeli oppression, which transforms the victimizer into the victim and the Arab into "the new Jew". According to Darwish the Israeli cannot be satisfied in empowering his memory with the inclusion of the armed fairy tale and the uniform of the victim—he has also to destroy the Palestinian memory and deprive the Palestinian of his relation to the place, the history, and the Arab space. Before long, says Darwish, the Israeli will claim to be the real Palestinian.[44]

---

41   Ilan Gur-Ze'ev, "Was Hitler really defeated?" in: *Philosophy, Politics and Education in Israel*, Haifa 1999, pp. 57–98.

42   Taha al Matukal, *A Song from Ansar 3*, Ramalla 1989, p. 63 (in Arabic).

43   Mahmud Darwish, "The identity of absence", *Mifgashim* 7–8 (Autem 1987), p. 27.

44   *Ibid.*

This position of Darwish and Said is rich, deep and challenging. A central element of it, however, is that *it is committed to justify one violence against its opposing violence* on the ground that one narrative and one claim for a homeland is more valid than the other. More specifically, in the Israeli-Palestinian struggle over the representation of rights, victimhood and authenticity Said sides with the Palestinian myths, claims, and interests, while denouncing the Jewish symbolic and non-symbolic violence—neglecting the essential lesson of Adorno which he claims to follow, that any collectivism, any use of violence, any normalizing apparatus is a but a challenge to overcome, not a homeland to be domesticated by.

Palestine, which swallowed Israeli and Palestinian identity, which swallowed Judaism, is Said's colonialist project. Deconstruction is here recruited for Palestinian ethnocentricity, which becomes a universal transcendental project. By conquering the Jewish claim for responsibility to justice, swallowing its narrative and its sites of origin, legends and pretensions, the Palestinian people becomes not "simply" a collective which is less than a century old, only recently formed with not much a reason for being proud of its culture and education, but much more than that, a historical power and an ancient rich universally valid moral voice and unmatched cultural project. Within it Said, as a Jew can find nowhere his home, but everywhere his homelessness. Here the loss of the homeland is inseparable from the actual violent struggle for its recapturing. On this matter Said is uncompromising, as one can see in his rejection of the present "peace process" and appeasement attempt between the Israelis and the Palestinians. Said's favoring actual continuation of the war until the final defeat of the Israelis, their surrender of the land/hegemony, and their acceptance of their historic role as victimizers represents the postcolonialist devotion to ethnocentrism, violence and victory.

At the same time it also shows that he too refuses to face the implications and challenges of normalizing education—and avoids the struggle of overcoming its violences of which his project is one of the most advanced apparatuses. The struggle between two rival narratives over questions such as "Who is the ultimate victim of history?" "Whose homeland is Israel/Palestine?" And "Who is the real Jew?" is a unique manifestation of the ongoing general function of normalizing education which is committed to the production of collectives, their quest for territorial homeland and their realms of self evidence which simultaneously produces also their "Jew" as a danger/threat/colonizer. This necessity of fabricating the "Jew" is essential to the life and death between rival narratives that manifest meaninglessness while producing "meanings", "values", "we" and the "Jew" as the ultimate Other, the ultimate victim who is presented as the ultimate danger/threat/colonizer as part of the *danse macabre* of vivid, creative narratives.

While both the Israeli and the Palestinian sides are committed to controlling the space, they are also committed *to controlling its "true" representation* or effectively destroying the rival, "false", narrative within a framework in which homeland is a metaphysical entity. Here the Palestinian patriots and the Israeli patriots join forces. In other words, here it is seen in special clarity how normalizing education creates rivals both as *prisoners* of "their" narratives and as essential agents for its own self-reproduction.

Diasporic philosophy offers a gate to overcome the temptation of "critique" and "emancipation" in response to the call of Love of Life, creativity and responsibility. The aim of counter-education is to prepare us for a worthy Diasporic response, to create not in an oppressive manner but as part of let-be in a Godless world, situating ourselves as *becoming-towards-the world*. Diasporic philosophy never "at the same time" offers refusing to dwell and find pleasure in self-forgetfulness "within" the narrative of each of the smilingly rival camps, overcoming not only both narratives—but also the play within which they are actualized, destroyed and replaced by younger, more effective, productive, violent and suggestive narratives. Counter-education that is born out of the roots of Diasporic philosophy, therefore, has no "homeland", not even as a telos, yet it is so rich and disillusioned that it can find everywhere intimacy so that homelessness is its home.

Jewish negative theology, Heidegger's concept of facing the Ge-stell and Benjamin and Adorno's concept of Messianism without a Messiah, or negative utopianism, are some of the places a Diasporic counter-education committed person will visit in order to empower the struggle against normalizing education.

The Holocaust and the Nakbah, as well as the struggle over the uncontested status of being the ultimate victim and the owner of the authentic claim to homeland, are inseparable. They represent the tragic essence of every education as a process of normalization within a *Same* as homeland. Normalizing education is inseparable from "reality" in the sense of being that which necessarily produces war over existence, over representation and over space. Within this process, as part of the dance of narrative's meaninglessness producing "meaning" it produces also fears, holy and "unavoidable" struggles for national liberation and ideology critiques, which are aimed at defeating and conquering the other's representation apparatuses, claims to homeland and even its homelessness.

Counter-education should not offer an alternative version of homeland, not even an alternative to the nationalistic, patriotic education, not even to the critique of all versions of forming collectives and controlled love of "homeland". As the Holocaust and Nakbah teach us, this is an important anti-dehumanization lesson. But this is still within the framework of normalizing education. Counter-education must challenge all versions of the Same, the truth, fixed sense of reality and predestined love.

In face of this, my responsibility awakens me to challenge the continuum of the Same and refuse the abandonment of the human's responsibility to himself as the shepherd of being.[45] Counter-education, however, cannot become an instrument, not even a paved way. Within counter-education there is only *a chance* of sensitivity to an alternative self-education and readiness to the one presented by Edward Said's postcolonialist concept of being a genuine Jew. To the degree that Judaism offers Messianism without a Messiah it is Jewish, but there is nothing exclusively Jewish in this kind of exile. An ontological exile can never become a prelude for a nationalistic violence di-

---

45   Martin Heidegger, "Letter on humanism", *Ibid.*

rected against the illegitimacy of the Other's narrative and its violences. Living in such an exile cannot be part of a sentimental gaze or longing for a lost home, nor for a new or renewed collectivism, truth or love. It must not neglect the life-and-death struggle between narratives and collectives as well as conflicting commitments to truth, justice and creativity. At the same time, however, it is *exiled* from the quest for victory in the homeland which produces these endless struggles and it sees these wars for meaning and the Same as a manifestation of meaninglessness and exile. The irony of counter-education exiles it even from the safe haven of the tragic sense of normalizing education. In this exile, however, creative improvisation and responsibility, not abandoning responsibility, cynicism or the quest for mere pleasure or power, have the last word. Homelessness is the home of counter-education and as such it cannot appease itself with the self-assurance of the misery of the loss of the quest for a homeland of its own. It cannot even abandon its responsibility to revisit the quest for a given or a lost homeland and the violences that struggle over hegemony in producing and representing Holocausts and Nakbahs. And so the counter-educationalist must be involved and committed in the actuality, and challenge the victimizations and the productions of truths, memories and identities. It is a must to be involved and resist injustice. In this sense the quest and the struggle for dialogue are a concrete moral-political situatedness. As such counter-education is always on the verge of being transformed into another version of normalizing education and creating its own "homeland" or, at best, a quest for an alternative concept of exile. Still, while being involved in this dialectical sense, counter-education is never at home even in this exile, is not identical with that which it refers too, ready for its call—that which is absent. The religiosity, which is manifested in this readiness in face of the presence of the absence of God as homeland and as being exiled from homeland, can never be at home with itself. This dangerous existence, while contradicting itself and endangering its negative dialectics, opens the possibility for never totally abandoning the refusal of the temptations of the immanently violent quest for dwelling in the Garden of Eden, for God, or for "homeland worthy of the name". Even self-reassuring exile from any form of Same cannot become its homeland. This is the only kind of hope possible for counter-education. And where there is hope there is "room" for love, even if never a safe "home".

CHAPTER 13

PHILOSOPHY OF PEACE EDUCATION IN A POSTMODERN ERA

Peace education is currently enjoying the support and appreciation of most theoretical orientations and political establishments. Enlightened modernists and "soft" postmodernists, multiculturalists, feminists, critical thinkers, and liberals all celebrate the new fashion.

An interesting set of assumptions is central in the current general appreciation of peace education. It is important to note the conviction that peace should be sought, and longed for, or struggled for. Another central assumption is that peace is the opposite of violence or conflict and that it is possible to differentiate them. Still another central assumption is that it is possible to educate for peace or for the promotion of peace, in one way or another, and that it is justified and desirable to invest the proper means to do so. In this paper we wish to question these assumptions. We will argue that peace education is normally part and parcel of the reality it pretends to change. The division between peace and violence (or conflict) is not unproblematic. The kind of differentiation will determine the preferable version of peace education yet the whole project should be able to justify the preference for peace. As an ultimate goal, the justifications that are common in current peace education, we will argue, not only serve various violences, which peace education fails to reflect and challenge: peace education is one of the manifestations of their presence. We will conclude by addressing the possibilities for an alternative to the current trends in peace education.

PEACE EDUCATION: CONFLICTING TRENDS AND THEIR IMPLICATIONS

In this paper we do not reconstruct in detail the similar or conflicting tendencies in current peace education. Suffice it to pinpoint the variations in the propositions, the aims, and their orientations. Under such circumstances, in fact, it is quite misleading to speak about "peace education" as a monolithic entity. We would do better to speak of the various theories and practices within current peace education. In this paper "peace education" as a general term is an abstraction and its usefulness carries a price. We will try to justify this price.

Most of the current peace education activities manifest much good will but less theoretical framework and philosophical elaboration concerning the propositions, aims, methods, and evaluation of the results and their meaning. We think that a lot of the difficulties and shortcomings that the peace education practitioners face are not challenged on account of the lack of conceptual work and reflection. In a certain sense this is not always a bad thing, since at times the naivete of the practitioners and their public is a productive or potentially productive element in normalizing educational process. At times philosophical work is understood as unnecessary, artificial, or even dangerous for this educational cause. This attitude also holds concerning the modernism-postmodernism divide of discourses.

Many peace education versions work within the framework of modernistic-oriented technical reason. This manifests various positivist, pragmatic, and functionalist views of knowledge, paying scant attention to the social and cultural context and the violence which produces the yardsticks and the conceptions of knowledge, values, strivings, and imagination, as well as their own identity. There is however an additional idealist moral dimension, which we will have to address with special sensitivity. This dimension concerns the concept of universal human rights. The source of many of these versions of peace education is religious (mainly Christian); others are humanist of various kinds. However they are all united in tying resistance against violence or the prevention of conflicts to human rights as an a-historic, essential, universalistic phenomenon.

The concept of universal human rights is prima facie modernistic-oriented. It is rooted in an essentialist concept of the human subject as an entity whose characteristics are universally valid. Its telos, ends, or potentials are conceived as rooted in its essence. This concept is related to peace education even before it acquired its current title, formalization, and institutionalization at the end of the 19th century from John Dewey and after World War I from the progressive educational movement.

Like many other activists of peace education of his day (except the pacifists), Dewey did not base his peace education on moral grounds but on pragmatic political arguments.[1] But here too, as everywhere else, Dewey's pragmatism is founded on Enlightened concept of the aim of knowledge and of the potentials of the human subject, and is to be seen as part of the humanist tradition even after its rhetorical divorce from metaphysics.

The realization of human potentials by humanist education accompanied by social changes, Dewey thought, would prevent the conditions for war. And since he understood peace as the absence of war, he had much hope in the restructuring of the curriculum and the pedagogy in order to enhance the education of a reflective and a non-dogmatic public, which would not easily be manipulated into warfare. Within such a framework

> History is not the study of heroes, but an account of social development; it provides us with knowledge of the past which contributes to the solution of social problems of the present and the future. [Therefore,] before starting with history as such it would be a good idea to identify the important problems of the present-day society…[2]

---

1   Charles F. T. Howlett, "John Dewey and Nicholas Murray Butler: Contrasting Conceptions of Peace Education in the Twenties", *Educational Theory*, 37: 4 (Fall 1987): 448.

2   John Dewey, "Lectures in China 1919–1920", in: Robert W. Clopton and Tsuin-Chen (eds.), *John Dewey: Lectures in China, 1919–1920*, Honolulu: University of Hawaii Press 1973: 277.

Since he identified peace with the elevation of humanity and the development of rational and pragmatically enlightened human capacities, he understood the development of geography and history studies as instruments for peace. His project was not directed solely to the American situation or for a limited time, but was part of a liberal-universalistic orientation sensitive to differences, contexts, and changes. Yet it remained fundamentally contextual: Western, humanistic, liberal, and enlightened. In general this also holds for the work of the central figure in peace education during the last generation, Johan Galtung. Galtung believed that

> Ultimately, peace research is an effort to put Man together again, an effort to transcend all these borders and divisions discussed in this paper, in order to arrive at something more truthful to the miracle that is Man.[3]

Some scholars think that peace education continues the progressive education articulated by Dewey. Within this trend Friesen and Weiler hold that current feminist and multicultural peace education advocates Dewey's appreciation for democratic principles when it maintains that its approach will further social progress and global stability by enhancing understanding among nations.[4]

This trend in peace education is part of a larger effort to integrate emancipatory dimensions in Dewey's thought and neo-Marxist tradition with some aspects of current postmodernist discourses, as manifested in the work of Henry Giroux. [5] These efforts are always highly problematic, as evinced by the various efforts to construct a postmodern critical pedagogy in face of the need to obtain a difficult or an impossible balance among the autonomy of the subject and her contingency, the possibility of a priori value judgments, universal validity of truth claims, and the possibility of a non-repressive communication. Not only do various modern orientations take part in peace education, but "soft" postmodernists too, in both the practice and the philosophical justifications of essentialism, universalism, and transcendentalism. But so far, the only work that explicitly set itself the task of articulating a postmodern critique of current peace education has failed to realize its promise in all but its title.[6] Some trends in the Israeli multiculturalist and peace movements are bona fide manifestations of this phenomenon.[7] In the case of peace education the coexistence of these

---

3   Johan Galtung, *Peace: Research, Education, Action: Essays in Peace Research*, I, Copenhagen 1975: 262.

4   John W. Friesen and Edith Elizabeth Weiler, "New robes for an Old Order: Multicultural Education, Peace Education, Cooperative Learning and Progressive Education", *The Journal of Educational Thought*, 22: 1 (April 1988): 50

5   Henry Giroux, *Teachers as Intellectuals: Toward a Critical Pedagogy of Learning*, New York: Bergin & Garvey, 1988, p. 160.

6   Ian M. Harris, "Editor's introduction", *Peabody Journal of Education*, 71: 3 (1996), pp. 1–11.

7   Ilan Gur-Ze'ev, "Modernity, postmodernity and multiculturalism in Israeli education", in: Ilan Gur-Ze'ev (ed.). *Modernity, Postmodernity, and Education*,(Tel Aviv: Ramot Tel-Aviv University Press, 1999, pp. 7–50.

two trends is inexorably modernist in its assumptions, even when using a fashionable "soft" postmodern rhetoric in feminist, multiculturalist, and critical arenas. At the same time a large part of peace education field activity and theoretical elaboration is modern, and even pre-modern, as in the case of various religious educational centers. Another part of the activity is run or heavily supported by governmental agencies, and still another part by the United Nations. Substantial work is done by NGOs.

The postmodern sensitivity to the contingent stance of values and truth claims, the refusal to accept universal validity claims, as well as the rejection of any general theory, of foundationalism, essentialism, and transcendentalism, are in direct conflict with Enlightenment's modern ideals and its philosophical tradition. Their implicit conservation

without their re-articulation or transformation should be addressed. Galtung[8] already identified the unreflective use of the term peace education and the lack of theoretical elaboration of the foundations of the practitioner's work in this field. Galtung himself, however, worked within the modernist framework and certainly did not challenge peace education and standard peace research from a postmodernist orientation. So far, the only work that explicitly set itself the task of articulating a postmodern critique of current peace education has failed to realize its promise in all but its title.[9]

Some feminist-oriented peace education programs explicitly connect themselves to Dewey's philosophy and its concept of problem solving via the practice of conflict resolution. They do so while emphasizing the importance of "value clarification" as a reaction to current attempts to rationalize patriotism and justify ever-growing investments in armament. The idea here is that

> Children must learn to be peacemakers in order to survive in the nuclear age. They need an education that affirms life and encourages new thinking about conflict, progress, and peacemaking. Feminist educators can play an important role in peace education by helping children understand the connections between militarism and patriarchy.[10]

> The central part of patriarchy and sex roles is sometimes complemented by a retreat to human nature and universal rights that feminist peace education is committed to.[11]

The lack of a social-oriented philosophical elaboration of peace education made possible the positivistic views about "conflict resolution" within media studies and com-

---

8   Johan Galtung, "Violence, Peace, and Peace Research", *Journal of Peace Research*, 6 (1969): 167,

9   Ian M. Harris (ed)," *Peace Education in a Postmodern World*, a special issue of *Peabody Journal of Education 71: 3* (1996).

10   Ruth S. Meyers, "Peace Education: Problems and Promise", *Women's Studies Quarterly XII: 2* (Summer 1984): 21.

11   Brigit Brock-Utne, *Educating for Peace: A Feminist Perspective*, (New York : Pergamon Press, 1983).

munication in the 1980s and the great hopes of using the Internet in the service of peace education during the 1990s.[12]

Even peace education within the framework of current critical pedagogy has sometimes an essentialist conception of human rights and a positivistic conception of true critical knowledge in the service of peace education. This is occasionally so even when moral imagination is prized as against instrumental rationality and technical reason.[13] This trend is rooted already in the thinking of the Frankfurt School thinkers in the first phase of their thought[14] and in the concept of dialogue of Paulo Freire and even in present-day thinkers of critical pedagogy such as Henry Giroux.

This line of thinking is also highly evident in some current multicultural discourses which affirm difference, contingency, and anti-fundamentalist-oriented pedagogy. Here again, the very possibility of a postmodern dialogue among differences and of border crossing overcoming ethnocentrism is ultimately founded on modern universalistic conceptions of the good (or at least on universal pragmatic) and a fundamentalist conception of human nature and human rights. This is so even when explicitly educational thinkers like Giroux align themselves with the "soft" postmodern critique of the Enlightenment and its fundamentalism, universalism, and transcendentalism.[15] The relation between peace and human rights and the potential tension between multiculturalism and humanism is identifiable also in major UNESCO declarations, where the United Nations' commitment to self-determination and the independence of states is covered by an explicit, uncompromising commitment to a humanist conception of universal human rights.

In UNESCO's Medium-Term Plan for 1977–1982 we read that it "condemns all violations of human rights as a threat and contrary to its very spirit". The struggle for peace and action to promote human rights are recognized as inseparable. Their linkage "constitutes a coherent conceptual framework". UNESCO[16] states in this spirit that

> There can be no genuine peace when the most elementary human rights are violated, or while situations of injustice continue to exist; conversely, human rights for all cannot take root and achieve full growth while latent or open conflicts are rife... Peace is incomplete with malnutrition, extreme poverty and the refusal of the rights of people to self-determination... The only lasting peace is a just peace based

12 Marcia L. Johnson, "Trends in peace education", http://www.indiana.edu/~ssdc/pcdig.htm, 15.11.1999.
13 Marguerite K. Rivage-Seul, "Peace education: Imagination and pedagogy of the oppressed", *Harvard Educational Review*, 57: 2 (May 1987), p. 157.
14 Ilan Gur-Ze'ev, *The Frankfurt School and the History of Pessimism*, Jerusalem: Magnes Press, 1996. (in Hebrew).
15 Henriette Dahan-Kalev, "Mizrakhim in Israel: A Postmodern Point of View", in: Ilan Gur-Ze'ev (ed.). *Modernity, Postmodernity, and Education*, Tel Aviv: Ramot Tel-Aviv University Press, 1999.
16 UNESCO, "Thinking Ahead 1977", p. 62, in: Brock-Utne, 1983: 2.

on respect for human rights. Furthermore, a just peace calls for the establishment of an equitable international order, which will preserve future generations from the scourge of war.

The universalistic-oriented conception of human rights in the modern sense can be traced to the Virginia Bill of Rights and to the 1776 American Declaration of Independence, as well as to the 1789 French declaration. It can also be traced to Kantian philosophy. Yet all these are founded not only on Locke's and Rousseau's conceptions of natural law, but on Western traditional fundamentalism within which natural law and human nature are developed.

Such conceptions are highly problematic in today's philosophical and political discussions regardless of one's self-positioning. As postmodernists, modernists, humanists, feminists, or post-colonialists, feminists, multiculturalists or other representatives of the postmodern influence, such thinkers are highly committed to challenging the modern universalistic and essentialist conception of human rights. They favor contingency, localism, difference, and uniqueness as the starting point for a declared non-Western-ethnocentric-oriented peace education. Within the various "soft" postmodern trends the politics of rights is founded on contingent, fragile, temporary coalitions of minorities, which represent real, changing interests and passions, replacing Western ethnocentric universalized concepts such as human rights.[17] Constituent thinkers of this trend do not take part in today's celebrated peace education even when they are involved in actual communal, ethnic, race, and gender conflicts, such as in the case of bell hooks, Peter McLaren, and Elizabeth Ellsworth. Here we do not address this issue but limit ourselves to developing the argument that both "left" and the "right" supporters of peace education are united in moralizing politics. This objectifies a certain discourse for the totalization of an order in which there will be no room for an autonomous subject and free spirit. Harmony, instead, will endure in perpetual "peace".

Moralizing politics is not too problematic for conservatives. As displayed by some of the "soft" postmodern rhetorics of peace education, it is also a serious challenge for some of the radical critics of Western meta-narratives. It is an issue to be addressed by the critics of the existing relations between politics and moral philosophy in essentialist terms, as part of the naturalization of inequalities, marginalization of the Other, and self-reproduction of the white man's domination and its structural and direct violence.

Karl Schmidt was quick to challenge the humanist way to peace under the banners of universal human rights and moralizing politics. He ridiculed the humanist attempt to legitimize "just wars" in the name of future peace and present human cosmopolitan rights. Habermas criticizes Schmidt for ultimately justifying all wars[18] and Schmidt is rightly blameworthy on this point.

---

17   Linda Alcoff, "Culture Feminism versus Post-Structuralis", *Journal of Women in Culture and Society, 13: 31* (1988), pp. 405–435
18   Juergen Habermas, "Two hundred years' hindsight", in James Bohman and Matthias Lutz-Bachmann (eds.), *Perpetual Peace: Essays on Kant's Cosmopolitan Ideal*, London and Cambridge: MIT Press, 1997, p. 141.

More than that, Schmidt, along with other proto-Nazi writers such as Ernst Juenger, is to be blamed for aesthetisizing and moralizing all forms of heroic or effective national violence. But does Habermas's critique really respond to Schmidt's challenge to the concepts of "just war" and world peace as a (justified) violent realization of human rights? The difference here is between those who think that successful wars are all justified—or at least not provable as unjustified—and those who claim that only "just wars" are justified. We do not attempt to establish a postmodern position according to which there is no way to distinguish Schmidt's critique from Habermas's defense of humanist universalism and their concepts of the justification of war and the commitment to peace. We do claim, however, that from current postmodern critique and from traditional critical theory it is possible to place a serious challenge before the concepts of peace and violence presented within peace education as this is represented by declared modernists and postmodernists alike.

In our questioning of current peace education some aspects of Schmidt's critique will be further developed by questioning the concepts of "peace", "violence", and "education" that are normally taken for granted by peace education practitioners and theorists. Amazingly, it is Galtung, the positivist theorist of peace research, who suggests the most advanced questioning of the concepts of peace and violence within this tradition.[19] His pupils and critics alike refrained from investing too much energy in the fundamental questions of peace education.

THE CONCEPT OF PEACE IN CURRENT PEACE EDUCATION

The lack of conceptualization within the current framework of peace education has been noted by a number of writers. Salomon's words are highly relevant:

> What is peace education? What is the core of peace education, its defining attributes? What, if anything, distinguishes its most prototypical instantiations from other, similar fields? ...Numerous programs are called "peace education", ranging from violence reduction in schools to learning about war and peace, and from democratic education to the cultivation of self-esteem. Subsuming all of these under the superordinate category of peace education tends to blur important distinctions, such as between the kind of peace education that is carried out in areas of conflict, such as northern Ireland, and programs designed for more peaceful regions. Similarly, too wide a category tends to lump together programs designed to cultivate universal peaceful outlook with programs aimed at promoting a peaceful disposition toward a particular group, race or nation to replace collective sentiments of hatred, discrimination, and hostility.[20]

---

19 Galtung (1969).
20 Gavriel Salomon and Baruch Nevo, "Peace Education: An Active Field in need for Research", paper presented at a Peace Education Conference, The University of Haifa, (November 7–8, 1999), pp. 5–6.

While accepting part of Salomon's critique it is worth observing that that very critique makes indiscriminate use of various and conflicting ideological and philosophical conceptions of peace education. More important still is that like the thinkers whom he criticizes for lack of conceptualization, he too treats "peace" as an unproblematic concept and does not invest much effort in conceptualizing his own project. True, there is here a beginning in the direction of a general conceptualization of the field and tackling its major problematic; but following Galtung, Salomon distinguishes negative and positive peace, adding that

> One needs, perhaps, to distinguish here between peace in the sense of harmony and the absence of tension and conflict on the individual, micro level, and peace in the sense of the absence of war, armed conflict or violence, on the collective, macro level.[21]

Other scholars, such as Reardon, identify peace with reconciliation, and the prospects for achieving peace with conflict resolution[22] and education for reflection grounded in shared values.[23]

This trend is also manifested in UNESCO's 1998 declaration on the occasion of World Teacher's Day. Teachers are presented as peace builders who shape the future within a positivistic conflict-resolution orientation:

> Building the foundations for peace is as much a challenge for teachers as it is for those who sign peace treaties. Conflict resolution and the implementation of peace settlements feature regularly in the news, but today on World Teachers' Day, we should ask ourselves how much such peace efforts would achieve without the unheralded contribution of the world's 50 million peace teachers? Day after day and year after year, teachers build the very fabric of peace. They transmit the knowledge, values and attitudes, the skills and behavior which ensure that peace is not just the absence of conflict but becomes a way of life for all, putting into daily practice the concept that social justice is essential to universal and lasting peace.[24]

This positivistic orientation might have a positive concept of peace, not just a negative one which conceives peace as an absence of national conflicts, as do Salomon and

---

21   *Ibid.*, p. 6.
22   Betty A. Reardon, *Comprehensive Peace Education: Educating for Global Responsibility*, New York and London: Teachers College Press, 1988, p. 69.
23   *Ibid.* 72.
24   UNESCO, ILO UNDP and UNICEF launch a joint message on occasion of World Teachers' Day, October 1998, http://mirror-us.unesco.org/opi/eng/unescopress/98–209e.htm (4/01/2000).

many other peace education researchers and practitioners. However, it is important to note that while accepting Galtung's positive concept of peace[25] and even when relating to the social context and its structural violence,[26] the UNESCO declaration conceives peace as an absence of conflict that is to be achieved by solving "social injustice" through the teaching of conflict resolution skills. This declaration conceives peace and social justice as positive and desirable, in contrast to violence and injustice, which are undesirable. According to the UNESCO's declaration, this is the aim of teachers as educators, and this is actually what teachers universally do in their daily work.

We claim that the work of the 50 million teachers referred to by UNESCO is one of the main mechanisms of perpetuating violence and injustice. This is not because they are doing such a poor job, but on the contrary, because around the world teachers, together with the other manipulations of normalizing education, are doing it so well. The current human reality is to be challenged by a critical addressing of the fundamentals and the context of the concept of peace that these teachers/educators are committed to, and certainly not by a search for new routes for improving their present "achievements".

Within this trend there is a strong positivistic conviction that conflict resolution skills are a matter of professional knowledge and good didactics. There is here a belief that these skills, fundamentally, might be taught along with the quest for justice, in the most concrete and specific manner.[27] Some of the positivist writers within this trend even see peace education as a successful conflict-solving process in which the decline of violence is to be detected by a measurable promotion of schools' efficiency and productivity.[28]

As the UNESCO declaration shows, not all peace education researchers and thinkers neglect the social context and the challenge of actual power relations within which peace education and its rivals are produced. Winch, for example, is a peace education thinker who rejects the conception of positive peace. Winch stresses the inevitability of social conflict and suggests that peace is not merely the absence of conflict, but entails "learning to live with conflict in a constructive manner.[29] Within this framework personal fulfillment is essential for world peace, or in Ross's words "the individual must be helped to develop his full potential for constructive, peaceful living".[30]

Peace education within the multicultural discourse emphasizes diversity as a precondition for peace, in contrast to the concept of reproducing shared values and a homogeneous kind of reflection towards universal solidarity and responsibility as analyzed by liberal peace educators and most of the theorists of civil education. Rennebohm-Franz's statements are paradigmatic in this context:

---

25 Galtung (1975): 29.
26 *Ibid.* 251
27 Benjamin Chetkow-Yanoov, "Conflict-resolution Skills Can be Taught", *Peabody Journal of Education*, 7: 3 (1996), pp. 12–28.
28 Harris, 1996.
29 Friesen and Wieler, 1988: 51.
30 *Ibid.*

> With multiple versions of ways of coming to know our world as well as multiple versions of presenting and sharing understandings, we begin to weave an educational tapestry that reveals the complexities, diversities, commonalties, and interconnectedness of many human experiences. Understanding multiple versions is the beginning of learning how to weave a global multicultural peace tapestry rich in many colors, textures, and styles.[31]

Freire, Rivage-Seul, and many other critical educational theorists such as McLaren and Giroux tried to give voice and place to the perspective of the marginalized, to empower those whose voice has been silenced. Rivage-Seul tries to develop an alternative peace education based not on hegemonic perspectives and interests but on the contrary, on those of the silenced, based on Freire's concept of moral imagination which, it is hoped, will transcend "the bounds of technical thought".[32] However, peace education within the framework of this traditional Freirerian framework is universalistic and essentialist, and at bottom conceives hierarchical relations between teacher and students as a precondition for educational progress.[33] The writers who are committed to developing the possibility of the oppressed raising their voice conceive the potential for the universalization of knowledge and the articulation of the facts as a precondition for an emancipatory peace education.

> Since all human beings are inevitably interrelated on a limited planet, the pursuit of a material advantage on the part of some inevitably affects the ability of others to meet their basic needs. Therefore, persistence in the cult of the superfluous necessarily violates the others' basic freedom, understood as the liberty of each to choose whatever does not endanger the material basis of the freedom of any other).[34]

This conception of human essence is impossible to separate from the conception of the possible emancipation manifested in "peace". Under the influence of Marcuse and the positive utopian tradition Rivage-Seul cites Hinklammert to hint in the direction of emancipatory, critical, peace education:

> Transcendental imagination envisions full human life in which there no longer exists a disjunction between sensual hunger and its equally sensual satisfaction... It is a question of imagining fullness in which there is no need for institutions... There is neither perfect competition

---

31 Kristi Rennebohm-Franz, "Toward a Critical Social Consciousness in Children: Multicultural Peace Education in a First Grade Classroom", *Theory into Practice*, 35: 4 (Autumn 1996), p. 266.
32 Rivage-Seul 1987, p. 160.
33 Ilan Gur-Ze'ev, "Toward a Nonrepressive Critical Pedagogy", *Educational Theory*, 48: 4 (1988), p. 463.
34 Rivage-Seul 1987, p. 162

nor planning. It is the spontaneity which comes from the recognition of all as subjects, and which is not thinkable except by means of an imagination of a fluid nature friendly to human beings. [35]

All these diverse conceptions of peace are united in conceiving "peace" as desirable, on the one hand, and as a manifestation of the reduction or complete elimination of violence and the realization of human potential free and just intersubjectivity, on the other. We think that this conviction should be challenged.

IS PEACE A MANIFESTATION OF OR THE ELIMINATION OF VIOLENCE?

In Book IV of *The City of God against the Pagans*, St. Augustine establishes the sources of peace and violence and articulates their essence and characters. Since the various trends in current peace education share the same general concept of peace, which is traceable not only to the Enlightenment's thought but even to earlier Christian and Greek sources, it is worth resorting to St. Augustine even if he is not the sole influence or the earliest. As we will show, while being one of the sources for the concept of peace dominant in present peace education, the Augustinian concept is much richer and is of more value in the presentation of the concepts of peace and violence in the postmodern elaboration.

> I distinguish two branches of mankind: one made up of those who live according to man, the other those who live according to God. I speak of these branches also allegorically as two cities, that is, two societies of human beings, of which one is predestined to reign eternally with God and the other to undergo eternal punishment with the devil. For at the very start, when the two cities began their history through birth and death, the first to be born was the citizen of this world, and only after him came the alien in this world who is a member of the city of God, one predestined by grace and chosen by grace, one by grace an alien below and by grace a citizen above.[36]

St. Augustine's framework distinguishes two entities and two histories within which the separation of peace and violence acquires its full meaning. But for St. Augustine, contrary to current major trends in peace education, this is a dialectical historical process. He follows it in presenting an imperative to transcend history and its violences. We will return later to this aspect of the division between peace and violence's historical existence and its transcendence. However, already at this stage it is important to stress his grounds for the preference of peace: its relation to true belief in the right way to the redemption of humans and the world.

---

35 *Ibid.*
36 Saint Augustine, *The City of God Against the Pagans*, IV, XVI., London and Cambridge: W. Heinemann, 1957, p. 415.

Here St. Augustine follows the Socratic tradition and connects redemption to the possibility of transcendence as attaining the light of the true knowledge.[37] This is one of the preconditions for the totalizing dimension of Western education and its being swallowed, reproduced, and re-presented within the hegemonic violences. The present peace education has lost its theological sources and its theological conceptualizations. It has also lost its humanist as well as its total commitment to the imperatives of reason and to the revolutionization of the general human condition towards its full emancipation.

While speaking in the language of moral politics, present-day peace education fails to submit non-contingent justifications for its claims, practices, and hopes for a state of peace that is not a mere violent/stable, political construct. However, it is exactly in the present-day postmodern condition and in the current globalization process that there is no room for a serious challenge to the hegemonic claims for knowledge by the totally other than the present reality or by an alternative, vivid Spirit. Within the present reality there is no room for a new Moses, Jesus, Buddha, Marx, or Hitler. Even the supposed alternative Spirit of Humanism was rapidly domesticated in the Middle East and in Iran itself by the logic of capitalism and instrumental rationality. Within the present modern and pre-modern conditions the otherness of the Other is terrorized while proclaimed as evil, sin, or a dangerous epistemological or dogmatic gift. In the most efficient assault, such as the assaults currently taking place in today's postmodern arenas, such as the cyberspace, it is presented and functions as an irrelevant element; it is being ironized or even internalized within the global pleasure machine as a mere meaningless "link", "site", "item", or "experience", namely as an ornament or a plaything to be used for a passing moment in a context where there is no transcendence or escape from meaninglessness.

This conception is immanently committed to totalizing information and to purging the threatening gift or "saving" humanity from its danger by all necessary means. Here normalizing education, purging the Other of his or her epistemological otherness, structural violence, and the "direct" individual and collective violences are inseparable. One of our aims should be to unveil the relation between the success of these violences and their invisibility as a manifestation of mental health and collective stability, order, and "peace" as an order of things which prevents reflection, resistance and transcendence. Within the theological tradition this resistance to the given reality is conceived as openness or quest for "redemption". Peace is conceived within this framework as "the return of the multiple to unity, in conformity with the Platonic or Neoplatonic idea of the one".[38]

It is important to note, however, that within history, for St. Augustine it is impossible to conceive "the city of God" disconnected from "the earthly city": they are always to be conceived in their mutual relations. More than that, while real peace is

---

37   Plato, "Phaedo", *The Portable Plato*, New York: Viking Press, 1950, p. 201.
38   Emmanuel Levinas, "Peace and proximity", in: Adriaan T. Peperzak, Simon Critchley, and Robert Bernasconi (eds.), *Emmanuel Levinas: Basic Philosophical Writings*, Bloomington: Indiana University Press, 1996, p. 162.

only to be conceived within "the city of God", its rival city strives for peace too. The division is not only, as in current peace education, between a state of peace and a state of violence (or conflict), but in parallel also between two essentially different states of peace. One could also say, between two different sets of violences, one secular, the other sacred violence, namely "peace".

"The earthly city" is in constant "pursuit of victories that either cut lives short or at any rate are short-lived".[39] Yet as the manifestation of successful violence, these victories contain also goods, although only "the lowest kind of goods". Among these "lowest kinds of goods" attained by warfare St. Augustine counts "earthly peace".[40] The point that is important for St. Augustine, which is forgotten by today's peace education, is that (earthly) peace is only attainable by warfare:

> Thus to gain the lowest kind of good it covets an earthly peace, one that it seeks to attain by warfare; for if it is victorious and no one remains to resist it, there will be peace...[41]

According to St. Augustine there are higher goods than a earthly peace; these "belong to the city above, in which victory will be untroubled in everlasting and ultimate peace".[42] This other kind of peace is totally other than the peace that is tenable in the earthly city, and it is even conditioned by transcending from the peace that the earthly city and its victories can offer.

On the one hand, St. Augustine represents a Western philosophical tradition which after being secularized by Kant, Hegel, and Marx could lead to a kind of universalism within which idealists, pragmatists, and even (very) "soft" postmodernists could share peace education.

Within peace education as developed by pragmatists, feminists, multiculturalists, and certainly by positivistic-oriented functionalists who strive for social stability and free, prosperous national and international markets, all trends relate to human rights and resist direct and explicit violence in the name of universal rights such as freedom from persecution or exploitation. Here the division between peace and violence is clear-cut, and the very commitment and quest for peace is left unaddressed and is unproblematized.

It is St. Augustine, more than present peace education theorists and practitioners that follow his essentialism, who seriously addresses the issue of peace and problematizes the quest for peace in relation to the essence of the human and her ultimate goal. In Augustinian terms the ideal and the reality, which peace education strives for, is the earthly city in its most severe form. For St. Augustine this is something unavoidable in this world, yet it is a challenge to overcome in order to be redeemed.

---

39   St. Augustine (1955): XV., IV: 425.
40   *Ibid.*
41   *Ibid.*
42   *Ibid.*, p. 427

We see St. Augustine's doctrine and the educational attitude he represents within Western thinking not solely but also as part of a violent control of Western consciousness and as a manifestation of epistemological violence against its disciples. At the same time, however, it is worth acknowledging its dialectics and its transcendental element. It contains an antagonism to the whole order of which "peace" as a desire, as an ideal, and as a reality, is but a part. As such it is a constant challenge to this order, while being part of it, and it contains an important emancipatory potential. This dimension of challenging the hegemonic realm of self-evidence and the imperative for overcoming philosophy and existence is surely missing in the concept of peace which functions in the various trends in current peace education.

Following St. Augustine we claim that what in the political arena is called "peace" is one of the extreme manifestations of successful terror. Levinas sees the seed of this condition already in "Greek wisdom" and pinpoints its violent nature in which human peace is awaited on the basis of the truth:

> Peace on the basis of the truth—on the basis of the truth of knowledge where, instead of opposing itself, the diverse agrees with itself and unites; where the stranger is assimilated... Peace on the basis of the truth, which—marvel of marvels—commands humans without forcing them or combating them, which governs them or gathers them together without enslaving them, which through discourse, can convince rather than vanquish...[43]

This totalizing concept of peace in its relation to true knowledge allows effective dehumanization of humans and their formation into collectives. At its peak it makes possible and secures consciousness, which is committed to "true" solidarity. It creates and generously awards the willingness of the individual to sacrifice herself for the collective, its security, ideals, values, and horizons. As such it is part and parcel of the violence which produces borders, wars, and Others as objects of education, destruction, redemption, emancipation, or deconstruction. Yet it is a concept of peace conditioned by abandonment of reflection and transcendence. It is a manifestation of one's being swallowed or constructed by the ruling realm of self-evidence. With the assistance of good parents, devoted teachers, supporting friends, beautiful texts, and endless other ways it produces brave warriors to protect its borders and destroy its internal and external enemies. As such, it actually manifests human forgetfulness of its goal, domestication, tranquilization that reflects the victory of normalizing education. It is peace as "repose among beings well-placed or reposing on the underlying solidity of their substance, self-sufficient in their identity or capable of being satisfied and seeking satisfaction".[44]

43   Levinas (1996), p. 162
44   *Ibid*, 163

This concept of philosophy, which was dominated by the Platonic quest for light and love of truth, is embarrassed and feels guilty in current Western thought. It finds it hard to

> Recognize itself in its millennia of fratricidal, political, and bloody struggles, of imperialism, of human hatred and exploitation, up to our century of world wars, genocides, the Holocaust, and terrorism; of unemployment, the continuing poverty of the Third World. [45]

Levinas does not explicitly say it but he implies that actually there exists a resemblance between this quest for the Platonic light and the violence which governs/constitutes Westerns reality. Postcolonialist thinkers implement this concept of Levinas and Derrida for re-reading the direct and symbolic violence and counter-violence between Western colonialism and its marginalized cultures in the third world and within the Western realm itself.[46]. Adorno and Horkheimer showed in a fascinating manner how this tradition was galvanized[47] and how instrumental rationality is responsible for the control of nature and the control of nature within humanity, as a trend which leads to the Holocaust, to Stalinism as well as to their liberal alternates.[48]

The concept of peace that is at the basis of peace education (in all its different versions) is to be seen as part and parcel of the same reality which it is committed to overcome. As the critical theory of Adorno and Horkheimer shows, it is much more than what Levinas calls "an embarrassment" for the West, as if it were a misfortune that could be overcome within the tradition of instrumental rationality which made it possible it in the first place. But the critical theory of Adorno and Horkheimer and the philosophy of Levinas do share an understanding that the struggle against the governing violence and the challenge to the epistemological, cultural, political, and economic misfortune afflicting today's human is possible. This challenge, according to these two philosophical trends, is to be developed from within the Judeo-Christian tradition by the pursuit of the option encapsulated as "the wisdom of Jerusalem". Within their utopian pessimism they present an alternative concept of peace to the one that is hegemonic in current peace education and the philosophical frameworks from which it borrows its concepts, strivings, dreams, and fears. Later we shall return to the alternative concept of peace and peace education; first we have to present current oppositions to this kind of utopianism.

For all their differences, neo-Marxist thinkers such as Adorno and Horkheimer share with Levinas a common understanding, belief, or narrative. Within it the autonomous subject is not an empty concept, freedom is an imperative, knowledge is

---

45 *Ibid.*
46 Iain Chambers, "Waiting on the end of the world?" in: David Morley and Kuan-Hsing Chen (eds.), *Stuart Hall: Critical Dialogues in Cultural Studies,* London: Routledge, 1996, p. 209.
47 Max Horkheimer, *Eclipse of Reason,* New York: Oxford University Press, 1974.
48 Max Horkheimer & Theodor Adorno, *Dialectics of Enlightenment,* translated by John Cumming, New York: Herder and Herder, 1972.

possible, and responsibility is highly relevant in challenging the reality in which the absence of peace or false "peace" has the upper hand. The Frankfurt School critical theory too emphasizes the responsibility of the subject to resist the hegemonic realm of self-evidence. These two philosophies are highly skeptical and ironist, yet they reject the kind of relativism that made possible most forms of current postmodern discourses even in their "soft" versions. However, central figures of current postmodernism too are challenging the philosophical assumptions of current peace education. Postmodernists such as Foucault, Derrida, Leotard, and Baudrillard, as well as post-colonialists such as Homi Bahba and Gayatri Spivack, constitute a considerable challenge to the various naive humanist concepts of peace education from the "left".

As we have seen, the conceptualization that divides peace and violence parallels the division between true and false knowledge. This division provides the unification of peace and truth. In parallel it provides a conception of the essence of the human being and an appropriate ethics. This provides the West with a metaphysical preference for peace and the justification of peace education. The philosophy of Foucault is a serious challenge to this project. According to Foucault

> ...one's point of reference should not be to the great model of language and signs, but to that of war and battle. The history, which bears and determines us, has the form of war rather than that of language: relations of power, not relations of meaning.[49]

Within the Foucaultian project, peace education does not differ from any other regime of truth which produces subjects, knowledge, and values within a history which has no "meaning". Like all others, this regime too should be subject to analysis not in accordance with good intentions, "truth", and a natural or sacred "faith in the human" or God, but "in accordance with the intelligibility of struggles, of strategies and tactics" without "evading the always open and hazardous reality of conflict", without "avoiding its violent, bloody and lethal character by reducing it to the calm Platonic form of language and dialogue".[50]

The concept of peace, which makes possible peace education as resistance to the various manifestations of national, ethnic, racial, and gender repression, is seriously challenged by the Foucaltian project. Here "the understanding of the ways within which power manifests itself resist the very concept of repression".[51] It denotes the productivity of power and represents the subject, be it a "victim" or a "victimizer", as one of the manifestations of contingent, meaningless, aimless power relations. In contrast to the traditional Western concepts of violence, now truth itself "isn't outside power".[52]

---

49   Michel Foucault, *Power/Knowledge; Selected Interviews and Other Writings 1972–1977*, edited by Colin Gordon, translated by Colin Gordon, Brighton, Sussex: Harvester Press, 1980.
50   *Ibid.*, 115.
51   *Ibid.*, 118
52   *Ibid.*, 131

Foucault, like some other postmodernists, deconstructs the quests and the concepts that allow transcendent, orchestrated, essential change by human autonomy or reason. Traditionally the very possibility of transcendence made reflection possible. It also allowed a concept of a difference, which makes a difference of the kind that "peace" is supposed to be in relation to "war". People who refuse to accept the omnipotence of epistemic violence, namely that there is no difference that makes a difference, he considers naive; such people find it difficult to acknowledge

> that their history, their economics, their social practices, the language
> that they speak, the mythology of their ancestors... are governed by
> rules that are not all given to their consciousness... [53]

PEACE EDUCATION AS A NORMALIZING EDUCATION

Peace education is but one version of normalizing education. A systematic critical reconstruction of peace education should also challenge its positive utopianism. Within this positive utopianism in relation to the stance of "peace" a special role is played by conceptions that allow hierarchical relations, asymmetries, positive value judgments, and guarded existential horizons. These are developed and delivered by the ideal educator/teacher, trainer, mediator, or facilitator. This Utopia determines not only her/his relation to the student but to human communication in more general terms, within a broader concept of education. This positive Utopia determines the entire set of concepts, yardsticks, and strivings available to the student. Yet here objects, norms, persons, and events are inseparable from the struggles between conflicting representation apparatuses and the meta-narratives within which they dwell.

The philosophy and politics of representation as well as the life-and-death struggles between narratives and their colonialist imperative and other "dangerous" issues of that kind are absolutely foreign to peace education, which is committed to a positive Utopia of undistorted dialogue and peaceful consensus among adversaries. As such peace education cannot reflect on the preconditions for the kind of educational discourse within which it is positioned and it cannot reflect on the violences that it serves and others that it tries to resist.

Within this project the various violences of the nameless kind are untraceable and unchallenged. It is important, however, not to conceive this situation as mere blindness and passivity: this special situatedness of peace education is what makes other violences explicit and addressed. As such it allows their categorization, articulation, and evaluation. The unreflective consumption and the productive internalization of violences of the first kind allows the transparency of "evil" and the quest for peace within a stable realm of self-evidence. It is important to note the productivity of the theoretical limits of peace education; it produces not only the refusal to problematize the concepts of knowledge, representation, communication, consensus, intersubjec-

---

53   Michel Foucault, *The Archeology of Knowledge*, translated by A. Sheridan Smith, London: Tavistock
     Publications, 1995, pp. 210–211.

tivity, and the avoidance of treating the social, cultural, and historical dimensions of the context within which peace education flourishes. At the same time it also reproduces the dichotomies between victims and victimizers, good and evil, light and darkness, and ultimately gives birth to a positive Utopia which makes possible the quest for "peace" and peace education of the kind of "the earthly city".

Within current peace education, therefore, it is impossible to problematize the hegemonic concept of "peace" or the concept of "violence". Nor is this peace education competent to question the concepts of justice/injustice and of human subjects and "their" subjectivity, or to resist the powers and the apparatuses which produce, reproduce, and destroy collectives, individuals, their identities, knowledge, skills, perspectives, consciousness, and contexts. It is no wonder that within peace education there is no problematization of issues such as the representation of "reality", and the Other and his/her otherness in terms of potential violence, mistakes, threats, and refusal to acknowledge the true and the just. The politics of recognition, the politics of representation, and the life-and-death war raging between and within narratives and truth regimes are unmentioned, unchallenged, and unaddressed. As a result there is no reflection on the possibilities for creating a critical distance from the realization of their relation to the capitalistic globalization and the world division of work and the room it makes for well intentioned intellectuals and Western peace activists.

It is wrong to decontextualize peace education and detach it from the capitalist globalization and the world order. We think there is a heavy human cost to the acceptance of this order as a yardstick and guide for peace education. This is why we think it is important to address the reasons for peace education's disregard for the hegemonic culture industry and neglect of a critical perspective for evaluating the reaction to the violences which produce, reproduce, represent, and consume the present order of things. Peace education refrains from tackling the fundamentals of the order within which narratives, armies, merchants, priests, parents and teachers, establishments, nations, and ideologies struggle for hegemony. This struggle is for hegemony over truth and justice. It is the very same hegemony that allows the invisibility of the violence that manipulates, constructs, or destroys the material base, the consciousness, and the violences of the rival narratives and establishments which they serve and represent.[54]

Peace education in all its versions avoids questioning life itself and refrains from questioning the positive, constitutive role violence plays within it. It avoids addressing the status quo as a protection and reproduction of an order whose very existence implies the destruction of other possibilities for life and the production of concepts of "justice" as part of the elimination of possibilities for other, alternative violences within this dynamics.

The real aim of peace education is revealed as the fortification of the existing order and the preservation of the invisibility of the hegemonic violence, even when it claims to give voice to the silenced and challenges the injustice inflicted on the marginalized or the oppressed. The ultimate yardstick of this concept of peace is the productivity of

---

54   Ilan Gur-Ze'ev, *Destroying the Other's Collective Memory*, New York: Peter Lang, 1999.

the existing symbolic and material order without questioning its own legitimization as a narrative knowledge.[55]

Epistemic violence[56] is a precondition for to the explicit, unmediated use of violence, which as such is granted a name and is addressed as a "conflict" or a "violence". It is realized in the formation of conceptual apparatuses, knowledge, consciousness, ideological orientations, and consensus or self-evidence. This is the aim of normalizing education, in the service of the self-evidence and the hegemonic order of things.[57]

Only when this violence is successful in producing the subject[58] and her self-evidence as well as the horizons of her predetermined consensus is it possible that she and her compatriots/rivals will become good soldiers and destroy the Other while manifesting bravery or activating efficient violence to save the collective or ("her")self.

Without effective educational apparatuses (teachers and schools are only one element in a much richer arsenal) there will be no room for the subjectification of the subject (who actually functions as an object) and for successful delegitimization of all other language games and their subjectifications. In the absence of normalizing education or in face of its deconstruction it will be difficult to establish a stable consensus which will provide a suitable legitimization of the hegemonic narrative and its social matrix of power. In such a utopian situation it will be impossible to actualize an effective direct collective violence which is normally conceived as a just, unavoidable, use of force.[59]

The various versions of peace education with their special relations to the concept of universal human rights share a modernist view of consensus, which should be addressed. Some of the peace education theorists and activists share very naive conceptions regarding the role of rationality, good intentions, or openness in the meeting with the Other as sure ways to guarantee a change in attitude to the Other and consensus.[60] Even in its most advanced forms, for example, the Habermasian project, within this modernist orientation the concept of truth is based on a consensus of a collective universal subject. But the very notions of consensus, truth, or norms, which are ideally articulated freely and jointly in an undistorted dialogue, are challenged by postmodernists such as Lyotard in a manner which is extremely relevant to the rhetoric of peace education. For Lyotard,

> Consensus is only a particular state of discussion, not its end. Its end, on the contrary, is paralogy. This double observation... destroys a belief

---

55   Jean-Francois Lyotard, *The Postmodern Condition: A Report on Knowledge*, translated by Geoff Benington and Brian Massumi, Manchester: Manchester University Press, 1991, p.27.

56   Michel Foucault, *Madness and Civilization: A History of Insanity in the Age of Reason*, translated by Richard Howard, New York: Tavistoc, 1965, pp. 261–262.

57   Ilan Gur-Ze'ev, Jan Masschelein, and Nigel Blake, "Reflectivity, reflection and counter-education, Studies in: *Philosophy and Education* 20 (2001), pp. 93–106.

58   Homi Bhabha, "Culture's in-between", in: Stuart Hall and Paul de Gay (eds.), *Questions of Cultural Identity*, London: Sage, 1996, pp. 54–55.

59   Gur-Ze'ev, *ibid.*

60   In: Salomon and Nevo, 1999.

that still underlines Habermas's research, namely, that humanity as a
collective (universal) subject seeks its common emancipation through
the regularization of the "moves" permitted in all language games and
that the legitimacy of any statement resides in its contributing to that
emancipation.[61]

Normalizing education is founded on an unchallenged consensus and it is committed
to securing its self-evidence. As part of its function it is very important for normalizing
education to conceal its foundations and avoid transparency (or secure only a certain
kind of critique and transparency, which is the same thing) of the apparatuses it uses.
This is in order to reproduce the subjectification or the human subject as some-thing
and not as some-one. This process includes the production of his/her potential vio-
lence/productivity and the aims, ideals, interests, and strivings for love and peace—as
well as categories such as "justice". All these enable the subject to function as an agent
of the reproduction of the system. In "peace" the invisibility of the violence, which
guarantees the present order, is best secured, the hegemonic violence is unchallenged,
and counter-violence is successfully delegitimized. In "peace" the subject is efficiently
sent off on the quest to realize her human potentials to become other than what she
is constructed to be. In such a "peace" and stable normality[62] forgetfulness rules and
humans are not ready to be called upon by their destiny. Normalizing education sets
for them the relevant quests, or real dreams, goals, and enemies, and all the rest is a
history of struggling efficiencies—until something totally other intervenes and challenges the hegemonic self-evidence and the order of things. The constant subjectification of the subject goes on unchallenged.

The process of subjectification does not relate solely to individuals. This kind of
objectivization and closure is no less present in the normalization of collectives. Normalizing education cannot reproduce the horizons of the collective and the closure of
its identity without the enclosure of the Other and her otherness. Yet, as Stuart Hall
puts it,

> The unities which identities proclaim are, in fact, constructed within
> the play of power and exclusion, and are the result, not of a natural and
> inevitable or primordial totality but of the naturalized, overdetermined
> process of "closure.[63]

This is an implicit critique of the agenda of peace education and its propositions. It
problematizes the concept of violence, which makes possible the will for preventing "unjust" violence between and within opponent collectives. It problematizes the

---

61   Lyotard 1991, pp.65–66.
62   Dan Bar-On, The Indescribable and the Undiscussable; Reconstructing Human Discourse After
      Trauma, Budapest: Central European University Press, 1999, p. 261.
63   Stuart Hall, "Introduction: Who Needs Identity?" in: Stuart Hall and Paul du Gay, 1996, p. 5.

hidden procedure of legitimization/delegitimization and the very possibility of an unproblematic evaluation and consensus.

It is also important to question the unproblematic introduction of conflict resolution skills and knowledge. From the postmodern perspective these strategies are revealed as one of many conflicting voices fighting over the position of silencing their Others, in a context of constant semiotic bombardment. Peace education is unveiled as a position situated in the narrativization of the individual and collective "self". As such, it is part and parcel of the conflicting violences competing over hegemony. In this space hegemony ensures its own veiling as violence by producing its justification, or in the case of a final defeat of its rivals by ensuring totality, closure, sameness, harmonious order, and "peace". In relation to Levinas's concept of war we can say that in "peace" the "same does not find again its priority over the other" since the otherness of the Other has totally vanished.[64] This is where the project of conflict resolution skills within peace education is situated.

Propagating and bestowing conflict resolution "skills" is ultimately nothing less than a mode of violence which is committed to reproducing the present order of things and its ideals. There is no room here for the totally other except for the given facts, quests, and ideological horizons. This holds as long as it is instrumental and effective, yet it is precisely where it is practically most needed that its impotence is most dramatically manifested. This is manifested in the case of the Israeli/Palestinian struggle. In not even one of the many peace education projects in this spot on the globe is there an attempt to challenge the dialectics of the Israeli Independence Day and its concept of the Holocaust-Exile-Redemption, or the Palestinian concept of the Nakbah. The violences of the two representation systems of the conflicting memories and their instrumentalizations within the rival ethnocentric collectives[65] are taken for granted by all of today's peace education projects. Conflict resolution skills education is threatened even by approaching an issue such as relating to the national day of triumph/defeat. It fears treating it as part of the questioning of who are "we" and what is worthy life or death for "us". It turns away from questions such as what kind of togetherness is possible/bearable/longed-for and what are the ways to approach such a future—along "practical" questions which are for each of the parties fundamentally life-and death struggle worthy questions. It refuses questioning the language that should be the language of the dialogue/conflict or: what are the starting points, the horizons and the aims of the dialogue/struggle within which peace education is promoted/rejected?

Research has illuminated the first steps of departing from the safe ground of "coexistence" projects within the present order into less restricted and controlled elaboration. It manifests the structural asymmetry and its violences, which are intent on maintaining Israeli hegemony within which peace education, "dialogue aimed at peaceful coex-

---

64 Emmanuel Levinas, "Philosophy and the Idea of Infinity", in: *Collected Philosophical Papers*, translated by Alphonso Lingis, Dordrecht: M. Nijhoff, 1987, p. 51.

65 Ilan Gur-Ze'ev, "The Morality of Acknowledging/not Acknowledging the Other's Holocaust/Genocide", *Journal of Moral Education*, 27: 2 (1998), pp. 161–178.

istence", and conflict resolution projects flourish. The moment of departure from the hegemony of one side dictating the agenda of "peace" for its Other is also the moment of exposure of what education in conflict-resolution skills is dedicated to veiling and protecting. Even the most advanced research on this issue in Israel/Palestine still treats it with positivistic optimism and speaks of "dilemmas" in realizing ideal coexistence paradigms in the asymmetrical intercourse within which peace education is realized.[66]

The current swelling Palestinian demand in Israel is to problematize the status quo and challenge this order and the kind of peace it longs for. The Israeli hegemonic ideologies and central political powers have so far refused to question, let alone abolish the structural violence which establishes the conditions not only for the systematic oppression of the Palestinians citizens but also of securing the very existence of the State of Israel. This trend is not totally disconnected with the hegemonic Palestinian attitude of denying the legitimacy of any Jewish sovereign existence in Israel, or Palestine, as they insist on calling it. For the Palestinians' part, peace education and dialogue should lead, ultimately, to nothing less than regaining Palestine and the abolition of the Zionist project. Only within this context is each of the struggling collectives willing to promote projects furthering conflict resolution skills and those oriented to achieving "just peace". This only shows how education in conflict resolution skills within peace education takes part in the reproduction of symbolic, mental, economic, cultural, and political struggles in this arena. It is an arena that hosts many competing camps contesting for hegemony over representing "reality" as it really is, reality as it actually should be interpreted, or as it should be best deconstructed/reconstructed. It is served or reproduced by subjects whose agency guarantees the invisible violences which name the Other, his violences, injustice, mistakes, and potentials for improvement which will render possible making peace with him. This "earthly city" produces representations of reality, which pretend to be different, more accurate, or more just than competing representations and evaluations of "reality". It produces subjects who will strive to reproduce, change, or destroy this "reality" and its representations or evaluations as part of the meaninglessness which ultimately fills the whole of such a world of competing representations, evaluations, interpretations, and consensuses.

Peace education within critical, feminist, multiculturalist, and ecological-oriented groups dwells on the same quicksand, even when using functionalist or pragmatic orientations instead of an idealist or transcendentalist rhetoric. This is so as long as these groups do not address the challenges presented here.

All this, however, does not mean that we should accept all of Lyotard's, Foucault's, or Levinas's alternatives. Nor does it imply that there are no emancipatory dimensions in different versions of peace education or that there is no difference that makes a difference between the victim and the victimizer, war, general health care, and well-being, poverty, and illiteracy. But it does mean that there is a need to decipher the

---

66   Ifat Maoz, "Multiple conflicts and Competing Agenda: A Framework for Conceptualizing Structured Encounters Between Groups in Conflict: The Case of Coexistence Project of Jews and Palestinians in Israel", *Journal of Peace Psychology* (forthcoming).

material, historical and political context of normalizing education and challenging it with a counter-education that will not be anything other than one more version of normalizing education.

If counter-education ought seriously to address violence and be committed to peace, and we do believe that this is implicit in its essence, counter-education should not follow the positive Utopia of peace education and its naive universalistic essentialism. It should address and overcome its philosophical assumptions and challenge the politics of peace education while avoiding the kind of universalism and violences it is committed to overcome. It should avoid, at the same time, reintroducing violence as "justified" counter-violence. This attempt is embedded in its negative Utopia.

While introducing itself as a Utopia, counter-education cannot find comfort in an abstract negativism which negates the illusions of consensus among individuals and collectives that are produced to perpetuate meaninglessness and productivity of contingent symbolic economy. It should not abandon the imperative of transcendence as the human mode of existence. Its Utopia, however, must be a negative Utopia. Within it there are no positive universals such as "justice" or "human rights" but transcendent negative imperatives for openness such as responding to injustice and worthy suffering. Within it there is no commitment to universal "truth" but an infinite responsibility to transcending the fabricated "truths" and their violences which they represent and serve. Within counter-education there is rejection even of the universal validity of the pleasure principle, and it represents, instead, the presence of pain and the possibility of transcending it into worthy suffering. Counter-education offers a need for a radically different concept of peace and an alternative conception of education. This, however, should be not only in face of the naivete or violence of the hegemonic concepts of peace and education within current peace education.

Counter-education should today face the changing postmodern conditions, and within it the questions of responsibility (ethics), life (ontology), and knowledge (epistemology). Violence in the era of cyberspace and violence within cyberspace present us with additional challenges on the psychic, conceptual, and political levels, and counter-education should address it also by concrete political action. Within this arena the responsibility of the subject, and the very possibility of a subject and responsibility, are impossible to be conceived in the traditional way. However, violences are not to be understood as opposed to "real" responsibility. Violences signify irresponsibility (of the Other) and are to be understood as making possible the violences of counter-ethics and counter-responsibilities.

The possibility of a non-repressive consensus, the possibility of meaning, the possibility of justice in respect of the cyberspace dwellers and the hardware producers who work for less than 50 dollars a month and are structurally deprived of the potentials of their work, needs a brave reconceptualization. Counter-education not only has no positive Utopia; it also looks for a new language that has not yet been born. This does not mean that it should be silent and passive before the current reality.

The responsibility of counter-education is not naive. It acknowledges the importance of deconstructing the naivete and violence of the quest for challenging injustice and violence. Yet it refuses relativism and escapism. It is a serious commitment, a responsibility in a Godless world where the logic of capitalism has the upper hand.

The impetus of counter-education springs from the *ethical I*. Yet the responsibility of the *ethical I* has no words; it is pre-rational even if it is always historically embedded.

Counter-education acknowledges that an unavoidable rupture deprives the *ethical I* of the moral I[67]. There is a rift between the pre-rational ethical responsibility toward the Others and the rational/moral dialogue with the others, which does not negate their otherness. Such a dialogue is not a given reality, it is a Utopia. The Utopia of such a dialogue is a negative Utopia, a concrete negative Utopia.

Only as concrete negative Utopia is the dialogue able to produce a conversation that is not a contingent manifestation of power relations and symbolic economies, that merely reflects the omnipotence, and the whole-presence, of simulacra. Such a negative Utopia acknowledges not only reason, politics, and compromises, but also the presence of power in the formatted, conceptualized, manipulated, otherness of the Other. This is as far as its negative dimension is concerned. As a concrete Utopia it is present as an actual potential to be realized, and it is realizable even in microscopic arenas and for instant hindrances of the continuum. Its historical situatedness enforces its presence within concrete power-relations which it addresses within its openness to infinity,[68] to the totally other than the given reality. These power-relations which govern its context constantly attempt to invade the dialogue, to cause a perpetual distortion that permits no ideal speech situation. As such, the dialogue is committed to transcend the realm of self-evidence and its agencies within the dialogue and its participants. Its awareness of its conceptual and historical situatedness as well as its commitment to reflection and to its own transcendence constitutes a central difference between it and peace education. As such, it cannot avoid being a concrete praxis.

The realization of negative Utopia is the imperative of counter-education. Even when realized to a certain degree on a specific occasion it can never offer peace of mind or symmetrical relations. Yet it can offer sensibility to be called upon by something totally other, by the Other as a demand for responsibility, seriousness, and love. One should ask, facing counter-education, but what about positive manifestations of meaning, truth, consensus, justice, and peace? Counter-education does not promise such gifts. These, in their positive form, remain in the hands of peace education and its rivals.

---

67   Ilan Gur-Ze'ev, Jan Masschelein, and Nigel Blake, "Reflectivity, Reflection and Counter-Education", p. 103. Ilan Gur-Ze'ev, "Postmodernism, Values and Moral Education in Israel", in: Yaacov Iram, Samul Scolnicov, Jonathan Cohen and Elli Schachter (eds.), *Crossroads: Vlues and Education in Israeli Society*, Jerusalem: Ministry of Education Chief Scietist's Office, Jerusalem: Ministry of Education Chief Scietist's Office, 2001, pp. 91–155 (in Hebrew).

68   Levinas 1987, pp. 47–60.

CHAPTER 14

POST-COLONIALISM, NEW RACISM, NEW ANTI-SEMITISM, AND THE BOYCOTT OF ISRAELI ACADEMIA (A LECTURE PRESENTED AT THE OXFORD GBPES 2006 CONFERENCE)

On April 22, 2005 the British AUT (Association of University Teachers) decided to boycott my university, the University of Haifa, among other Israeli academic institutions. In its own words, "the council delegates also agreed to circulate to all local associations a statement from Palestinian organizations calling for an academic boycott of Israeli institutions".[1] The AUT conceived this act as a strong, necessary, manifestation of its self-conception, its responsibilities, and its competence as articulated on May 26, 2005 on the occasion of revoking its decision to boycott Israeli universities:

> UK higher education has a long and proud tradition of defending academic freedom. The struggle to maintain academic freedom whenever it is under threat is one that AUT will always support and this principle will continue to guide our work.[2]

On the one level, the decision did not surprise me at all. On another level, it was a very difficult decision for me. Not only because it called unjustifiably for boycotting my colleagues and friends at my own university. Without understating the importance of this very personal level, it became a serious challenge to any discourse between my identity as a human, who treats so personally, so seriously, the Enlightenment tradition, and my conceiving of myself as a Diasporic person; a Diasporic human who takes earnestly the challenge of edifying while overcoming Judaism and its commitment to cosmopolitanism, to anti-dogmatism, to Love of Life, and to the happiness/worthy suffering of the eternal-improviser.

Overcoming Judaism and prevailing over the Enlightenment's ideals are important dimensions of the Diasporic philosophy and counter-education that I try to reconstruct, articulate, and offer as a relevant new cosmopolitanism in the era of the histori-

---

1   "Israel universities—statement by AUT general secretary Sally Hunt", http://www.aut.org.uk/index. cfm?articleid=1201 (21.1.2006).

2   "Israel boycotts Revoke—AUT Statement", http://www.aut.org.uk/index.cfm?articleid=1235 (21.1.2006).

cal triumph of globalizing capitalism and disorientation.[3] It is a counter-education that is committed to refusal to abandon ourselves and reminds us that the possibilities for Diasporic life are closely connected to *academia* as community of the homeless enduring improvisers, as a non-territorial place for the struggle for transcendence in face of the exile of Spirit. As we shall see in the following, academia is a *Diasporic ideal* and is very different from the university.[4]

Here one has to carefully differentiate between the university as an institution (which historically has taken part in the power-games and challenged the academic ideal while committing itself to its realization) and the Diasporic essence of the historical realizations of the academic ideal. Today, in face of the omnipotence of globalizing capitalism the academic ideal and academic freedom are challenged by new, more sophisticated limitations, instrumentalizations, and are faced with *the transformation of academic freedom into its opposite*. This process is hardly challenged theoretically, and certainly it is not addressed politically by the academic community worldwide, with very few exceptions.

To the best of my knowledge the Brazilian academic community and the Israeli academic communities are among the very few who have tried to organize themselves and offer a strategic, thoughtful, collectivist resistance. Theirs was an attempt to resist the global structural transformation of present-day universities, and the actual transformation of the aim of academic education, and the meaning, actuality and future of academic freedom. How may we understand that the transformation of the academic ideal and the restructuring of the organization and power-relations in the universities, which are actually going on before our eyes, with neither theoretical nor political resistance on the part of the academic community, all over the globe?

Failing to offer philosophical, educational or political resistance to the *transformation of academic freedom into its opposite*, namely to its becoming a productive element of the capitalistic culture industry, the academic community that still felt part of the emancipatory ethos (of disenchantment with the closure of the immanence of myth to transcending mature human life) has begun to treat academic freedom more in relation to fashionable politically-correct topics, adding new, internal, barriers and limits to the actual attempt to struggle for the realization of academic freedom. It is my claim that rearticulated academic freedom as *the life of the eternal-improviser*,[5] who challenges any consensus, closure and "home" while she struggles for a new togetherness, creativity, Love of Life, and refusal of injustice, is what has been assailed by the boycott decision of the British Association of University Teachers. Again: these are the same colleagues of mine who failed to offer a critical reconstruction of the instrumentalization of the academic ideal and the reification of academic freedom as part of

---

3   Ilan Gur-Ze'ev, "Critical theory and critical pedagogy", in: Ilan Gur-Ze'ev (ed.), *Critical Theory and Critical Pedagogy Today*, Haifa: Faculty of Education, University of Haifa, 2005.

4   Ilan Gur-Ze'ev, "The university, the eternal-improviser, and the possibility of meaning in a post-modern era", in: Ilan Gur-Ze'ev (ed.), *The End of Israeli Academia?* Haifa: Faculty of Education, University of Haifa, 2005, pp.193–251 (in Hebrew).

5   Ilan Gur-Ze'ev, *ibid.*

the post-Fordist economy, and who failed to realize their responsibility in all contexts where academic freedom is perverted, demolished or falsely realized as part of the new normality of the McWorld.

Why is it so that the explicit attempt to use the weapon of boycott in the service of "defending academic freedom wherever it is under threat" is *a hazard to academic freedom*, the academic ideal, and the other manifestations and arenas of Diasporic life, and to the struggle for overcoming dogmatism, collectivism, and "consensus" as a manifestation of effective, invisible, symbolic violence?

Here we would be well advised to distinguish between the call to boycott the Israeli universities "in defense of academic freedom around the globe" and a different agenda, a very different agenda, that of using the academic arena and its vocabulary to promote separatist interests and act more effectively in the political sphere. In both cases politics and academia, and the presumption of a difference between politics and academic life, will give birth to a call to overcome or to resist the separation between academic life and "external" power-relations and go into the realization of the responsibility of the *ethical I* that are beyond the commitments, standards and expectations of the scientific "neutral" endeavor. Actually, according to this assertion, which here I will call "postcolonialist", it is academic life at its height, as we can see in the history of science and in the biographies of its heroes such as Socrates, Bruno, Galileo and Einstein, and Marcuse.

Here, dear friends and colleagues, I would like to say a word or two about the use of the concept of "postcolonialism" on the present occasion, since I am not quite satisfied with this articulation and I only use it in the absence of a better one. "Postcolonialism" on the present occasion has for me three levels: political, psychological and philosophical. On each of these levels, Western and non-Western postcolonialists meet under unequal terms. Western intellectuals who are recruited to the postcolonialist camp do not merely surrender to a specific academic fashion enthusiastically accepted in all the capitals of former and present colonialist countries. It is not that they are swallowed by this fashion unacknowledged and blindly, as they are trained to as "free customers" in the capitalist market and its culture industry and follow a "trend" or a politically-correct code. Actually, it is a much more dangerous and deep-rooted challenge.

The present disciples of "postcolonialism" are in a passionate, quasi-religious search of something genuine, radically, spiritually and existentially new. That "something" is quasi-authentic, quasi-ecstatic, and might offer a kind of self-forgetfulness that compensates for the absence of telos, lack of courage and transformation of authenticity into its opposite. In this sense the current postcolonialist quest is genuine. In a way it is *totally new*. This is because never before did humans find themselves with a moral quest in face of the exile of the gods/criteria/codes/universal-existential validity claims/values. In symbolizes and realizes a quest for a new human beginning in an era of the exile of the preconditions for Utopia, disorientation and mistrust of any value, general theory, narrative or even responsibility to a specific ethos, sensibility or sentiment.

The postcolonialists' search is taking place. It is taking place in a Godless, de-territorialized world for redemption and for home-returning: *for purification*. For purification of themselves as Westerners, as Westernized whites, as intellectuals, as humans laden with an unbearable moral burden. As such they lack the conceptual apparatus not only to be cured, but even to relate to the possibility of redemption from their guilt feelings and committing themselves to redeem the victims of colonialism/globalizing capitalism/paternalist history/monotheism/phallocentrism while combating "America", "monotheism", or, "the Jew in the form of Zionist/Israeli".

Present-day postcolonialism in its broader sense (or in its form as "anti-phallocentrism") is articulated within the framework of their infinite moral responsibilities toward two, conflicting, concepts of victimization: responsibility to challenge the dialectics of *"the Jew" as the ultimate representative of the Other* and as the internal, repressive-colonialist essence of the Jewish-Christian world, on the one hand, and responsibility for self-redemption by resisting/transforming the memory and the practice of the Western *Jewish-Christian victimization* of the non-Western and the Western marginalized Other.

"Postcolonialism" in the broader sense of the word, as a Western decontamination or redemption, cannot offer an emancipatory re-education without sacrificing the most precious dimension of its Diasporic essence: the anti-dogmatism, the universal and eternal mission of homelessness and refusal of the promise of power, victory and unhindered control of the "home" as represented by Judaism and as addressed so earnestly in the history of Christianity. It cannot avoid striving against these dimensions in the praxis and negative theology of Judaism and in Christian theology which traditionally dialectically opposed and resisted modern and postmodern manifestations of colonialism and offered a transcendent alternative. Within the Christian tradition itself the negation of the Diasporic essence of Judaism is essential, and anti-Semitism or anti-Diasporic commitment is essential to Western tradition and its true colonialist nature. *Present day postcolonialism, actually, continues this colonialist, anti-Semitic, anti-Diasporic impetus.*

Psychologically, politically, and philosophically, Israel, as an idea and as an institutionalized manifestation of Jewish nationhood, has to be not only de-legitimized and condemned as a prima facie realization of Western "colonialism"—as a much needed *ramification* in face of Western guilt feelings. Israel must be condemned as prima facie "colonialist" and cannibalistically torn into pieces and eaten, together, in a sacred feast of the totem animal in a Godless world. This kind of Western postcolonialist cannibalism is actualized in order to make possible forgetfulness of the primordial, eternal Sin of Western violent colonialism as the realization of Jewish monotheism.

The postcolonialist agenda, as one of the manifestations of the ramification *sentiment*, philosophical escape and political alternative, contains much more than normally understood in this concept. Actually it also contains a moral-political commitment to "*anti-phallocentrism*" in its forms and manifestations. This attitude of negation of all forms of Western or "Jewish" violence is crucial for understanding the various kinds and the essence of postcolonialism in its narrower sense; it might enable us to see differently the deep foundations and the richer context of the academic politics actualized by the AUT even if it is not the sole factor. One has to see the AUT agenda in a broader perspective in light of so many other calls to boycott the state of Israel, to de-legitimize its very existence and legitimize "counter-violence" summoned for the destruction of this supposed garrison/agent of "Western colonialism" or of "America" in the heart of the oppressed/humiliated Arab world.

Most, if not all, the initiators of the call to boycott Israel in general and Israeli universities in particular are self-declared postcolonialists. Fundamentally, these post-colonialists do not call for the boycott of the Israeli universities in light of the threats to academic freedom in Israel, as one might be mislead to understand from the AUT declaration. As I will try to show, today they strive for nothing less than the de-legiti-mizing and destruction not only of the State of Israel but of Israeliness itself. Namely, they want to reeducate the colonizers in light of postcolonialist counter-education, so that not only will the productive violence of the victimizers stop, but a new era of edification and solidarity will be made possible. This perspective is also central to important trends in current peace education, as one can see in the work of Ilan Pappe, one of the initiators of the academic boycott agenda, my colleague and a partner to an ongoing critical dialogue.

> Why I am against the AUT Israel Boycott of Israeli Universities: The second meeting, which discussed the AUT resolutions, contained a rather unpleasant discourse. References were made to 'rich and power-ful Zionists' and certain well-known Palestinian leaders and academics were described as 'collaborators'.[6]

The issue under consideration is *protecting academic freedom* and countering its viola-tion in Israel: this is the official claim of the AUT, and provisionally I shall take it at face value. However, let us give the pro-boycott representatives an opportunity to overcome our suspicion that their agenda is philosophically ungrounded, academi-cally unfounded, morally wrong, and politically dangerous.

Before going into this I cannot omit a personal note. It is a very non-academic note. A very non-academic note of the kind that I have avoided for many years, since my first participation in the Oxford GBPES conferences which was in 1995. I will begin my personal note by relating to a routine, almost banal event in the Near East. In April 2002 another suicide bomber exploded himself in Israel. This time it was inside the Matsa Restaurant, a Palestinian-owned restaurant where Palestinians and lower and middle class Israeli Jews meet daily, especially at weekends, enjoy each other's company, and the simple yet delicious Palestinian dishes. The restaurant is located a three-minute walk from my apartment.

The explosion killed nine and wounded dozens of Israeli Jews and Palestinians. It was a year before another terror explosion was perpetrated in a school bus killed many children; and only by sheer chance did Mae, the daughter of Alona, my wife, miss

---

6   John Strawson, "Why I am against the AUT Israel Boycott of Israeli Universities", http://www.zion-ism-israel.com/strawson_on_zionism.htm (4.5.2005).

this bus, on which she normally came home from school, so she was saved. On that occasion I naturally received many letters from friends in Israel and from all over the world. One letter, from a very dear friend, begins with the following words:

> I read of the enormous explosion yesterday in Haifa—are you OK? And your family and friends? It is easy to feel for individuals, but I can have no sympathy for the nation of Israel whilst Sharon is allowed to behave as he is doing. His behavior is intolerable. My opinions are widely shared and perhaps the majority view here, of those who follow the story.

The letter, from a committed humanist, a philosopher and an educator, was very difficult for me. The depth of refusal of empathy, as well as refusal of an honest, critical evaluation of the situation was so strong, and was nourished by such deep and pre-conceptual emotions and drives, so I felt at that time, that it was an enormous challenge for me to face. Where is the critical thinker here? And where is the presence of the human here, standing before innocent men and women, children and the elderly, Jewish and Palestinian dead—with empathy? And I felt it as a grandson of Keyla, who barely escaped being slaughtered by her neighbors in the Kishiniev *pogrom* in 1904 with so many other Jews, only for being Jews. I felt it as a son of Robert Wiltcheck, my beloved father, whose entire family was wiped out by the Germans in the Holocaust, and who himself escaped only after being beaten to death, so they thought, and who, after being tossed into a mass grave, raised himself up, severely wounded, back to life; I felt it as the husband of Alona, whose father, Alik, barely saved himself in the Second War World in Lithuania. It is interesting to note that the Nazi army went into Lithuania in June 1941. The Nazis were not fast enough to kill most of the Jews in Lithuania—not because the Jews fled or were saved but for the following reason: most of the 250,000 Jews in Lithuania, a community that had lived there for many centuries, were killed by their own neighbors even before the Nazis could close in on them in the service of their death-industry. In Butrimonys, where Alik lived with his family, most of the 800 Jews were killed with hammers, knives, stones, and bare hands by their own Christian friends and neighbors; such was the fate of 95% of the Jews who lived in Lithuania, and in many other countries. Whence came such hatred, and whither did it go after the war was over? What transformations and new syntheses and connections did anti-Semitism establish in the intellectual sphere, in world politics, and in the collective psyche of various collectives on our planet? These were among the questions I asked myself while the blood in Matsa Restaurant was still warm and vital, and the words in the letter of my postcolonialist friend still hurt me so deeply.

I cannot avoid presenting this personal note, in relation to the call for boycotting the Israeli academics. To put it even more clearly, I cannot avoid asking myself in what forms, and in what new garb, are the old and new forms of anti-Semitism having their say here under the banner of the commitment to the protection and enhancement of academic freedom? I know that putting this issue so clearly and directly is an embarrassment for many of my friends, who feel so much better when discussing such issues under the umbrella of politically-correct rhetoric, pure analytic maneuvers, or other tactics of avoidance of fundamental philosophical, existential, and political challenges. Alright—I take the more dangerous way. At the same time I go into the issue of boycotting the Israeli universities not as an Israeli patriot. Far from it. It is my intention to question the grounds of the pro-boycotting representatives as one of the most radical critics, not of the 1967 Israeli occupation of the Palestinian lands but of the very existence of the state of Israel[7] as an alternative to the Diasporic mission of the Jewish people on the one hand, and of overcoming Judaism and monotheism as such, on the other. Time and again I am accused, as a writer and academic, of constituting a threat to Israeli culture and a danger to its youth. In his "Israel's Academic Extremists" Salomon Socrates says about my work:

> Ilan Gur-Ze'ev, at the School of Education at the University of Haifa and one of Israel's more bizarre figures, is a 'philosopher of education'. He goes well beyond the usual academic anti-Zionism and argues that Israel's original sin lies in its trying to teach its children that the Holocaust somehow implies that Israel has the right to exist. He believes that the Holocaust was no greater a horror than that perpetrated by Zionists against the Palestinians. He looks upon school violence as something progressive and positive.[8]

I cannot avoid going into it because I see here a problematic so great that it cannot be explained by the poverty of the arguments and the ignorance concerning the facts of the supporters of the boycott agenda, and, yes, in light of my own emotional involvement.

This is the reason why in my talk I shall refer to the *facts* of the matter as central dimensions, and this is also the reason why I came here, maybe the only one who came here to this symposium, with an orderly and organized file of documents relevant to the issue under consideration.

Relating to the facts, even the contested, manipulated, violently controlled machineries of representation of the facts, still has to address principles and standards. Here I begin my argumentation:

1. The pro-boycott supporters have to present us with good reasons and consistent criteria for their unique initiative against radical critics of Israel such as myself and my colleagues. They should do so, to my mind, after the systematic, orderly presentation of their concept of academic freedom and after a detailed presentation of the practices of enhancement and protection of their version of the concept of academic freedom. They should elaborate on the relation between their academic ideal and their conception of academic freedom that they claim is today under threat in Israel (more than in all other places where they neither conduct,

7   Solomon Socrates,
8   Solomon Socrates, Middle East Quarterly (Fall 2001). See also: http://www.bigcampaign.org.uk/ newsmequarterly.html

nor call for, protest and counter-measures). Between their concept of academic freedom and their actual protection of academic freedom they should be able to offer a consistent linkage within which the boycott of the Israeli universities would be rationalized and justified. But not only have the supporters of the boycott failed to convince us here, *they have not even bothered to present either their academic ideal or their concept of academic freedom.* They insist on using academia in the service of their specific political agenda, while claiming the opposite—that they are struggling for the protection and enrichment of academic freedom.

2. At this stage I will not insist on this last requirement, although I will insist on a *clarification of the concept of the academic freedom* which is at stake here. Amazingly, we all have to admit that never have the supporters of the boycott of Israeli academia presented us with *their* concept of the academic ideal and its relation to their concept of academic freedom. This makes their agenda philosophically unfounded. Still, we may forgive them this, and present them with a minimal request: *Please explain your criteria for boycotting a state or an academic institution in order to enhance academic freedom, or to promote academic freedom, in that state or in that institution.*

3. It comes as quite a surprise to many of us, but this is the truth: the pro-boycott agenda representatives *refuse to offer us an orderly, hierarchical, list of criteria for deciding whether to boycott or not to boycott a state or an institution. This makes their agenda morally indefensible,* since they deny accountability on the one hand and do not allow a fair defense by the accused (such as myself) on the other. This is not only an impossible philosophical position and a morally indefensible claim: it is even an embarrassing political position. Unless on the grounds of pure hate, surrendering to ignorance, or the most primitive manipulations, how is it possible to call on us to join in a boycott without offering us the *criteria* for deciding whether a state or an institution is to be boycotted?—that is, if we are in the business of boycotting in the name of academic freedom and the academic ideal at all!

4. After presenting us with a list of their criteria and its hierarchy, I argue, the pro-boycott supporters should present us with *a detailed report on the political conditions of all universities in the world* and of the state of academic freedom in each state in the world. This would enable us to try to chart the state of academic freedom worldwide and allow us to achieve a reasonable, morally defensible realization of the agenda of struggling for the defense and elevation of academic freedom all over the world. I think we cannot concede the requirement that they convince us that they are making reasonable, balanced, and honest use of the principles and criteria, being fully aware of the state of academic freedom in the various states and institutions. This would be without preferring some to others, or at least while setting forth for us the principles that enable or direct us not to apply the criteria *even-handedly* in the case of China vs. Britain, Tajikistan vs. France, or Syria vs. Israel, Sri Lanka vs. Panama. But a rich set of topics is found here, without any explicable, orderly presentation of the challenges they pose or

their possible solutions by the boycott supporters. They abandon responsibility by not offering us their solutions to such challenging issues as:

A. What are the desirable relations of the academic ideal, academic freedom, academic practice, and world politics?

B. Should academics as such go into politics within academic practice and as part of their commitment to the academic ideal?

C. Should academic freedom serve political agendas of national liberation, and if it should, then under what principles, within the framework of which political philosophy, and under what constraints or criteria?

D. What are the constraints and criteria of responsibility of individual academics to the policies of their institutions? What are the constraints and criteria of the responsibility of academic institutions to the political agenda of the states within which they exist?

E. In case of disagreement on such matters, how can one take academic freedom seriously on the one hand, and call for collective academic action such as a boycott on the other?

5. Have the pro-boycott agenda supporters presented us with their work of implementing their criteria and principles *in relation to all nations and institutions*? Have they made even the slightest attempt to convince us that they have *the relevant information about the state of academic freedom in the relevant nations and institutions to be compared* (and struggled against if and when academic freedom is disregarded or oppressed in these locations)? Have they implemented the concepts and the criteria in a consistent, reasonable, and intellectually honest manner? Unfortunately, they have not. Actually, they have not even convinced us that any serious *judgment* was involved here, certainly no scholarly, rational, and honest judgment.

6. In the absence of meeting these basic academic requirements, which we insist on even with our BA students in the first year of their studies at the university, one cannot defend either the rationale or the moral ground of the decision to boycott Israeli universities. Things would appear very different if the pro-boycott representatives satisfied the minimal requirements of academic reasoning and human honesty; if they took even the first steps in presenting us with their criteria and concepts in relation to their study and their detailed review of the various degrees of violation of these ideals and concepts in different states and institutions in the world. If such preconditions for a reasonable and honest discussion were fulfilled, then most probably the first in the list of nations to be boycotted would be those in which are found the most fervent supporters of boycotting me and my colleagues in Israel. It would not be a great surprise for me if top in the list, if organized according to the degree of violation of academic freedom, would be Syria, Sudan, Egypt, Palestine, North Korea, Iran, China, and many, many more centers of postcolonialist support for the destruction of Israel and of supporting boycotting its universities and academics.

Were we also to refer to the state of *unofficial* and structural destruction of academic freedom, as in the case of *implementing capitalistic rationality in academic research* and life, and were we not content to condemn formal and explicit violations of academic freedom alone, we might then be obliged to conclude that not only Palestine, Sudan, or Syria, but even the United States of America should be boycotted under such a criterion, before we got to Israel on such a list.

But why should we go into the business of boycotting each other in academia in the first place? Do we not need today a more open, free, and undisrupted critical dialogue, and not more silencing and boycotting of each other? What is your answer to this question, in light of your academic ideal and your concept of academic freedom? Any attempt to meet these challenges will be highly dangerous for the pro-boycott activists, and they will do everything to prevent such an open discussion. Instead, they will call you, at a philosophical conference as ours, to "action—no endless and useless philosophical talk". These people, who hasten to silence some of us, or most of us, in the name of politically correct policy while vaunting their moral superiority, are the true enemies of academic freedom and of human edification. The last thing we should do, I would suggest, is boycott them.

6. The pragmatic dimension is also to be considered. Even if we agree on the legitimacy or the justification of academic boycotts in situations of the most extreme and rare kinds, we should take into consideration its potential fruits. Here I would suggest to differentiate between (1) a principle to be realized—at all cost, whatever the circumstances and regardless of the outcomes, and (2) boycott as an instrument to achieve specific desirable goals. In the second instance, when boycott is favored as both legitimate and effective, I suggest distinguishing between (I) boycotting as a political instrument of the academic community for saving or enhancing academic freedom in some parts of the academic world and (II) academic boycott in the service of a kind of political involvement that the academic community finds justified, legitimate, and practical, in the sense of promoting freedom, a human rights agenda, and so forth. In 6(2), 6(I), and 6(II), the legitimacy and justification of the principle of boycott as a realization of academic freedom are not enough. Before their implementation *one has to be convinced that the fruits of this realization actually promote the agenda of emancipation or academic freedom.* That said, one has to consider whether the act of boycott that might be instrumental in one society will not be counter-productive in another. More specifically, one might ask if the act of boycott, in general, is universally effective, regardless of the unique contexts, or if it is contextual and should be considered also in light of its actual consequences. In the case of Israel, I dare to suggest that even before an orderly study of this question an academic boycott would lead to the strengthening of ethnocentrism and to the empowerment of ultra nationalistic-oriented policies, and would certainly threaten academic freedom and humanistic-oriented agendas in more general terms. But what is the relation between the academic ideal, academic freedom, and emancipatory politics in the first place?

7. The university was ever a daughter of this world, part and parcel of human history, part of an ever-changing systems of networks, powers, interests, evils, and naiveties, and of worldly love and actual improvements in the human condition. But it was also more. The university also contained the quest for God or the love of dogma and security. The university, in our historical moment of the triumph of globalizing capitalism, is not a totally new reality in this respect. Yet historically, it also contained something foreign, a negative utopia in the form of the academic ideal.

The quest is a manifestation of the free human spirit, the quest for *alethea*, for overcoming the self-evident and compulsory, as an ever-unveiling, ever-renewed building of the Tower of Babel. This process of unveiling, of overcoming the self-evident, the consensual "truth", and the political-correct is the arena where academic freedom—when true to itself—can breath, where it becomes relevant not as a parody of itself, but as a manifestation of the otherness of the human who refuses consensus and challenges normalized education, where the Diasporic, free, spirit is alive even in academia, even if never more than an exile, and never as a dweller.

Academic freedom is never to be institutionalized, dogmatized, or even secured. Its Diasporic essence will never become domesticated. Still, as such, counter-education in universities can do so much to prepare the ground for its appearance, for its never-totally-realized presence. This ideal is not to be disconnected from the ideas of true knowledge and the enduring improviser. These ideas have became so problematic in face of the historic transformation of Fordist ways of production into post-Fordism within the framework of the McWorld and the change in the stance of knowledge and of the human subject. The transformation of the human in face of the McDonaldization of reality from Some-one into Some-thing; the instrumentalization of knowledge and the reification of human relations, representations, identities and objectifications changed the ways academic freedom is being misused, absorbed, and manipulated.

> The nature of knowledge cannot survive unchanged within this context of general transformation. It can fit into the new channels, and become operational, only if learning is translated into quantities of information. We can predict that anything in the constituted body of knowledge that is not translatable in this way will be abandoned and that the direction of new research will be directed by the possibility of its eventual results being translatable into computer language...[9]

Within this framework *the academic ideal* as a potential realization of counter-education is being exiled, or even worse, absorbed, by the process of rearticulating and restructuring the university according to the imperative of the capitalist logic and the

9   J. F. Lyotard, *The Postmodern Condition*, Manchester: Manchester University Press, 1991, p. 4.

imperatives of the post-Fordist, "flexible", "free" market.[10] Academic freedom is not demolished—it is being rearticulated in face of the needs of the "risk society" and the "truths" and imperatives of current globalizing capitalism. In many respects, according to the young Marx, this is the true universal realization of the essence of Judaism. The other, corresponding universal realization of the essence of Judaism was the Enlightenment and the scientific revolution in which the history of modern university plays a special role. Today these two conflicting-corresponding ways of the universal realization of Judaism have clogged the fertilization of a rich, dialectical, antagonism between the truth of the logic of capitalism on the one hand, and the Enlightened quest for truth and academic freedom on the other.[11] These conflicting concepts of Diaspora concluded their historic antagonism in a grand triumph of one of them over the other: *the logic of capitalism is unquestionably victorious in our historical moment. It has absorbed the Enlightened quest for truth, justice and maturity.* But its triumph has summoned oppositions of various kinds, one of which is the "postcolonialist" camp. We can articulate it in still other words: the domestication of humans and the fabrication of actuality as a worldly Garden of Eden has defeated the Diasporic quest and the Diasporic nomadism as an eternal, improvising responsibility for creation, love, and non-ethnocentrist togetherness. This absorption is concluded by restructuring not only the universities but also the aim of the universities and the academic ideal. Accordingly, today, all over the globe where post-Fordism flourishes, and the McWorld and not the world of Jihad or obsolete totalitarianism has the upper hand, academic freedom is rearticulated.

Now, *academic freedom becomes the freedom of the university as an institution to discipline and to rationalize its "academic workforce"!* It is the most sophisticated manner of transforming academic freedom into its opposite. This, as part of restructuring the relations between the social context, the university, the academic ideal, and academic freedom in the actuality of the McWorld and in face of the world of Jihad. In Israel this process is presently triumphantly taking place, overcoming without hindrance the weak and pathetic resistance offered by the academic community in recent years.[12]

8.   The triumph of abandoning the historical process of *modernization* under ideological umbrellas such as the Enlightenment's liberalism and socialism for *globalization* and instrumental rationality is far from remaining unchallenged in

---

10   Ilan Gur-Ze'ev, "The university, the eternal-improviser, and the possibility of meaning in a postmodern era", in: Ilan Gur-Ze'ev (ed.), *The End of Israeli Academia?*, Haifa: 2005, pp.193–251. (in Hebrew).; Ilan Gur-Ze'ev, "The 31th floor: The tower of the university of Haifa and Zionist phallocentrism", in: Yehuda Shenhav, *Merhav, Adama, Bait*. Jerusalem and Tel Aviv: Hakibutz Hame'uhad and Van Leer Institute, pp. 257–261 (in Hebrew).; Ilan Gur-Ze'ev, "The Catch of Limor Livnat", *Ma'ariv*, 13 Jan. 2002, p. 6.; Ilan Gur-Ze'ev, "What should we strike about?" *Ha'aretz*, 28 Oct. 2001, p. 2b.; Ilan Gur-Ze'ev, "The end of academia?" *Ha'aretz*, 15 June 2001, p. 15b.

11   Ilan Gur-Ze'ev, "The university, the eternal-improviser, and the possibility of meaning in a post-modern era", in: Ilan Gur-Ze'ev (ed.), *The End of Israeli Academia?*, Haifa: 2005, p. 221.

12   Ilan Gur-Ze'ev and Yair Censor, "The struggle of the Israeli Universities for the defense of academic freedom", in: (ed.), *Toward the End of Israeli Academia?* Haifa: Haifa University, Faculty of Education, 2005, pp. 92–109 (in Hebrew).

our day. The logic of current capitalism and its postmodern culture industry is being challenged today by fundamentalism of various kinds, of which the world of Jihad is the most coherent and promising. Of much relevance here are neo-Marxist and postmodern anti-globalization NGOs that are united in their postcolonialist agenda. This postcolonialist agenda is committed in its two wings to an anti-racist education. This anti-racist education is based on "anti-phallocentrism" and commitment to postcolonialism that is reduced to a critique of the traditional "Eurocentric", "Western", "Judeo-Christian" concept of knowledge. Such an educational commitment is focused on the cultural fundamentals of "the West" and its colonialist manifestations such as its immanent "orientalism" that is conceived as stemming from the Western Platonic concept of truth/light and its "Jewish" monotheism that inflicts on the Other the most terrible violence in the name of an inescapable one truth, justice and order. Enlightenment here is conceived as an immanent manifestation of Western racism under the delusion of universal validity of truths, values and emancipation. This is why the Western canon, higher culture, academic tradition and its "racist", "ethnocentristic" concept of academic freedom are criticized here for their "whiteness" or for being violently "phallocentristic", or simply for manifesting "Western" concepts of freedom, education, and academia.

9. The present debate concerning the protection of academic freedom is situated within a framework where the various universities in the world are located broadly within three different cultural, political, and economic arenas:

   I. *Universities located in non-democratic societies*, where there is no room for academic freedom in the sense of the Western academic ideal. In societies such as present-day Iran, Syria, Tajikistan, China, Angola, Sudan, Palestine, and so many other countries, academic freedom is impossible, or it is possible solely as a bad joke.

   II. *Universities located in societies that enjoy a certain degree of democracy* and commitment to the academic ideal and are not yet totally absorbed by politically correct censorship on the one hand, and the implementation of the logic of the market on the other. Here it is very difficult to generalize countries, and within certain countries one should go individually into the study of the situation in each of the academic institutions and the different faculties within each university. Nevertheless, most broadly, in France, Germany, and Israel one might find genuine realizations of academic freedom. Yet it is only as a struggle, as a realized unstable and temporary possibility, a concrete negative utopia. That is why broadly speaking the Israeli academic community is so devoted to cultural critique and to actual resistance to Israeli ethnocentrism under very problematic circumstances.

   III. *Universities located in societies in which the logic of the post-Fordist ways of production and the politically correct moral police have overcome the academic ideal* and the potential of academic freedom.

10. If in this conference we seriously relate not to the justification of academic life and academic ideals in the service of political manipulations, but to the issue of

defending academic freedom even by political means, then one has to wonder if
we are not facing here a coalition of the worst enemies of academic freedom: of
those who are actually interested in oppressive political agendas that make use
of the issue of academic freedom in Israel in service of their implicit or explicit
old anti-Semitism and new anti-Semitism, or Palestinian patriotism, whose goals
have very little to do with the responsibility for academic freedom and more to do
with boycotting and ultimately with the complete destruction of Israel, and those
who are dogmatic politically correct agents of various kinds. I have still a fresh
memory of an invitation I received from a Palestinian friend who respects my ongoing critique of Israel's policies to teach in the University of al-Quds. "Be aware,
however", my friend added, "that you will have in your class only the older and
the weaker among our students". "Why is that?" I asked my friend in surprise.
"What is wrong with a heterogeneous class that will include many lively young
women and men?" "OH!" my friend said. "Oh! You still don't get it, do you? The
older students at our university are so weak that even when you talk with them
freely they will not throw you out of the window!... You don't know our students!
With a free spirit as yours under normal academic conditions in the university
of al-Quds in no time you will find yourself thrown out of the class through the
window and you might be hurt". Occasionally the disciples of the industrializa-
tion of the universities will join this "anti-Western" coalition. This is because the
academic freedom that is still realized in Israel is a threat to their commitment to
de-humanize humanity and to constitute a human subject who will be nothing
more than a sophisticated, productive, pragmatic-oriented producer-consumer.

11. All members of this coalition, most probably, will say to us:

> Do not go into the facts of the matter, Ilan, please, it is only a lo-
> cal issue. Here we are serious philosophers who are devoted to going
> into the elaboration of the principles involved in the issue of academic
> boycott—leaving unchallenged the reality that led to the decision to
> boycott the University of Haifa and other Israeli universities.

I say, let us ask what were the psychic, philosophical and political preconditions for
the consensus around the boycott agenda and its true interest, roots, and presump-
tions. Only then, I suggest, may we move on to the question of the possibilities and
limitations of academic freedom in face of pre-modern reality (self-imposed refusal of
critical thinking and free discussion), modern reality (external, institutional oppression and prevention of free dialogue and critical thinking in all human spheres), and
post-modern reality (where the logic of the market, McDonaldization of Spirit and
politically correct moral police cooperate to exile genuine academic freedom).

But even if we come to an agreement, and one of the members of our communities
thinks differently—should we force him or her to abandon his or her understanding
and go into action, maybe boycotting him or her until he or she accepts our understanding of academic freedom? Not only would I not recommend such an action. It
is my suggestion that we go farther into the concepts of knowledge, freedom, subject,

and academia, and challenge the positive utopia, the naivety, and enrolment in the triumph of the enemies of genuine academic freedom that made this discussion unavoidable and so relevant. Ironically, this is the gate, the only gate, through which the hope for realized academic freedom might come. This is because genuine realization of academic freedom (as against academic training and preparation for its appearance) is not a dweller of the university as an institution, is not part of a reality of any institution as such. The essence of freedom in "academic freedom" is transcendence; exiled from academic reality in daily life and in the framework of the politics of knowledge. And yet, at certain moments it bursts in, manifesting **the totally other**, and making possible authentic creation and reflective thinking even in today's academia, overcoming its successful boycott by conventional thinking, consensus, fear, and hate.

In this sense, we should thank the pro-boycott representatives for the opportunity they have afforded us. Thank you.

NAMES INDEX

Adorno, Theodor, 2, 14, 16, 19-22, 24-27, 31, 34-35, 39-53, 55-56, 58-62, 67, 71, 74-75, 78-79, 81-82, 84, 89-96, 99-110, 112, 123, 132, 164, 173, 174-176, 178-179, 181, 204, 211, 244, 255, 282, 283, 285-286, 303
Alcoff, Lynda, 168, 294
Apollo, 157
Apple, Michael, 16, 18, 66, 75, 191, 262
Anaximander, 25
Aronowitz, Stanley, 2, 89, 92, 112, 164
Aristotle, 84, 251
Arnold, Matthew, 123
Augustine, St., 2, 13, 213, 299-302

Baudrillard, Jean, 256, 304
Bauman, Zygmunt, 125
Beck, Ulrich, 27, 61, 207-208, 217-218
Benhabib, Seyla, 86, 168
Benjamin, Walter, 16-19, 24, 31, 41, 43, 47, 49, 52, 56, 58, 80, 82, 85, 87, 89, 92, 94-97, 99-102, 105-106, 117, 153, 177-179, 230, 244, 286-297
Bergson, Henri, 21
Bhabha, Homi, 171, 307
Biesta, Gert, 15-16, 121
Bloch, Ernst, 121-122
Burbules, Nicholas, 15-16, 74-76, 81, 112-113, 115, 121, 128, 131, 167
Butler, Judith, 162, 290

Camus, Albert, 25
De Castell, Suzanne, 117, 122
Castro, Fidel, 69, 71, 79

Deleuze, Gilles, 25, 49, 124, 150, 157, 165, 171-173, 176, 181, 225-226, 242-243
Derrida, Jacques, 2, 23, 25, 87, 120, 165, 304
Descartes, Rene, 222
Dewey, John, 72-73, 128, 172, 290-292
Dionysus, 57, 142, 157, 161, 223, 226-227, 232, 233
Duarte, Eduardo, 15-16

Ellsworth, Elizabeth, 89, 95, 99, 121, 157, 159, 161-165, 167-168, 171-172, 175-176, 185, 294

Feuerbach, Ludwig, 182
Foucault, Michel, 70, 75, 79, 83, 85-87, 94, 120, 127-128, 137-150-151, 154, 163, 165, 168, 176, 247, 255, 258, 304-305, 307, 310
Freire, Paulo, 18, 66-72, 74-75, 77, 79-82, 86-87, 89, 91-92, 94, 112-113, 115, 117, 121-122, 128, 153, 156-158, 160, 162-163, 166, 175, 180, 293, 298
Freud, Sigmund, 2, 60, 73, 84, 97, 245
Fromm, Erich, 89

Giroux, Henry, 15, 27, 53, 65-68, 72-79, 81, 86-87, 89, 91-94, 98-100, 112-115, 121-122, 153, 15-157, 162, 175, 189, 291, 293, 298
Gruschka, Andreas, 15-16
Gramsci, Antonio, 67
Guattari, Felix, 49, 124, 165, 171-173, 242
Guevara, Che, 69, 122
Gur-Ze'ev, Ilan, 1-2, 8, 10, 12, 14, 18-20, 23, 25-26, 36, 37, 39, 42, 44, 51, 53, 59, 62, 84, 91-92, 9495, 103, 117, 119, 126-127, 129, 133, 135, 145, 147, 149-150, 152, 154-158, 169, 172, 174, 180, 194, 203, 209-211, 221, 223, 229, 231, 244-245, 259, 264, 265, 269, 281, 283-284, 291, 293, 298, 306-307, 309, 312, 314, 319, 324

Habermas, Juergen, 56, 68, 78-79, 119, 124, 164, 72, 185, 197-201
Hegel, Georg Wilhelm Friedrich, 41, 44, 75, 74, 97, 100, 102, 107, 115, 256, 301
Heidegger, Martin, 14, 16, 21, 25, 27, 35, 51, 79, 84-86, 96, 103, 109, 119, 135-147, 152, 169, 176, 193, 203-204, 229, 236, 255, 286
Heilman, Elizabeth, 15-16
Heraclites, 25, 84
Hooks, Bell, 153, 157-158, 294
Horkheimer, Max, 14-16, 19-24, 27, 31, 34, 39-62, 66-68, 70-72, 7-75, 77-80, 82, 84, 88-97, 99-110, 112, 117, 121, 123-124, 155, 175-179, 181, 183, 220, 223, 303

Jonas, Hans, 21, 53

Kafka, Franz, 2, 25

SUBJECTS INDEX

Absolute, 23, 28-29, 33, 41, 43, 47, 49, 52-54, 57-60, 100, 102, 105, 107, 115, 1881, 200, 215, 239, 242-243, 246, 305

Aesthetic, 9, 13, 23, 31, 62, 89, 96, 109, 130, 154, 165, 181, 198, 210, 214, 216, 222, 230, 256

Affirmation, 10-11, 56, 232

Agency, 67, 95, 154, 157, 174, 196, 229, 239, 266, 310

Alienation, 13, 28-29, 41, 44, 91, 96, 100, 103, 107, 109, 125, 130, 132, 134, 137, 192-193, 195, 199, 20, 223, 235, 237, 264

Alterity, 9, 62, 125, 269

Auschwitz, 45, 110, 274, 284

Authentic, 20, 22, 26, 28-31, 33, 35-36, 48, 53, 62, 69-70, 84, 88, 98, 129-130, 133, 126-143, 145-149, 154, 175, 198, 218, 225, 227, 233, 272, 275, 278, 281-283, 285-286, 315, 327

Autonomy/Autonomous, 29, 34, 42, 50, 52, 65, 67, 71, 74-75, 77, 80, 84, 87, 93, 96, 101, 103, 108, 119, 123, 126, 129-130, 133, 151, 163, 170-171, 173, 178, 185-186, 192, 194-195, 200, 204, 213, 225, 237, 240-241, 243-245, 255-256, 291, 305

Barbarism, 19, 42, 101, 110

Beauty, 20, 22, 27-28, 30, 51, 96, 129, 152, 164, 171, 179, 183, 200, 202, 216-217, 226, 233, 240, 247-248, 302

Becoming, 9, 15, 18, 20, 22, 24, 26-28, 30-31, 33-37, 49, 51, 79, 97, 135, 147, 149-150, 152-153, 158, 171-173, 181-18, 199, 223, 225-226, 229, 255, 261, 267, 283, 286, 314

Bildung, 88, 98, 101

Body, 13, 20, 29, 77, 93, 152, 170, 173, 188, 198-200, 202, 210-217, 219-224, 227-229, 239, 255-256, 275, 291-292, 297, 323

Bourgeoisie, 267

Capital/ist, 5, 10, 18, 79, 85-86, 93, 95-96, 118, 120-123, 126, 131, 150, 163, 167, 181, 196, 203, 209-212, 214, 218-222, 224, 226-227, 236, 238, 242, 245, 257, 259, 306, 314-315, 323

Canon, 29, 75, 93, 113, 160, 189, 325

Chaos, 15, 22, 197, 253

Christian/ity, 2, 10, 13-14, 42, 58, 70, 98, 101, 213-217, 241, 243, 268, 290, 303, 316, 318, 325

Class, 5, 13, 18, 32, 68-69, 72, 74, 84, 90, 117, 120, 123, 125, 132-133, 158, 160-161, 166, 175, 199, 207, 215, 246, 274, 317, 326

Collective/collectivism, 2, 6-10, 12, 14, 16, 21-22, 24-25, 29, 29, 31, 34, 36-37, 39, 44, 55, 62, 65, 68-70, 74, 77, 79-83, 88, 107, 114, 123, 147, 149, 152, 154-155, 164, 166, 176-177, 180, 182-183, 186, 210-211, 218-222, 226-228, 232-233, 242, 245, 254, 259, 261, 263-265, 267-269, 272-274, 277-279, 281, 283, 285-287, 295-296, 300, 302, 306-311, 314-315, 318, 321

Colonialism, 28, 70, 150, 163, 169, 201, 258, 303, 316-317

Commodity, 41, 44, 45, 72, 82, 104, 123, 178, 211-212, 215, 218, 237, 241, 245-247, 260

Communication, 15, 17, 30, 55, 111-112, 116-117, 119-120, 124, 133, 135, 170, 187, 190, 197, 249, 252, 254, 256, 291, 305

Community, 2, 8-9, 23, 37, 52, 54-55, 57, 59, 69, 77, 91, 118, 147, 168, 189, 202, 211, 218, 229, 274, 214, 318, 322, 324-325

Consciousness, 11, 31, 44, 49, 67, 70-71, 74, 78-80, 82-83, 85, 87, 91, 93, 98, 102-104, 107, 112, 114, 116, 125, 127, 136, 139, 154, 160, 162-163, 178, 193, 198, 207, 211, 218, 222, 229, 232, 234, 239, 241-242, 245, 254, 262, 264-265, 298, 302, 305-307

Conservative, 75, 92-93, 139, 252-253, 256, 258-259, 294

Consumption, 11, 27, 31, 41, 93, 100, 122-123, 125, 155, 207-208, 211, 215, 218, 222-225, 241, 245, 248, 251, 256, 281, 305

Context, 1, 16, 33-34, 36, 4, 52, 58, 61-62, 66, 69-70, 76, 79-80, 82, 84, 86, 88, 93, 104, 109, 113-116, 118, 120, 122, 126-127, 132, 136-137, 139, 148, 150, 152-153, 156, 158-159, 175, 177-178, 181-182, 185, 189, 191, 193, 195, 197, 208, 215, 219, 222-223, 232, 236, 238-239, 243, 245, 248-249, 252, 254, 257, 264, 265, 267, 272, 290-291, 297, 300, 306, 309-312, 315-316, 322, 324

Printed in the United Kingdom
by Lightning Source UK Ltd.
123096UK00001B/72/A

9 789087 900717